P9-DTI-571

RENEWALS 458-4574

RENEWALS 691-4574
DATE DUE

WITHDRAWN
UTSA LIBRARIES

Critical Issues
in U.S. Health Reform

Critical Issues in U.S. Health Reform

EDITED BY
Eli Ginzberg

WESTVIEW PRESS
BOULDER • SAN FRANCISCO • OXFORD

*This book was made possible with support from
The Commonwealth Fund's Health Care Reform Program.*

*The statements made and the views expressed in this book
are those of the authors and do not necessarily reflect those
of The Commonwealth Fund.*

All rights reserved. No part of this publication may be reproduced or transmitted in any form or by any means, electronic or mechanical, including photocopy, recording, or any information storage and retrieval system, without permission in writing from the publisher.

Copyright © 1994 by The Eisenhower Center for the Conservation of Human Resources, Columbia University

Published in 1994 in the United States of America by Westview Press, Inc., 5500 Central Avenue, Boulder, Colorado 80301-2877, and in the United Kingdom by Westview Press, 36 Lonsdale Road, Summertown, Oxford OX2 7EW

Library of Congress Cataloging-in-Publication Data
Critical issues in U.S. health reform / edited by Eli Ginzberg.
    p. cm.
  Includes bibliographical references.
  ISBN 0-8133-8870-8. — ISBN 0-8133-8871-6 (pbk.)
  1. Medical care—Finance—Government policy—United States.
2. Health care reform—United States. 3. Medical policy—United
States. I. Ginzberg, Eli, 1911–
RA395.A3C85 1994
362.1'0973—dc20   94-7920
                                               CIP

Printed and bound in the United States of America

The paper used in this publication meets the requirements
of the American National Standard for Permanence of Paper
for Printed Library Materials Z39.48-1984.

10   9   8   7   6   5   4   3   2

Library
University of Texas
at San Antonio

Contents

SEP 2 0 REC'D

PART FOUR
Private-Public Sector Roles and Responsibilities

Foreword

Widespread support exists for a substantial restructuring of our health care system. Universal health insurance coverage and containment of health care costs are embraced by Americans across the social, economic, and political spectrum. Yet while these issues have finally been propelled to the top of the domestic policy agenda, the problems leading to the current crisis have evolved over time and provide a record of useful lessons from former initiatives.

This volume acknowledges the value of that history in examining the complexities of reform and the implications of policy choices. Nationally recognized health care researchers who have authored the following chapters bring their insightful knowledge and expertise to analyses of the major issues raised by reform proposals. Each proposal will be defined and differentiated by how it addresses several crucial areas, such as mechanisms for financing and cost control; the responsibilities of federal and state governments, employers, and individuals; and the level of competition, regulation, or new administrative structures required. The fate of public programs and how vulnerable groups will be provided for, as well as the fate of specialty providers, academic health centers, and graduate medical education, are also major concerns. These chapters provide a thorough and careful examination of these difficult issues, in the context of our past and present situations, as a method of reaching agreement on the best way to proceed in achieving our goals.

The daunting scope of this task demands an ongoing, informed dialogue between all parties in the debate to understand the system as it stands now and the ramifications of change. As the debate evolves, information, analysis, and communication are vital. The mission of The Commonwealth Fund's Health Care Reform Program, of which this book is a product, is to illuminate the intricacies of the U.S. health care system and options for its future. To this end, we owe special thanks to the contributing authors of this volume, and to Eli Ginzberg, who in his capacity as editor is uniquely qualified to synthesize the topics discussed here and predict the challenges ahead.

Karen Davis
Executive Vice President, The Commonwealth Fund

Acknowledgments

This book could not have been produced in record time without the wholehearted cooperation of the contributors.

The principal responsibility for editing the manuscript was carried by Christopher Zurawsky. Anna Dutka, a long-time member of the staff, assisted.

The principal responsibility for making the manuscript print-ready rested with Shoshana Vasheetz, who once again demonstrated her great skill in staying on top of multiple flows of paper in varying stages of editing. Gregory Grove managed the technical requirements of the tabular materials.

Special thanks go to Matthew Held of Westview Press, who has been a strong ally of ours over many productive years.

Eli Ginzberg, Director
The Eisenhower Center for the
Conservation of Human Resources
Columbia University

PART ONE

Framework

1

Setting the Scene

Eli Ginzberg

The first obligation of the editor is to convey to the reader the reasons for undertaking this collaborative effort and the purposes that it aims to serve. I shall speak to each in turn. The book aims specifically to contribute to the debate on health reform that dominates the political arena in 1994. For the better part of three decades since the passage of Medicare and Medicaid, neither the public nor the Congress paid serious attention to issues of cost, effectiveness, and equity in the financing and delivery of medical services to the American people. However, once the presidential campaign of 1992 got underway and once President Clinton entered the White House, health care reform moved rapidly toward the top of the domestic political agenda. Since many aspects of health care reform have been little studied and less understood, a volume directed to illuminating many of the critical dimensions of the prospective reforms was an inviting challenge, one that has engaged the authors and the editor, with due acknowledgment to The Commonwealth Fund for its interest and support.

Although the chapters that follow have addressed most of the reform agenda, the volume does not presume to cover all of the important issues. Two issues in particular are conspicuous by their absence: the future role of biomedical research and technology; and the multiple adjustments that are needed in the numbers, education and training, and utilization of the 10 million persons who comprise the health care workforce. Further probing could probably identify other elements of reform that would justify more attention than they have received. Nevertheless, the book can claim to address more definitively than any other current source the major issues involved in reforming the health system. We hope it will prove useful to the many parties to the discussion and debate that will shape the legislation Congress is likely to pass by early fall 1994.

Any attempt to summarize the principal arguments, conclusions, and recommendations contained in the successive chapters of the book would be neither practical nor desirable. However, a brief overview of the scale and scope of the critical issues that concern the various authors will help to set the scene.

Let me note first the structure of the volume as a whole. The chapters are organized thematically under four major subdivisions—framework, benefits and cost controls, public programs, and private-public sector roles and responsibilities. Alternative sequences and groupings were considered but the above schema appeared to provide the approach of choice.

In his opening chapter under the rubric of "Framework," Professor Joseph P. Newhouse explores a number of interrelated aspects of the financing of health care in the United States, raising such questions as whether the concern with the steeply rising expenditure trend is justified; the extent to which expenditure trends in the U.S. parallel or differ from those in other advanced countries; the principal causes for the accelerating outlays; the implications of the fact that two of the nation's largest spending programs (Medicare and Medicaid) are funded by government; and whether the public is receiving reasonable value for its money.

The second contribution, by David Mechanic, deals with the issues of equity and efficiency. In exploring these basic dimensions of our health care delivery system, Mechanic examines the role of the health sector in the context of the larger society and the extent to which the public differentiates between the influence of health care services (medical care) and of such societal factors as class, education, and race on health status.

Mechanic also considers the special role that access to health care plays in a society with gross differences both in income and wealth and in health status and need for care. Broadening his analysis of health care policy in a modern, changing economy and value system, Mechanic examines the trade-offs between more spending and more effective therapeutics; the inevitability of rationing; and the issue of who should do the rationing. He reminds the reader that given the interdependencies between the health sector and the evolving society no health reform program can provide permanent answers.

Part Two of the book, Benefits and Cost Controls, starts with a chapter on benefit design by Thomas Rice. As Rice notes in his introduction, the average citizen confronting proposals for health reform is concerned primarily with how his/her benefits are likely to be affected by the potential changes and what the corresponding costs will be. With this reminder of the importance of benefit design in any serious proposal for health reform, Rice focuses on the criteria that should guide the development of an acceptable benefit package. He presents five organizing principles and examines each in turn.

Turning first to the question of "eligibility for coverage," Rice assesses the pluses and the minuses of providing universal coverage, i.e. inclusive of everyone, foreigners and visitors not excepted (the case in Great Britain), unlike the Clinton plan which would exclude undocumented immigrants. Closely related issues are the standardization of benefits and what, if any, should be the role of supplemental insurance. As has been demonstrated elsewhere, it is difficult if not impossible in a society with vast differences in income and wealth to preclude the voluntary purchase of supplemental insurance. Its perpetuation, however, precipitates new difficulties at the same time that it resolves old ones. Other criteria stipulated by Rice relate to the choice of services to be covered and the restrictions on covered services.

These challenges are confounded by the substantial degree of uncertainty about the efficacy and cost-effectiveness of specific services; and—more profoundly—the continuing transformation of medical care by advances in research and technology. How to ensure access to an agreed-to package of stipulated services is the closing issue raised in Rice's chapter.

A related exploration of the benefits theme, more micro-focused, is provided by Howard Goldman and his colleagues, Richard Frank and Thomas McGuire, who examine the complexities of designing a mental health benefit and follow this with a brief consideration of long-term care. Contrasting the major structural differences between coverage for acute care services and mental health services, the authors call attention to the shallowness of mental health coverage provided by private health insurance; the severe restrictions on volume of mental health service utilization by private insurance; and the special role of state government in the provision of long-term institutional care for psychiatric and mentally impaired individuals.

In developing these themes the authors provide selected data that illuminate the parallels and differences between mainline medical care and mental health care. Reviewing the ways in which different groups of health care reformers have proposed to deal with the special case of mental health services, they examine first the principle of "parity" which they compare with three alternative programmatic criteria: protection against catastrophic financial consequences; encouragement of cost effective treatment; and the control of costs.

Much of their analysis is focused on the treatment of mental health under the Clinton reform program, and the compromises in benefits and implementation adopted by the White House for reasons of cost. Their concluding section on long-term care emphasizes the fact that although a home and community health care benefit has been added, the Clinton plan fails to provide, now or in the future, for expanded nursing home services.

Stuart Altman and Donald Young, the chair and the executive director of the Prospective Payment Assessment Commission respectively, are well-positioned to provide an in-depth evaluation of past and future approaches to "Controlling Payments for Hospital Services." The authors trace the significant changes over time in the flows of dollars to hospitals primarily via private insurance and the key governmental programs, Medicare and Medicaid, with close attention to the adequacy of hospital revenues and the issue of cross-subsidization.

The chapter looks next at the changing trends in hospital services—the declining role of inpatient care—and the consequences of this major structural shift for both hospital expenses and quality of care. Against this background the authors confront some of the priority issues involved in health reform, in particular the problem of the uninsured and the multiple adjustments in current and future payment mechanisms that would be needed if universal coverage were instituted.

The heart of their analysis is directed at alternative mechanisms to control spending growth—a rate-setting strategy, managed competition, and global budget-insurance premium controls—and the implications of each for the financing and delivery of hospital care. The special strength of the chapter derives from the authors' in-depth knowledge of the interactions between broad public policy and the detailed administrative and financial arrangements required to ensure the ability of the hospital sector to meet its multiple, complex societal obligations.

Paul Ginsburg's chapter on "Physician Fee Controls" is also the work of an insider with extensive experience in designing and administering the fee and volume controls recently adopted by Medicare to reimburse physicians for the treatment of its beneficiaries. He is the long-term executive director of the Physician Payment Review Commission (PPRC), an advisory body to the Congress.

Ginsburg reviews the characteristics of the Resource-Based Relative Value Scale (RBRVS) now used to determine physician fee schedules and the steps taken by the PPRC to refine the scale, making allowance for geographic adjustments. He then turns to the critically important arena of expenditure targets, including balance billing, and a review, mostly positive, of experience with payment reform.

Ginsburg examines the treatment of fee-control under different proposals for health reform including single-payer and all-payer settings. These are transitional issues that must be addressed in moving toward a more comprehensive system of global budgets. His concluding section deals with rate setting under the Clinton proposal.

The last contribution in Part Two was prepared by David Lawrence and James Lane of the Kaiser Foundation Health Plan and is concerned with "Cost and Quality Issues: An HMO Perspective." The authors introduce their analysis with the observation that group-practice HMOs are a uniquely American institution and their conviction that distinct advantages will accrue to a society that continues to rely on competition rather than on government regulation as a means of controlling costs and increasing value. Their argument is supported by an examination of the relationships between costs and quality.

The authors explore the reasons for the more rapid growth of the IPA and network models than traditional staffed HMOs. Noting the limited capacity of group model HMOs to expand, they review the influence of these archetypical HMOs in reducing hospital costs and enhancing quality. In assessing the claims and counter-claims for the contribution of HMOs, the authors respond to four widespread criticisms: favorable patient selection, inadequate participation in Medicare and Medicaid, volume discounts, and a failure/inability to keep cost increases below general health care increases.

Despite the pessimistic outlook for group practice HMOs in the health care market, they emphasize the potential of such organizations to take the initiative in undertaking outcome studies (as Kaiser-Permanente has done), given their large enrolled population, and learn from empiric data how costs can be effectively controlled and quality improved.

The third section of the book, sub-titled "Public Programs," contains four chapters, which address respectively Medicare, Medicaid, Government Employees Health Insurance Plans, and a Public Data System.

Marilyn Moon of the Urban Institute in Washington, D.C. is the author of "The Role of Medicare in Reform." Noting the importance of Medicare as the critical provider to the elderly and the disabled, and the many successes that it has achieved since it became operational in 1966, Moon examines some of the unique issues confronting Medicare, notably its political vulnerability due to its disproportionately large share in the federal budget.

She reflects on the relatively high proportion of Medicare spending for people "at the end of life" and raises questions about the size of the "saving" that could be achieved by pursuing a different set of policies. In terms of the contentious issues of technology and the need for long-term care, Moon points out how Medicare has been "twisted" to cover some of these costs that are not dealt with in a straightforward manner.

The second part of her chapter deals with the lack of an integrated approach in reform options and calls attention to the differences in benefits (and payments) that will confront the population below age 65 and the Medicare-eligible population if the Clinton reforms are enacted. She explores what she calls the "Medicare wedge," referring specifically to the future consequences of Medicare's current policy of underpayment. Moon suggests needed modifications in the benefit structure and in premiums and cost sharing if the imminent tensions between the population below age 65 and the elderly population are to be contained and the total health care system administered effectively and economically.

Diane Rowland, who is currently the Executive Director of The Kaiser Commission on the Future of Medicaid, is the author of the chapter entitled "Lessons from the Medicaid Experience." She begins with a brief review of the role and structure of Medicaid and assesses many of the accomplishments of Medicaid, calling attention to the vulnerable populations that Medicaid serves, the improved access it offers its enrollees, and the reduced financial risks and burdens that enrollees face.

There is also the dark side of Medicaid, with its well-known shortcomings including limited coverage, limitations of services for those who have coverage, limitations in access to care, and rising costs. The concluding sections of Rowland's chapter are directed to a broad set of lessons for reform and a focused discussion of what the Medicaid experience can contribute to the Clinton reform agenda.

Cathy Schoen and Lawrence Zacharias, with the assistance of Gloria Santa Anna and Susan Kelly, present an in-depth evaluation of the experience of "Federal and State Public Employees Health Benefit Programs." With over 19 million enrollees and $33 billion of annual expenditures, these programs can shed considerable light on the pending health reform proposals.

The authors emphasize that large "purchasing alliances" to provide low cost health insurance can go in any of several directions: use their purchasing power to negotiate the best possible prices from providers; serve as intermediaries that rely on competition between managed care plans to provide low cost services for good value; or adopt a hybrid approach exemplified in the Clinton proposal.

In their analysis of the Federal Employees Health Benefits Program they are in agreement with many previous assessments that the plan has serious programmatic flaws. It can best contribute to the present reform debate by calling attention to what it did poorly in the past and the reasons for its shortcomings.

Their data-rich analytically-penetrating discussion is focused for the most part on state public employees health benefit programs where they also find many weaknesses although these are somewhat balanced by the recent movement toward more effective cost controls. A considerable body of information from California and Minnesota reveals that these systems are no longer "just purchasers" but are much more actively engaged in controlling costs. One of the most valuable parts of their analysis addresses the twin issues of risk distribution and risk adjustment. Their ambitious and far-ranging chapter concludes with a number of critical issues about the future of these state programs in an era of Clinton reforms.

The last chapter in Part Three, contributed by Lynn Etheredge, a Washington-based health care consultant, is directed to the urgent need for "Public Data Systems." Etheredge agrees with the President's view that much in our present health care system is "broken" but he takes a somewhat different tack when it comes to fixing it. The author is convinced that in the absence of a reliable data base and of report cards for accountable performance any serious attempt at reform is at best quixotic, at worst impossible. Hence his insistence that early, serious attention be paid to putting a proper data system in place. In fact, he responds to his own challenge by indicating what needs to be included in the report cards. He also identifies work undertaken by others that can move the process ahead.

Raising the question of the potential users of report card information, Etheredge offers a number of relevant replies. The concluding part of his essay is directed to the urgent need for the development and improvement of health sector economic data without which it will be impossible to monitor health care expenditures, prices and volume at national, state and local levels. No matter which reform plan is finally adopted, Etheredge emphasizes (correctly), its ability to meet its challenges and responsibilities will be conditioned upon the operation of a reliable data system, one that lends itself to ongoing improvement.

We come now to Part Four—Private-Public Sector Roles and Responsibilities—which contains three ambitious and insightful chapters directed respectively to the potential of private health insurance, the administrative apparatus of reform, and global budgets to advance and achieve the goals of health care reform. Stan Jones, a specialist in health insurance, explores the capability of private health insurance to achieve the goals of health reform. By way of introduction to his analysis, he presents a "domino theory" of cost containment and quality assurance and inquires whether the existing market can be improved to accomplish the desired objectives. Developing a progressive set of models Jones calls attention to medical underwriting and risk selection, and notes the reasons that insurers have traditionally sought to avoid working closely with providers. He observes that insurers are conservative risk managers and that employers are poor managers of plan competition.

The second part of Jones' chapter explores the preferred level of federal and state action needed to improve the insurance market. He considers seriatim: regulate insurers and encourage employees; regulate insurers and mandate employer and individual purchasing; charter insurers and replace employers; make insurers the equivalent of public utilities; replace insurers and employers with government.

Professor Lawrence D. Brown, of the Columbia School of Public Health, contributes a chapter entitled "The Administrative Perils of Political Progress: Implementation Challenges in the Clinton Health Plan" in which he focuses on a much neglected facet of current reform, namely the role of administration once Congress (and state legislatures) take far-reaching actions to remodel the nation's health care financing and delivery systems. He begins his enlightening analysis by laying out some of the major administrative challenges of health policy reform, which he categorizes under the headings of structure, technology, and environment.

In looking at structure, Brown juxtaposes the systemic reforms that are the goal of the President's proposals—some alternative proposals as well—and asks how the National Health Board (NHB) will interact with the states; the states with regional alliances; and the regional alliances with the health plans that will have to shape and reshape themselves in response to federal, state, and regional alliance directives.

Brown then looks at technological dilemmas, which, oversimplified, can be defined as the mechanisms in place or needed to carry out a host of complicated new tasks such as proper risk adjustment which is the precondition for effectively functioning regional alliances. Or to take another example: the machinery that will be required to control and improve quality.

Mediating between government and groups is the descriptor for Brown's exploration of "Environmental dilemmas." He notes that "universality" and "affordability" have long eluded U.S. society and, as another analyst has observed, "partially contradict one another." How will the inevitable conflicts between private sector groups and state and federal governments be managed? Brown is sufficiently intimidated by his own analysis of the immensity of the administrative complications associated with the Clinton reform proposals to ask at the end of his chapter whether we might not be well advised to pursue a less ambitious set of reforms.

The concluding chapter on "Global Budgets and the Competitive Market" is the joint product of Harold Luft and Kevin Grumbach of the University of California, San Francisco. The authors start their chapter by examining "global budgets" in Canada and Western Europe where they have been in use for decades. They extrapolate from this experience the implications of global budgets for hospitals, physicians and other services in the U.S. and draw up a trial balance sheet of its advantages and disadvantages as a cost control device.

The second part of their chapter is a similarly perceptive and even-handed treatment of managed competition with specific reference to Enthoven's proposals. The authors caution that the competitive approach has a "certain degree of income inequality built into it which must be contained by various regulatory policies."

The concluding section of the analysis directs itself to managing competition and global budgets under the Clinton plan, and emphasizes that controlling payments to health insurance plans will, by themselves, not be adequate; payments to providers of services must also be controlled.

Ultimately, two key challenges confront the U.S. health care system in finding the appropriate balance between regulation and competition. First, who should be in charge of regulating global budgets at the level of specific provider units? And second, if authority over global budgets is delegated to HMOs, how should their levels of payment be determined?

2

Open Issues in Financing and Coverage

Joseph P. Newhouse

Health care costs and health care cost containment have been a staple of political dialogue for over two decades. In the din over costs, however, a key distinction between *high* costs and *rising* costs is often lost. Much of the rhetoric about cost containment in the United States focuses on the reasons for high costs, including large numbers of inappropriate procedures potentially induced by excessive fees, and high administrative costs in the small business insurance market.

The evidence that costs are excessive is persuasive (Brook and Mc-Glynn 1991), but most of the commonly alleged causes have not changed substantially over time (for example, high administrative costs in the small business market); thus, they cannot readily explain why real (inflation-adjusted) costs continue to increase. Yet it is the *increase* in health care costs that has brought the issue to the political boiling point; if health care costs were still at 1960—or even 1970—levels, it is unlikely that President Clinton would have made health care reform the top domestic priority of his first term. There is good reason for the President's concern. The ever increasing share of the economic pie that goes to medical care means there is less for everything else. In economic jargon, the increase comes at an ever higher opportunity cost; that is, it becomes ever more painful to gain access to additional resources for medical care.

The Causes of Rising Costs

Health care spending as a proportion of the Gross Domestic Product (GDP) has steadily risen; health care now takes over 14 percent of our GDP, a figure projected to rise to around 17 to 19 percent by the year 2000. In a rather short time almost one dollar in every five will be devoted to producing health care services. Moreover, during the 51 years from 1940 to 1991 real per capita health care spending has risen by a factor of nine (Table 2.1).[1]

What precipitated this increase? In earlier work (Newhouse 1992, 1993) I attempted to quantify the effect on cost of some commonly mentioned causes: aging; more widely available insurance; rising incomes; expanding physician ranks; defensive medicine; and steady price increases for goods and services that do not experience significant increases in productivity. Examining more closely the effects of aging and physician supply will illustrate the method. Had all else remained constant, this would have caused about a 9 percent increase in spending, or about 1 percent of the increase that actually occurred.[2]

More physicians. Many believe that an increasing supply of physicians drives up spending (twenty years ago it was commonly held that each new physician cost about $250,000, but the source of this dubious figure was never clear). Even if the increased supply of physicians were an independent cause of rising expenditures, it was also a response to some of the factors listed above, such as the aging of the population, which increased the demand for physician services.

But the degree to which the physician boom is an independent cause of increased spending is not clear. For better or worse, the United States government conducted an immense natural experiment in the late 1960s and early 1970s when its policies roughly doubled the number of medical school graduates (graduation rates both before and since have remained relatively stable). Table 2.2 shows the change in spending by decade as a function of the increase in the physician supply in that decade. Clearly, the increased production of physicians starting in the late 1960s did not accelerate the rate of health care spending. This evidence, however, is far from conclusive, in part because the increase in the number of physicians coincided with a slowdown in the economy, which has a retarding effect on health spending. Nevertheless, the data in Table 2.2 ought to give pause to those who assert that simply reducing the number of physicians will markedly reduce the dollar flow to health care. Other explanations are needed to understand the increase in health care costs from 1940 to 1970.

Because factors like aging and the greater availability of physicians do not appear to account for much of the spending increase, one is left with a large, unexplained residual in the health care cost rise. The exact size of the residual is uncertain, but taking four percent per year as a rough estimate of the historical increase in real per capita costs, the residual is at least one percentage point and probably close to two. The majority of this remainder likely results from the increase in medical capabilities. Admittedly, testing such a hypothesis could prove difficult because there is no ready quantitative measure of the increased capabilities, but it is hard to imagine what else could account for a residual of this magnitude.

Table 2.1   Increases in Real Personal Health Care Spending Per Person, United States, 1940-1991

Decade	Annual % Increase in Health Spending	Annual % Increase in GDP/Person	End of Period Per Person Real Spending (1940 = 100)
1940-1950	3.7	3.1	144
1950-1960	3.7	1.5	207
1960-1970	5.8	2.5	364
1970-1980	4.1	1.7	544
1980-1991	4.7	1.2	899

Sources: Health Care Financing Review, various issues; Economic Report of the President. GDP deflator used to deflate personal health care spending.

There are four arguments that support the preeminent role of rapidly advancing diagnostic and therapeutic technique in health care's significantly expanded cost structure. The first is non-quantitative and simply lists medical technologies that we did not have several decades ago: invasive cardiology; cardiac surgery; non-invasive imaging; renal dialysis; organ transplantation; intraocular lens implants; motorized wheel chairs; advanced hearing aids; operations on joints (especially hips and knees); and biotechnology. Although some technology reduces unit costs, resulting increases in volume may still cause total spending to rise; this appears to have happened, for example, with respect to laparoscopic cholecystectomy (Legorreta, et al. 1993). Overall, it is clear that much of what is taken for granted in today's hospitals was simply unavailable even as late as 1970.

Second, the Prospective Payment Assessment Commission (ProPAC) has estimated how much of the Medicare program's hospital spending increase can be attributed to specific new technologies. Their figure for two recent years was 0.7 percent per year, but as an estimate of the overall increase in cost attributable to technological change, this is surely low because it only counts certain items and does not account for the spread of existing procedures into new populations (ProPAC 1991 pp. 57–58).

Table 2.2   Increase in Real Per Person Personal Health Care Spending and Physician Per Person, By Decade, 1930-1990

Decade	Annual Percentage Increase Physicians Per Person	Annual Percentage Increase Real Dollars Per Person
1930-1940	0.6	1.4
1940-1950	-0.1	3.7
1950-1960	-0.1	3.7
1960-1970	1.1	5.8
1970-1980	2.4	4.1
1980-1990	2.0	4.5

Sources: Newhouse (1992); Health Care Financing Review, various issues. GDP deflator used to deflate personal health care spending.

Third, use of medical services, as measured by hospital days per person or physician visits per person, has not changed significantly from 1960 to 1990. Virtually all of the increase in hospital spending (which over the years has constituted about 40 percent of total spending) is seen in cost per admission or cost per patient day. Although inconclusive, this is consistent with the idea of an association between rising costs and new technological capabilities.

Finally, other industrialized countries have also experienced similar rates of cost increase (Table 2.3).[3] Thus, peculiarities of the U.S. financing system, like the non-taxable nature of employer-paid premiums, do not appear to have much affected the rate of increase in health care spending, although they are a cause of high levels of spending in general in the U.S. (Table 2.3).

Percentage increases in the other countries are, however, based on decidedly less spending (Table 2.3). This is consistent with America's greater levels of investment in each new technology. For example, suppose a new diagnostic test costs two dollars. If, before the new test is available, the U.S. spent $2,000 per person on health care and buys 40 tests, its spending goes up eighty dollars or 4 percent. If another hypothetical country of the same population spent half as much per person ($1,000) and buys 20 tests,

Table 2.3   Rates of Increase in Real Health Spending Per Person, G-7 Countries, 1960-1990 (Annual Percentage Increase)

Country	1960-90	1960-70	1970-80	1980-90	Real Spending Per Person, 1990
Canada	4.7	6.1	3.7	4.3	$1,770
France	5.5	7.8	5.3	3.3	1,532
Germany	4.4	5.6	6.3	1.4	1,486
Italy	6.1	8.9	6.2	3.4	1,236
Japan	8.2	14.0	7.1	3.7	1,171
United Kingdom	3.7	3.7	4.4	3.1	972
United States	4.8	6.0	4.2	4.4	2,566

Source: Schieber, G. J., Poullier, J.P., and Greenwald, L.M.: U.S. Health Expenditure Performance: An International Comparison and Data Update.   Health Care Financing Review 13(4) : Tables pages 4-7, Summer 1992. GDP deflator used to deflate personal health care spending.

its spending also goes up 4 percent. The next year there may be another innovation, and the story may repeat itself. The key point is this: Even if the U.S. were overinvesting (of course, the other country could be underinvesting) and even if better technology assessment led the U.S. to reduce its rate of new test purchases by half so that it bought at the rate of the other country, after a transition period the U.S. rate of spending increase would still be 4 percent per year, just like the other country.

This is not an argument against assessing new technology—though that is difficult to do with no agreed upon method for valuing benefits— but rather an argument that better technology assessment has more to do with the level of costs than with a steady rate of increase in spending. In particular, the consistent rate of cost increase appears to be influenced significantly by the rate of medical innovation, whereas the level of costs appears to be influenced by the extent to which any given innovation is adopted (that is, the number of patients who receive it). Traditional technology assessment has tended to focus on the latter issue.

Innovation can be viewed in two contexts: process innovation, which lowers the cost of producing an existing good or service; and product innovation, or the creation of new capabilities.[4] Medical innovation has seen a great deal of the latter, from antibiotics to transplantation. How much process innovation it has seen is unclear, but one could argue that the heavily insured U.S. market effectively paid for anything that benefitted the patient, thereby skewing innovation toward product innovation. Some hope that increased emphasis on costs, whether through budgeting or by cost-conscious choice-of-plan by consumers, will raise the amount of process innovation.

Such an outcome is plausible, but the size of the effect on process innovation is in doubt. For many medical treatments the U.S. represents less than half of the world market. Thus, an alteration in the American market is not necessarily a decisive factor in the innovator's manufacturing or sales strategy. Moreover, the rest of the world, at least for the past ten or fifteen years, has arguably practiced cost containment, thus providing a market for process innovation. Therefore, a shift in this country toward a greater emphasis on cost containment will increase the rewards to a developer with a process innovation (e.g., a cheaper artificial joint or lens implant), but that does not imply that there was previously no market for such innovation.

It is difficult to determine if health care reform will have any effect on the rate of scientific innovation.[5] One can safely assume that entrepreneurs will not bring new products to market if they do not believe they can recoup their costs of research and development. Thus, the issue becomes society's willingness to pay for new advances through either higher global budgets or higher insurance premiums and taxes in a managed competition market. Given the experience of the past five decades, there is every reason to expect that as long as we are willing to pay, we will continue to see innovation.

The real question then is what other goods and services we are prepared to give up in order to have more medical innovation. In the short run, health care waste and inefficiency means that in principle we do not necessarily have to give up any valuable goods and services to have additional innovation. But savings from less waste are certainly limited— though just how limited is a matter of dispute—and there is no assurance in any event that cost containment initiatives will simply eliminate waste. Thus, sooner or later we must decide whether we wish to continue to direct a greater share of our resources into medical care, thereby enjoying the fruits of medical innovation but relinquishing possibly preferable goods and services (Schwartz 1987).

Public budgets. Independent of the debate over resource allocation for health care, there is a special problem with respect to financing Medicare and Medicaid. If costs increase in the private sector because of enhanced capabilities, the government has three choices: 1) it can allow the costs of Medicare and Medicaid to increase, financing the increase through higher taxes, decreases in other government spending, a larger deficit (an option for the federal government, but not for most states), or through increased beneficiary payments based on premium hikes or higher payments at the point-of-service; 2) it can try to control costs in the government programs; 3) it can try to control all medical spending.

Medicare and Medicaid's greatly increasing costs historically have been financed by the first two methods. There is, however, something of a political consensus that taxes should not rise, nor should decreases elsewhere finance the increased spending. There is a reluctance to expand the deficit further, and increasing the deficit relative to GDP is not a viable strategy over the long run in any event. Further, today's elderly face a substantially lower tax rate, while today's youth, and future generations, face a particularly striking increase because of the cost to service the debt resulting from the deficit (Table 2.4). Thus, the current rejection of higher tax rates or deficits to support Medicare has some support in arguments over intergenerational equity. Increased payment by beneficiaries also is not politically popular, nor is it even feasible for most of the Medicaid population and the poorer segment of the Medicare population. Thus, financing increased spending in Medicare and Medicaid is not a politically attractive option.

Controlling only Medicare and Medicaid costs, however, raises the very real possibility that providers will shun beneficiaries of these programs. Therefore, this is also not an attractive option. That leaves the third option, controlling all health care costs, which in the long run will cause a

Table 2.4   Intergenerational Accounting: Lifetime Taxes as a
Percentage of Labor Income (by Cohort, Net of Transfers
Received) to Balance Government Spending and Taxes Over Time*

Generation's Age in 1990	Males	Females
80	21.8%	35.7%
60	26.4	34.4
40	30.6	30.6
20	33.6	32.5
0	33.9	32.9
Future Generations	71.5	69.3

* Assumes 6% discount rate.

Source: Auerbach, Gokhale, and Kotlikoff (1994), based on figures
from the Office of Management and Budget. The high tax rates for
older females reflect the allocation of their pro rata share of sales
taxes and their modest labor incomes prior to recent decades.

drop in the rate of expenditure-increasing innovation. Between 2005 and
2010 aging may raise health care spending by about .4 to .5 percentage
points annually, and that rate will increase as the post-war baby boomers
reach 75 years of age.[6] If new technology adds one to two points to growth
in real per capita health spending, as the above argument suggests, aging
and technological change would boost real spending by roughly 1.5 to 2.5
percent per year. Other factors such as income growth and a possibly
lower rate of productivity growth in health care would tend to raise this
figure even further. An economic growth rate of 1 to 2 percent implies that
in the long run either health care's share of GDP will continue to climb, or
capabilities that would have otherwise been realized will be rejected. In
the short run, as already noted, these outcomes can be avoided through
reductions in waste and inefficiency.

The cost shift. Private health spending is often thought to be increasing
because the government does not pay its share and shifts costs to private
payers. Although fees paid to physicians and hospitals are lowest for
Medicaid and highest for private payers, with Medicare falling in between

(Prospective Payment Assessment Commission 1992; Physician Payment Review Commission 1993), it is less clear that cost shifting is a major catalyst for increasing private health care spending.

Gross figures on the proportion of hospital and physician revenues paid for by Medicare and Medicaid do not suggest that the burden of financing medical care in the past decade has swung markedly toward the private sector (Table 2.5). Thus, the data do not support the view that cost shifting is the major culprit behind rising costs in the private sector. If cost shifting was increasing, the share of hospital and physician revenue from the government should have fallen over time, but as Table 2.5 shows, the share of Medicaid spending for hospital services and of Medicare spending for physician services actually climbed substantially from 1980 to 1991. Medicare spending for hospital services and Medicaid spending for physician services has essentially maintained its share.

Despite the recent slow but steady increase in the elderly portion of the population (from about 11 to 12 percent), Medicare spending has actually dropped by .4 percentage points, implying a modest shift in Medicare hospital costs. And the modest rise in the number of older Americans cannot account quantitatively for the increase in physician spending. (The long-term disabled are also eligible for Medicare, but their share of the population has remained constant at 1.3 percent and thus cannot account for the increased share of physician spending paid by Medicare.)

The Medicaid proportion of the population also appears to have been fairly constant (see especially Table 2.5, Note 1). Furthermore, with the proportion of the population without insurance rising, these data imply that Medicaid financing has been shared between the public and private sectors. (Such public/private financing acts as part of the rationale behind the need for disproportionate share payments in Medicare and Medicaid.)

In sum, these data suggest that rising expenditures in the private sector are not primarily the result of cost shifting. Data supporting the contrary point of view include decreasing hospital margins on public program patients relative to private payers and decreasing fees in the Medicare and Medicaid programs relative to private payers. There are three ways to understand these discrepancies. The first is that the data on revenues in Table 2.5 do not consider costs; however, there is no *a priori* reason to believe that the percentage increase in costs among public programs greatly exceeds that among private programs, though it is hard to know because of uncertain cost estimations. Second, the data on margins are based on accounting costs, which in effect designate to public and private payers such fixed costs as the administrator's salary. Because there is no absolutely consistent way to determine margins, their meaning in this context is problematic. Third, fee data do not account for any volume offsets, which are included in the data on revenue.

Table 2.5   Government Spending as a Percentage of Total Spending

	1980	1991
Hospital		
Medicare	25.8%	25.4%
Medicaid	9.5	15.0
Physician		
Medicare	18.9	23.1
Medicaid	5.0	4.9
Medicare recipients as share of population		
Elderly	10.8	12.1
Disabled	1.3	1.3
Medicaid recipients as share of population	9.5	11.3

Sources: Expenditures: Health Care Financing Review, Winter 1992, pp. 23-24. Beneficiaries: 1993 Green Book, pp. 138, 1648. Total population: Statistical Abstract, 1991.

Who Pays for Health Care Reform?

The Incidence of Employer Paid Premiums

Most popular debate about who pays for health care assumes that the checkwriter bears the cost. It is also often implied that employers shoulder the cost of employer-paid premiums (see, for example, Levit and Cowan 1991). Standard microeconomic theory does not support these conclusions, however, nor does empirical research, which determines that 80 to 100 percent of employer-paid premiums are actually financed by lower cash wages (Gruber and Krueger 1991; Gruber, in press).[7] The economic intuition is that employers are most concerned with total compensation, while the employee monitors the division of that compensation between cash wages and fringes. Therefore, the employer has an incentive to divide the compensation package to satisfy employee preferences in order to attract the most highly qualified labor force available at a given level of total compensation.

The fact that most employer-paid premiums are ultimately at the expense of wages or other fringes such as pensions has several implications:

1. It partially accounts for the slow rise in cash wages; between 1980 and 1992 the ratio of average compensation to average earnings rose 5.7 percent (Lawrence and Slaughter 1993). Thus, if fringes were 20 percent of payroll in 1980, they would have increased to 24.3 percent in 1992, with a commensurate decrease in the share of cash wages.
2. It may explain why some firms do not offer insurance. Individuals who can obtain heavily subsidized health insurance through their spouse's employer would prefer to have higher cash wages (or other fringe benefits) rather than health insurance. Thus, there is a demand for jobs that offer no health insurance but correspondingly higher cash wages.
3. It shows that premium-based financing, whether nominally paid by the employer or the employee, is regressive, because the ultimate effect is similar to a head tax (but see the discussion below of capped premiums). Thus, any shift to financing based on payroll or income taxes would lead to a more egalitarian distribution of income.
4. It disproves the standard refrain that rising health care costs makes American business less competitive. Unless total compensation changes, there is no effect on price and hence no effect on American competitiveness.

Suppose, however, that the evidence that the financial impact of employer paid premiums are (mostly) shifted to wages was incorrect and that instead product prices rose as a result of rising employer-paid health insurance premiums. Even that would not impair American competitiveness. Exchange rates for the dollar for foreign currencies would adjust just as inflation in prices generally does (the value of the dollar would fall), so that on balance there would be no effect on the overall competitiveness of the economy. (The price of imports to consumers, however, would rise.) Any exchange rate adjustments, however, would have differential effects by firm. Exporting firms (or firms that compete domestically with imports) with a relatively high proportion of health care costs—for example, the auto companies—would be worse off, whereas similar firms with a relatively low proportion of health care costs—for example, the computer game industry—would be better off.

The popular notion that health care costs are reflected in prices and not wages may result in part from the common assertion that health care costs add several hundred dollars to the price of a car. The implied assumption is that if health care costs were lower, the car's cost would be lower. In fact, the most likely outcome of lower health care costs is that the price of the car would not change much, but cash wages of auto workers would be higher.

The conclusion that the effect of employer paid premiums is ultimately on wages does not apply to the health care costs of retirees. Such unfunded obligations of the firm cannot be shifted to current employees in the form of lower cash wages without losing those employees to other employers. Assuming the firm has already chosen a profit-maximizing price, those costs will fall on the shareholders.

Redistribution, Part One

Because redistribution generally tends to be resisted by the political system, the amount of redistribution that is part of any health care reform plan importantly affects the likelihood it will be enacted.[8] Unfortunately for advocates of health care reform, health care is such a large industry that any large scale reform of health care financing must inevitably entail considerable redistribution.

We normally think of redistribution as occurring across income classes, and whatever financing method is used to achieve universal health insurance will almost surely require such redistribution. The uninsured are disproportionately poor or near poor, and for them to bear the full cost of a premium is unthinkable. Indeed, this is a prime reason why the Clinton proposal includes subsidies for those out of the labor force who have incomes below 250 percent of poverty, and subsidies for firms whose premiums would exceed 7.9 percent of payroll (the 7.9 percent figure is reduced for small firms and low-wage firms).

For companies that receive subsidies, however, financing is not what it seems—namely, a premium or head tax—but rather a payroll tax; that is, the subsidy converts the employer financing from a head tax into a tax proportional to earnings. An example will clarify how the employer-paid premiums are in effect a payroll tax if premiums are capped. Suppose a firm currently has a payroll of $1,000,000 and pays 10 percent of payroll, or $100,000, in health insurance premiums. Under the Health Security Act this firm would pay 7.9 percent of payroll (or less) in premiums—that is, $79,000—and receive a check from the Treasury for the remaining $21,000.

Suppose the company adds a worker with annual earnings of $15,000. The payroll rises to $1,015,000, and the firm must pay 7.9 percent of its new payroll in premiums, or $80,185; that is, it must pay an additional 7.9

percent of $15,000 ($1,185) to add a $15,000 worker. If it had instead added a $40,000 worker, its premiums would have risen to 7.9 percent of $1,040,000, or $82,160. The nearly $2,000 additional the firm must pay to add the $40,000 worker illustrates the payroll-tax nature of the financing.

If the firm does not receive a subsidy, the situation is markedly different. In this case, whether the firm adds a worker earning $15,000 or $40,000, it pays a fixed additional amount, the premium for another person. Assume that, as I have argued above, the firm-paid premium is shifted back to wages. Then the $40,000 worker bears more of the cost in the subsidized firm than in the non-subsidized firm.

One of the Administration's arguments against a tax-financed single-payer scheme is that it implies an amount of redistribution that is not politically feasible. This is one reason the Clinton Administration proposed financing universal coverage through employer-based premium payments. Ironically, the proposal nonetheless creates substantial redistribution because of the subsidies. Of course, the subsidy itself will be financed out of general revenues, which consist primarily of the individual and corporate income tax. But this is the lesser part of the redistribution. Because no firm is currently subsidized, the Clinton proposal effectively shifts the incidence of the employer-paid premium from lower-earning to higher-earning workers in forms whose payments are capped.

But there is more redistribution in the President's Health Security Act than just across income groups. Health care costs differ widely by geographic area, and therefore any health care reform, whether financed by taxes or premiums, has scope for substantial redistribution in this dimension. Table 2.6 lists per capita expenditure on hospital, physicians' services and drugs in selected states in 1991. These data contain some errors because their numerator includes services produced for residents of other states or countries (exports) and excludes services produced for the state's own residents in other states (imports). Rough adjustments for exports and imports based on Medicare data would modestly reduce the spread in spending among the states, but substantial differences would remain.

Any portion of health care reform financed by federal taxes has the clear potential for interstate redistribution (e.g. the subsidies for firms). As with redistribution by income group, the Clinton plan, which relies primarily on locally paid premiums, would have less geographic redistribution than a tax-financed single-payer plan, but the scope of geographic redistribution is nonetheless substantial. Although premium-financed reform, with premiums community rated for a given geographic area, will not redistribute across those areas, there is clear potential for redistributing within those areas; for example, if a city is combined with its surrounding rural area and all persons are charged the same premium, those living in the rural area will almost certainly pay more, on average, than

Table 2.6   Per Person Expenditure for Hospitals, Physicians, and Drugs, Selected States, 1991

State	Spending
Massachusetts	$ 2,370
Maryland	1,930
Virginia	1,730
Utah	1,460
Mississippi	1,440
United States	1,880

Source: Health Care Financing Administration, unpublished data.

they do now. Nor is this issue limited to urban and rural residents; metropolitan areas within a given state can differ by a factor of two or more in per capita spending. Insofar as political support is diminished by who loses, it may not matter that much whether the redistribution is within an area or between areas.

Redistribution, Part Two

There are well-known inequalities in the delivery of health care services; in particular, that the uninsured receive fewer services (Weissman and Epstein 1993). Indeed, the uninsured population is the standard example of problems with access to medical care in America. Any universal entitlement to health insurance enacted as part of health care reform would remedy this. The uninsured—and a great many people are at risk of such a predicament over an extended period (Swartz 1994)—are clear beneficiaries of any widespread entitlement.

Nevertheless, even with such a benefit, several access problems could remain. First, the poor and minorities receive fewer services even when insured by the same insurance policy. This is true for Medicare patients (Gornick 1993; Ayanian et al. 1993), as well as for those insured privately. For example, blacks insured as part of the RAND Health Insurance Experiment had only 58 percent as many treated acute care episodes as non-blacks, controlling for insurance plan and many demographic factors including income and education (Newhouse and the Insurance Experiment Group 1993, p. 102). Thus, even universal entitlement could fail to resolve some access problems.

Second, virtually all health reform proposals envision competition between health care plans. Even the proposed single-payer plans would not end risk contracting, meaning that the government would contract with competing plans for necessary services for a stipulated dollar amount per person per month, as it now does in the Medicare program. If the premium charged by these plans cannot be satisfactorily adjusted for risk—and the evidence to date on that score is discouraging (Newhouse 1994)—those whose expected costs are substantially above the premium paid to the plan on their behalf may well find that they are not welcome at any plan (i.e., may be quietly encouraged to leave). Although this represents another type of obstacle to health care system access, any plan that welcomed such patients could find itself quickly out of business.

Third, one must ask exactly what a universal entitlement enables one to receive, and beyond that, how much inequality there will be, based on income, in the receipt of health care services? Suppose the universal entitlement is a very generous package of benefits. Because it is more expensive it will require greater redistribution, thus jeopardizing its enactment. On the other hand, a less generous package raises two issues: 1) Can there be supplementary insurance, or will selection behavior (purchase of insurance by bad risks) defeat it? and, 2) How "less generous" is the less generous package to be?

Experience with Medigap suggests that supplementary policies might exist in spite of selection behavior, but the frequency of medical underwriting in individual policies, as well as pre-existing condition exclusions, suggests they might not.[9] Even if supplementary insurance exists, experience with Medigap points to high administrative expenses.

Medical capabilities are becoming ever more expensive. For the lower-income population to receive those capabilities the upper-income brackets will require even more money. If the upper group wants to pay to have these capabilities for themselves, but is only willing to pay a modest amount to make them available for the low-income population, there could be ever more stratification of medical services in this country overtime.

What Is Being Bought?

A substantial body of thought—fueled by at least 25 years of writing by economists—holds that the marginal dollar in medical care buys very little; in Alain Enthoven's felicitous phrase, we are engaged in flat-of-the-curve medicine.[10] I began this essay with the distinction between high costs and rising costs. Further, I suggested that because of technological change, even if one believed in flat-of-the-curve medicine at a given point in time, one could not necessarily infer that the increased health care spending over time was "flat-of-the-curve" because it was being spent on new capabilities.

Nonetheless, many believe that the U.S. has not received much for its greatly increased health care spending. An often cited figure is that the U.S. spends more than any other country, but its life expectancy rates do not begin to correspond to its expenditure rates. I close this essay by questioning this statement on two levels.

First, a substantial part of the increased capabilities of medicine has little to do with life expectancy. For example, many of the innovations I cited above—improved intraocular lenses, better hearing aids, non-invasive imaging, artificial hips and motorized wheel chairs—have little to do with fending off death. The benefits gained from these advances are simply not measured by life expectancy.

Second, the argument about "no correlation with mortality" can be countered on its own grounds. Hadley (1982) presented data across states showing a negative correlation between medical utilization and mortality rates at a point in time. Additionally, Table 2.7 shows data for the G-7 countries on the change in real per person health care spending from 1960 to 1990 and on the change in life expectancy for males and females at birth and at age 60. Although I do not wish to place great emphasis on seven observations, there is a striking overall correlation between the change in health spending and the change in life expectancy. Japan, Italy, and France had the greatest relative increase in spending, and (with the exception of males at age 60 in Italy) had the greatest relative change in life expectancy. Indeed, if the null hypothesis of no linear relationship between the life expectancy change and the spending change is tested, the null can be rejected in three of the four cases at the 1 percent level and in the fourth case at the 5 percent level.[11]

The usual argument that the U.S. has a relatively low life expectancy considering its high spending ignores the many factors other than spending that affect life span. Many of these elements may be rather stable, for example, cultural dietary norms. Any stable variables will be held constant in looking at changes and hence will not affect the results, but they

Table 2.7 Change in Real Health Spending Per Person and Change in Life Expectancy, At Birth and at Age 60, G-7 Countries, 1960-1990* (Ranks in Parentheses)

Country	Annual Percent Change in Real Health Spending Per Person	Annual Percentage Change in Life Expectancy, 1990/1960			
		Birth		Age 60	
		Males	Females	Males	Females
Canada	4.7 (5)	0.26 (5)	0.28 (5)	0.36 (7)	0.62 (5)
France	5.5 (3)	0.27 (4)	0.32 (3)	0.65 (2)	0.72 (2)
Germany	4.4 (6)	0.28 (3)	0.30 (4)	0.48 (4)	0.63 (4)
Italy	6.1 (2)	0.33 (2)	0.37 (2)	0.38 (6)	0.65 (3)
Japan	8.2 (1)	0.50 (1)	0.51 (1)	0.99 (1)	1.04 (1)
United Kingdom	3.7 (7)	0.20 (7)	0.19 (7)	0.44 (5)	0.40 (7)
United States	4.8 (4)	0.22 (6)	0.25 (6)	0.56 (3)	0.53 (6)

* Canada life expectancy change 1961-1986. Some countries' series terminate in 1989.

Source: Calculated from data in Health Care Financing Review, Summer 1992.

will affect results if levels are considered. Thus, looking at changes is a better (though still highly imperfect) test of the relationship between medical spending and mortality rates. Moreover, the usual argument ignores increases in spending in other countries; because spending in those countries has been increasing at about the same rate as in the U.S., there is no strong reason to think that the U.S. should improve relative to them.

Recapitulation

This analysis has emphasized several points:

1. Concern with health care costs is certainly legitimate; we have good reason to believe we overspend, and the steady increase in health care costs comes at an ever higher opportunity cost—that is, diverting ever more resources into health care becomes increasingly painful.

2. A principal cause of increasing health care costs is the enhanced capabilities of medicine. Although for some years we could maintain the historical rate of change by reducing waste and inefficiency, this ability is limited and at some point we will likely face the hard choice of paying higher costs (implicitly giving up other goods and services) and not having the same capabilities. Just where this point lies is debatable.

3. There is a special problem with respect to Medicare and Medicaid. Because expenditure-increasing forces affect these public programs as well, the Congress and the President can either allow expenditures to increase—meaning some combination of a tax increase, a deficit increase, or increased payments by beneficiaries—try to control the costs of these (or other) programs, which may jeopardize the access of these beneficiaries, or try to control all costs, which could force us to forego some medical care we would have been willing to pay for.

4. The amount of redistribution will greatly affect the chances of health care reform enactment. In addition to common redistribution across income groups, which universal coverage would certainly entail, there is likely to be substantial geographic redistribution as part of any major change in health care financing. In addition, the nature of the subsidies in the Administration's bill implicitly redistributes money from some, but not all, high-earning workers to some low-earning workers.

5. Access is likely to remain at issue after financing reform, but its nature may change. The most prominent group among those thought to have an access problem now are the uninsured, including those

with pre-existing conditions, though others face obstacles of trans-
portation or language. Clearly, any universal insurance program
will end the problem of no insurance as we know it.[12] In its place a
new type of access problem may arise because of incomplete risk adjustment; insurance plans may not wish to treat patients on whom
they expect to lose money. Also, the poor and the minorities may
continue to receive inadequate care. Supplementing a basic benefit
package will certainly incur relatively high administrative costs, and
such a coverage scheme could fail completely if only poor risks buy
in.

6. Although there is a popular perception that increased spending has
not bought any benefits, the ultimate gain, longer life, could not be
expected to capture many of the benefits. Moreover, there is some
evidence that more spending does reduce mortality. The perception
that the U.S. spends a great deal of money but does not improve its
life expectancy rates relative to other countries ignores the fact that
those countries are also increasing their spending on medical care in
about the same proportion as this country. Indeed, sketchy evidence
suggests that large, developed countries that increased expenditures
relatively more also increased life expectancy relatively more.

Notes

1. The numbers in Table 2.1 differ somewhat from those in Newhouse 1992,
1993 because I deflate by the GDP deflator rather than the GDP deflator for con-
sumption. Although I believe the latter is preferable conceptually, the OECD uses
the former, and I believe the reduction in potential confusion realized by using the
same deflator more than offsets the possible gains from using the GDP consump-
tion deflator. In any event, the differences are not large.

2. Accounting for aging within the over-65 group (i.e., the increased fraction of
those over 85 years old) would not change this conclusion. Note that the ratio of
spending by the elderly to the non-elderly is not a universal constant. For example,
it is a factor of five in Japan, which, when combined with higher aging rates in the
1990s, means aging is a substantially more important factor there.

3. The more often cited percentage of GDP figures give a somewhat different
picture; the U.S. not only spends more but, particularly in the 1980s, the share of
U.S. GDP spent on health care has increased more rapidly than in the other G-7
countries. Although real health care costs per person did grow more rapidly in the
U.S. in the 1980s, the U.S. economy also grew less rapidly; in other words, the percentage of GDP spent on health care is also influenced by the behavior of the de-
nominator.

4. If the price of a new capability before it exists is regarded as infinite, the two
types merge.

5. More precisely, the issue is the degree to which the rate of technological
change will be affected by binding global budgets.

6. This calculation comes from Census projections of the population (U.S. Department of Commerce 1991, p. 16) and the assumption that the over-65 population spends about three times as much per person as those under 65. Adjusting for the aging of the elderly (i.e., the growth of number of those over 85) would raise this figure slightly.

7. This statement ignores the fact that employer-paid premiums are paid with before-tax income, and cash wages would be taxable. Accounting for the tax treatment would shift some of the costs back to taxpayers. Also, at the minimum wage the employer-paid premium cannot be shifted.

8. Recall Machiavelli's warning to his prince: "There is nothing more doubtful of success, and more dangerous to carry through than initiating changes in a state's constitution. The innovator makes enemies of all those who prospered under the old order, and only lukewarm support is forthcoming from those who would prosper under the new. Their support is lukewarm partly from fear of their adversaries, who have the existing laws on their side, and partly because men are generally incredulous, never really trusting new things unless they have tested them by experience. In consequence, whenever those who oppose the changes can do so, they attack vigorously, and the defense made by the others is only lukewarm."

9. This discussion assumes that the public plan is not a secondary payer; if it is, supplementary insurance would effectively not exist.

10. Indeed, the RAND Health Insurance Experiment results largely bears out the view that the additional services induced by abolishing initial cost sharing represent on average flat-of-the-curve medicine (Newhouse and the Insurance Experiment Group 1993).

11. Spearman rank correlations are significant at the 5 percent level for all but the change in life expectancy for males at age 60. This analysis could clearly be extended to include other countries, although in a weighted regression the addition of smaller countries would carry proportionately less weight. The principal point, however, is that one should pay less attention to cross-section regressions of levels of mortality rates on levels of health spending than to similar regressions in first differences (or analogous regressions of the final level controlling for the initial level).

12. However, illegal immigrants will still be uninsured.

References

Auerbach, Alan J., Jagadeesh Gokhale, and Laurence J. Kotlikoff. 1994. "Generational Accounting: A Meaningful Way to Evaluate Fiscal Policy," *Journal of Economic Perspectives*, 8(1): 73–94.

Ayanian, John Z., I. Steven Udvarhelyi, Constantine Gatsonis, et al. 1993. "Racial Differences in the Use of Revascularization Procedures After Coronary Angiography," *Journal of the American Medical Association* 269: 2642–2646.

Brook, Robert H. and Elizabeth McGlynn. 1991. "Maintaining Quality of Care," in Eli Ginzberg, ed., *Health Services Research* (Cambridge, MA: Harvard University Press).

Gornick, Marian. 1993. "Physician Payment Reform Under Medicare: Monitoring Utilization and Access," *Health Care Financing Review* 14(3): 77–96.

Gruber, Jonathan, "The Incidence of Mandated Maternity Benefits," *American Economic Review*, in press.

Gruber, Jonathan and Alan Krueger. 1991. "The Incidence of Mandated Employer Provided Insurance: Lessons from Workers' Compensation," in David Bradford, ed., *Tax Policy and the Economy*, vol. 5 (Cambridge, MA: MIT Press).

Hadley, Jack. 1982. *More Medical Care, Better Health?* (Washington, D.C.: The Urban Institute).

Lawrence, Robert Z. and Matthew J. Slaughter. 1993. "International Trade and American Wages in the 1980s, Giant Sucking Sound or Small Hiccup?" *Brookings Papers on Economic Activity, Microeconomics 2*, pp. 166–226.

Legorreta, Antonio P., Jeffrey H. Silber, George N. Costantino, et al. 1993. "Increased Cholecystectomy Rate After the Introduction of Laparoscopic Cholecystectomy," *Journal of the American Medical Association* 270: 1429–1432.

Levit, Katharine R., and Cathy A. Cowan. 1991. "Business, Households, and Governments: Health Care Costs: 1990," *Health Care Financing Review*, 13(2): 83–93.

Newhouse, Joseph P. 1992. "Medical Care Costs: How Much Welfare Loss?" *Journal of Economic Perspectives* 6 (3): 3–21.

———. 1993. "An Iconoclastic View of Cost Containment," *Health Affairs* 12 (supplement): 152–171.

———. 1994. "Patients at Risk: Health Reform and Risk Adjustment," *Health Affairs* 13 (Supplement), in press.

——— and the Insurance Experiment Group. 1993. *Free for All? Lessons from the RAND Health Insurance Experiment* (Cambridge, MA: Harvard University Press).

Physician Payment Review Commission. 1993. *Annual Report, 1993* (Washington, D.C.: The Commission).

Prospective Payment Assessment Commission. 1991. "Report and Recommendations to the Congress, March 1, 1991" (Washington, D.C.: The Commission).

———. 1992. "Medicare and the American Health Care System: Report to the Congress, June 1992" (Washington, D.C.: The Commission).

Schwartz, William B. 1987. "The Inevitable Failure of Current Cost Containment Strategies: Why They Can Provide Only Temporary Relief," *Journal of the American Medical Association* 257: 220–224.

Swartz, Katharine. 1994. "Dynamics of People Without Health Insurance," *Journal of the American Medical Association* 271: 64–66.

United States Department of Commerce, Statistical Abstract. 1991. (Washington: Government Printing Office, 1991).

Weissman, Joel S. and Arnold M. Epstein. 1993. "The Insurance Gap: Does It Make a Difference?" in Gilbert S. Omenn, ed., *Annual Review of Public Health*, vol. 14 (Palo Alto, CA: Annual Reviews).

3

Equity and Efficiency Considerations

David Mechanic

Health reforms inevitably build on existing structures, professional groupings and preexisting forms of organization. Their implementation commonly reaffirms and reinforces existing patterns and priorities, but they also provide opportunities to rethink directions and introduce innovative features that address both neglected and emerging problems. Thus debate on health reform is an opportunity to think carefully about health and medical care efforts and the future roles we would like them to have. The Clinton health reform proposals, however ambitious, are but the first step in a long-term process of rethinking how to promote health and contain illness and disability.

In a nation characterized by racial, ethnic, economic and geographic diversity, commitment to universal health care coverage contributes to a sense of national identity and cohesiveness across social strata and regions. Medicine has a sustaining and integrative role in society. It provides a legitimate context where people can bring a broad range of problems, some highly personal or stigmatized, and receive a sympathetic hearing and tangible assistance. Credibility and trust in medicine has diminished, as in all our social institutions, but patients' physicians, and the sophisticated institutions that support their efforts, still retain a high level of support and influence. As the authority of the family, church and community has eroded with social changes, health care has assumed a growing role in areas of behavior and social functioning that go well beyond the diagnosis and treatment of disease as narrowly construed. Some may lament this growing medicalization of life's many problems, but such demand substantially derives from the way patients experience and seek help for their troubles.

There is now overwhelming evidence of the relationship between psychosocial adversity and people's sense of physical distress and a link between such distress and the occurrence and course of disease.[1] Patients commonly seek care in response to a wide range of problems in living and often represent such distress through physical complaints, a process known as somatization.[2] The medicalization of psychosocial domains occurs not only because people commonly experience and express their distress in this way but also because of the ingenious capacities of health care specialties to define new areas of expertise and service products.

It is now commonly understood that health status is only dependent in limited ways on the medical care system and that broader cultural, socioeconomic and environmental influences importantly shape health outcomes. Economic deprivation and social disorganization are associated with the prevalence of somatic, psychological and behavioral disorders and their concomitants including stress and adversity, misuse and abuse of alcohol and drugs, physical and psychological abuse, high risk-taking, poor health behavior, and violence.[3] These problems often are interlinked or clustered together and occur with high prevalence in disadvantaged populations. While medicine is only a small part of efforts needed to address such challenges, the priorities that shape health initiatives and the organization of care can make medicine more or less relevant.

Two additional challenges in the areas of prevention and the management of chronic disabling disease also raise important questions about the role of medical care relative to other levels of intervention. Preventive efforts at the community level remain highly underdeveloped while many resources are invested in medical care to identify asymptomatic conditions or early manifestations of disease. While some preventive interventions such as immunizations and pap smears are cost effective,[4] others remain uncertain and questionable. In endorsing prevention as a goal, we need to carefully discriminate between initiatives offering a reasonable advantage and others, like the annual medical exam, which have dubious value.

While medicine commonly offers remarkable acute interventions in times of crisis, it often fails in the needed longitudinal management of chronic disabling disease that coordinates with other supportive agencies and contributes to helping persons function in preferred and less restrictive community environments. The Clinton health care reform proposals reflect recognition of the needs and complexity of this area and offer some potential for addressing chronic illness and long-term care issues, but these remain incidental to the major proposed initiatives. Changes in the medical care system that serve persons with chronic disabling illness more appropriately are likely to serve us all well by refocusing the priorities and goals of health care on promoting patient function and quality of life.[5]

Determinants of Health and Levels of Intervention

Social disadvantage is one of the major determinants of poor health, and it is central to any consideration of how to increase the effectiveness of health investments. Health risk occurs in a social context, but our conceptions of the problem are individualistic and moralistic. Failure to address the broad determinants is likely to seriously limit our efforts to achieve a higher level of population health.

Socioeconomic status is a major correlate of almost every aspect of health and welfare in our society from prematurity and infant mortality to disability and premature death.[6] Recent studies show that despite significant advances in health, and high expenditures, disparities in health by socioeconomic status have been increasing.[7] Some of our ghetto areas have health indices resembling developing countries.[8] The underlying causes of the disparities associated with disadvantage are diverse and complex, but it is evident that access to medical care by itself will not do a great deal to achieve parity in health status.[9]

Schooling and income impressively predict health status and longevity. An important part of the schooling effect is due to income which is correlated with it, and the access to material goods and a quality environment it provides, including availability of medical and other health services. Most studies show, however, that education has an independent effect on health indicators when income is controlled. Schooling is typically associated with scope of knowledge, self-concept, social participation, an inclination to defer rewards for future benefits, and a sense of personal control and efficacy.[10] Research in behavioral health increasingly finds that personal attributes such as sense of personal control, empowerment, optimism and related characteristics, and the strength of social ties either protect individuals from risk or ameliorate the effects of adversity.[11,12] Individuals with these characteristics have a greater stake in their communities, are more active in engaging their environment, seek and acquire appropriate information more effectively and appear to cope more successfully. Feelings of control and empowerment derive from social arrangements and personal networks giving individuals a sense of meaningful participation and attachment and a stake in the welfare of others and their own futures. Countless studies show a link between alienation and anomie and high levels of pathology and risk-taking.

The prevalence of morbidity and disability in disadvantaged populations requires extensive medical expenditures, but often these investments come too late to interrupt trajectories of risk, pathology and disability. Health care reform will inevitably increase these expenditures through enhanced insurance coverage and a variety of special programs in response to the need for increased access and earlier intervention. But even these initiatives appear relatively late in the intervention process and focus primarily on the individual. There is a need for a realistic assessment about how much can be achieved by improved access and isolated efforts to change individual behavior, in contrast with broader interventions to reconstruct communities, to promote the healthy development of children and youth, and to improve employment opportunities and conditions. Income support of poor families may do more to promote health than anything we attempt in the health sector, but opportunities for such simple trade-offs across sectors are not realistic policy options in the context of our politics.

Much of what we understand as behavior conducive to health is a natural consequence of certain life patterns and everyday activities. Aside from differences in biological endowments, individual health depends on how households make decisions, their investments in the health and education of family members, and the attitudes and values they promote.[13] Developing healthy communities depends on strengthening community standards and norms that encourage schooling, community participation, and responsibility toward others, and that are widely shared and continually reinforced. There is value, of course, in programs to reduce cigarette smoking, substance abuse and other health damaging behavior, but there are limits to remedial interventions on an individual level. Community approaches are needed to enlist families, businesses, schools, churches and other voluntary organizations in promoting community standards and providing meaningful opportunities that give people a stake in their futures. Our knowledge base for such interventions remains uncertain, and many needed changes involve highly controversial political decisions. It is incontestable, however, that many of the diseases and injuries that flow into the medical care system result from vast social inequities in the community, detachment from community standards, high risk-taking, fatalism, substance abuse, and violence.

Although health interventions can be introduced in a variety of ways, curative efforts often come too late in the illness trajectory. Curative medical care is typically our central focus not because it offers the best opportunities to enhance health but rather because the ill, injured and disabled who seek remedies for their pain and distress are motivated in ways different from those who are well. Illness and disability are tangible and evoke sympathy in a way that risk and probability do not, and it is easier to motivate people in search of relief than those who are only statistically at risk and feel invulnerable. There is also greater public compassion for those already ill and disabled than for those who are merely seen as potentially at risk, which distorts our investment choices among interventions.

In the broadest sense, health is a product of the ecological and social environment and one's place in it. It depends on the sustaining factors and risks in the person's social context including nutrition, shelter, economic security, meaningful participation, freedom from hazards and violence, and numerous other conditions. It encompasses individual's coping skills for dealing with life challenges, and the social institutions that support and sustain these, social networks and community connections, and one's sense of having some control over one's life and fate. Through organization and planning, more often on a community than on an individual level, individuals and groups can develop supportive and protective structures that increase favorable life chances. When they function well, they motivate the young to develop needed skills and supportive attachments, and empower individuals and community groups. Interventions that build communities and enhance social development may have little directly to do with health, but their efforts may be more pervasive than more specific health-directed interventions.

A second level of intervention is in the area of public health. While at the first level health outcomes are an indirect result of structures built around other essential goals, public health addresses health outcomes directly at the community level and involves such issues as air and water quality, sanitation, immunization, infectious disease control, injury prevention, containment of chronic disease, and health behavior. Increasingly, health departments have moved from traditional functions focused on communicable diseases to behavioral interventions designed to reduce smoking, substance abuse, and risky sexual behaviors. Other key functions include disease screening, prenatal and child care, immunization, and public education. The Clinton proposals presuppose that as universal coverage is enacted, health departments could devote fewer resources to directly providing medical care and give greater attention to health issues at the community level.

Public health is a powerful point of intervention but in practice is caught between the interests of clinical medicine and those of economic, political and religious groups.[14] Medical practitioners have always been protective of their domain and have resisted public health programs that are potentially competitive with clinical practice or that provide free services to potential paying customers. At the community level, public health interventions often come into conflict with groups who see their interests or values threatened. Such issues as gun control, pregnancy services, family planning, and sex education will continue to be contentious regardless of their public health implications. At the governmental level, public health interests crosscut other political entities including housing, sanitation, policing, traffic control, and social services, making it difficult to exercise authority. The core power of departments of public health ironically comes less through public health practice and more through their authority to regulate hospital and nursing home reimbursement rates and to administer certificates of need and related regulations. Thus, public health realizes its greatest influence and prestige when it departs from its historic responsibilities, but these new responsibilities ultimately have less influence on health. Shifting the balance of public health toward a community approach to controlling health risks and promoting safer behavior offers difficult challenges but also important opportunities.

A third level of intervention is in primary medical care, commonly a patient's point of first contact with the medical care system. Primary care typically refers to a generalist-physician with training in family medicine, general internal medicine or pediatrics, and for forty years the nation has been agonizing over the decreasing corps of such doctors.[15] Despite numerous government programs to revive primary care, the erosion of the role continues with fewer medical students selecting these specialties. The reasons have been well known and widely debated for years. Especially notable causes of primary care's demise include the lower pay and prestige afforded such practitioners, the extended responsibility that such physicians must assume for their patients' well-being, the increasing complexity of medical knowledge and the difficulty and uncertainties associated with practicing across the entire medical spectrum. The relatively low priority and prestige given to primary care in medical education, and inadequate training in primary care skills, exacerbate the problem. The learned orientations physicians commonly bring to many of the problems they see in primary care lead them to think of such work as boring and relatively trivial.

The primary care issue transcends having sufficient numbers of physicians to perform this role. Primary care should be a mind-set and philosophy that examines the problems patients bring to doctors in a longitudinal and community perspective and uses the knowledge gained about the patient over time to manage care more broadly than is possible in episodic relationships. To the extent that primary care is done well, it gives more than lip service to prevention and health maintenance, and manages chronic disease so as to avoid or delay exacerbations and promote function and quality of life.[16] We are presently in a process of transition in which the traditional curative orientations of medicine are increasingly challenged by new conceptions of how to evaluate appropriate and effective care. To the extent that new criteria oriented to function prevail, the primary care role should be elevated in conception. Elevation in status will depend on changing economic incentives and educational practices.

Freedom to choose one's physician, and to change physicians when dissatisfied, is not simply an amenity but has importance for constructive use of primary care opportunities. Patients are more likely to be satisfied with professionals they choose, and choice also facilitates trust and cooperation in treatment. With the increasing importance of behavioral morbidity and the need to assist patients in modifying lifestyles or accommodating to the constraints of their life situation, cooperation in treatment and in health maintenance is especially important. Choice also functions to disengage patients and practitioners who have conflicting perspectives and tastes, and reduces tensions and dissatisfactions.

Addressing the Technologic Bias

The goals of universality, broadness of coverage and choice conflict to some degree with the objective of constraining health expenditures. Such constraints in the American context will be fairly loose, reflecting varying opinions on how fast medical costs should continue to grow relative to the economy as a whole. Even the most draconian proposals seek only to slow growth to about the level of advances in the economy overall and would allow a high level of technology. Despite this, it is difficult to conceive of any level of realistic investment that can accommodate all that technology might make possible in the coming years, and any reasonable accommodation that does not shortchange other important social needs will require constraints on how we develop and use medical technology. This requires that we thoughtfully face the technologic bias that so dominates health care in America.

Most people accept the analyses of the deficiencies of our health care system and the need for more thoughtful use of resources, but when they or their loved ones are ill they typically want all the potential that science makes possible however uncertain and whatever the cost. There is a growing consensus that new technological developments substantially accelerate health care costs,[17,18] but the public persistently supports the development of new technologies and their rapid adoption even when efficacy remains unknown. People have almost insatiable interest in new medical possibilities, and the mass media has made advances in technology a common and often exciting news topic. There will be inevitably a growing disjunction between what people come to expect in the way of technology and our capacity to finance all that they would like. Taming medical technology and its applications will require significant modifications of public understanding and attitudes. It also requires major modifications in how physicians think about and use the technologies available to them.

Physicians have been trained to pursue what Fuchs has called the technologic imperative,[19] an inclination to use interventions, however costly, that promise any possible benefit however small. Although third party coverage, and fee-for-service incentives, encourage physicians to intervene actively in uncertain situations, the technologic imperative is also deeply supported and reinforced by medical education and the common culture. Some doctors obviously manipulate the reimbursement system to maximize income, but the impulse to act aggressively in uncertain situations rather than wait and observe is deeply ingrained in conventional practice and has been a major aspect of the acceleration of expenditures on technical procedures. This bias is not only expensive, but it probably subjects patients as well to more discomfort and risk than is necessary or desirable.

Ethical dilemmas also complicate decisions about ending futile life-supporting treatment. At one extreme physicians and medical institutions commonly impose expensive, active therapies in seemingly hopeless situations on patients and their families who neither seek nor want them. The growing public interest in living wills, health powers of attorney, and assisted suicide suggest that at least some sector of the population prefers a less active response to extension of life when little prospect for any reasonable quality remains. But the obverse is true as well when families demand continuation of futile therapies and seek court judgments to restrain doctors from discontinuing expensive therapies that offer no hope. A recent court judgment requiring continuing life supports for an anencephalic infant in intensive care after four months at almost $1,500 a day illustrates the dilemma.[20] While physicians caring for the baby saw no prospect for benefit, the mother insisted on life supports on the basis of her religious beliefs. Since the patient's health care plan was paying for continuing treatment, the mother faced no financial risk. Such cases are not representative of typical practice, but they are emblematic of the complications of decision making present in many medical encounters. We will have to devise better ways of defining limits and appropriate protections.

With increasing scientific and technical capacities affecting care at every phase of the life cycle, the implications of the technologic imperative become more daunting. With advances in imaging techniques and other diagnostic procedures, we now have the capacity to create detailed images of all parts of the body and to monitor a vast range of biological reactions. Advances in genetics and molecular biology make possible a whole new range of tests and future interventions. As we apply these technologies to screening and evaluation, we inevitably identify apparent pathologies whose significance is unknown and often inflated, or other problems for which we have no remedies. In clinical situations early identification of potential abnormalities can result in exaggerated estimates of the prevalence of disease and overly optimistic assessments of the value of treatment. Many of the attributable benefits are often due to biases of lead time and length that can make an intervention appear efficacious when its true impact is negligible or even harmful. As Black and Welch observe, "despite clinicians' best intentions, many patients may have been labeled with disease they do not really have, and many have been given therapy they do not really need."[21]

As we sensitize the public to the possibilities of threat within their bodies, and the technical potential for early screening and intervention, we not only invite anxiety, but we stimulate patterns of medical help-seeking and intervention that substantially increase expenditures.[22] The point is not that we should not aggressively pursue medical progress and effective preventive interventions whenever possible, but we must elicit greater caution in the use of expensive interventions, especially before we have firm evidence that people's lives can be extended and improved by such means.

The development of new tests to screen for asymptomatic disease encourages help-seeking, but the conditions screened for may be so uncommon that the cost of each condition detected becomes extremely exorbitant.[23] Many such tests have a high rate of false positive results, meaning that many patients are unnecessarily alarmed and often must be subjected to additional costly, and sometimes highly intrusive, diagnostic procedures. Positive findings encourage aggressive treatment even when the need for intervention is uncertain or lacking.[24] In some instances, harm results from the diagnostic and treatment process. Thus, medical innovations that are introduced widely before being properly evaluated can stimulate demand, increase costs and promote possibly harmful activities of doubtful usefulness and low cost-effectiveness. The tendency to act in uncertain situations, and the incentives that support such activity, reinforce this process.

Although there is much inappropriate use and waste, such patterns are neither systematic nor easily eliminated. Despite very large variations in practice, particularly involving procedures of uncertain efficacy, the frequency of performing particular procedures is not highly correlated with professional norms of inappropriate use or abuse.[25] Nor does high utilization of a particular medical technology predict high use of other technologies within the same practice area. In the long run, the growing body of outcomes research and sophisticated practice guidelines may help constrain utilization within a more narrow range, but given the rapidity of development of medical knowledge and technology, such research cannot be a panacea. It is unlikely that even greatly expanded research efforts can keep up with the growing complexity and pace of change inherrent in the applications of technical procedures and screening and diagnostic practices.

The issue of cost effectiveness for various populations is different from what individuals might prefer in avoiding risks. Economic analysis might demonstrate that a screening test involves very large costs for each year of life potentially saved, but once individuals are told they may be at risk, they may not be so easily persuaded by economic assessments. From a personal perspective, the theoretical life saved, however costly, may be their own. The public is often receptive to more frequent testing than may be cost-effective, and such preferences are reinforced by the weak link between utilization and payment. This is a compelling reason to make consumers more cost conscious in their demands for medical care.

Rationing Approaches

Not fully understanding how variations in practice arise, or the reasons for them, our options for constraining cost are relatively crude and less selective than desirable. Among these methods are limitations on capital investment in technology that constrain its availability, the use of patient cost-sharing to delay utilization, requiring providers to function within fixed prospective budgets, and utilization management. Most approaches to containing costs share some elements of each of these approaches, but the relative mix may vary a great deal.

Constraints on technology may be applied in its initial development or in its subsequent accessibility. The United States maintains an enormous biomedical enterprise which provides a continuing stream of new innovations. Although the goal is to identify effective interventions that ultimately reduce the need and demand for care, major innovations are typically "half-way" technologies that delay mortality and maintain function but also increase costs.[26] It would be possible, at least theoretically, to guide biomedical advances with more emphasis on cost-saving technologies and those more oriented to prevention.[27] Much of the demand for research, however, is motivated by the presence of disabling chronic disease and patterns of illness and disability most commonly found among the elderly. Some have advocated shifting priorities away from research and development affecting the elderly,[28] but such a view is likely to be received with great public skepticism.

One effective method for controlling expenditures on technology is to control its availability and accessibility. Rationing technology results in queuing and establishment of priorities for treatment. By any kind of efficiency standard, American health care is highly wasteful and its enormous capacity encourages utilization in situations of marginal usefulness. Most countries in the world put tighter constraints on the availability of expensive technical procedures than we do and use queuing as a rationing mechanism. In many instances where the procedure is not urgent and may be of uncertain necessity, waiting may be useful in that it gives both clinician and patient some opportunity for reflection and may encourage consideration of more conservative approaches to diagnosis and treatment. When options are fully understood, patients may prefer more conservative alternatives than their physicians favor.[29] If the controls are too severe, however, or if access is poorly distributed geographically, persons more immediately in need of services may experience delays as well as those whose needs are less urgent or more uncertain. We have not really tested the threshold of public impatience and its level of tolerance for delays in access. There is much room to tighten up on our uses of technology before the public experiences any serious sense of constraint, but given the crudeness of selection processes and queuing, some who can benefit may find access difficult. The American public is highly demanding, and it is unlikely that it will tolerate the levels of resource constraints common in some other western countries.[30]

At the service level, there are two basic rationing options consistent with universality and broad coverage, but both alternatives are imperfect. The first deters utilization by imposing significant cost-sharing, the second by managing care through global budgets so that resource use is considered carefully in relation to patient need and potential benefit. Cost-sharing substantially affects the demand for care, but as the RAND Health Insurance Experiment demonstrated, it functions as a general barrier to care affecting access where care is appropriate and efficacious as well as where it is of little value.[31] Cost-sharing also affects the poor more than the affluent. Tying cost-sharing to income is a potential remedy, but implementation is difficult and administratively burdensome.

Alternatively, coverage can be broad if there is sufficient control over triage to more expensive specialty care, high cost technologies and inpatient treatment. The idea of a case manager/gatekeeper who must function within constraints allows the retention of a broad and flexible benefit but restricts the patient to services deemed medically necessary. This limits the choices patients can make about their care, but if choice is preserved in a meaningful way at the primary care level, many patients may not find such an approach incompatible with expectations. To the extent that patients trust their primary physician and are convinced that the doctor is fully committed to their welfare, many, given reasonable incentives, would accept some limitation on their freedom of choice. The Clinton proposals seek to provide such incentives through the financial savings available to citizens who choose a low cost plan. It remains unclear whether the financial incentives are large enough to achieve their purpose, and if they are, whether locking patients into limited networks will result in significant dissatisfaction.

A further approach is utilization management (UM) which can be used concurrently with cost-sharing or prospective budgets. In UM, expensive utilization and intervention decisions are reviewed by predetermined standards or through a process of second opinions. Major approaches include precertification and concurrent review of inpatient care, case management of expensive episodes, and second surgical opinions. These management devices are typically combined with other organizational innovations including employee assistance programs and preferred provider plans. Although there are few controlled evaluations of managed care,[32] the existing literature suggests that UM can reduce utilization and costs by a meaningful amount for the insurance plan.[33] It is less clear to what extent costs are being shifted to consumers, their families, and the medical care system which must accommodate to UM processes and related "hassles." More important, it remains unclear whether UM is sufficiently selective to reduce costs without affecting the quality of patient outcomes.

Health Maintenance Organizations

There is little evidence of major differences in quality between HMOs and traditional forms of care. Both sectors are characterized by variations in performance that are much greater than the differences between sectors. HMOs probably have similar variabilities in practice patterns as those found more generally, but they can be restrained more easily by administrative measures. In theory, doctors who are practicing under other than fee-for-service arrangements are more inclined to make resource decisions on the basis of clinical need and potential benefit rather than financial incentives, but a less ideal process may result from such factors as administrative pressures, learned practice patterns, preferences for activities and patients who are more interesting and attractive, and other personal needs and inclinations. Studies consistently show that fee-for-service patients feel their doctors are more responsive than those in prepaid practice.[34] This may be due to a variety of reasons including the possibility that those in prepaid settings are more attuned to the standards of their colleagues and administrative pressures than the preferences of their patients.[35] Whatever the cause, such differences require continued monitoring.

Basic to understanding how HMOs function are the administrative and reimbursement arrangements that affect physicians. Doctors are trained to give high priority to professional responsibility and will not easily sacrifice the patient's welfare to organizational goals. Thus, such broad incentives as sharing of savings among a large group may have no perverse effects, but strong income incentives specific to each doctor may create irresistible pressures. A 1987 survey found that 23 percent of for-profit plans made primary care practitioners personally responsible for exceeding utilization targets,[36] and such incentives were associated with lower patient utilization.[37] How we pay professionals should reflect public priorities, and acceptable income incentive structures have to be differentiated from those that cross ethical lines. The view that physicians should be health advocates only and not responsible for allocation is unrealistic, but incentive structures should not push too strongly in any one direction. All forms of payment, whether fee-for-service, capitation, or case-payment have both advantages and limitations, and all can be gamed. More complex reimbursement systems make such manipulation more difficult, and as we develop better approaches remuneration could reflect not only skill level and effort required but also patient satisfaction, peer assessment, and even patient outcomes.

As the opportunity to change providers when one wishes becomes more restricted, the integrity of procedures for dealing with conflict and grievances become more important. Health plans will have to develop easily understood and accessible complaint and grievance procedures to allow doctor-patient and patient-plan conflicts to be adjudicated without litigation. Such procedures have not been prominent but will become increasingly important, particularly in the transition period when large numbers of people shift from a traditional fee-for-service model to various forms of more restrictive managed care. Experience in the Medicare program and elsewhere suggests that the public does not fully understand the constraints involved in moving from fee-for-service to capitated practice, and considerable public education will be needed.[38]

The prepaid group practice structure offers many organizational possibilities to make use of a broader mix of health professionals and special services, to put emphasis on prevention and patient education, and to increase the flexibility of care within a global budget. The effective development of such programs could in theory increase responsiveness to populations with special needs such as the frail elderly, persons with chronic illness and disadvantaged minorities. Some prepaid group practices have introduced meaningful innovations including outreach efforts, specialized clinics for chronic patients, and prevention and patient education programs, but these potentialities are largely underdeveloped. Although prepaid group practice was the generic model that stimulated public policy interest in HMOs, independent practice associations (IPAs) are the fastest growing type of HMO. IPAs have the advantage of offering a wider range of physician choice, but in using individual practitioners and traditional practice situations they offer less innovative potential. It is unclear that this alternative will provide either the cost-savings or opportunities for innovation suggested by the performance of the more outstanding prepaid group practices.

Challenges in Primary Health Care

The crisis in primary care has persisted for decades because, despite our rhetoric, we have been unwilling to develop the structures and incentives that could seriously redress the imbalance between primary and specialty care. We have invested considerable resources over the years in subsidies for training primary care doctors and for inducing doctors to practice in underserved areas, but these programs have been at the margins of mainstream efforts and have not seriously affected the incentives that drive the practice of medicine.

Central to the Clinton proposals are forceful measures to redress the persistent imbalance through regulation of residency programs as well as with incentives for entering primary care. These proposals seek eventual parity between primary care and specialty positions, although modifying the residency mix by itself will not reach this goal for several decades.[39] The Clinton program also proposes significant retraining efforts, although in the short run many physicians may take on primary care roles, in part or whole, without significant retooling. There continues to be a widespread assumption among doctors that anyone can do primary care. But successfully establishing a meaningful primary care system involves both changes in organization and in clinical perspective.

Primary care is not simply a description of a type of practitioner but more importantly represents a set of functions embedded in a system of care that carefully articulates functions and responsibilities. Several points follow: First, worldwide experience with primary care personnel points to considerable potential for provider substitution. Given our history, the large number of doctors we have, our affluence, and public expectations, it is unlikely that practitioners other than physicians will be dominant. But as we think of reorganizing how we provide care, it is evident that primary care nurse-practitioners and physician assistants can play a larger role. In some contexts they might function as independent practitioners, where doctors are in short supply, for instance. But it is more likely that they will join teams in organized health care settings, emphasizing prevention and health maintenance. A large body of research impressively demonstrates that they can perform these responsibilities effectively.[40]

Second, the way in which functions are articulated between primary care and other services is arbitrary and can be modified to fit the conditions and circumstances that prevail in a particular geographic or practice area. In many European systems, there is a historical separation between primary care and inpatient care. Although this pattern is unlikely to apply to American practice, the actual scope of responsibility of primary care will differ depending on the availability of other services that patients can access including minor surgery, prenatal and maternity care, etc.

Third, despite the assumption that anyone can do primary care, it typically requires fundamentally different attitudes, practice strategies and skills in the management of uncertainty and a much broader range of considerations in treatment. As the case manager/gatekeeper, the primary care physician is trained to moderate the technologic bias and to consider carefully potential false positives and the cost and benefits of watchful waiting versus aggressive interventions. Newly trained primary care physicians increasingly are acquiring the tools of clinical epidemiology and the decision sciences, linking their decisions to knowledge about patterns of morbidity in general populations. They also need to be sensitive to the social and behavioral factors that motivate a patient's behavior toward illness and that affect the course of disease. Functioning as a gatekeeper is an uncertain venture, but primary care offers protections by encouraging doctor-patient continuity and increasing the probability that over time the doctor will know patients in a way that sharpens judgment about their illness behavior.

To the extent that managed competition or other efforts to induce people into HMOs succeed, they will be more instrumental in restructuring primary care than many of the special programs that operated over the last forty years or that are now being proposed. As more patients enter managed care systems, specialists will have greater difficulty sustaining an independent practice and some will be attracted to primary care either on a full-time or part-time basis, particularly if inequalities in remuneration are narrowed. In the short-run, we will probably see many doctors mixing primary and specialist roles, but if the advantages of primary care as a different practice mode are to be achieved we will need to develop coherent systems that build on a community orientation and a biopsychosocial perspective.

Primary care has a number of key functions. As the point of first contact with the formal system of care it encompasses a broad range of complaints involving not only physical and emotional morbidity but a host of psychosocial ills. The primary physician, or a primary care team, not only assesses a problem and determines how care should proceed, but assumes continuing responsibility for the patient, providing most routine treatment and management, preventive services and health education, counseling, and social and emotional support. The primary care physician also supervises the referral process, ideally taking responsibility for integrating services received to reduce unnecessary duplication, ensure that the overall pattern of care makes sense, that appropriate communication occurs among the practitioners involved, and that patients understand their treatment and what is expected of them.

Patterns of illness in the community are changing, making new and often complicated demands on the medical care system. Young people, relatively immune from the historical perils of childhood infection, now face escalating behavioral risks and morbidity due to social conditions. With the weakening of family and community structures, increasing permissiveness, and the presence of a mass culture of excitement and violence, young people have many temptations and opportunities for high-risk activities. Similarly, significant risks for many adults arise from their own behaviors which may not be easy to modify but which should be on the doctor's agenda. Most chronic illness is concentrated in the older ages, and the challenge is not only to use medical technology wisely to promote function and quality of life but also to help mobilize social resources and activate peoples' social networks so that they can maintain their independence and pursue valued activities. Psychosocial issues complicate illnesses and play a large role in the problems people bring to doctors, making it essential that they be taken into account. This is particularly true for disadvantaged populations whose life problems may not only contribute significantly to their illnesses but can vastly complicate treatment and rehabilitation.

The dilemmas are difficult. How much can we really expect of primary care physicians who practice in an environment of increasing cost constraints that puts them under expanding time and productivity pressures and diminishes the value of their accumulated knowledge? We expect far too much of the individual doctor and give far too little attention to system development that will make it easier for physicians, working with nurse practitioners and other professionals, to address the wide range of problems inherent in many patients' illnesses.

Medical challenges are increasingly encountered in the area of chronic disease and disability and the interventions that can prevent or delay adverse consequences. Physicians can offer palliative relief to reduce pain and discomfort, and there are impressive opportunities for successful management through the use of assisted technologies. But much of the future potential lies in helping patients to develop new skills and find an acceptable way of living that allows continued functioning and independence.[41] In accomplishing this, the emphasis is as much social as medical, and effective communication plays a large role. Benefits accrue from primary health care personnel and patients working together over time to fit the required medical regimen into the constraints of the home environment and the demands of the patient's life. Simple exhortation to change behavior is ineffectual and discouraging for both practitioner and patient.

Physicians trained in traditional ways, and lacking special skills in these areas, naturally consider this an unrealistic approach. For many doctors, writing a prescription is easier than communicating with patients. But communication is central to every aspect of doctor-patient transactions, including eliciting an accurate history and assessing the complaint, achieving compliance with a suggested regimen, and scheduling treatments around a patient's daily routine. Reaching these goals requires understanding how patients think about their illness and how they organize their lives.

Despite an erosion of confidence, doctors continue to have much influence with patients, particularly when a strong and trusting relationship is sustained. Doctors, however, often have an inflated view of how they affect patients' behavior because of their particular location in the trajectory of care. They tend to overestimate their treatment efficacy because patients often seek help at the peak of their distress and in the normal course most would show improvement anyway.

In contrast, physicians typically view themselves as ineffectual in altering habits like smoking and often seem frustrated by the suggestion that they take more responsibility in attempting to change such harmful behaviors. The vast majority of patients, given brief counseling by a physician and a pamphlet on how to stop smoking, will be unaffected. Indeed, only about 5 percent will abstain for one year or more in response to physician efforts.[42] This might seem like a small yield to the doctor, but it is probably cost effective given the minimal effort and resources involved and the deleterious effects of continued smoking. Thus, the appearances of success and futility at the clinical level may be at variance with the broader realities of risk and disease.

It is unreasonable to anticipate that even much-improved primary care could compensate significantly for the social and environmental difficulties faced by our most disadvantaged groups. Yet is has been evident that the types of episodic services typical among these populations, commonly provided at emergency rooms and hospital outpatient departments, are extremely expensive and often inappropriate. Such groups, with their complex sociomedical problems, need a longitudinal relationship with a primary care setting that can easily link with a variety of medical, social and welfare services. This is especially critical for persons with disabling chronic disease whose welfare depends on appropriate integration of medical and social services. Community health centers with an expanded vision of clinical responsibility and a willingness to engage the disadvantaged at a community as well as a clinical level have achieved reduced morbidity rates and high patient satisfaction.[43,44] Such efforts should be emphasized as we begin to more seriously address characteristic health problems of high-risk populations.

A broader community approach offers the opportunity to intervene in ways that reduce disability, prevent secondary complications, and ultimately empower patients. Such programs not only promote aggressive outreach that assists patients in typical ways and helps them access needed services in related systems, but also contribute to community development efforts, energizing people to take more responsibility for their own problems. It may seem too ambitious to attempt to coordinate health care with initiatives in nutrition, schooling and housing, but health care isolated from such vital services in deprived communities offers little hope for addressing the noxious behavior patterns that not only contribute to poor health but undermine functioning more generally.

Given the diverse economic, social and behavioral factors contributing to social breakdown and poor health, it may seem counterintuitive to place such emphasis on health initiatives. There are, at least, two reasons to do so. First, patients bring most problems to the medical care system, and there is more trust in medicine than in most other public institutions. Thus, there are opportunities for intervention not easily identified elsewhere. Also, given the softness of public support for social initiatives directed to the disadvantaged, health and medicine remain among the most legitimate and accepted means of making a significant contribution. Health initiatives will not reduce poverty, or even significantly reduce health disparities, but they offer a publicly acceptable way to promote normal development and improved health outcomes.

Concluding Thoughts

There is broad agreement on the desirability of containing medical care costs, but an unwillingness to acknowledge that any constraint that reduces waste and unnecessary services will inevitably reduce some useful services as well. Although there is massive waste and inefficiency in our system of care, the degree of uncertainty concerning effectiveness and our limited understanding of practice variations inevitably means that we cannot cut the fat without losing some muscle. Although all of the cost-constraining tools available to us are merely crude rationing devices which share similar disadvantages, I favor the fixed budget because I believe that health professionals are best able to determine the need for any particular medical service, and the tastes and preferences of patients.[45] Physicians, of course, will make errors of judgment and are not immune from irrational influences, but I believe that the professionalism of doctors would work credibly better than other economic mechanisms, provided that such competence is taken seriously and that the system of care is reasonably well funded, with targeted incentives not excessively distorting clinical decision making.

While there is an emerging core consensus that reform is required, few interests are open to yielding any advantage they presently hold. Any rational resolution will create losers as well as winners, but the basis for choosing among competing interests has to be understood clearly by the public and perceived as fair. Values and guidelines for choice require articulation and explanation. Medical care has many functions including prevention and cure, and there is a need to achieve a better balance between how we make our investments and what we know to be cost effective. In a system already heavily weighted toward curative interventions, initiatives that contribute to preventing illness and promoting health should be elevated in importance. Our priorities ought to fit, as well, the changing demography of the population, the shifting patterns of disease distribution, and emerging new and old threats to health. This criterion argues for more focused attention on children and behavioral pathology on one hand, and on chronic disease and rehabilitation among the older population on the other hand. Further, it should be clear that the distributional effects of health reform are fair to those most disadvantaged and responsive to the growing inequalities in health status in our nation.

The health care debate becomes more distorted as each of the many advocates picks away at proposals that appear to be less than optimally beneficial to their cause. Experience throughout the world indicates that no health system achieves its full potential in a single leap. Rather, they evolve through iterative stages that reflect accommodations to the public and professional communities and an appreciation of the need to fine-tune various financial and organizational features. To the extent that we view health reform as an evolving process, we will have better opportunities to achieve reasonable solutions built around widely shared principles. The current style of debate has a high probability of stalemate and may squander an unusual opportunity to make significant progress in addressing difficult problems in the financing and organization of care.

A common ploy in the debate is to alarm the public with the threat of rationing and to suggest that lifesaving measures may not be available when needed. Beyond the apparent fact that care has always been rationed by insurance availability, copayment levels, geography, and accessibility of facilities, the public must come to understand that the risks of too much care have to be weighted against the risks of too little under some circumstances. Any thoughtful debate requires that the public grasp some of the limits of medical aggressiveness. In the context of American culture, with its high public expectations, vigilant media oversight, and propensity to protest and litigate, strong tendencies toward underservice will be held in check. Larger risks derive from unquestioning faith in the value of unproven technologies.

Whatever the fate of the Clinton health care reform proposals, major changes are inevitable. We can drift toward a new equilibrium or we can attempt to control the direction of change by imposing clear goals and priorities. To a major degree, medical practice is shaped by emerging knowledge and technology, and by patterns of morbidity, risk and financing. But health care is also a cultural institution and its framework is in no sense predetermined. Only the future can tell whether we have the wisdom to constructively use this unusual opportunity to take a giant step forward in providing health care.

Notes

1. George Brown and Tirril Harris, *Life Events and Illness* (New York: Guilford Press, 1989).

2. G. Richard Smith, Jr., *Somatization Disorder in the Medical Setting*, DHHS Pub. No. (ADM) 900–1631 (Rockville, MD: National Institute of Mental Health, 1990).

3. Lu Ann Aday, *At Risk in America: The Health and Health Care Needs of Vulnerable Populations in the United States* (San Francisco: Jossey-Bass, 1993).

4. Louise Russell, *Educated Guesses: Making Policy About Medical Screening Tests* (Berkeley: University of California Press, 1994).

5. Mark Schlesinger and David Mechanic, "Challenges for Managed Competition from Chronic Illness," *Health Affairs* 12 (Supplement) (1993): 123–137.

6. John P. Bunker, Deanna Gomby, and Barbara Kehrer, eds., *Pathways to Health: The Role of Social Factors* (Menlo Park, CA: The Henry J. Kaiser Family Foundation, 1989).

7. Gregory Pappas, Susan Queen, Wilbur Hadden, and Gail Fisher, "The Increasing Disparity in Mortality Between Socioeconomic Groups in the United States, 1960 and 1986," *New England Journal of Medicine* 329 (1993): 103–09.

8. Colin McCord and Harold P. Freeman, "Excess Mortality in Harlem," *New England Journal of Medicine* 322 (1990): 173–77.

9. Nancy E. Adler, Thomas Boyce, Margaret Chesney, Susan Folkman, and Leonard Syme, "Socioeconomic Inequalities in Health: No Easy Solution," *Journal of the American Medical Association* 269 (1993): 3140–45.

10. David Mechanic, "Socioeconomic Status and Health: An Examination of Underlying Processes," in *Pathways to Health: The Role of Social Factors*, eds. John Bunker et al. (Menlo Park, CA: The Henry J. Kaiser Family Foundation, 1989), pp. 9–26.

11. James S. House, Karl L. Landis, and Debra Umberson, "Social Relationships and Health," *Science* 241 (1988): 540–545.

12. Judith Rodin, "Aging and Health: Effects of Sense of Control," *Science* 233 (1986): 1271–76.

13. Jonathan Feinstein, "The Relationship Between Socioeconomic Status and Health: A Review of the Literature," *Milbank Quarterly* 71 (1993): 279–322.

14. Paul Starr, *The Social Transformation of American Medicine* (New York: Basic Books, 1982).

15. Charles Lewis, Rashi Fein, and David Mechanic, *A Right to Health: The Problem of Access to Primary Medical Care* (New York: Wiley-Interscience, 1976).

16. Institute of Medicine, *Disability in America: Toward a National Agenda for Prevention* (Washington, DC: National Academy Press, 1991).

17. Joseph P. Newhouse, "An Iconoclastic View of Health Cost Containment," *Health Affairs* 12 (Supplement) (1993): 152–71.

18. Henry J. Aaron and William B. Schwartz, "Managed Competition: Little Cost Containment Without Budget Limits," *Health Affairs* 12 (Supplement) (1993): 204–15.

19. Victor R. Fuchs, "The Growing Demand for Medical Care," *New England Journal of Medicine* 279 (1968): 190–95.

20. Linda Greenhouse, "Hospital Appeals Ruling on Treating Baby Born with Most of Brain Gone," *New York Times*, Sept. 24, 1993, A10.

21. William C. Black and Gilbert Welch, "Advances in Diagnostic Imaging and Overestimations of Disease Prevalence and the Benefits of Therapy," *New England Journal of Medicine* 328 (1993): 1237–1243.

22. Arthur Barsky, *Worried Sick: Our Troubled Quest for Wellness* (Boston: Little Brown and Co., 1988).

23. Louise B. Russell, *Is Prevention Better than Cure?* (Washington, D.C.: Brookings Institution, 1986).

24. Louise B. Russell, "The Role of Prevention in Health Reform," *New England Journal of Medicine* 329 (1993): 352–54.

25. M.R. Chassin, J. Kosecoff, R.E. Park, C.M. Winslow, C.M. Kahn, N.J. Mernick, J. Keesey, A. Fink, D.H. Solomon, and R.H. Brook, "Does Inappropriate Use Explain Geographic Variations in the Use of Health Care Services: A Study of Three Procedures," *Journal of the American Medical Association* 258 (1987): 2533–37.

26. Lewis Thomas, "On the Science and Technology of Medicine," *Daedalus* 106 (1977): 35–46.

27. Kenneth E. Warner, "Effects of Hospital Cost Containment on the Development and Use of Medical Technology," *Milbank Quarterly* 56 (1978): 187–211.

28. Daniel Callahan, "Adequate Health Care and an Aging Society: Are They Morally Compatible," *Daedalus* 115 (1986): 247–67.

29. John E. Wennberg, "Outcomes Research, Cost Containment and the Fear of Health Care Rationing," *New England Journal of Medicine* 323 (1990): 1202–04.

30. Henry J. Aaron and William B. Schwartz, *The Painful Prescription: Rationing Hospital Care* (Washington, DC: Broookings Institution, 1984).

31. Kathleen N. Lohr, Robert H. Brook, Caren J. Kamberg, George A. Goldberg, Arleen Leibowitz, Joan Keesey, David Reloussin, and Joseph P. Newhouse, *Use of Medical Care in the RAND Health Insurance Experiment: Diagnosis- and Service-Specific Analyses in a Randomized Controlled Trial*, Pub. No. R-3464-HHS (Santa Monica, CA: RAND Corporation, 1986).

32. General Accounting Office, *Managed Health Care: Effect on Employers' Costs Difficult to Measure*, GAO-HRD 94–3, October 1993 (Washington, DC: U.S. Government Printing Office).

33. Dominic Hodgkin, "The Impact of Private Utilization Management on Psychiatric Care: A Review of the Literature," *The Journal of Mental Health Administration* 19 (1992): 143–157.

34. Harold Luft, *Health Maintenance Organizations: Dimensions of Performance* (New Brunswick, NJ: Transactions Publishers, 1987).

35. Eliot Freidson, *Profession of Medicine: A Study of the Sociology of Applied Knowledge* (New York: Dodd-Mead, 1970).

36. Alan Hillman, "Financial Incentives for Physicians in HMOs: Is There a Conflict of Interest?" *New England Journal of Medicine* 317 (1987): 1743–48.

37. Alan Hillman, Mark Pauly, and Joseph Kerstein, "Do Financial Incentives Affect Physicians' Clinical Decisions and the Financial Performance of Health Maintenance Organizations?" *New England Journal of Medicine* 321 (1989): 86–95.

38. David Mechanic, Therese Ettel, and Diane Davis, "Choosing Among Health Insurance Options: A Study of New Employees," *Inquiry* 27 (1990): 14–23.

39. David Kindig, James Cultice, and Fitzhugh Mullan, "The Elusive Generalist Physician: Can We Reach a 50 Percent Goal?" *Journal of the American Medical Association* 270 (1993): 1069–73.

40. Loretta Ford, "Advanced Nursing Practice: Future of the Nurse Practitioner," in *Charting Nursing's Future*, eds. Linda Aiken and Claire Fagin (Philadelphia, PA: J.P. Lippencott Co., 1992), pp. 287–99.

41. DeWitt Stetten, "Coping with Blindness," *New England Journal of Medicine* 305 (1981): 458–60.

42. M.A.H. Russell, P.H. Stapleton, P.H. Jackson, P. Hajek, and M. Belcher, "District Programme to Reduce Smoking: Effect of Clinic Supported Brief Intervention by General Practitioners," *British Medical Journal* 295 (1987): 1240–44.

43. Diane Dutton, "Social Class, Health, and Illness," in *Applications of Social Science to Clinical Medicine and Health Policy*, eds. Linda H. Aiken and David Mechanic (New Brunswick, NJ: Rutgers University Press, 1986), pp. 31–62.

44. H. Jack Geiger, "Community Health Centers: Health Care as an Instrument of Social Change," in *Reforming Medicine: Lessons of the Last Quarter Century*, eds. V.W. Sidel and Ruth Sidel (New York: Pantheon, 1984), pp. 11–32.

45. David Mechanic, "Professional Judgment and the Rationing of Medical Care," *University of Pennsylvania Law Review* 140 (1992): 1713–54.

PART TWO

Benefits and Cost Controls

4

Who Gets What and How Much

Thomas Rice

The centerpiece of any health care reform legislation is its benefits package. The first thing most Americans ask when they hear about such a proposal is, "What's in it for me?" The next question, of course, is "How much will it cost?" Although obvious, these questions have occassionally been forgotten, with disastrous consequences. Probably the major reason that the Medicare Catastrophic Coverage Act was repealed just a year after its passage, was that many elderly Americans—particularly wealthier ones with supplemental insurance coverage from a former employer—believed that it provided them with no extra benefits, but would cost them a great deal more.[1]

Benefit design usually identifies the specific services and providers that will be covered or reimbursed by health insurance. Indeed, much of the publicity surrounding President Clinton's Task Force on Health Care Reform focused on which benefits were "in" versus which were "out." Some examples: Early in the Task Force's deliberations it appeared that mental health would be covered as completely as acute care, but this idea was squelched as the estimated cost of the reform plan escalated; one of the key strategies for obtaining support from the elderly was the inclusion of prescription drug coverage; and an issue that continues to be controversial is whether elective abortion should be covered (like most current plans and programs, the Clinton reform proposal includes this benefit).

This chapter, however, does not focus upon these specific issues (although two of them, mental health and long-term care, are addressed in Chapter 5). Rather, it focuses on perhaps more subtle and critical issues

The author wishes to express his appreciation to E. Richard Brown, Jon Gabel, and Robert Valdez, who reviewed the manuscript and provided a number of useful suggestions.

surrounding benefit design under a reformed health care system. Specifically, it explores the following:

1. eligibility for coverage;
2. whether benefits need to be standardized and the role of supplemental insurance;
3. criteria for choosing the services to be covered;
4. restrictions on covered services; and,
5. ensuring financial access to services.

Policymakers need to address these fundamental issues before finalizing the list of services and eligible providers to be covered under a health reform plan.

Eligibility

The first issue that needs to be addressed in designing a benefits package for a reformed health care system is: Who is eligible to receive the benefits? Stated another way, should coverage be universal, and if not, who won't be covered?

Guaranteeing universal coverage is highly desirable not only from an equity standpoint, but as a mechanism to control costs. This is true for two reasons. First, by including everyone in the system, the methods developed by the government to control expenditures will apply to the entire population. This concept has been well-stated by the Canadian economist Robert Evans:

> If providers have access to a significant uninsured or privately insured patient sector, or if they can at their discretion impose additional charges on patients, then the bargaining power of the reimbursing agency is undercut and cost control becomes more difficult if not impossible.[2]

Second, if everyone is part of the system, then it is unnecessary to have in place a parallel system that serves as a safety net for the excluded population. To illustrate, the Clinton Administration's reform plan does not provide the basic benefits package to undocumented immigrants. They will be able to receive coverage, however, "through emergency and other health services as provided under current law." Furthermore, "health care institutions that serve a large number of patients who are not eligible for coverage [will] continue to receive federal funding to compensate for their care."[3]

Universal coverage should preclude the need for such arrangements. If everyone has the same package of benefits—particularly if they are fairly comprehensive—then there is no need for such a safety net or for additional reimbursements to providers who treat uncovered individuals. In addition, there will be a reduction in administrative expenses for verifying eligibility, documenting costs for treating uncovered individuals, and so on. Finally, providers would not need to "cost shift" the expenses of treating uncovered persons to the insured population, and long-term savings could result from providing adequate primary care in a timely fashion.

One concern—for potentially short-sighted economic reasons—is that some of the most needy people will not receive basic benefits. But it is also possible to design a system where the opposite occurs, that is, economically secure people will be excluded from the system. But that, too, would work against both the equity and cost-savings goals of reform.

If wealthier people are excluded from universal coverage, the vast majority are likely to purchase coverage on the private market. This market, which would not be subjected to the same controls as the one in which universal coverage is granted, would likely be considerably more expensive. Furthermore, providers will tend to prefer to treat patients in the private market because payment rates are likely to be more lucrative—particularly if there are strong premium controls in the larger market. This is essentially what has happened in Germany, where about 10 percent of the population—generally, the wealthiest—can join private insurance plans that provide more benefits and pay higher rates to providers. There is increasing evidence that such a system causes increased costs, and compromises the quality of care received by those without private health insurance.[4]

The U.S. Medicaid program provides a more glaring example. By excluding the middle and upper classes, the program has been besieged by problems involving ineffective access to care and low quality. In summary, then, for both equity and cost-control reasons, coverage should be universal under a reformed health care system.

Standardized Benefits and the
Role of Supplemental Insurance

Once eligibility criteria are established, it becomes necessary to determine the format in which benefits will be offered. There are two prime candidates—minimum benefits or standardized benefits. Minimum benefit standards mean that all insurance plans must at a minimum cover certain services, but can offer others as well. In contrast, under "standardized benefits," insurers must offer a specified list of benefits; more or fewer benefits cannot be sold. (Although standardization of benefits usually implies more extensive coverage than minimum benefits, this does not always have to be the case.)

The issue of minimum versus standardized benefits applies mainly to reform proposals in which private insurers continue to sell coverage. In a completely public system benefits tend to be standardized, although people are usually free to purchase supplemental coverage.[5] In a mixed public-private system, however, a choice must be made. The Clinton Administration has opted for standardized benefits in its health care reform proposal.

There are several reasons to believe that standardized benefits are more effective than minimum benefits. One concerns adverse selection. With minimum benefits, individuals can choose the benefits that they wish to purchase over and above those specified in the minimum benefits package, and they are likely to purchase those that they are most likely to use. This will tend to drive up the premiums for these benefits, making them less affordable. In contrast, if such benefits are standardized, then their cost will be spread over the entire population, including non-users.

An even greater problem with minimum (as opposed to standardized) benefits, is that it makes it difficult for consumers to shop because they are usually faced with "apples and oranges" choices. Suppose, for example, that the minimum benefits package does not cover prescription drugs, dental services, or home health care; furthermore, among policies that do, each has a different schedule of benefits and requires different cost-sharing. A consumer facing an array of such insurance policies, all sold at different premiums, will find it extremely difficult to determine which is the best bargain. In contrast, if benefits are standardized, then it is much easier to pick a policy based on the premium charged for a standard set of benefits.

The main argument against standardization is that it bars consumers from choosing the exact configuration of benefits that they want. The central policy question, then, is whether there are sufficient gains to offset this loss of consumer sovereignty. To address this question, it is useful to look at the experience of the "Medigap," the Medicare supplemental health insurance market.

The Medigap market has been harshly criticized since the inception of the Medicare program for providing inadequate benefits for premiums paid, as well as various agent and company abuses.[6] To address this problem, Congress approved the "Baucus Amendments" in 1980, which required (among other things) that all Medigap policies conform to minimum benefit standards. It soon became apparent, however, that this did little to solve the market drawbacks because even though companies complied with the legislation, each sold policies with different benefits, making comparison shopping nearly impossible.

The extent of the problem can be seen in the results of a recent study of Medigap policies sold by some of the largest Medigap insurers just prior to the enactment of standardization legislation. It found that of the nine companies providing prescription drug coverage, each offered a different configuration of benefits ranging from, "annual deductibles of $50, $100, $200, or $250; patient coinsurance rates of 20 percent, 25 percent, or 50 percent; and maximum company annual liabilities of $300, $500, and unlimited."[7] It should be kept in mind that this is one of only many differing benefits, several of which show the same degree of heterogeneity.

In 1990, Congress passed legislation that dramatically changed the face of competition in the Medigap market.[8] Rather than allowing companies to market whatever coverage they wished, so long as it met the minimum standards established by the Baucus Amendments, it required coverage to be standardized. Since the summer of 1992, companies have been limited to selling only policies that exactly conform to ten standardized policies developed by the National Association of Insurance Commissioners. Although it is too early to know how the legislation has affected Medigap premiums, preliminary findings suggest it has resulted in a substantial decline in consumer complaints filed with state insurance departments.[9]

Once a decision is made about the format of benefits, rules must be established regarding supplemental insurance—that is, private insurance policies that cover any remaining health care expenses (including patient cost sharing) not covered under the health plan's benefit package.

There are some potential disadvantages to allowing the sale of supplemental insurance. First, it leads to in an inequitable distribution of insurance coverage. In the Medigap market, for example, practically all studies have found that minorities and individuals with lower incomes are less likely to purchase coverage, even though they tend to have more serious health problems.[10] Second, it results in the use of more services.[11] This is of special concern for coverage of the patient cost-sharing requirements under a reformed system. If the system requires, say, a ten dollar copayment or 20 percent coinsurance for use of a service, but this is covered by a supplemental insurance policy, then the use of services will be higher, which in turn may raise total expenditures for the health system. Because the supplemental insurer is responsible only for the copayment amount, and not for any of the health system's extra expenditures, this means that the health system is providing an implicit subsidy to the insurance company.[12]

With respect to the first issue—whether people should be allowed to purchase supplemental insurance—it would be very hard to prevent them from doing so. Traditionally, this country has not prevented people from purchasing the types of coverage they desire. Evidence from the RAND Health Insurance Experiment indicates that most people say they would be interested in purchasing supplemental policies that cover their cost-sharing requirements.[13]

The second issue, regarding the implicit subsidy for supplemental insurance, can be addressed, however. Under the Clinton Administration's plan (which also requires the standardization of such supplemental benefits), it is stipulated that "the price of any cost-sharing policy ... shall take into account any expected increase in utilization resulting from the purchase of the policy. ..."[14]

Criteria for Choosing Covered Services

The specific services covered under a reformed health care system should be drawn from a cogent set of criteria. These criteria should be selected from issue areas that are of concern to policymakers, such as ensuring access to care, preserving quality, and controlling expenditures. Therefore, the establishment of such criteria is a necessary step in determining the services that ultimately will be covered under reform.

One set of criteria, recently developed by Linda Bergthold, lists four alternative benefit-design approaches: (1) primary care; (2) catastrophic care; (3) fee-for-service; and (4) health maintenance organization (HMO).[15] Although this is a useful list, it combines two issues that perhaps should be treated separately—how patient cost-sharing requirements are assessed (the first and second), and how providers are paid (the third and fourth).

The framework presented here is quite different from Bergthold's, although it also includes four alternative criteria for benefits design—public health, medical effectiveness, cost-effectiveness, and microeconomic. A public health model stresses the importance of keeping people healthy. This includes ensuring a physical and social environment conducive to good health, promoting healthful behaviors, and detecting incipient illnesses before they become more serious. Some of these activities (e.g., protecting the environment and ensuring adequate housing) go beyond what we might expect to accomplish through our nation's medical care system, particularly during times of scarce public resources. The one thing that the public health model stresses with respect to the medical care system is the availability and use of preventive and primary care services.

Thus, adopting the public health model implies that we stress the provision of primary care services, including regular check-ups, immunizations, and early screening for diseases. All of these would therefore be encouraged, not only through public health education, but also by reducing economic barriers to medical care. If there are patient cost-sharing requirements built into the health plan's benefit structure, these requirements would not apply (or would be much lower) for these services since their provision is essential to the success of the public health model.

A benefits model based on medical effectiveness would not cover services that provide little benefit to patients. Unlike the public health model, which would probably provide incentives for the provision of primary care, medical-effectiveness criteria would not necessarily favor the provision of one type of service over another, as long as neither has been demonstrated to be of little medical value. Although it would be difficult to implement such a model with the information currently available, advances in medical-effectiveness and outcomes research will make it more feasible to use such criteria in the future. (In the past, most public and private insurers have refused to pay for "medically unnecessary" care, but it has been extremely difficult to implement such policies because of disagreements over what care is truly unnecessary.)

A cost-effectiveness model goes a step further, stating that services not only need to be medically effective, but that they must also pass a cost-effectiveness test. That is, services that bring marginal gains at very high costs would not be covered because resources could be better spent for other types of services. One commonly cited example is expensive therapies delivered in the last weeks or months of life. Cost-effectiveness is one of the criteria that the state of Oregon has used in developing its proposed list of covered Medicaid services. Included in the list of services that will not be covered are such procedures as liver transplantation for patients with alcoholic cirrhosis of the liver, and breast reconstruction after mastectomy for breast cancer.[16]

The microeconomic model differs from the others, focusing not so much on professionals' evaluations of the worth of services, but rather on consumer valuations. Under this model, the services that should be covered most completely by health insurance are those whose quantities are least responsive to price changes. In contrast, if some services, like primary care, exhibit high price sensitivity, their coverage should be less complete.

It must be stressed that these models are not mutually exclusive; it is possible to use more than one at a time. In fact, the Clinton Administration's reform proposal appears to use three of the four (excluding the microeconomic model), although it seems to conform most closely to the public health model. The proposal specifies a list of covered preventive services (including check-ups, which traditionally have not been covered by insurance), and requires no coinsurance for preventive services, including prenatal and well-baby care. There are also a number of other initiatives concerning prevention, such as enhanced prevention research and a requirement that over 50 percent of new medical residents be trained in primary care specialties.

Medical-effectiveness criteria are also explicitly included in the Clinton proposal, and the benefits package omits any service "that is not medically necessary or appropriate."[17] This may have little effect in the short run, since medical necessity research is still in its infancy. Over time, however, one would expect such criteria to be used more widely. Cost-effectiveness criteria may become even more important further down the road, since cost is one element that will be considered in the development of practice guidelines.

Coverage Restrictions

Access to Affordable Coverage

One of the major problems with the U.S. health care system is that many people are prevented from purchasing affordable private health insurance. In a recent article, Donald Light listed and discussed dozens of techniques employed by insurers to keep less healthy people from obtaining coverage or to reduce the likelihood that a medical claim will be paid.[18]

An argument can be made, however, that individual insurers are not to blame. Because insurers must compete on the basis of premiums, each feels compelled to use the same coverage restrictions as others do in order to stay in business. What is needed, therefore, are strong rules for all insurers that guarantee the availability of affordable universal coverage. One way to achieve this, of course, is for the government to provide coverage to everyone (e.g., adopt a single-payer system, such as by enrolling the entire population in Medicare). Another is to continue to rely on private insurers, but make them abide by certain principles.

Three general rules are critical. The first is that insurers not deny insurance coverage to any person or group, so that those people in poor health are not excluded from coverage. The second is that insurance policies provide coverage for all health problems; refusing to cover the cost of specific diseases like AIDS would be prohibited. Although these two rules would do much to improve the equity of the health care system, they do not solve the problem, because insurers may decide to charge some people or groups higher premiums, based on their medical condition or other factors. Thus, it is also necessary to require that the premiums charged be the same for all individuals and groups, a concept known as "community rating."[19] All three of these rules are incorporated into the Clinton Administration's reform proposal.

Cost-Sharing Requirements

The remainder of this section will focus on another coverage restriction— patient cost sharing. Economists often argue that if people have to pay for something, they will use less of it. Cost sharing in the medical care sector is therefore supposed to dissuade people from seeking as much care as they would if the care were free. In other words, it is designed to make people "think twice" before obtaining a medical service.[20]

The first decision that needs to be made is whether a reformed health system should require patient cost sharing. This issue has been the subject of great debate, with some proponents of a single-payer, Canadian-style system arguing that patient cost sharing would be unnecessary if the United States were to implement their reform proposal. Most other analysts have concluded that cost sharing is one of a series of necessary elements of a reformed health care system, and that without such requirements, cost control will be all the more difficult.

Cost sharing is certainly not an ideal way to constrain growth in medical care expenditures. One reason is that it appears to reduce the provision of highly effective and less-effective services by the same amount.[21] (In this respect, one might view the use of cost sharing as a "meat-cleaver" approach to achieving certain policy aims.) Another reason is that it imposes the greatest hardship on those with lower incomes. Indeed, an argument can be made that if cost-sharing requirements are to be included in a health care reform plan, they should be related to each person's ability to pay.[22]

Nevertheless, for pragmatic reasons it is probably necessary to include cost-sharing requirements in a reformed health care system. The vast majority of fee-for-service plans, and a growing majority of HMOs, now require cost sharing; its removal would increase health care utilization and expenditures. The counter argument—that Canada has managed quite well without instituting cost sharing—is not very convincing because a Canadian-style system would probably operate much differently (and not as cost-effectively) in the United States.

Two examples illustrate this point. First, in Canada real physician payment rates have fallen dramatically over the last twenty years. Between 1971 and 1985, real physician fees dropped by almost 20 percent in Canada while rising more than 20 percent in the United States.[23] Such cuts would be difficult to achieve in this country given the strong political power of the medical community. Second, the rationing of medical equipment in Canada has significantly limited the availability of high technology for the average hospital.[24] This, in turn, has resulted in waiting lists for elective procedures. The U.S. General Accounting Office found that nearly every hospital surveyed in Ontario has waiting lists for CT scans, MRIs, cardiovascular surgery, eye surgery, orthopedic surgery, lithotripsy, specialized physical rehabilitation, and bone marrow transplants, when these procedures were used on an elective basis.[25] This is something that Americans claim they are unwilling to accept. Public opinion polls show support for national health insurance dropping from 73 percent to 36 percent if it would result in longer waits for receiving services.[26]

Having said this, estimates of the savings that can be achieved through cost sharing, although certainly real, are probably overstated. Most are based on the findings from the RAND Health Insurance Experiment, a randomized controlled social experiment that took place between 1974 and 1982. The problem with using these estimates is that patients in the experiment comprised only a tiny proportion of physicians' practices. As a result, the decline in utilization of services that occured when high cost-sharing requirements were imposed had almost no effect on physicians' practices. Thus, these physicians had almost no incentive to "induce demand" for services in an attempt to recoup lost revenue.[27] When, as in a national health care plan, cost-sharing requirements are applied to a large proportion of patients, physicians may respond by inducing more utilization—a move that would result in higher medical expenditures.[28]

Once a decision is made to impose patient cost sharing, several other issues must be addressed. These include determining the level of coinsurance or copayments, deductibles, out-of-pocket maximums, and maximum benefits. The last is easiest to handle: Because the purpose of insurance is to provide protection against a financial catastrophe, insurance policies should have no maximums on lifetime payments; but if they do, these maximums should be high enough (i.e., in the millions of dollars) so that they are almost never reached.

Similarly, patient out-of-pocket maximums should be set at a relatively affordable level, for two reasons. First, if a person reaches his or her maximum during a year, it is likely to be because of a hospitalization. In such a situation, a patient has little control over his or her expenditures. Since cost sharing is aimed at getting people to reconsider discretionary expenses, it does not apply to instances in which they are hospitalized. The other group likely to exceed the maximum consists of those with chronic illnesses; again, the associated expenses tend to be less discretionary. The second reason for a reasonably low out-of-pocket maximum relates to the primary purpose of insurance, which is to reduce the risk of incurring a financial catastrophe. Consequently, the limit on out-of-pocket expenses must be lower than the amount that could be defined as being catastrophic.

Defining exactly what this maximum should be is harder, in part because private insurance policies now cover such a wide range. In 1990, about two-thirds of policies have out-of-pocket maximums between $500 and $2,000.[29] The Clinton Administration's reform proposal sets a limit of $1,500 for individuals and $3,000 for families; although appropriate for the middle class, these would appear to impose a serious burden on people with lower incomes who are not eligible for Medicaid. The proposal does provide subsidies to lower-income individuals and families to help pay these expenses, but the total amount of subsidies available will be capped. A more equitable arrangement would base such maximums on family income.[30]

One important point to be made about out-of-pocket maximums is that currently, none exist under the Medicare program. (There would have been a maximum under the Medicare Catastrophic Coverage Act, but that was repealed.) A shortcoming of the Clinton Administration proposal is that it sets an out-of-pocket maximum for the non-elderly, but not for Medicare beneficiaries (with the exception of prescription drug purchases).

Coinsurance rates currently are typically 20 percent in the fee-for-service sector, and $5 to $10 per visit in HMOs.[31] There would appear to be no overriding reason to change these (except to waive them for selected services, as discussed earlier), and indeed, these are consistent with the ones proposed by the Clinton Administration. The same is true of deductibles in the fee-for-service sector, which in 1993 averaged about $225 for individuals and $550 for families.[32] Again, these are consistent with the rates proposed by the Clinton Administration of $200 and $400, respectively.

Ensuring Financial Access to Services

Perhaps the most misunderstood aspect of health care reform is the equating of universal access to insurance with adequate access to services. It is commonly believed that if everyone is given (or required to purchase) health insurance, access problems will be solved—at least in urban and suburban areas. This simply is not the case; understanding this point is critical to designing an equitable health care system.

The problem, in a nutshell, is this: To providers, a patient's financial attractiveness is proportional to how much they will be paid for treating that patient. (This is especially true under proposals like the Clinton Administration's, which prohibits providers from "balance billing"—that is, charging patients in excess of the health plan's fee schedule.) Patient's whose insurers pay providers less will not get the same treatment as those whose plans are more generous.

This contention is supported by the experience of the Medicaid program, where provider payment rates tend to be much lower than those paid by private insurers and by Medicare. A large body of research demonstrates that provider willingness to treat *any* Medicaid patients, as well as the number of Medicaid patients they see, is related to states' Medicaid fees for physician services.[33]

The issue for health care reformers, then, is how to ensure that all patients are worth substantially the same to providers. One sure method is to establish a single-payer system (like Canada) or an all-payer system (like Germany, France, and Japan). An all-payer system would maintain the current array of private and public insurers, but would require that they each pay the same price for hospital and physician services.[34]

Currently, the favored reform approach in the United States is managed competition. Although the Clinton proposal allows states to form their own single-payer systems and establishes all-payer systems for people who opt to stay in fee-for-service, it is largely based on the principles of managed competition. The issue, then, is how this access issue can be addressed under managed competition.

A pure managed competition model, such as that espoused by the Jackson Hole Group, is likely to result in the continuation of multi-tiered medicine because wealthier people will be able to afford much more expensive health plans than the poor and near poor.[35] These plans will be able to pay providers more, and as a result, will be more attractive to providers. If provider payments between plans differ too much, most providers may eschew participating in the cheaper plans, just as they have shied away from treating Medicaid patients in the past.

The Clinton Administration's proposal has two provisions that may help ensure more equitable access. The first is that contributions for subsidized individuals (Medicaid beneficiaries and other poor and near-poor) will be based not on the lowest-cost plan in an area (as is the case in most managed competition proposals), but rather on the average-cost plan. This will mean that to receive a typical insurance policy, poorer people will have to pay less of their own money in premiums. Second, the plan allows (but does not require) regional purchasing alliances to keep premium charges by health plans no more than 20 percent above the average of all plans. If the alliances take advantage of this provision, they could keep down the amount of the difference between the highest and lowest-cost plans. This, in turn, may limit how much of a difference exists in provider fees across plans, and in turn, the degree to which access to care is equal as opposed to multi-tiered.

Conclusions

Benefit design issues constitute some of the most important decisions to be made by legislators and policymakers seeking to reform the U.S. health care system. Often, however, discussions of benefits focus on fairly narrow (albeit important) issues concerning what services will and will not be covered. In this chapter, we have tried to show that benefits design constitutes a much broader set of questions. Several conclusions were reached.

First, to as great an extent as possible, coverage under a reformed health care system should be universal. Universal coverage is not only the most equitable approach, but is instrumental in getting a handle on health care costs as well. The universality of coverage helps ensure that there will not be a large portion of the population outside of the health care system subject to cost-control regulations. Furthermore, it limits the need for a large safety net for those requiring further assistance. Almost all other countries have been able to achieve universal coverage without sacrificing cost control; the United States should be able to do so as well.

Second, benefits under a reformed health care system should be standardized. Allowing private insurers to market whatever benefits they wish (so long as they meet minimum standards) may sound like an attractive way to maximize consumer choice, but it is not. Without standardization, it is extremely difficult for consumers to choose the health plans that provide the most benefits per premium dollar. Similarly, given that supplemental insurance is likely to exist under a reformed health system, those benefits should also be subject to standardization similar to current regulations governing the Medigap market. The premiums charged for these policies should also be regulated to reflect the additional utilization and costs they will generate for the rest of the health care system.

Third, it is necessary to adopt a cogent philosophy governing the design of the benefits package. Four alternative approaches have been presented—public health, medical effectiveness, cost-effectiveness, and microeconomic. It is possible, however, to merge these as well (as evidenced by the multiple criteria included in the Clinton Administration's health reform proposal). For example, the public health model might be used to justify more thorough coverage of preventive and primary care services, while the cost-effectiveness model could be employed to exclude the use of extremely costly medical technologies that provide only marginal benefits.

Fourth, certain coverage restrictions should be outlawed, including any barriers that prevent persons from choosing whatever health plan they wish, or those that result in some people being charged more for coverage than others. Some barriers, however, will have to be retained—notably, patient cost-sharing requirements. Although there are many valid ways to design these requirements, one key is to ensure that no one suffers catastrophic financial consequences as a result of medical costs. Consequently, there should be no limit on how much coverage a person receives over his or her lifetime, and there should be an affordable limit on annual out-of-pocket costs.

Finally, to ensure equitable access to care, it is necessary to make all patients equally attractive financially to providers. The best way to achieve this is by requiring that all public and private insurers pay the same rate to providers for treating a given patient, as is done under single-payer and all-payer systems. Such an approach, however, is not consistent with a more competitive plan like managed competition. Thus, other mechanisms would be needed to ensure that the end result is not merely a continuation of multi-tiered medicine.

Notes

1. Thomas Rice, Katherine Desmond, and Jon Gabel, "The Medicare Catastrophic Coverage Act: A Postmortem," *Health Affairs* 9 (Fall 1990): 75–87.

2. Robert G. Evans, "Financing Health Care Coverage in Canada: Universal Coverage with Stable Costs," *Beitrage zur Gesundheitsokonomie* (Stuttgart, Germany) (1986): 276–318.

3. "President Clinton's Health Care Reform Proposal," Early Draft (Washington, D.C.: The White House, September 7, 1993).

4. Jere A. Wysong and Thomas Abel, "Universal Health Insurance and High-risk Groups in West Germany: Implications for U.S. Health Policy," *The Milbank Quarterly* 68 (1990): 527–560.

5. It could be claimed that a system like Canada's does not have standardized benefits because different provinces cover different services. Within a province, however, benefits are standardized.

6. For example, see: U.S. House of Representatives, Select Committee on Aging, *Abuses in the Sale of Health Insurance to the Elderly in Supplementation of Medicare: A National Scandal*, Committee Pub. No. 95–160 (WASHINGTON, D.C.: U.S. GOVERNMENT PRINTING OFFICE, 1979).

7. Thomas Rice and Kathleen Thomas, "An Evaluation of the New Medigap Standardization Regulations," *Health Affairs* 11 (Spring 1992): 200–201.

8. For a discussion of this legislation see: Rice and Thomas, "An Evaluation of the New Medigap Standardization Regulations," pp. 194–207.

9. Peter D. Fox, Thomas Rice, and Lisa Alecxih, "The Medigap Reform Legislation of 1990: Implications for U.S. Health Care Reform," submitted for publication to *Health Affairs*.

10. For a review of the literature, see: Thomas Rice, Nelda McCall, and James Boismier, "The Effectiveness of Consumer Choice in the Medicare Supplemental Health Insurance Market," *Health Services Research* 26 (June 1991): 223–246.

11. For a review of this literature, see: Nelda McCall, Thomas Rice, James Boismier, et al., "Private Health Insurance and Medical Care Utilization: Evidence from the Medicare Population," *Inquiry* 28 (Fall 1991): 276–287.

12. For a discussion of this issue, see: Bryan Dowd, Jon Christianson, Roger Feldman, et al., "Issues Regarding Health Plan Payments Under Medicare and Recommendations for Reform," *Milbank Quarterly* 70 (1992): 423–453.

13. Susan M. Marquis and Charles E. Phelps, "Demand for Supplementary Health Insurance," RAND Pub. No. R-3285-HHS (Santa Monica, CA: The RAND Corp., July 1985).

14. H.R. 3600, The Health Security Act (Clinton Administration), p. 243.

15. Linda A. Bergthold, "Benefit Design Choices Under Managed Competition," *Health Affairs* 12 (Special Supplement, 1993): 99–109.

16. Robert Steinbrook and Bernard Lo, "The Oregon Medicaid Demonstration Project—Will it Provide Adequate Medical Care?," *New England Journal of Medicine* 326 (Jan. 30, 1992): 340–344.

17. H.R. 3600, The Health Security Act (Clinton Administration), p. 86.

18. Donald W. Light, "The Practice and Ethics of Risk-Rated Health Insurance," *Journal of the American Medical Association* 267 (May 13, 1992): 2503–2508.

19. Because less healthy people may, on average, choose health plans different from those chosen by healthier people, it may also be necessary to compensate insurers that are unfortunate enough to get an "unfavorable selection" of patients. For a discussion of these issues, see: James C. Robinson, "A Payment Method for Health Insurance Purchasing Cooperatives," *Health Affairs* 12 (Special Supplement, 1993): 65–75.

20. Thomas Rice, "Patient Cost Sharing for Medical Services: A Review of the Literature and Implications for Health Care Reform," *Medical Care Review* (forthcoming in 1994).

21. Kathleen N. Lohr, Robert H. Brook, Caren J. Kamberg, et al., "Effect of Cost Sharing on Use of Medically Effective and Less Effective Care," *Medical Care* 24 (Supplement, 1986): S31–S38.

22. Thomas Rice and Kenneth E. Thorpe, "Income-Related Cost Sharing in Health Insurance," *Health Affairs* 12 (Spring 1993): 21–39.

23. Morris L. Barer, Robert G. Evans, and Roberta J. Labelle, "Fee Controls as Cost Control: Tales from the Frozen North," *The Milbank Quarterly* 66 (1988): 1–64.

24. Dale A. Rublee, "Medical Technology in Canada, Germany, and the United States," *Health Affairs* 8 (Fall 1989): 181–184.

25. U.S. General Accounting Office (GAO), *Canadian Health Insurance: Lessons for the United States* (Washington, D.C.: GAO, June 1991).

26. Robert J. Blendon and Karen Donelan, "The Public and the Emerging Debate Over National Health Insurance," *New England Journal of Medicine* 323 (July 19, 1990): 208–212.

27. Rice, "Patient Cost Sharing for Medical Services," (forthcoming).

28. Unfortunately, there is no direct evidence on this point one way or another. The only related study is: Marianne C. Fahs, "Physician Response to the United Mine Workers' Cost-Sharing Program: The Other Side of the Coin," *Health Services Research* 27 (April 1992): 25–45. The author examined one large multispecialty group practice in Western Pennsylvania that provided care, almost exclusively, to mine workers and steel workers. The mine workers experienced an increase in cost sharing requirements in the late 1970s, while the steelworkers did not. This study found that physicians responded to the imposition of cost sharing on their UMW patients by changing their practice behavior for non-UMW patients. This response took the form of raising their prices for ambulatory care to non-UMW patients and increasing their inpatient lengths-of-stay. Fahs concludes that, "when the economic effects of cost sharing on physician service use are analyzed for all patients within a physician practice, the findings are remarkably different from those of an analysis limited to those patients directly affected by cost sharing" (pp. 25–26).

29. Cynthia Sullivan and Thomas Rice, "The Health Insurance Picture, 1990," *Health Affairs* 10 (Summer 1991): 104–115.

30. A proposal for implementing this appears in: Rice and Thorpe, "Income Related Cost Sharing in Health Insurance," pp. 21–39.

31. KPMG Peat Marwick, "Health Benefits in 1993" (Washington, D.C.: KPMG Peat Marwick, 1993), p. 27.

32. KPMG Peat Marwick, "Health Benefits in 1993," p. 25.

33. For a literature review, see Physician Payment Review Commission (PPRC), *Physician Payment Under Medicaid*, Pub. No. 91–4 (Washington, D.C.: PPRC, 1991), pp. 38–44.

34. Thomas Rice, "Including an All-Payer Reimbursement System in a Universal Health Insurance Program," *Inquiry* 29 (Summer 1992): 203–212.

35. Thomas Rice, E. Richard Brown, and Roberta Wyn, "Holes in the Jackson Hole Approach to Health Care Reform," *Journal of the American Medical Association* 270 (Sept. 15, 1993): 1357–1362.

5

Mental Health Care

Howard H. Goldman, Richard G. Frank, and Thomas G. McGuire

Reforming mental health care within the context of general health care reform presents a special opportunity and a significant challenge. Improving access to care and controlling costs are goals shared by health and *mental* health care reform proposals. The task is complicated by special characteristics of the mental health services system: (1) insurance coverage for mental health services is far more limited than for general health care services; (2) supply and demand responses for mental health services exceed those in general health care, leading to the imposition of special demand-side cost control mechanisms; and (3) there is a large, publicly operated system of state and local mental health services designed to provide care to indigent individuals and to those who have exhausted their insurance benefits.

In addition to the large group of Americans with no insurance at all, there are many individuals with partial coverage who are not insured for substance abuse and mental illness services. In 1991, 15.6 percent of the population had no health insurance while an additional 5.3 percent had no coverage for mental health and substance abuse (MH/SA) care.[1] Furthermore, of those with insurance, most are underinsured for MH/SA care. In some instances, certain types of services are not covered and most are limited. In addition, restrictive annual and lifetime caps on expenditures expose individuals and families to the risk of catastrophic financial losses. These limits are stricter than those imposed on general health care services, both in private insurance and in public programs, such as Medicare and Medicaid.

As with general medical services, there is a wide range of mental health services. Some services are targeted at severe and disabling problems; others are directed at less serious conditions. The demand for some of these services is very responsive to out-of-pocket costs, while for others it is not. High demand for some mental health services has led to almost universal limitations on coverage (e.g., higher co-payments to limit demand). Only recently has there been any attempt to tailor benefits to differential patterns of price responsiveness, such as higher Medicare copayments for psychotherapy but not for medication management visits.

Limited benefits for MH/SA insurance coverage have been possible because of an elaborate system of publicly operated and categorically funded MH/SA services. State and local resources accounted for 38 percent of all mental health services expenditures in 1990. The public mental health care system has always served the poor and uninsured, and in recent decades it has expanded to include the underinsured and those whose coverage has been exhausted or who cannot afford high out-of-pocket costs.[2] For over 150 years the public mental health system, in effect, has reinsured the private mental health system, allowing it to survive by shifting costs. The public system absorbs the private system's bad risks, difficult patients, and high-cost cases. Because the public system historically has been underfunded and has provided charity care, it has been perceived as inferior to the private care system. The result: A "two-class" system of care.

Reforming mental health care means addressing dilemmas faced by the insurance market, especially those relating to severe and persistent mental disorders. These issues include strong demand response, unimaginative and needlessly restrictive cost control mechanisms, and a constant shifting of responsibility between the public and private mental health services systems.

This chapter contains a brief introduction to the mental health service system, followed by an analysis of current policy issues as seen from the perspectives of mental health policy advocates and analysts. Also included is an overview of mental health service coverage as proposed in the Clinton health plan. The chapter concludes with a discussion of obstacles faced when providing long-term care for individuals with severe and persistent mental illness, and, in a broader context, how long-term care should be approached in health care reform.

The Scope of the Problem

Over the course of a year, 28.1 percent of the adult population in the United States is affected by a diagnosable mental disorder, including alcohol and other substance abuse disorders. Of those individuals, only 28.5 percent (8 percent of the adult population) sought mental health or substance abuse services. In addition, people without a diagnosable disorder also seek care, thus boosting the share of those receiving some form of mental health-related service in any given year to almost 15 percent of the adult population. Specialists render care to only 5.9 percent of the population, the remainder seek help from general physicians, other human services workers, and voluntary agencies. Severe disorders affect between 2 and 3 percent of the population, and about one million citizens currently receive Social Security Administration disability payments because of severe mental illness.[3]

The specialty mental health service system spans numerous facility types and a variety of individual provider groups, and it is highly differentiated with respect to the populations served. As noted, there is a "two-class" system of public and private providers and a "two-tiered" system of acute and long-term services. State and county mental hospitals provide care to indigent, forensic and the most disturbed patients. Veterans hospitals and military neuropsychiatric facilities serve former members of the armed services and active duty personnel. General hospital psychiatric units and private psychiatric hospitals provide care to individuals with private insurance, Medicare or Medicaid. Community mental health centers, partial hospital programs, residential treatment centers, substance abuse detoxification and rehabilitation centers, and a host of psychosocial rehabilitation programs, generally are either publicly operated or provide services funded by grants and contracts from public agencies. Psychiatrists and other physicians deliver services, along with non-medical providers such as nurses, social workers, psychologists, occupational therapists, substance abuse and other types of counselors (e.g., rehabilitation and pastoral), and a variety of psychotherapists. Licensure for independent practice varies from state to state, while insurance coverage for their services differs from policy to policy.

In 1990, approximately 10 percent of all personal health care expenditures ($225 per person) in the United States were spent on mental health and substance abuse services. Expenditures vary, however, among population groups. It is estimated that uninsured individuals, who are disproportionately severely impaired, incurred $399 in costs in 1990 compared to $117 for those covered through employer-based insurance. About 40 percent of all expenses for mental health and substance abuse services is financed through private insurance or out-of-pocket expenditures, 38 percent is paid by state and local government, and the remainder is covered by the federal government through its contributions to Medicaid, Medicare, the Department of Veterans' Affairs, and block grants to states.[4]

Characterizing the Problem for Health Care Reform

In general, cost control issues dominate the discussion surrounding inclusion of benefits for mental health, alcohol and other drug abuse services in health care reform. Concerns about the insurability of mental disorders and the "value" (i.e., effectiveness) of providing services also enter the debate. Among mental health policy analysts and advocates, similar concerns focus on coverage details and on how insurance benefit design will affect cost, quality, and the dynamic balance between the public and private sector.

With respect to cost, the questions are how much is the right amount, who will pay, and how will the costs be financed and distributed? Although some argue that the current level of expenditures is inadequate, this also can be viewed as an issue of equitably allocating resources to meet wide-ranging mental health needs. Existing financial and organizational arrangements have led to expenditure patterns that are generally considered to be inadequate. A case in point: About 65 percent of all expenditures go to institutional treatment, in part because effective community-based treatment programs exist but are not in widespread use.[5]

The divergent sources of private and government expenditures, coupled with the significant discrepancy between the mental health costs of employed populations ($117 per annum) compared with those without insurance but cared for by public agencies ($399 per annum), pose a significant barrier to redistributing the financial burden.[6] Furthermore, even within sectors there are enormous variations in the level of expenditure. For example, the state mental health agency in New York State spends $118 per person per year, while the state agency in Iowa spends $17.[7]

Severe mental illnesses, such as schizophrenia, manic depressive illness, and severe major depression bring ruinous costs to bear on individuals suffering from these illnesses. Accounting for roughly 40 percent of all MH/SA expenditures, severe mental disorders meet the classic criteria for insurable conditions: They are relatively rare, have great financial consequences, and their onset is not under a patient's control. Although the lion's share of mental health care expenditures are paid for these and related illnesses, a significant portion of care is provided for less severe mental disorders and emotional problems, which challenge the standard approaches to the design of health insurance and thus warrant special attention.[8]

A recent report of the National Advisory Mental Health Council concluded that "[F]or persons with severe mental disorders, the chances of obtaining significant benefit through treatment have never been better."[9] Once viewed as undefinable conditions with only non-specific treatments, mental disorders can now be reliably diagnosed and specifically treated. A wide range of biomedical and psychosocial treatments may be focused on specific conditions with demonstrated efficacy. In many cases, the effectiveness and cost-effectiveness of these treatments has been well documented.[10] As with general medical services, however, gaps remain between the availability of efficacious treatments and their effective application in practice. This is due to technical problems in matching patients to appropriate treatments, problems in adherence to accepted treatment protocols (both by patients and practitioners), and limited access to insurance and other resources that would open the doors to effective treatment.

As noted above, there is a wide range of conditions that may be defined as "mental health" problems. Although a disproportionate share of expenditures are devoted to those with diagnosable conditions with significant impairment, some of the treatments can be (and are) used by individuals with no diagnosed condition. For example, approximately 45 percent of individuals who use services are considered "sub-threshold cases."[11] Many of these people may experience considerable suffering, and their treatment (often with psychotherapy or counseling) predictably brings relief. It is their care, however, that provokes concerns about inappropriate utilization and the insurability of mental health care.

There are two principal economic concerns underlying the existing coverage of mental health care in private insurance: "moral hazard" and "adverse selection."

Adverse selection occurs when a plan offers relatively generous coverage for a broad set of disorders that often are persistent (low incidence but high prevalence), encouraging individuals at high risk of using services for those conditions to enroll disproportionately. Obviously, such plans incur significant costs covering such care. Faced with systematic risk selection, the incentive encourages such plans to compete on the basis of their ability to avoid "bad risks." This wasteful form of competition results in the "underprovision" of mental health care coverage in private insurance.

Moral hazard is a problem for general medical services as well as for mental health services, but the evidence suggests greater demand for the latter, thus justifying special restrictions. Empirical evidence of a higher degree of price-responsive demand for some mental health services (e.g., psychotherapy), when mental health care is compared to general medical services taken in the aggregate.[12] A similar problem occurs in some hospital-based treatment. The insurance structure distorts the economics of demand in the setting choice for individuals. Hospital care is usually well-covered for 30 days, whereas alternatives to the hospital (e.g., partial hospitalization or residential substance abuse rehabilitation) typically are not covered. Consequently, hospital care becomes a relatively economical option for the beneficiary.

The experience with Medicare and several self-insured companies, such as IBM, indicates that mental health services can be covered with predictable levels of annual expenditure. If cost-shifting can be controlled and case mix severity distributed more evenly, mental health and substance abuse services can be insured and costs controlled. Through a combination of prospective, cost-based, and managed care cost containment techniques, these services can be covered like any other health care services. Models for doing so generally call for the use of supply-side payment mechanisms, managed care, and some application of cost sharing to control utilization and cost.[13]

The current state of affairs reveals a tangle of multiple payers and diverse providers competing for scarce resources, each trying to shift the costs to some other payer or provider. This set of conditions is duplicative, wasteful and inequitable, offering limited coverage to roughly 80 percent of the population and none to the rest, who depend on a highly variable "two-class" system of state and local mental health and substance abuse services, available in some jurisdictions and not in others.

Contrasting Views of Reform

Prior to the 1992 presidential election, mental health services researchers and mental health care advocates engaged in a number of exercises to prepare for health care reform and, hopefully, the inclusion of mental health care benefits. Much of their work, notably a set of reform principles, has shaped the current debate.[14]

There are three important principles that might guide mental health services public policy under national health care reform: (1) provide protection against the catastrophic financial consequences of mental illness or substance abuse disorders; (2) encourage cost-effective treatment choices; and (3) control costs. These goals will be discussed in more detail below.

The central tenet of one approach to correcting the failure in the insurance market is to offer "non-discriminatory" coverage, meaning that the same rules of benefit design and cost containment should be applied to mental health and general health care services alike. Restrictions would not be imposed on the basis of diagnosis alone.

Mental health advocates have extended this approach into a principle called "parity," i.e., providing the same benefits for mental health services that are available for general health services. The term, however, is misleading. In practice, parity means "no special limits," but special benefits (perceived as advantageous) are acceptable. For example, advocates support exemption of psychiatric hospital care from Medicare's Prospective Payment System and continue to back benefits for mental health services not currently covered by general health care benefits (e.g., partial hospitalization). Pure adherence to a policy of parity would argue that these services should be covered (or not) exactly as general health care services—without exceptions. On the basis of parity, advocates often vigorously oppose the higher copayments for psychotherapy without accepting that it is a unique service which has special properties (e.g., unusually price-responsive demand). A standard based on the even-handed application of insurance benefit design principles would prevent the arbitrary application of rules perceived as advantageous or disadvantageous to MH/SA care.

A coalition of 33 advocacy organizations recently recommended "a broad array of coordinated acute and rehabilitative services ... consistent with the individual's clinical needs."[15] The benefit package combined elements of Medicare (for acute care) and Medicaid (for rehabilitative, supportive, and long-term care). The emphasis was on coverage for adults with the greatest treatment needs (to protect against catastrophic financial loss) but services for less severe illnesses and for children and adolescents were also included in the recommended benefit package. The mix of recommended services underscored the need to cover alternatives to institutional care in order to promote substitution of less costly (and usually more desirable) care. These advocacy goals generally were in keeping with well-known insurance principles. First and foremost is the emphasis on providing protection against financial ruin stemming from the treatment of severe mental illnesses. Second is encouraging the use of services to meet individual clinical need according to the best available information about effectiveness.

The point is illustrated by Medicare's differential coverage of psychotherapy and "medical management" (often for psychotropic drug management). This benefit design feature now is being recommended for the basic benefit package in health care reform. The recommended coverage of medical management is no different from the coverage of office visits for any other medical illness (i.e., parity). Prior to the introduction of this policy, many office visits were billed as "psychotherapy," often incurring higher overall costs to both patients and payors. In contrast, medical management is a relatively low-cost service, generally less costly and less price-responsive than psychotherapy. Individual patients, however, may need frequent visits (often at least weekly), thus incurring substantial costs. Many consider medical management to be the outpatient "service of choice" for patients with serious and prevalent illnesses. In particular, for patients with moderate to severe depression, brief (20-minute) visits have been shown to be comparatively cost-effective when used in combination with an appropriate regimen of antidepressant medication.[16] This policy provides an example of benefit design based on insurance principles and data on effectiveness.

We now turn to elimination of the "two-class" system of mental health care in the United States. This can be accomplished by providing universal coverage for a broad array of services, while recognizing the need for a residual set of public services for everyone with certain care needs not covered by the national benefit. Accomplishing this goal requires that health care reform policies delineate, as clearly as possible, the respective responsibilities of health plans and the public mental health system. This is essential for eliminating duplication and preventing cost shifting and the "dumping" of patients. It is particularly important to deter such practices and protect the most impaired beneficiaries, who should continue to be covered for specified services by national health insurance, even when some of their care is provided by the public sector.

The President's Proposal for Health Care Reform

Three benefit options for mental health care reform have been considered: (1) a comprehensive package that fully integrates mental health and substance abuse services into the larger health care system; (2) a package of acute and rehabilitative services that would retain a well-defined role for the existing public sector delivering only long-term and some rehabilitative services; and (3) a benefit extending the current median level of coverage under typical private insurance for the uninsured, leaving a substantial role for the public sector for providing services beyond the basic benefit. The President's proposal also recommends the full integration of mental health and substance abuse services with the medical system by 2001, but its plan for implementing that future vision involves a combination of benefit elements from options (2) and (3).

Defining Full Integration

From the patient's perspective, full integration of mental health and substance abuse services means that there would be no difference between insurance coverage for mental disorders and coverage for other health problems. A health plan would provide clinically necessary care for all stages of a mental illness or substance abuse disorder. There would be no special financial or other benefit-design limitations imposed on mental health services or on beneficiaries with mental disorders. That means an end to the "two-class" system of services and to higher copayments and deductibles, separate limits on length of stay or visits, and different policies with respect to out-of-pocket costs, including annual and lifetime limits.

The fully integrated plan promises to accomplish all of the goals for mental health care reform except cost control. A comprehensive array of services would be available to meet the acute, rehabilitative, and long-term care needs of beneficiaries. The benefit design would encourage the substitution of cost-effective alternatives to institutional care but would also provide financial protection against catastrophic personal expenditures. Individuals with the most severe and persistent disorders would be protected without severely restricting coverage for others with less disabling impairments.

The "two-class" system of care would be eliminated; patients would be less likely to be shifted to a publicly-operated service system when they exhaust their resources. Duplication of effort and resources between the two systems would be reduced dramatically. Care could be better coordinated and provided in a less-fragmented service system. The cost containment goals of such a system would be reinforced by a managed care system operating within a global budget.

The case for full integration was predicated on a body of evidence suggesting that the current system was broken and that the proposed models could fix it. As noted above, there was evidence that mental health services were insurable and cost effective. Furthermore, it was generally accepted that typical current insurance coverage failed to meet its goal of providing financial protection. The financial risks associated with illnesses causing the greatest impairments were not adequately protected by policies offering only 30 days of inpatient coverage, 20 psychotherapy visits, no coverage for alternative services of proven cost-effectiveness, and low annual and lifetime limits (e.g., $10,000). The limited data available suggested that the costs could be managed through a combination of creative utilization management and payment system techniques (such as capitation, prospective budgets, and performance contracts), so that aggregate MH/SA costs would increase only modestly.

Implementing Full Integration

In spite of this evidence, and the potential to reach reform goals, implementation of the fully integrated plan was delayed until 2001 because of three complex problems: risk adjustment, financing the reform, and managing the new system.

Financing. The money needed to finance the system is not immediately available, in part because the more than $20 billion in state and local mental health expenditures is distributed so unevenly. They would need to be allocated differently to provide the resources to pay for full integration with no rise in government appropriations. Under a national benefit in a fully integrated system, citizens in states which currently provide few resources for mental health and substance abuse services would be entitled to the same services as those living in more generous commonwealths. To pay for the reform without increasing costs, it would be necessary to direct public resources away from states currently spending more than the average and toward states spending less. Legislation needed to finance such a system raises the following constitutional questions: How can the Congress compel one state legislature to continue appropriating re-

sources for mental health services delivery in another state? Are legislators willing to allocate public resources that will ultimately be controlled
by "private" health plans?

One means of adjusting for interstate differences in state and local
spending is compensatory federal spending, perhaps coupled with compensatory federal taxation to finance it. Even assuming that a redistribu-
tive formula could be developed, its political feasibility is questionable. It
would either be too costly, or the increase in taxation to support such redistribution would be blocked in Congress by the majority of states that
spend less than the average. The federal government already spends over
$5 billion on matching funds for Medicaid mental health expenditures
and more than $4 billion on V.A. mental health services, block grants for
alcohol, drug abuse, and mental health services, and other federal programs, Medicare excluded.[17] Those funds are essential to financing the
rest of health care reform and paying for the portion of the premium to be
devoted to mental health care.

Another possible financing mechanism is redistribution of current private expenditures, especially those that are already a part of employer
contributions. Overall increases in business contributions to premiums
will be necessary to pay for whatever benefits are offered through mental
health care reform, but this is no different from the general problem of financing health care reform, except for the significant state-to-state variation in public mental health expenditures. Clearly, it will take time and
careful thought to develop a financing mechanism for the fully integrated
plan. Whether this requires a delay until 2001, however, is less certain.

Managed care. An integrated system depends on close management of a
budget allocation for mental health and substance abuse services, because
the benefit package has little or no other cost-containment mechanisms.
The usual array of demand-side cost controls and limits will not be used
under the fully integrated plan. Instead a set of capitation rates, prospective budgets, contractual arrangements, and individual utilization management techniques will be implemented to control costs. The managed
care approach poses a number of problems for beneficiaries who may not
have a clear sense of their benefits or who may not function well as consumers, especially those individuals with severe and persistent illnesses.
They may be systematically undertreated in a delivery structure featuring
fixed resources and incentives to give less care rather than more. Although there are no explicit limits on coverage in the fully integrated system, that does not imply that there will be no limits on care.

Studies of supply responses under various methods of prospective
payment demonstrate the ability of these mechanisms to control costs by
reducing overall utilization. In fact, supply responses for mental health

and substance abuse services exceed those seen for general medical care. This is especially true for inpatient care.[18]

The evidence for similar responses to utilization management is much more limited. Many approaches are being tried, but they have yet to be comparatively evaluated. We know from several demonstrations that it is possible to control costs using managed care techniques. Again, it is in the area of pre-authorization for inpatient care that the greatest savings emerge. For instance, the Minnesota Consolidated Chemical Dependency Fund reduced expenditures by 16 percent in one year by shifting treatment from inpatient to community-based settings; Aetna's managed care efforts resulted in an estimated $35 per enrollee annual reduction in costs; and a CHAMPUS case management program and capitated-contract provider arrangement in the Tidewater area of Virginia saved about 30 percent on mental health and substance abuse expenditures.[19]

These experiences are typical of what is reported in the literature, but because the evidence is from special studies in special populations, there are questions about their applicability to national health care reform. There is concern that insufficient national experience with managed mental health care still exists. Some policymakers doubt that the present managed mental health system is sufficiently developed—a mature management system would be the cornerstone of the fully integrated plan—and such misgivings have prompted the postponement of implementation until 2001.

Risk selection and monitoring. Given a policy of universal coverage and a prohibition on underwriting against "pre-existing conditions," health plans may experience biased selection. Despite a variety of protections against the withholding of insurance coverage, there are still opportunities for beneficiaries to be underserved or "encouraged to leave" a plan. The President's proposal counters incentives for plans to "risk select" and protects them against adverse selection through (1) risk adjustment to premium, (2) utilization and enrollment monitoring, and (3) setting treatment practice standards. Risk selection is particularly problematic for individuals with severe and persistent impairments, who may cost the plan a great deal of money but who may also be grossly underserved.

For managed competition to work, beneficiaries must be able to assess the quality of services and change plans if they are dissatisfied. Conversely, for a plan to remain financially solvent it must not have a disproportionate share of costly cases. A plan that provides high quality mental health services to individuals with disabling impairments requiring costly care is likely to attract beneficiaries seeking quality care for life-long problems, as well as those leaving plans that they consider to be unresponsive to their needs. It will be necessary to protect these "high-quality" plans and their disabled beneficiaries from either financial hardship or subsequent undertreatment in the face of higher than expected demand.

Three mechanisms are available for achieving that protection. Unfortunately, none is well-developed enough for immediate implementation, thus providing another reason for delayed implementation of a fully integrated plan. One proposed method is risk adjustment, but it is difficult to identify variables which predict utilization accurately enough to be used as premium adjusters. Another method would relate premium to costs (rather than attempting to predict utilization). A third possibility is reinsuring a plan that covers individuals with severe mental disorders. It could be paid for certain types of costs incurred once a threshold of expenditures had been reached by individuals identified as disabled. The latter represents a form of risk sharing between the alliance and the plan. All of these methods require further refinement before they can be used in health care reform.[20]

The Proposed Benefit—A Compromise

The initial MH/SA benefit included in the President's proposal follows a traditional approach to insurance coverage. The benefit designed for implementation at the beginning of health care reform is a compromise between the innovation of the fully integrated plan and current coverage. Although it improves upon existing insurance in some important ways, the initial benefit falls short of the objectives set by mental health advocates.

The entire MH/SA benefit is summarized in Table 5.1. It covers a wide range of services, including many treatment modalities rarely covered in current private insurance policies. The range of services is more typical of the package offered in the most comprehensive Medicaid programs, and features many alternatives to hospitalization (such as crisis residential services and partial hospitalization) and rehabilitative services. Case management services are also covered, a provision that is important for several reasons. Compared to traditional coverage, this benefit better meets the needs of beneficiaries, especially those with severe impairments. In addition, coverage of alternatives to hospitalization offers an opportunity for substitution of less restrictive and lower cost services.

Although the benefit is comprehensive in terms of the types of services and providers covered by the plan, there are significant cost control mechanisms in place to limit use of the wide array of services. In addition to controls on cost imposed by global expenditure limits and changes in the basic organization of service delivery (such as the use of HMOs and individual managed care arrangements), the MH/SA benefit is laden with traditional cost-containment mechanisms. Strict annual limits are imposed on the use of inpatient care and the range of residential and non-residential alternatives to hospital services. In addition, a one-day deductible is required for each admission. The proposal also features a complex system of "trades" against the inpatient benefit, further eroding protection. There also are limits and higher co-payments (50 percent in point-of-service and out-of-network plans) on psychotherapy and other ambulatory services, with the exception of medical management and diagnostic services. Furthermore, many of the out-of-pocket expenditures do *not* count toward the annual catastrophic limit.

The MH/SA benefit is a mixed bag with respect to protecting beneficiaries against significant financial loss. First, like the rest of the health care reform proposal, there are no exclusions due to pre-existing conditions, a reason often cited by insurers to deny coverage to individuals with a history of mental illness. Second, there are no lifetime limits on coverage. These are both major advances, but the remainder of the package suffers from many of the shortcomings of traditional coverage. In particular, the MH/SA benefit continues to expose individuals and their families to the risk of catastrophic losses and maintains the "two-class" system of care. In addition to the exclusion of many types of personal expenditure from the out-of-pocket limits, the restrictions on inpatient and residential services increase the risk of catastrophic loss and transfer to the public mental health system. Furthermore, the system of trades allows a beneficiary to swap the most important financial protection in the benefit for extended coverage of psychotherapy.

The 30-day inpatient and residential care benefit (with its complex mechanism for a 30-day extension and its potential for reduction through the system of substitutes and trades) represents the most important compromise between protection and concerns about cost. As noted above, the public mental health system historically has provided catastrophic protection to individuals with mental illnesses and addictive disorders, especially for the uninsured and, to some extent, for the underinsured. The President's proposal eliminates the role of the public mental health system for the uninsured, but it leaves a "two-class" system of care in place to deal with the widespread underinsurance characteristic of the MH/SA benefit. Furthermore, if Medicaid is folded into the ultimate plan and the MH/SA benefit is limited to the standard benefit, the demand on the public sector from severely impaired and disabled Medicaid beneficiaries would increase further.

Although the proposed fully integrated system will take time to implement, the current initial benefit does not facilitate the transfer of responsibility from the public system to private health plans. Because of limitations in the benefit, the public system will need to retain (and possibly expand) its acute care capacity to handle patients who are transferred

Table 5.1 Health Security Act Proposed Mental Health and Substance Abuse Benefit Plan

Service	Coverage	Copayment in Lower Cost Sharing Plan or In-Network Combination Plan	Cost Sharing in Higher Cost Sharing Plan or Out-of-Network Combination Plan
Inpatient hospital and residential services[a]	Prior to January 1, 2001 treatment is subject to an aggregate annual limit of 30 days. A maximum of 30 additional days shall be covered for an individual if a health professional designated by the health plan determines in advance that 1) the individual poses a threat to his or her own life or the life of another individual; or 2) the medical condition of the individual requires inpatient treatment in a hospital or a psychiatric hospital in order to initiate, change, or adjust pharmacological or somatic therapy.	No copayment	1 day deductible 20% coinsurance. Payments count toward out-of-pocket limit.
Intensive nonresidential treatment[b]	Prior to January 1, 2001, covered days are through a trade for inpatient days at the rate of two intensive non-residential days for one inpatient day, until the 30 day inpatient limit is reached.	No copayment	1 day deductible 20% coinsurance. For mental illness, payment on first 60 days done as trade count toward out-of-pocket limit.
	An additional 60 days may be provided if a health care professional designated by the plan determines additional treatment is medically necessary or appropriate.	For additional 60 days, $25 per visit. Not counted toward out-of-pocket limit.	For additional 60 days, 50% coinsurance. Not counted toward out-of-pocket limit.
Prescription drugs	Medical necessity	$5 per prescription. Payments count toward out-of-pocket limit.	$250 deductible; 20% coinsurance. Payments count toward out-of-pocket limit.

Table 5.1 *Continued*

Service	Coverage	Copayment in Lower Cost Sharing Plan or In-Network Combination Plan	Cost Sharing in Higher Cost Sharing Plan or Out-of-Network Combination Plan
Screening and assessment, diagnosis, medical management, crisis services, somatic treatments	Medical necessity	$10 per visit. Not counted toward out-of-pocket limit.	20% coinsurance. Not counted toward out-of-pocket limit.
Psychotherapy and collateral services	Prior to January 1, 2001, 30 visits per year. Additional visits may be covered at the discretion of the plan to prevent hospitalization or facilitate earlier discharge. Inpatient benefits are reduced 1 day for each 4 additional visits.	$25 per visit. Not counted toward out-of-pocket limit.	50% coinsurance. Not counted toward out-of-pocket limit.
Outpatient substance abuse counseling and relapse prevention	Substance abuse counseling and relapse prevention will be covered based on an exchange of 1 inpatient day for 4 visits. Prior to January 1, 2001, after an individual receives residential or intensive nonresidential treatment, 30 visits in group therapy.	$10 per visit. Not counted toward out-of-pocket limit.	20% coinsurance. Not counted toward out-of-pocket limit.
Case management	Defined as assisting persons "in gaining access to needed medical, social, educational and other services." Available if a health professional designated by the health plan determines the individual should receive such services.	No copayment	No insurance

[a] Includes general and psychiatric hospital, residential treatment and residential detoxification centers, crisis residential programs, mental health residential treatment programs, therapeutic family or group treatment homes, community residential treatment or recovery centers for substance abuse.

[b] Includes partial hospitalization, day treatment, psychiatric rehabilitation, home-based services, ambulatory detoxification, behavioral aide services.

Source: The Clinton Health Security Plan, 1993.

from health plans when their benefit limit is reached. This service pattern is personally and clinically disruptive, and the resulting care often would be inferior, duplicative, and costly to society.

Earlier proposals in the health care reform process called for a 90-day inpatient and residential benefit to cover virtually all acute care episodes, leaving to the public system responsibility for longer-term care. The 90-day limit fit clinical patterns (the nature of care generally changes after three months of hospitalization) and the historic pattern of use (almost all individuals in private insurance plans accrue fewer than 90 days in a year). The current proposal fits neither scenario, and the impact on public and private systems is likely to be significant. Data from the Center for Mental Health Services indicate that 54 percent of people in state mental hospitals use fewer than 30 days per year. That is care that would be covered privately under the current proposal. Whereas data from MEDSTAT Systems, Inc., indicate that approximately 30 percent of private users of inpatient MH/SA services use more than 30 days per year and might then be transferred into the public system.[21]

The 30-day extension of the benefit may help deflect some of these transfers to the public system. On the other hand, there is the risk that health plans will seldom seek the extension, preferring instead to transfer these difficult and expensive patients (and their treatment costs) into the public system. As noted, the system of substituting days in alternative non-residential services and trading days for outpatient visits may also result in no inpatient coverage for individuals who have the greatest need and are at significant risk of incurring hugh costs. They, too, will turn to the public sector for their care.

On balance, and in spite of these weaknesses, the President's proposal represents an improvement over the current state of affairs. It would provide MH/SA coverage to millions of uninsured Americans, and it would improve the package of services for about half of the insured population. In 1992, median benefits consisted of 30 or fewer days of inpatient care, very limited coverage of alternatives to the hospital, and 20 psychotherapy visits with 50 percent co-payments.[22] The resources to be allocated to health plans for MH/SA services are substantial, but not great enough to eliminate the public mental health system. Duplication of services and the retention of a "two-class" system of care will add costs and reduce the value to beneficiaries and taxpayers. This is the price of compromise and a long transition.

Long-Term Care and Mental Health Care Reform

As the previous sections have indicated, one of the most challenging aspects of mental health care reform has been identifying a method for incorporating treatment for individuals with severe and persistent mental disorders. These people require a mix of acute care, rehabilitation, and long-term care services. The President's proposal addresses the acute care needs of patients in a comprehensive fashion, but the rehabilitative and long-term care services receive limited attention. The fully integrated mental health and substance abuse system proposed for 2001 would begin to address all three types of care and treatment in a comprehensive way. The same is *not* true for long-term care in the general population. There is no definite timetable set for fully integrating nursing home and other long-term care into health care reform.

Although a thoughtful discussion of long-term care is beyond the scope of this chapter, it will conclude with a brief examination of the President's proposals for long-term care and the following related questions: What does the dilemma of the interim care of individuals with rehabilitation and long-term care needs tell us about the problem of long-term care more generally? What are beneficiaries who need long-term care to do while waiting for the new millennium and a fully integrated system?

The President's reform plan proposes to consolidate existing long-term care programs under programs such as Medicaid and create a new home and community-based services program. It also suggests tax incentives for disabled individuals to return to work, and new federal standards for private long-term care insurance. The proposal essentially contains no new residential long-term care benefit.[23]

The home and community-based care provisions of the Health Care Reform proposal expand existing supportive services for individuals with difficulties performing activities of daily living. The aim is to improve quality of life and promote community tenure among individuals who would previously have been admitted to nursing homes. This portion of the health care reform proposal would be funded at an increasing level over a ten-year implementation period, ultimately reaching $38 billion. Resources would be allocated via a formula grant to the states, and eligibility would not be means-tested but would require severe cognitive disability or other mental impairment.

Home and community-based supportive services are available to individuals who need constant supervision because of the danger of harm to themselves or to others. They can also be used by people with multiple and significant behavioral problems, or by those who are unable to administer their own medications. Personal assistance services would be available under the plan for all qualified individuals, subject to a standardized assessment of need and an individual care plan. Other rehabilitative and long-term care services, such as case management, homemaker, respite, habilitation and rehabilitation, and adult day services *may* be provided, but such provision is not required.

While waiting for the fully integrated system, individuals with substance abuse and mental disorders who need long-term care will turn to the public sector. Some will receive long-term residential care in state-operated facilities; others will have non-residential services provided directly or under contract from community-based providers. They are lucky that a safety net of such services will fill the gap between the basic benefit and their needs. Individuals with general medical impairments (especially those with moderate impairment) who need more intensive or extensive rehabilitation and long-term care services than provided in the package offered by the President will either wait for further reform or be admitted to nursing homes or other supported residential settings.

As challenging as it has been to include mental health and substance abuse services in health care reform, the problem of financing a system of long-term care services is at least as problematic. For individuals with mental illness, it is those with long-term care needs who strain the existing system most. Yet they are the same people for whom insurance protection is most imperative and for whom the system must be reformed with care.

Notes

1. National Co-Morbidity Study (Ann Arbor, MI: University of Michigan Survey Research Center, 1991.)

2. Bernard Arons, Richard Frank, Howard Goldman, Thomas McGuire, and Sharman Stephens, "Mental Health and Substance Abuse Coverage Under National Health Reform," *Health Affairs*, forthcoming 1994.

3. Darrel Regier, William Narrow, Donald Rae, Ronald Manderscheid, Ben Locke, and Frederick Goodwin, "The de facto U.S. Mental and Addictive Disorders Service System: Epidemiologic Catchment Area Prospective One-Year Prevalence Rates of Disorders and Services," *Archives of General Psychiatry* 50 (1993): 85–94; National Advisory Mental Health Council, "Health Care Reform for Americans with Severe Mental Illnesses," *American Journal of Psychiatry* 150 (1993): 1447–1465.

4. Grayson Norquist and Kenneth Wells, "Mental Health Needs of the Uninsured," *Archives of General Psychiatry* 48 (1991): 476–480; Arons, et al., "Mental Health and Substance Abuse Coverage."

5. David Mechanic, "Strategies for Integrating Public Mental Health Services," *Hospital and Community Psychiatry* 42 (1992): 797–801.

6. Norquist and Wells, "Mental Health Needs"; Richard Frank, Thomas McGuire, Darrel Regier, Ronald Manderscheid, and Albert Woodward, "Data Watch," *Health Affairs*, forthcoming 1994.

7. Theodore Lutterman, Vera Hollen, and Michael Hogan, *Funding Sources and Expenditures of State Mental Health Agencies: Revenue/Expenditure Study Results—Fiscal Year 1990* (Alexandria, VA: National Association of State Mental Health Program Directors, 1993).

8. National Mental Health Advisory Council, 1993.

9. National Mental Health Advisory Council, 1993.

10. National Mental Health Advisory Council, 1993, directs the reader to the *Psychopharmacology Bulletin* 29(4) (1993) for detailed reports; William Hargreaves and Martha Shumway, "Effectiveness of Mental Health Services for the Severely Mentally Ill," in *The Future of Mental Health Services Research*, Carl Taube, David Mechanic, and Ann Hohmann, eds., DHHS Publication No. (ADM)89–1600 (Washington, D.C.: Department of Health and Human Services, 1989).

11. Regier, et al., "de facto," 1993.

12. Thomas McGuire, "Financing and Demand for Mental Health Services," in *The Future of Mental Health Services Research*, Taube, et al., eds., 1989.

13. Richard Frank, Howard Goldman, and Thomas McGuire, "A Model Mental Health Benefit in Private Insurance," *Health Affairs* 11 (Fall 1992): 99–117.

14. Chris Koyanagi, Joseph Manes, Richard Surles, and Howard Goldman, "On Being Very Smart: The Mental Health Community's Response in the Health Care Reform Debate," *Hospital and Community Psychiatry* 44 (1993): 537–542 which includes the position statement of 33 mental health organizations; H. Richard Lamb, Stephen Goldfinger, David Greenfield, John Nemiah, John Schwab, John Talbott, Allan Tasman, and Leona Bachrach, "Ensuring Services for Persons with Chronic Mental Illness Under National Health Care Reform," *Hospital and Community Psychiatry* 44 (1993): 545–546.

15. Koyanagi, "On Being Very Smart," position statement, pp. 539–542.

16. Steven Sharfstein and Howard Goldman, "Financing the Medical Management of Mental Disorders," *American Journal of Psychiatry* 146 (1989): 345–349; Irene Elkin, "National Institute of Mental Health Treatment of Depression Collaborative Research Program: General Effectiveness of Treatments," *Archives of General Psychiatry* 46 (1989): 971–982.

17. Arons, et al., "Mental Health and Substance Abuse Coverage."

18. Mark Freiman, Randall Ellis, and Thomas McGuire, "Provider Response to Medicare's PPS: Reductions in Length of Stay for Psychiatric Patients Treated in Scatter Beds," *Inquiry* (Summer 1989): 192–201; Kyle Grazier and Thomas McGuire, "Payment Systems and Hospital Resource Use: A Comparative Analysis of Psychiatric, Medical, and Obstetrical Services," in *The Economics of Mental Health Services*, Thomas McGuire and Richard Scheffler, eds. (Greenwich CT: JAI Press, 1987); Carl Taube, Judith Lave, Agnes Rupp, Richard Frank, and Howard Goldman, "Psychiatry Under Prospective Payment: Experience in the First Year," *American Journal of Psychiatry* 145 (1988): 210–213.

19. Dominic Hodgkin, "The Impact of Private Utilization Management on Psychiatric Care: A Review of the Literature," *Journal of Mental Health Administration* 19 (1992): 143–157; Robert Coulam and Joseph Smith, *Evaluation of the CPA—Norfolk Demonstration*, U.S. Defense Department Contract: MDA 907–87-C-0003 (Cambridge, MA: Abt Associates, Inc., 1990).

20. Mark Schlesinger and David Mechanic, "Challenges for Managed Competition from Chronic Illness," *Health Affairs* 12 (1993 supplement): 123–137.

21. Arons, et al., "Mental Health and Substance Abuse Coverage."

22. Hay-Huggins, Inc., *Psychiatric Benefits in Employer Provided Health Care Plans* (Washington, D.C.: Hay-Huggins, 1992).

23. Material on long-term care is derived from the Health Security Act proposal and from a presentation by Robyn Stone, Deputy Assistant Secretary for Planning and Evaluation, DHHS.

6

Controlling Payment
for Hospital Services

Stuart H. Altman and Donald A. Young

For almost one hundred years, the hospital has been the unchallenged engine of the American health care system, offering the newest technology and most advanced services, training physicians, and accounting for the largest share of national health care spending. The elaboration of the modern hospital has been closely linked to the financing of the services it provides. For many years, private, voluntary health insurance, generally obtained through the workplace, has been an important source of hospital revenue. With the passage of the Medicare program in 1965, the federal government also became a major payer of care, covering services furnished to the elderly. At the same time, the Medicaid program was enacted, with the federal and state governments sharing responsibility for payment for services rendered to certain low income groups.

Payment policies established by private and public policymakers have played a substantial role in shaping the organization and delivery of care. Of special importance was the decision by private payers to pay hospitals in relation to the cost or charges of the care they furnished to subscribers, regardless of the volume of services or the efficiency of production.[1] Initially, the Medicare and Medicaid programs also followed this approach.[2] Consequently, for many years hospitals could rely on a steady source of guaranteed revenue that would increase as they added new technologic capabilities and expensive services.

More recently, to control escalating costs, private insurers and government payers have questioned the need for inpatient care, attempted to control the level of hospital payment, and encouraged the use of less costly providers and sites of care. These new policies contributed to declines in the utilization of inpatient acute care services and created financial pressure for hospitals. They also contributed to the rapid growth in spending for services furnished in other settings.

Hospitals responded by seeking new sources of revenue. They rapidly expanded their capacity to perform ambulatory surgery and other outpatient services and developed specialized units to provide inpatient psychiatric, drug and alcohol treatment, general rehabilitation care, and subacute and skilled nursing services. Many hospitals now also offer home health and other community services. Hospitals are also developing networks with physicians, integrated delivery systems with other providers, and assuming some traditional insurance functions by sharing the financial risk of furnishing care to groups of enrollees.

Spending for specialized services furnished by hospitals and other providers continues to grow rapidly, while many Americans lack financial access to basic health services. Consequently, policymakers are calling for health care reform to slow the relentless growth in the cost of medical services and eliminate financial barriers to a basic level of care. There are substantial disagreements, however, on how to achieve these goals.

In this chapter, we focus on controlling payment for hospital services and identify issues policymakers are likely to confront as they evaluate various health care reform proposals. We begin our discussion with an examination of the sources of hospital revenue and the so-called phenomenon of cost shifting. We then discuss the changing composition of services and revenues among hospitals and other providers and suppliers and go on to identify important policy considerations affecting the distribution of hospital revenues across geographic areas, types of facilities, and types of services.

If health care reform is successful in reducing the rate of increase in payments, hospitals will have to reduce the rate of increase in their expenses to survive. Faced with revenue constraints and the need to slow cost growth, providers are quick to suggest that quality of care will be the first victim. We consider this possibility, including the effects of cost containment and expansion of coverage to the uninsured on service availability, delivery, and outcomes. We identify the major issues related to hospital care that policymakers will have to grapple with as they consider health care reform and we conclude by discussing how choices related to health care reform may affect the structure of health services delivery and the role of what we have traditionally known as a hospital.

Hospital Revenue Sources

In 1991, $288.6 billion was spent for inpatient and outpatient hospital services (Table 6.1). Non-federal, short term, acute care community hospitals received 86 percent of these revenues. The remaining 14 percent was di-

Table 6.1   Hospital Revenues and Annual Percent Growth, 1985–1991

Type of Hospital	1985	1986	1987	1988	1989	1990	1991
				Revenues in Billions			
Non-federal	154.9	165.8	179.4	196.7	215.8	240.0	268.9
Community	143.3	153.2	165.7	181.7	199.3	222.6	249.4
Inpatient	119.1	125.1	133.3	143.6	155.2	170.0	186.5
Outpatient	24.2	28.1	32.4	38.1	44.1	52.6	63.0
Non-community	11.7	12.6	13.7	15.0	16.5	17.4	19.5
Federal	13.3	14.0	14.9	15.3	16.5	18.1	19.7
Total	$168.2	$179.8	$194.2	$212.0	$232.4	$258.1	$288.6
				Annual Percent Growth			
Non-federal	6.7	7.0	8.2	9.7	9.7	11.2	12.1
Community	6.6	6.9	8.2	9.7	9.7	11.7	12.1
Inpatient	4.4	5.1	6.6	7.7	8.1	9.5	9.7
Outpatient	19.3	16.0	15.3	17.7	15.7	19.3	19.7
Non-community	7.5	7.8	8.7	9.5	10.3	5.3	12.0
Federal	8.5	5.4	6.1	3.0	7.8	9.6	8.9
Total	6.8	6.8	8.0	9.2	9.6	11.1	11.8

Note: Non-community non-federal hospitals include long-term care, psychiatric, alcohol and chemical dependency, and chronic disease hospitals.

Source: Health Care Financing Administration, Office of the Actuary.

vided about equally between federal facilities and non-acute care facilities such as psychiatric and long-term hospitals.

Most hospital care is now financed by third parties, with only 3.4 percent paid for by consumers directly out of pocket.[3] Between 1960 and 1991, the share of hospital revenue obtained through private health insurance remained stable at about 36 percent. With the implementation of the

Medicare and Medicaid programs, the share of government spending jumped promptly from 37 percent to 55 percent and has remained relatively constant since then. As Medicare and Medicaid spending grew, out of pocket spending by individuals and other government expenditures decreased as a proportion of the total. Most of the federal government spending for hospital care, other than Medicare and Medicaid, is for services furnished by the Departments of Defense and Veterans Affairs. State and local government spending includes subsidies to cover the uninsured and programs such as worker's compensation.

Most health care reform proposals would affect the mix and relationship among payment sources. Preferences range from the current blend of public and multiple voluntary private payers to a government-controlled single-payer system with universal coverage. To evaluate the implications of alternative proposals for the future of the hospital, policymakers must have a firm understanding of the relationship between hospital revenues and expenses by payer group, including the effects of third-party policy changes in the past decade.

Government Payers

The Medicaid program was the first major payer to move from the traditional reasonable cost/charges approach of paying hospitals, disallowing certain costs, such as those associated with non-patient care activities. In addition, some states used prospective payment systems for hospital outpatient services. Consequently, in 1980 Medicaid payments to hospitals averaged about 92 percent of reported costs.

A provision of the Omnibus Reconciliation Act of 1981, known as the Boren Amendment, gave states broad discretion to develop alternative Medicaid hospital payment methods, requiring them only to ensure that payments were sufficient to cover the costs of efficiently and economically operated facilities, while maintaining access and quality of care for Medicaid participants. In response, most states shifted to some type of prospective payment system that allowed them to slow the growth in hospital payments.[4] By 1989 Medicaid payment levels averaged 78 percent of hospital costs and their reimbursements for care to Medicaid patients lagged costs by $3.7 billion.[4]

The declining ratio of Medicaid revenues to costs has recently been partly reversed. In 1991, the average Medicaid payment to cost ratio was 82 percent, although Medicaid shortfalls had increased to $5.1 billion (Table 6.2). The improvement in payment to cost ratios was due in part to successful legal challenges by provider groups to the Boren Amendment and its implementation. In addition, Congress allowed states to provide substantial payment increases to hospitals that serve a disproportionate share

Table 6.2   Community Hospital Costs and Revenues, by Source, 1991

Payer or Other Source	Revenues (In Billions)	Percent of Total	Costs (In Billions)	Percent of Total	Ratio of Revenues To Costs
Medicare	$76.3	32.8	$86.3	38.4	0.88
Medicaid	22.7	9.8	27.8	12.4	0.82
Other government payers	3.2	1.4	3.2	1.4	1.00
Private payers	113.9	49.0	87.8	39.1	1.30
Uncompensated care *	n/a	n/a	13.4	6.0	n/a
State and local subsidies	2.6	1.1	n/a	n/a	n/a
Other operating **	8.9	3.8	6.0	2.7	1.47
Non-operating ***	4.9	2.1	n/a	n/a	n/a
Total	232.6	100.0	224.5	100.0	1.04

* Uncompensated care includes charity care and bad debt.
** Includes operating revenues and costs for sources other than patient care, such as gift shops.
*** Includes revenues from donations, grants, and other sources.

Source: Prospective Payment Assessment Commission analysis of data from
the American Hospital Association's Annual Survey of Hospitals for 1991.

of low income patients. States have also taken advantage of the ability to use provider taxes and donations to increase the federal share of Medicaid payments. As a result, between 1989 and 1991, Medicaid expenditures for hospitals rose from $22.9 billion to $43.4 billion,[3] the greatest portion consisting of disproportionate share hospital payments that by 1992 had reached about $18 billion. This increased funding, however, may not translate into large improvements in Medicaid and uncompensated care shortfalls since a part of it reflects intergovernmental transfers rather than new funds. In addition, Medicaid admissions have continued to increase, with hospital costs rising more rapidly than payments.[5]

There are currently large disparities in Medicaid payments across states, with payments ranging from 56 percent to 119 percent of costs in 1991.[6] Medicaid policies have also had a differential impact across types of hospitals. Overall, Medicaid losses as a percentage of total hospital costs averaged two percent, with public, major teaching hospitals suffering the greatest losses (3.4 percent of total costs), and rural disproportionate share hospitals the least (1.2 percent).

In 1983, Medicare followed Medicaid in replacing retrospective, cost-based reimbursement, with a prospective payment system (PPS). It was expected that a system of fixed payments, set in advance, covering all inpatient hospital services during an admission would slow the acceleration in hospital costs. In the early years of PPS, Medicare spending growth slowed, due primarily to a decline in hospital admissions. Payments per discharge, however, were higher than intended, with increases of 18.5 percent and 10.5 percent in the first two years. By the third year, the Medicare program had a firm grip on its payment level, with a per case increase of only 3.1 percent.[6] Subsequently, payments have increased about 5 to 6 percent a year, about 1 percent more than the annual increase in the hospital market basket measure of inflation.

Although PPS succeeded in braking the growth in Medicare payments to hospitals, it failed to affect the growth in hospital operating costs per case. In the first year of PPS, hospitals reduced the quantity of services furnished, especially length of stay, and costs per case increased only 1.9 percent. In the second year, costs per discharge rebounded to 10.6 percent. The annual increase in operating costs per discharge then declined slowly to 7.3 percent in 1991, an amount still 1.8 percentage points greater than payments.[6]

Because Medicare's reasonable cost methodology did not allow some hospital reported costs, in 1980, before PPS, its ratio of payments to costs was about 0.96, about the same as in 1988 under PPS.[7] By 1991, the ratio had fallen to 0.88, with hospital reported Medicare expenses exceeding revenues by $10 billion (Table 6.2).

In the first six years of PPS, aggregate Medicare payments exceeded hospital costs, leading to profits for many hospitals; since then costs per case have grown faster than payments and the majority of hospitals are now sustaining a loss on their Medicare inpatient business. At the same time, the overall financial status of hospitals, as measured by total hospital margins, is better today than it was in the years preceding PPS.

Many health care reform proposals would retain Medicare as a separate program, although significant changes in its policies are likely. Since Medicare is a major purchaser of hospital care, the PPS payment level will directly affect hospitals and indirectly the payments of other payers. The Medicare PPS has also stipulated special provisions to protect teaching, disproportionate share, sole community, and other hospitals that may need to be modified to conform with health care reform design decisions.

Policymakers will also have to consider the role of other government payers—worker's compensation, state and local government insurance plans, and the Civilian Health and Medical Programs of the Uniformed Services (CHAMPUS) which finances care for certain military retirees. In 1991, revenues of $3.2 billion from these sources equaled the cost of furnishing care to their beneficiaries.

Private Insurance

One of the most contentious aspects of health care reform will be the future role and responsibilities of private insurers and employers. Americans are unique among the industrialized nations in their preference for voluntary, private health insurance. Private insurance has historically favored coverage for hospital services over other personal health care services and accounted, in 1991, for 49 percent, $114 billion, of community hospital revenues.

The private health insurance market has experienced major changes in the past decade. Although there are more than 2,000 private insurance companies and plans, only a few dominate the insurance market, and very few plans dominate a local health services market, as Blue Cross plans once did. Many large companies, attempting to control spending for employee health care benefits, have assumed the financial risk of their employees' medical costs by self-insuring, and by 1990, 44 percent of employer-covered medical bills were paid through self-insured plans. Many small employers, however, do not offer any type of health insurance benefits to their workers. It is generally believed that insurance company marketing and pricing strategies including risk selection, experience rating, and discriminatory underwriting have contributed to the lack of coverage.[8]

Private payers also lack the power of government to set payment rates at levels they are willing to pay and for many years, simply paid hospitals their costs or charges. Payers are now attempting to control their spending, and hospitals are competing for patients. Some private insurers have effectively used "managed care" strategies to control the price and utilization of services. These strategies allow insurers to negotiate a lower payment in return for a guarantee that the insured group will use their services when needed. Consequently, there is more price competition and negotiation in many markets. Hospitals and payers have even joined forces in joint ventures, blurring the distinction between the payer and the service delivery roles.

The experience with private insurance in the past decade is instructive regarding the ability of hospitals to increase their revenues. For many years, payments from private payers have exceeded hospital costs of their enrollees and despite efforts to control spending, their share of hospital revenue relative to their costs is rising. In 1980, before Medicare and Medicaid began to tighten their reimbursement policies, payments from private payers accounted for 112 percent of their costs. After 1987, when the policies of government payers began to take hold, overpayment by private payers rose rapidly, reaching, by 1991, 130 percent of costs of care for their patients and providing hospitals with excess revenues of $26 billion (Table 6.2).

Hospitals have been able to increase this stream of excess revenue because most private payers continue to pay either full billed charges or negotiated discounts from charges. In 1980, hospital charges averaged 125 percent of costs.[6] As more private payers negotiated discounts off charges, or chose other payment methods such as negotiated per diems, hospitals simply responded by increasing their charges. Consequently, by 1991 the starting point for discount negotiations, the billed charge, had jumped to 153 percent of costs.

Information concerning costs and payment levels for payers using managed care and capitation strategies would be especially useful but unfortunately, insurer-specific data are lacking. An analysis conducted by the Congressional Budget Office indicated that, in 1989, 7 percent of hospitals lost money on their private patients. These losses could be related to effective managed care, other payment strategies or still other factors.[7]

According to a study by the Prospective Payment Assessment Commission, there is tremendous variation in the ability of insurer and employer groups to control the level of hospital payments. Analysis of a large employer data base showed hospital payments in 1991 ranging from 93 percent to 172 percent of hospital costs, with an average of 138 percent. Ninety percent of the group paid at least 115 percent of costs. These averages are somewhat higher than those for private insurance overall. The data base contained employers with PPOs, but not staff- and group-model HMOs. Better knowledge of the experience of HMOs could have a major impact on the health care reform debate.

Government Subsidies and Uncompensated Care

Providing financial access to care for all Americans may be the greatest challenge facing policymakers as they consider the merits of health care reform proposals, an issue that has engaged the nation intermittently since the second decade of this century.[9]

In the absence of universal health insurance, many hospitals have adhered to their origins as charitable institutions, furnishing services to individuals without the means to pay for their care. When the cost of care outstripped the ability of philanthropy to keep pace, state and local governments stepped in with financial support. The result was a still evolving system of public hospitals providing care to the poor and ensuring the availability of services to vulnerable populations. Today there are 1,500 general hospitals owned by states, counties, and other community entities. The dominant role of many of these hospitals as charitable institutions, however, has diminished over the years.

State and local governments provide direct subsidies to about 15 percent of hospitals.[7] The subsidies are an important source of revenue for many of these hospitals, helping to defray the cost of providing care to the uninsured. The contributions of state and local governments grew from $1.0 billion in 1980 to $2.6 billion 1991. During this time, however, hospitals' uncompensated care greatly outpaced the revenues from state and local governments. Uncompensated care costs, consisting of charity care furnished to the poor and bad debts, increased from $3.6 billion in 1980 to $13.4 billion in 1991 and despite enlarged government subsidies, rose from 5.4 to 6.0 percent of total hospital costs in the past decade.

The amount of uncompensated care a hospital furnishes varies widely among similar types of hospitals. For example, among urban disproportionate share hospitals in 1989, the proportion of total costs due to uncompensated care net of government subsidies ranged from 9.2 percent for the top 10 percent to 1.1 percent for the lowest 10 percent of these hospitals. Similar variations are found across the spectrum of hospital sponsorship and location.

This tremendous diversity in the distribution of uncompensated care costs suggests that the targeted policies of the past decade are not effectively protecting the most deserving hospitals. In particular, the Medicare teaching adjustment, and to a lesser extent the disproportionate share adjustment, are poorly associated with hospitals' uncompensated care load. State and local government subsidies also appear to be used for other purposes. In 1989, the subsidies exceeded the cost of uncompensated care for about 45 percent of hospitals.[7] Increased Medicaid disproportionate share revenues seem to go to offset current state subsidies and for other purposes than were intended by policymakers.

Nonpatient Care Revenue

In addition to patient care, hospitals have other sources of revenue, including small profit-making businesses such as cafeterias, gift shops, and parking concessions, which in 1991 generated $8.9 billion income at a cost of $6.0 billion.

The philanthropic heritage of hospitals also continues. Hospitals obtained $4.9 billion in nonoperating revenues from donations, contributions, endowment income, as well as grants and other earnings. These revenues are substantially cost-free.

Shifting Responsibilities

Hospitals have always subsidized costs that were not directly paid for by or on behalf of a specific individual. These unreimbursed costs fall into two broad categories: charity care provided to patients who are unable to pay as well as bad debts from people who are able to pay but do not; and underpayments from various payers for treating the patients covered by them. Hospitals' unreimbursed costs from uncompensated care and publicly insured patients rose from 7 percent of total costs in 1980 to almost 13 percent, $28 billion, in 1991. The relative shares of unreimbursed costs changed concomitantly. Uncompensated care rose modestly from 5.4 percent of total costs to 6.0 percent, totaling $13 billion, while losses from Medicare and Medicaid increased from 1.7 percent of costs to 6.7 percent, reaching $15 billion.

Nevertheless, aggregate industry revenues exceeded costs throughout this time. Hospitals were able to cover most of their unreimbursed costs with revenues from three sources, although their relative shares changed. Between 1980 and 1991, state and local government subsidies, as a percent of unreimbursed costs, fell from 27 percent to 10 percent, while other nonpatient revenue sources remained stable at about 30 percent. The share of unreimbursed costs paid by private insurers, however, rose from 37 percent to 55 percent, and 23 percent of all revenues from private payers were used to offset unreimbursed costs (Table 6.3).

These offsets were accomplished by increasing the prices hospitals charged to privately insured patients, a strategy known as "cost shifting." This practice of raising prices for some groups of buyers to compensate for lower amounts paid by other groups is common in the American economy and has historically been used by hospitals to subsidize care of the poor. It has come to attention recently, however, because the Medicare and Medicaid programs have successfully kept the increase in their payments below the increase in hospital costs. This does not necessarily mean that Medicare or Medicaid rates are too low. Medicare PPS payments were intended to create financial incentives for hospitals to decrease their costs for all payers.[10] Perversely, hospitals responded to the incentives by increasing revenue from private payers, rather than decreasing the rate of cost increases. The cost-shifting experience, however, is not uniform— there is wide variation across private payers in hospital payment to cost ratios and in the ability of hospitals to generate surplus revenue from private sources.[6]

Changing Trends in Hospital Services

The largest share of this nation's health care dollars continues to be used to purchase hospital services. Major cost-control efforts notwithstanding, between 1980 and 1991 spending for hospital care increased from $102 billion to $289 billion; even adjusting for general inflation, a rise of 70 percent was recorded.[11] Total personal health care expenditures, however, grew even more rapidly, and the share going to hospitals fell from 47 percent to 44 percent. As third party payers struggled to control their spending and inpatient admissions declined, hospitals expanded into new markets, re-

Table 6.3 Losses and Gains as a Percentage of Hospital Costs, by Source, 1981-1991

Source	1981	1983	1985	1987	1989	1991
Uncompensated care*	-3.3	-3.6	-4.4	-4.4	-4.4	-4.4
Medicaid	-0.7	-0.8	-1.0	-1.7	-2.5	-2.3
Medicare	-1.0	-1.2	0.4	-0.7	-3.3	-4.4
Private payers	5.0	7.0	6.7	8.2	8.9	11.6

* Net of government subsidies

Source: Prospective Payment Assessment Commission analysis of data from the American Hospital Association's Annual Survey of Hospitals.

ducing their reliance on revenues from traditional acute care services, and carving out new roles in the American health care system.

Cost control policies of third party payers, public acceptance of new medical and technologic capabilities, and increased competition from new post acute care and ambulatory care providers all contributed to changing the composition of hospital services. Alternative payment methods created financial incentives for hospitals to decrease the length of stay and intensity of services furnished during an admission at the same time that managed care, other utilization review strategies, and expanded benefits to encourage less costly ambulatory care were introduced to control hospital admissions. These policies had their intended effect on hospital utilization, with 5.5 million fewer hospital admissions in 1992 than in 1982, a drop of 14.5 percent despite a 10 percent increase in population. Rural hospitals were especially affected with a 34 percent decrease as against a 9 percent loss for urban hospitals. The average hospital length of stay also fell, from 7.2 days to 6.4 days.

The declining demand for inpatient care was accompanied by declining bed supply. From a peak of just over one million in 1983, the number of hospital beds fell 9.6 percent to 908,000 in 1992 as the result of downsizing, hospital mergers, acquisitions, conversions to other uses, and closures. In 1991, there were 471 fewer community hospitals than in 1981, a fall of 8.1 percent. State and government owned facilities and rural hospitals fared the worst, declining 18 percent and 12 percent, respectively. Demand declined even more rapidly, however, and hospital occupancy dipped from 76 percent in 1980 to 62 percent in 1992 (Table 6.4).[6]

Table 6.4   Trends in the Hospital Market, Selected Years

Year	Number of Hospitals	Hospital Beds Total (In Thousands)	Per 1,000 Population	Admissions Total (In Thousands)	Per 1,000 Population	Occupancy Rate (Percent)
1960	6,876	1,658	8.8	25,027	130	84.6
1965	7,123	1,704	8.4	28,812	140	82.3
1970	7,123	1,616	7.6	31,759	150	80.3
1975	7,156	1,466	6.6	36,157	160	76.7
1980	6,965	1,365	5.8	38,892	170	77.7
1985	6,872	1,318	5.3	36,304	150	69.0
1987	6,821	1,267	5.0	34,439	140	68.9
1989	6,720	1,226	4.8	33,742	130	69.6
1991	6,634	1,202	4.6	33,567	130	68.8

Note: Hospital market includes community, federal, long-term care, hospital units of institutions, psychiatric, tuberculosis, and other special hospitals.

Source: Congressional Budget Office. Trends in Health Spending: An Update, June 1993.

These unprecedented declines in inpatient hospital supply and utilization were initially accompanied by equally impressive drops in spending growth. Between 1984 and 1985, inpatient hospital revenues grew only 4.4 percent, but by 1991 annual revenue growth reached 9.7 percent,[3] in part reflecting a substantial expansion of specialty units providing psychiatric, rehabilitation, skilled nursing facility level, alcohol and drug, and other services, rather than traditional acute inpatient care.

Although the bulk of hospital revenues still comes from inpatient services, their share has been falling as hospitals expand their ambulatory services. Between 1980 and 1992, outpatient revenues increased from 13 percent to 25 percent of total revenues, reflecting shifts or substitutions for traditional inpatient services, and aggressive competition with other providers for new outpatient business. The number of hospital-provided ambulatory surgery procedures, for example, quadrupled from three million in 1980 to twelve million in 1991, and the share of hospital based home health agencies increased from 12 percent to 26 percent, generating $2.3 billion in 1991.[3]

The evolutionary spiral is spinning in still other directions. Hospitals are developing joint ventures with other providers and suppliers; many are entering into collaborative arrangements with physicians, and the most adventurous are moving into the financing arena and sharing the financial risk of providing care.

Hospital Expenses

Spending for hospital care is determined by the number of people receiving services and the cost per inpatient admission or outpatient visit. From 1985 to 1991, total hospital costs increased on average 9.5 percent annually. Population accounts for about 10 percent, or one percentage point, of this increase. During this time, hospital admissions continued to decline, while outpatient visits accelerated. The net effect was a decrease in admissions and visits per person, reducing costs by 0.3 percentage points (Figure 6.1). Policymakers should note, however, that while reductions in hospital admissions or slower growth in outpatient visits will reduce the growth in hospital spending, it will not necessarily slow the rise in total health care spending. Many people who would have received services from hospitals will obtain them in other settings. In some cases, the policies of third party payers or the technologic advances that are seen as cost reducing in fact lead to increases in overall expenditures as the mix of services and settings changes.[12,13]

Although the hospital share of total spending for care has declined, costs per admission and outpatient visit have continued to increase rapidly. To control hospital spending further, health care reform will have to slow the growth in expenses per case. These expenses include the labor, non-labor, and capital resources that go into the provision of hospital care and are responsible, respectively, for about 54 percent, 38 percent and 8 percent of outlays used to produce patient services, purchase malpractice insurance and provide administrative services.

There are three broad ways hospitals could slow the growth in expenses. They could produce fewer services during an admission or visit, increase efficiency by using fewer resources to produce each service, or pay a lower price for each unit of input they purchase.

Inflation in the general economy—over which hospitals have little control—is the single largest contributor to hospital cost increases, accounting for 43 percent of the total increase between 1985 and 1991. An additional 8 percent of the annual cost increase was due to price inflation specific to the health sector, in particular hospital wages and salaries, as well as pharmaceutical prices. The extent to which hospitals have control over this sector-specific inflation depends upon their negotiating ability and the complex interaction between supply and demand for labor and goods.

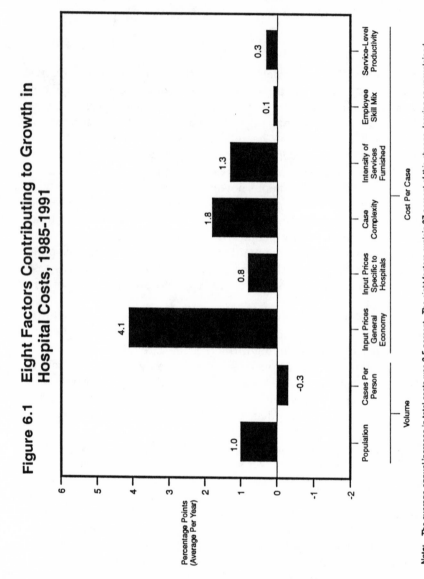

Figure 6.1   Eight Factors Contributing to Growth in Hospital Costs, 1985-1991

Note: The average annual increase in total costs was 9.5 percent. The eight factors explain 97 percent of this change, leaving an unexplained residual of 0.3 percentage points per year.

SOURCE: ProPAC analysis based on data from the American Hospital Association, Health Care Financing Administration, and Department of Labor.

As the composition of hospital admissions and visits has changed, the average complexity of the patients treated has intensified, accounting for 19 percent of the increase in expenses. It is expected that caring for more complex patients will require more resources, and, therefore, this factor is also generally beyond the control of hospitals. The increase in the number and complexity of services furnished, however, was greater than can explained by changes in case complexity. This additional increase in service intensity was responsible for 14 percent of the hospital cost growth. Over the period of this analysis, the growth in service intensity slowed, and it is likely that this area is a candidate for further reductions.

The final factor influencing hospital expenses is efficiency and productivity in the use of resources to produce the services furnished during an admission or visit. Productivity improvements can reduce hospital expenses by producing the same output with less resources or increasing output using the same amount of resources. In the past decade, case-mix adjusted hospital productivity has generally declined rather than increased. Between 1985 and 1991 diminishing productivity was responsible for a 3 percent annual increase in hospital costs.

While some of the factors pushing per case expenses higher and higher, such as general inflation, are outside hospital influence, reductions in other areas are possible. Hospital administrative costs are estimated to account for as much as 24 percent of hospital expenses.[14,15] Administrative services—patient billing, information systems and reporting, and quality and utilization management—may be altered by health care reform and could be substantial. Better use of hospital capacity could also result in large productivity gains.[16] The excess supply of hospital services includes the number of beds as well as inefficient use of technology and surgical capacity. Inefficiencies in the use of hospital capacity are also related to the rapid growth in ambulatory and other facility-based services. Policies aimed at improving the utilization of service capacity must consider the supply of services in all settings.

Hospitals may also be able to reduce the volume and intensity of services furnished during an admission. A number of studies have demonstrated large, unexplained variation in the use of hospital services across geographic areas and population groups, some of which represents services that do not contribute to improved quality of care. The paucity of sound medical evidence regarding the efficacy of many services and procedures, however, will hinder the passage of reform proposals that opponents believe may reduce services and affect access to high quality care.

Access to Quality Care

Most parties to the health care reform debate are agreed on the goal of ensuring access to quality care for all Americans. The contentious issue will be how to achieve this goal while slowing the growth in current spending. As the design of a health reform proposal unfolds, many providers, payers, and others opposed to specific policies will voice their fear that quality and access will suffer. Policymakers have faced similar concerns repeatedly in recent years, and they can bring to the debate the knowledge gained from research and experience.

The experience with the Medicare prospective payment system (PPS) is particularly enlightening. Shortly after PPS began, policymakers were inundated with complaints about the deterioration of patient care, the potential stifling of innovation, and intensification of the special problems of access facing beneficiaries who rely on rural or inner-city hospitals. Those living in areas where hospitals were threatened with closure also received much attention. Consequently, extensive research and analysis was directed to the impact of PPS on quality and access.

The studies generally found no evidence of systematic declines in access to quality care for Medicare beneficiaries. There were, however, dramatic changes in the pattern of service delivery, specifically, the unprecedented fall in hospital length of stay and the movement of surgical and other technology-intensive services to ambulatory settings. Increasingly, residents of rural areas bypassed their local facility in seeking hospital care, a trend that probably was a cause rather than a result of declines in rural hospital occupancy.

Access to quality care was preserved by various adjustments in this period of changing hospital utilization and financing. The erosion of acute inpatient services was compensated by the increased utilization of skilled nursing and rehabilitation facilities, home-based care and ambulatory services, and the impact of Medicare payment constraints was ameliorated by the ability to obtain increased revenues from private payers. Congress also provided additional financial protection to groups of hospitals it believed were especially vulnerable.

Other research findings, however, should be of concern to policymakers. Although hospitals and their physicians are believed to apply the same standards of care to all patients, in some cases the health insurance status of individuals appears to be related to the use of resources during an admission.[17] High-cost, medically discretionary procedures appear to be used less frequently for the uninsured, although the utilization of low cost procedures and tests that are medically necessary does not seem to differ. Hospital payer mix and financial condition also have been associated with lower expenditures and poorer quality of care in some facilities.[18] However, the factors underlying these relationships, and their implications, are poorly understood.

These studies illustrate the complexities involved in attempting to measure quality of care and apply the findings to policy. Most Americans report that they are highly satisfied with the care they receive from physicians and hospitals,[19] but the basis for this satisfaction frequently is not grounded in scientific evidence. Mechanisms for the review and oversight of hospital care have been in place for many years, although the lack of medical consensus regarding the benefit, appropriateness, and necessity of many diagnostic and therapeutic interventions limits the value of these activities. The review and oversight process also has been a source of tension, leading to the search for better methods to evaluate and improve quality of care. As weak as it may be, there is some information on the quality of hospital care to guide policymakers. There are few or no review and oversight activities and very little information regarding the appropriateness and quality of the care furnished in ambulatory and other settings.

Issues in Health Care Reform

Agreed: Policymakers designing a health care reform plan must find a technically acceptable solution to two problems—slowing the growth in current expenditures, now 14 percent of the nation's economic output, and expanding coverage for the many people who are uninsured. To be enacted, however, a proposal must also meet the test of political acceptability and be consistent with the desires of the American public as perceived by their political leaders. Traditionally, the public has favored pluralism, with a mix of for-profit and non-profit private sector providers delivering the care furnished to most citizens. The private sector has also been the first choice, on a voluntary basis, for financing the care, with the government assuming a role only as a last resort.

Advocates of comprehensive reform argue that the government must intervene to ensure that all Americans have access to a basic level of care. These observers are critical of both the voluntary nature of employment-based private insurance and the practices of insurance companies, for instance, the replacement of community rating with experience rating and other risk avoidance techniques to enroll the healthiest individuals in the interest of restraining premium increases and expanding market share. These practices are believed to have contributed to the rapidly increasing costs of insurance coverage for the most vulnerable population groups and threatened the availability of insurance for other workers. Many employers have chosen not to offer a health insurance benefit at any price. Moreover, the most vulnerable population groups, the poor, elderly, and sick, usually are not employed. To fill the gaps left by voluntary coverage in the workplace, the government will have to step in as it did with the passage of Medicare and Medicaid.

The proponents of a stronger role for government also point to the cost shifting experience of the past decade to demonstrate that no single payer, not even Medicare, has sufficient leverage to control total health care spending. Medicare and Medicaid both used government power to control payments with the hope hospitals would respond to the financial incentives and slow the rate of increase in costs for all payers. Hospitals, however, face even stronger incentives to expand their technologic capabilities, maintain good relations with the physicians who admit patients, and be perceived as state of the art. Rather than reducing cost growth, hospitals responded to payment constraints by generating revenues in excess of costs from other sources, especially private payers. Hence, concerted action by all payers is necessary to eliminate the opportunity for hospitals to evade the cost control policies of one payer by increasing revenues from others.

Those favoring a strong private sector role believe that a predominantly private, pluralistic financing and delivery system is necessary to ensure diversity and freedom of choice and to prevent government, or any other group, from gaining excessive power. True competition in the medical market, they are convinced, is the best way to establish the level of health spending that reflects the values and wishes of the general public. Government regulatory activities, subject as they are to political pressure, will not result in the hard choices needed to force efficiencies on hospitals, since regulatory authorities tend to protect the economic survival of the entities they are regulating.[20] Moreover, the associated administrative procedures and requirements will add substantial costs to the government as well as the private sector.

Health care reform policies will evolve in an environment with widely differing ideological and philosophical beliefs regarding the role and responsibilities of government and a more competitive private sector. The American public has generally strongly opposed government ownership or control of health care delivery, but at the same time has supported government financing of care for the poor and elderly. In addition, the public has embraced government support for research, funding for hospital construction, and a wide range of public health activities and has consistently backed tax policies that have subsidized hospitals and the purchase of insurance. The choices made by policymakers to resolve differences in strongly held opinions regarding the relative roles and responsibilities of government and the private sector may be the most important factor determining the financing and structure of the health care system for many years to come.

Covering the Uninsured

Despite its relative wealth and prosperity, the United States is the only industrialized nation that does not provide protection against the cost of illness for all its citizens. The failure of the prevailing system of private, employment-based insurance to serve the needs of the elderly and poor led to the passage of Medicare and Medicaid in 1965 and established the government as a major payer of care for the first time. Today, the problems continue as over 37 million Americans, almost 15 percent of the total population, lack health insurance coverage. Not all are poor or unemployed. In 1991, about 29 percent of the uninsured were in families earning between $20,000 and $40,000 a year, and for an additional 17 percent, family income exceeds $40,000. Further, 85 percent of the uninsured are in families headed by workers, and more than 60 percent of the uninsured workers were employed the entire year. Many smaller firms are dropping coverage of their employees. In 1991, one out of five firms with twenty-five to ninety-nine employees did not offer health insurance, and two out of three of those with less than twenty five workers. Clearly, linking health insurance, on a voluntary basis, to employment status is resulting in increasing gaps in coverage. As for public programs, in 1991, only 52 percent of the nonelderly population with incomes below the poverty level received publicly sponsored coverage.[21,22]

Estimates of the cost of providing coverage to the uninsured vary widely and are influenced by factors such as the benefits covered, the payment methods and amounts, cost sharing responsibilities, and the increased demand for services that coverage may generate. Universal coverage will provide hospitals with new revenue to cover the charity care they now furnish, as well as an expected increase in admissions and services for the previously uninsured. Covering the uninsured, however, will also result in decreases in other revenue. State and local governments are likely to eliminate or reduce their subsidies to hospitals, which in 1991 amounted to $2.6 billion. Depending on cost sharing policies, hospitals may see less revenue due to bad debts from individuals who do not pay their share of the bill. Medicare and Medicaid hospital payment policies have also provided additional revenue to disproportionate share hospitals (DSH) that treat a large number of the poor, including many teaching hospitals. President Clinton's health care reform proposal would eliminate most of these DSH payments, which are estimated to be $18 billion in 1993. Many DSH hospitals would also suffer under the President's proposal from substantial reductions in the special Medicare payments to teaching hospitals, although the plan would create a distinctive fund for academic health centers. Conceivably, too, voluntary gifts to hospitals by the public would be curtailed if universal coverage were enacted.

Policies that determine coverage for the uninsured, reductions in the level of the special Medicaid and Medicare disproportionate share and teaching adjustments, and decreases in the level of state and local government subsidies will also affect the distribution of payments across geographic areas and types of hospitals. In many cases, current policies have not done a good job of matching payments with the charity care burden of individual hospitals. Uncompensated care losses as a percentage of total costs vary widely by state, from 1.5 percent in Iowa to 9.9 percent in Mississippi. There are also large differences within types of hospitals. Some major teaching hospitals furnish almost no uncompensated care, in others uncompensated care accounts for more than 10 percent of total costs.[23] Hospitals that currently benefit from Medicare's disproportionate share and teaching policies, even though they do not care for a large share of the uninsured, are likely to see their special treatment end. Hospitals that have shouldered the largest share of the load, as well as those that have not received any special treatment, are likely to gain from the new policies. In addition, if insurance coverage leads to substantial increases in admissions to some hospitals that have been operating at low capacity, efficiency improvements may slow the growth in costs per case.

The greatest financial impact of expanded coverage, however, may be determined by the initial level and the annual increase in the payments for the services provided to those who become insured. If health care reform contains strong cost containment provisions, payment amounts will increase at a lower rate than hospital costs. Comprehensive reform could also increase the financial pressure on hospitals by reducing or eliminating opportunities for cross-subsidization.

Strategies to Control Spending Growth

Despite public concern with recent "cuts" in government and private health care spending, none of the past actions or future proposals actually cut spending. All they attempt to do is decelerate the annual growth rate which has recently been about 11 percent. The first set of questions facing policymakers must be answered by the political system. Does the American public truly want to slow the growth in spending for hospital and other health services? If so, how should it be done and by how much?

Numerous strategies to reform health care financing have been introduced in the Congress. The first model looks to a strong government role with rate setting. The second model, "managed competition," seeks to create more effective competition among health plans, based on the prices (premiums) they charge and the availability and quality of the services they deliver. The third model attempts to combine the efficiency of the managed competition approach with some of the cost containment features of government regulation of total health care expenditures, by controlling the rates of increase of health plan premiums.

A rate setting strategy aims to control spending by means of prospectively determined payment amounts for each service furnished that would apply to all covered services and all providers and suppliers of these services. The system could involve a single payer, the government, or multiple public and private payers following a single set of rules. Both a single-payer and an all-payer rate setting system could use the power of government to control the prices of individual units of service. Such systems, however, provide strong incentives to increase the volume of services furnished and may encourage new types of providers, excess or inappropriate capacity, and non-price competition for patients. Creating larger payment units, such as Medicare has done with diagnosis related groups (DRGs), can control the volume of services furnished during a specific episode of care, such as a hospital admission, but can also result in spending increases in other settings.

To control volume, other policies must accompany a rate setting system. One option is a volume performance standard that triggers a payment adjustment in future years if expenditure growth exceeds a predetermined target. Such an approach could apply to each type of provider group individually, or there could be an aggregate global budget target applicable to all groups. Although hospital-specific budgets have been used in other nations, they would be much more difficult to implement in this country because of the number and diversity of hospitals and other providers furnishing similar services. A rate setting system could also include a capitated payment option, similar to Medicare's risk-based program. Such an approach would be consistent with the direction of health care financing today and has the potential to control price and volume.

The second approach, managed competition, attempts to control spending through market forces by creating competition among alternative health plans. Under a pure form of such a market system, health plans would be free to pay hospitals and other providers at mutually negotiated rates. Its proponents expect that each plan would seek to minimize its costs, and therefore its premium, while maintaining an acceptable quality level of care. To lower their costs, health plans would be aggressive in seeking cheaper rates from hospitals and attempt tight management of hospital utilization. Hospitals would be more willing to negotiate lower rates for plans that guarantee increased patient flow. Such an approach would require a much more fundamental change in the health care delivery system than is expected under a government regulated rate setting approach. To its proponents, this is one of the major advantages of the managed competition approach. To its detractors, this strong push to an American health care delivery system dominated by large, independent, often for-profit, managed care health plans is an important reason to reject such an approach. There is also disagreement on how effective such market competition alone would be in slowing the growth in health care expenditures. Evidence to date indicates that managed care plans have been able to reduce expenditures for hospital care by 20 to 30 percent and total expenditures by about 10 percent. For the most part, these have been one time savings with future increased spending rates paralleling the experience of other systems. But, the managed competition advocates argue, this is before we have restructured the entire health care market as envisioned under a managed competition approach.

To ensure more effective spending control, President Clinton's health reform plan stipulates a third approach which, in addition to providing structural incentives to expand the degree of market competition, limits the amount each health plan can raise its premium. We have called this the global budget premium control system. The limitation on premium income would constrain the ability of health plans to pay more to hospitals and other providers and, therefore, force them to be tougher in their negotiations for price reductions. It would also put added pressure on such health plans to become more effective managers of the care used by their subscribers. In aggregate, such premium controls would create a global budgeting system. Unlike a rate setting system, however, there would be no micro-regulation by the government of what a hospital or other provider could charge for its services. Supporters of the managed competition approach fear that the premium controls would so restrict the ability of health plans to compete that the system would revert to that under rate regulation, which they contend is grossly inefficient.

The Effects on Hospitals

The effects of efforts to slow the growth in hospital and other health care spending will be determined by a mix of political and technical decisions by policymakers concerning specific reform strategies and design and implementation issues. The most important financing decision concerns how far and how fast to lower the projected baseline rate of spending growth. The continued rise in spending for hospital services reflects both a high base level and an annual increase more than twice the rate of population growth plus inflation in the general economy. Spending in other health delivery sectors is growing even more rapidly. Many policymakers believe that health care reform must both stabilize the base level and slow the annual growth thereafter. Estimating the spending effects of proposed policy changes, however, is a difficult task characterized by considerable uncertainty. Congress has assigned the responsibility for estimating the spending impacts of proposed legislation to the Congressional Budget Office (CBO).

The CBO has reported that a proposal stipulating incremental reforms of the current financing and delivery system will neither slow spending growth nor expand insurance coverage.[24] A managed competition plan without a global budget is expected to reduce the base level of spending as more people join HMOs and similar plans, but will not slow the annual increases thereafter, hence it effectiveness in controlling long-term spending growth is limited. The effectiveness of managed competition approaches, without budget limits, is also dependent on the inclusion of several highly controversial features, including changes in the tax treatment of employer provided insurance benefits.

According to CBO projections, the only proposals that will have a substantial effect on spending growth are those with some type of budget limit. An all-payer rate setting system with budget limits would slow the growth in spending moderately, with modest expansion of coverage. A single-payer system with a global budget, however, would produce large savings, while also providing universal coverage. The CBO anticipates that President Clinton's managed competition proposal would generate initial increases followed by long-run reductions. By the year 2000 it will realize lower expenditures and universal coverage. This proposal also contains a total spending control mechanism.

An effective spending limit could have wide ranging consequences for hospitals. An analysis by the Prospective Payment Assessment Commission (ProPAC) shows that if spending growth for inpatient hospital care were reduced from its forecasted annual rate of about 8.0 percent to 4.9 percent between 1994 and 1998, reductions in spending over this time would be $113 billion.[25] A 4.9 percent target represents the projected annual rate of increase in the gross domestic product (GDP), a standard favored by some policymakers. This target is similar to the average growth target contained in the President's proposal. The effect of such a target on hospital outpatient revenues is even more dramatic. There, the growth in spending would be reduced from a forecasted annual increase of 14.8 percent to 4.9 percent, a reduction of $160 billion over the five-year period (Table 6.5). More recently, however, ProPAC has reported that the growth in hospital real (adjusted for inflation) per capita costs has fallen from an average of 4.3 percent per year between 1985 and 1992 to 2.7 percent per year in the first eight months of 1993. If hospitals can maintain cost growth at this 1993 level, the effects of a budget limit or the premium cap proposed by the President would be substantially reduced. It is important to note, however, that if a budget limit were put in place, it probably would not be completely effective. In fact, CBO reduces its savings estimates to acknowledge that proposals will not be fully effective because of behavioral responses and other factors that are not accounted for by policymakers.

To achieve maximum effectiveness, a cost control strategy built on a global budget, or other spending limits, must apply to most of the payers for services and providers of care. The aggregate impact on hospitals of ef-

Table 6.5 Trends in Hospital Spending and the Impact of a Budget Target, 1993-1998

| | Forecasted Expenditures | | | | Savings With a Budget Target Based on GDP Growth | | | |
| | Hospital Inpatient | | Hospital Outpatient | | Hospital Inpatient | | Hospital Outpatient | |
Year	Amount (In Billions)	Percent Change	Amount (In Billions)	Percent Change	Amount (In Billions)	Percent Change	Amount (In Billions)	Percent Change
1993	$209.3	--	$81.2	--	--	--	--	--
1994	226.5	8.7	94.2	16.0	$5.9	4.9	$8.6	4.9
1995	245.2	8.3	108.8	15.5	12.9	4.9	18.7	4.9
1996	265.1	8.1	124.9	14.7	21.2	4.9	30.2	4.9
1997	286.3	8.0	142.6	14.2	31.1	4.9	43.5	4.9
1998	307.9	7.5	162.0	13.6	41.7	4.9	58.7	4.9

Source: Prospective Payment Assessment Commission. Global Budgeting: Design and Implementation Issues. Congressional Report C–93–01, July 1993.

fective spending controls will be determined by the rate at which spending will increase, the length of time hospitals will be given to adjust to new policies, the payers, populations, and services included in the reform scheme, and the choice between a rate setting and a managed competition strategy.

A rate setting approach, especially when combined with an option for capitation, would be consistent with current financing and delivery patterns. Hospitals would benefit if these policies led to more uniform pricing, billing, utilization review, and other administrative requirements. They would, however, lose the flexibility to generate additional revenue from one payer to offset losses from another. They also would be dependent on the ability of the administrative pricing system to adjust for factors beyond their control, avoid errors, and keep abreast of technologic advances, practice patterns and other changing hospital resource needs. The frequent policy changes accompanying the Medicare prospective payment system demonstrate the complexity of the task and the significant effects such changes can have for specific hospitals. The Medicare experience also illustrates the potential for the Congress to become involved in technical policies, at times for seemingly political reasons.

A managed competition design would require major restructuring of the financing and delivery system. Managed competition requires hospitals to develop and participate in health plans that would furnish all services to enrollees. Hospitals would be required to develop networks and alliances with other providers, physicians, and payers. Most, however, would have to alter longstanding relationships with physicians, other providers, and insurers. They would be expected to share the insurance risk with other plan members and to develop mechanisms to determine their share of plan revenues. Consequently, they would have to develop accurate information regarding expected costs of furnishing services to specific groups of enrollees in order to bid or negotiate with the plans and alliances. They would also be subject to the rules and requirements of the purchasing alliance. To ensure fairness, a payment system based on price competition would have to recognize in the price setting negotiations factors beyond the control of individual plans and providers, including geographic differences in the cost of labor and other goods, differences in patient mix and severity of illness, and cost differences involved in providing access to vulnerable populations, such as inhabitants of isolated rural areas or inner cities.

Health care reform strategies must also recognize that, in addition to direct patient care, hospitals serve other socially valuable functions. These include participation in the medical education of physicians and other health care personnel, clinical investigation, and the advancement of technologic capabilities and medical practices. Hospitals also are the nucleus of the medical system, and at times the only provider, as well as a major employer in many communities. They may be the only source of care for the poor. These important roles traditionally have been funded, at least in part, by patient care revenues. A plan that effectively reduced the growth in hospital revenues, without providing universal coverage, could severely limit access to care for the uninsured and other vulnerable populations, impede the training of health personnel, and slow clinical advances. Policymakers must decide whether to include in a health care reform plan the financial incentives and resources to serve these social needs.

Changes in the Financing of Care

The call for health care reform is coming on the heels of major changes in the organization and financing of hospital and non-hospital services. For many years hospitals were favored with virtually unlimited flexibility to price their services and obtain the revenue required to meet the technology-driven demand of the public. This favorable pricing environment allowed hospitals to cover costs that did not meet government criteria of reasonableness and to serve other societal needs. In the past decade, however, government and private buyers began to flex their purchasing muscles. The Medicare program moved to prospective pricing for hospital, physician, and other services that some see as a model for a single-payer or an all-payer rate setting system. Employers are increasingly self-insuring and pushing many of their employees into managed care plans, encouraging doctors and hospitals to enter into integrated, risk-sharing financing and delivery arrangements, and using their market power to select preferred providers and negotiate more favorable payment rates. Many observers see this employer trend as a step toward managed competition.

Rate setting and managed competition are both likely to continue to change the mix of payers and to shift power to the buyers of hospital services. The burden of the insurance risk has shifted substantially from private insurance to large firms that elect to self insure. A single-payer system would entirely eliminate the role of private insurers as a third party between the employer-financer of care and the provider who delivers services. An all-payer rate setting system would largely displace the traditional risk bearing insurance function. Managed competition would also alter the role of traditional private insurers by combining the insurance function with the service delivery function, as is now occurring with health maintenance organizations and other managed care strategies.

The two approaches would also have substantially different effects on consumers' choices regarding payers, providers, and physicians. A rate setting system would continue to allow subscribers the freedom to choose specific providers and physicians. Managed competition could follow the current managed care practice of many employers, restricting an employee's choice of insurers, plans, and providers. In many cases, however, managed competition may actually give individuals more choice through the plans that their employers' alliances offer. Some approaches, such as the President's, would offer greater freedom of choice, subject to additional cost sharing.

Both strategies envision an expanded role for government, but in very different ways that policymakers must consider. They could also result in the same overall reductions in the level of spending for hospital services if they included a global budget or other spending limits. They would likely, however, have very different effects on the distribution of spending across geographic areas, types of health care providers, and types of hospitals. Advocates of a government sponsored rate setting system question whether a competitive market, driven by price and the potential for profit, will make socially desirable and equitable allocation decisions. They also note the very high price in administrative costs that Americans pay for a pluralistic financing system. Supporters of managed competition maintain that the government is frequently an erratic and undependable partner, making allocation decisions for political purposes. They also note that health care is furnished in local markets that differ greatly across the country and that managed competition has the flexibility to meet local needs.

The choice of a government- or market-controlled strategy could have a pronounced effect on the future structure of health services delivery generally and hospitals specifically. There are currently large differences in the distribution of payments across types of providers (sectors), reflecting historical preferences in utilization, practice patterns, regulation, and financing decisions. A rate setting system with sector-specific budget limits could freeze the current distribution of payments among hospitals and other providers and suppliers in place. Although policymakers could alter the distribution of payments across provider sectors as part of the annual updating process, their decisions would play a major role in determining the future structure and capacity of the delivery system.

With a rate setting system and a global budget, policy decisions will determine the allocation of available funds across types of providers or types of services. These decisions could substantially alter the current rates of growth in the price and utilization of services across sectors. The equitable distribution of funds among sectors will be complicated by the increasing diversity of the delivery system. The acute care hospital is not the dominant provider that it is in other nations or once was in this country. Further, hospitals have been diversifying to generate additional revenue. They now actively compete with physicians and other providers, and many of the ambulatory and non-acute inpatient services they furnish are indistinguishable from the services furnished by these other providers. Policymakers would have to decide whether to have a single budget applicable to all providers or to set sector-specific budgets and if so, how many sectors to designate. Designating a relatively large number of sectors will provide incentives and opportunities for providers to evade budget limits by shifting services to other sectors. Hospitals, for example, could attempt to shift some of their outpatient services to a physician sector budget. A small number of sectors, however, could inappropriately penalize those providers who meet budget goals but see their payments reduced because others did not achieve their goals.

The budget also could be allocated to specific institutions, such as hospitals, and cover all the services furnished by that class of provider. An institution-specific allocation would hold a class of providers accountable for budget targets. Since the same service may be furnished by many types of providers, an institution-specific budget could result in different payment amounts across providers for the same service. Payment policies, consequently, could unfairly reward some types of providers at the expense of others and distort decisions regarding the appropriate and most efficient site of service delivery.

Rate setting policies could also have a large impact on service supply. A rate setting system can effectively control the price paid for each unit of service and provide incentives to reduce excess capacity and improve system-wide efficiency if volume growth is also controlled. The current payment and delivery system, however, stimulates competition for patient revenues, based on factors other than price, and has contributed to an expanded supply of services as hospitals and other providers move into new markets in an attempt to increase patient volume and revenues. The challenge to policymakers is to devise a method for controlling the growth in service volume as well as price. Setting and maintaining appropriate sector budgets will be complicated by large differences in volume growth across sectors. In 1994, for example, all of the growth in inpatient hospital spending is expected to be due to price increases. For outpatient services, however, volume increases are anticipated to account for 43 percent of the increased spending.

The policy decisions that determine the allocation of payments across sectors under rate setting with a global budget will be technically complex and a continuing source of political debate, with each type of provider demanding a larger share of the overall budget for its own budget. The decisions, however, will determine the future structure and supply of the delivery system and the role of hospitals in that system.

A managed competition strategy, especially if it contained spending limits, will also raise difficult technical and political issues. Managed competition requires the creation and effective functioning of a new entity, the regional alliance, and wide availability of competing health plans, which are envisioned to function like health maintenance organizations. Policymakers will have to develop a method that will distribute equitably an overall national budget target among regional alliances. Decisions will also be necessary regarding the populations and services the alliance budget is to cover and the methods of allocating funding to each health plan. Policies also must be developed to prevent plans from engaging in favorable risk selection. Health plans may, however, still enroll different mixes of sick and healthy individuals, and the allocation of funds to the plans must recognize different levels of risk.

With a managed competition strategy, individual health plans would make the decisions regarding the allocation of funds to specific providers of care. Since the health plans are to be composed of networks of providers and insurers, the membership of the plan could be an important determinant of the availability and use of specific types of services. Plans would have incentives to provide services efficiently by substitutions among provider sectors. They would also have an incentive to curtail the supply of costly or inefficient services, since they share the financial risk of furnishing care. Mechanisms would have to be developed, however, to ensure that plans funded and made available appropriate services in traditionally underserved areas. At times, individuals will also require services from providers that do not have an agreement or relationship with the plan, for example when traveling or in the case of a rare or unusual condition that can only be treated at a teaching or other specialty hospital. Policies must ensure adequate payment to these providers and at the same time protect the plan from excessive utilization or costs.

To create financially integrated delivery systems, managed competition will also require a careful reassessment of antitrust laws and policies. Providers, particularly hospitals, that now compete with each other are expected to enter into collaborative arrangements for the joint purchase and use of expensive equipment. They will also have strong incentives to reduce facility and equipment redundancies through mergers and sharing arrangements. In areas with less demand for certain services, however, one plan could be the sole provider of a service and use monopoly power to set prices to other plans at unreasonable levels. Plans in isolated areas will be at special risk, since they will have to purchase many complex and expensive services. The negotiations among providers regarding membership in available plans will also require the sharing of cost and price information. Such information could lead to collusion in setting prices for other plans that must purchase services. Policymakers will have to balance carefully the desire to use competitive forces to reduce the duplication of services and improve system efficiency with the need to protect plans and providers that may be disadvantaged by their geographic location, the patient populations they serve, or lack of power to negotiate effectively.

A managed competition strategy with health plans determining the distribution of funds and use of services across sectors may create more financial risk and uncertainty for hospitals than a rate setting approach. It is likely that hospitals will compete with physicians, other providers, and insurers for control of the networks and plans. The end result of the maneuvering could seriously affect the availability, distribution, and utilization of services. Proponents of managed competition contend, however, that an informed consumer will play the pivotal role in shaping the structure of the market through the choice of plans.

Managed competition and rate setting could also lead to large redistributions in total expenditures, as well as sector spending, across states and other geographic areas. For many years, reimbursement of providers by government and private insurers was based on the costs they incurred or the charges they requested, resulting in wide variations in health spending, service supply, and utilization among regions, states, and localities frequently bearing no clear relationship to health status or outcome.[6,26] Policymakers will have to decide whether payment policies should continue to reflect these historical differences or whether they should move to more uniform spending distribution across geographic areas.

The proposed rate setting strategies would follow the recent Medicare approach of setting uniform national base payment rates for hospital, physician, and other services that are adjusted only for those geographic factors that policymakers determine to be warranted. Managed competition without a budget limit would let market forces determine the geographic spending patterns through price competitive plans and the choices and preferences of an informed, price sensitive public. The President's managed competition proposal would allocate budget limits to each state and health care alliance based on the level of premiums in a base year. The annual per capita rate of spending growth thereafter would be uniform across areas. This proposal would also give additional power to the states to set their own policies regarding the operations of the alliances and plans. The President's proposal would offer the flexibility to serve state and local needs and preferences, within the premium limits. In the past, however, joint federal and state programs have been beset with conflicts over goals and responsibilities. Political as well as technical policymakers at the federal and state level frequently disagree on important matters, leading to differences in program implementation, policies, service delivery, and efficiencies across states. The policies that determine distribution of spending and the role of the states in the financing of care may have large effects on the availability and delivery of hospital services.

Changes in the Delivery of Care

Although the policies that set the aggregate spending base will affect hospitals' overall financial performance, a more important consideration is likely to be the annual rate of growth thereafter. The overall rate of growth in revenues will shape the future role of hospitals generally, and policy decisions that distribute available funds will determine the future of individual hospitals and the care furnished to their patients. Regardless of the reform approach, rate setting or managed competition, if it reduces the growth of a hospital's total revenues, the hospital will have to respond with reductions in expenses. Reductions could come from enhancing efficiency, curtailing administrative and overhead costs, or slowing the growth in direct patient care costs.

Rate setting and managed competition may provide very different incentives for the efficient utilization of capacity. Rate setting encourages providers to increase the number of services they furnish and to make site substitution decisions based on sector and budget allocations. Consequently, rate setting could continue to encourage the excess supply of services as providers diversify to maximize their revenue and attempt to shift costs to other provider sectors. While such decisions might be appropriate for an individual provider, the result might be declines in system-wide efficiency. Effective volume controls, plus the addition of regional health planning or other effective limits on capital formation, however, could ameliorate this problem. Since managed competition would provide a capitated payment to a plan, the providers participating in that plan would have an incentive to utilize their total service capacity in the most efficient manner possible. They would also have the flexibility to substitute services based on local circumstances. Whether market forces would be strong enough to force out of the system much of the excess capacity and ensure that new excesses are not created is a question. There is some evidence that such reductions are beginning to occur today due to market place pressure.

Many analysts believe that health care reform can also achieve large administrative savings by eliminating the need for hospitals to maintain the records and systems involved in billing multiple payers and negotiating with increasing numbers of managed care plans. The Congressional Budget Office has indicated that such savings are most likely to accrue from a single-payer rate setting system.

Savings that result from more efficient utilization of service capacity and reductions in administrative overhead will lower the aggregated spending base, but not the annual increase in the base. If health care reform also places tight limits on the growth of hospital revenues, the annual growth of hospital expense will also have to slow. The total annual increase in spending for inpatient hospital care reflects changes in the number of admissions and the payment for each admission. For a number of years, the per capita inpatient admission rate has been declining, with expense growth due entirely to annual increases of about 8 to 9 percent in the cost per admission, or about 4.6 percent above inflation. Since early 1993, however, the cost per admission has been increasing at only a 6.1 percent annual rate, which translates into a 2.7 percent increase above inflation.

Currently, the gross domestic product (GDP) is projected to increase about 5 percent a year. A budget target set at this level, that also maintained the current share of spending for inpatient hospital care, would require hospitals to reduce their annual increase in per case expenses less than 2 percent. It remains to be seen, however, whether the decrease in cost per case in 1993 reflects a new trend or is a one time phenomenon. It is possible that the annual increase in expenses could return to the higher levels seen for most of the decade, requiring even greater reductions in costs. This GDP target is similar to the average target proposed by the President under his global budgeting premium control system. Other aspects of the President's proposal, however, could further reduce the growth in current inpatient hospital revenues, requiring greater cost reductions. This is because other sectors, which are growing much faster than the GDP, are not likely to be constrained to that level. In order to bring total spending in line with GDP growth, hospital inpatient spending may need to be constrained to less than GDP growth. Since hospitals would not be able to cost-shift, meeting this budget target would also require that the revenue growth for the care of all patients, government and private, be at least equal to the level of the target.

The picture for hospital outpatient care is quite different. There, spending is increasing about 15 percent a year with growth in the volume of services accounting for about 40 percent of the rise. To meet a GDP growth target with the current sector allocation and volume growth at this level, the recent annual increase of 8 to 9 percent in expenses per unit of service would have to fall to minus 1 percent. Hospitals would not be able to maintain cost growth of this amount, and would have to reduce severely the amount of services they furnish to stay within the growth target. These substantial differences in the relative contributions of volume and price to spending growth in inpatient and other settings illustrate the importance of the decisions that will confront policymakers concerning the allocation of a spending target.

A spending target based on GDP growth will present a challenge to hospitals to limit the annual increase in expenses per admission or unit of service. There are a limited number of ways hospitals could respond to reduce their annual expense growth to 5 percent, or perhaps less. Hospitals have little control over inflation in the general economy or increases in the complexity of the cases they treat. They do have some control over the price and mix of labor and other goods that they purchase. They could negotiate more effectively with suppliers, slow the rapid increase in administrative salaries, and attempt to slow the rise in wages for nursing and other clinical personnel. The latter increases, however, have been caused in part by increased demand that could continue as more services are furnished to the uninsured. To control the rise in nursing wages, hospitals also may have to reduce demand by substituting other personnel or using nurses more efficiently. In 1993, for the first time in many years, hospitals slowed the increase in wages to the level of the general economy. It remains to be seen whether these constraints in the price of labor can be maintained over a longer period of time.

Hospitals also could increase their productivity by decreasing the number or mix of employees and other resources used to produce a unit of service. The experience of the past ten years suggests that productivity improvements leading to reductions in the growth of costs are certainly possible, but they are unlikely to achieve all the spending reductions that may be required. Consequently, hospitals may not be able to achieve stringent budget targets without reducing the amount of services they furnish. To maintain the quality of care Americans demand, hospitals and their physicians would have to eliminate services of little or no value, as demonstrated by numerous research studies, while maintaining those that are necessary and appropriate.[27] Some analysts, however, have questioned the methods and results of these studies, suggesting that they fail to recognize important differences in patient preferences and satisfaction.[28] The ability of hospitals to restrain the growth in expenses will be hampered by legitimate medical disagreements and, in many cases, the absence of a firm scientific and medical foundation on which to base difficult decisions.

Access to Quality Care

The effects of health care reform on access to quality care for Americans will depend on the political and technical choices of policymakers concerning the payment method, level, and distribution of available resources in concert with the behavioral response of payers and providers. Assessing the effects on quality of care will be especially difficult due to deficiencies in definitions and measurement tools. Physicians traditionally have been responsible for ensuring the welfare of patients and generally have carried out this task free of responsibility for the costs of their clinical decisions. In recent years, hospital representatives have complained that physicians do not confront the same financial imperatives they do to control costs and have called for a better alignment of incentives. While a rate setting system would maintain tensions between physicians and other providers, managed competition creates networks of physicians and other providers that jointly share the financial risk of medical decisions. Policymakers must consider whether it is in the public interest for the financial welfare of physicians to be too closely tied to that of other providers.

The Future of Hospitals

This nation and its political leaders are considering fundamental changes in the financing of medical care that could profoundly alter the future role of the hospital in the American health care system. For many years, the community hospital occupied a unique place in the medical landscape. Today, the hospital is an institution in transition. Its preeminence in the American health care system has diminished as the public turns away from traditional inpatient care and hospitals diversify into services that are also furnished by other providers. The seeds for the transition were sown many years ago when the escalating costs of modern medicine led a third party, a private insuring entity, to join the hospital-patient relationship.

As in the past, the future of the hospital will be determined by financing policies, especially the choice of an incremental or comprehensive health care reform strategy. An incremental strategy would continue to rely on voluntary, private insurance, with the government covering the elderly and some of the disabled and poor, leaving an increasing number of Americans without insurance. To finance care to the uninsured, hospitals would have to seek government subsidies or continue to generate additional revenues from private payers. Hospitals that treat a disproportionate share of the uninsured, especially public hospitals with a small share of private pay patients, would continue to face severe financial distress. The burden of providing care to the uninsured, however, crosses all types of hospitals, though not evenly within each group. Many hospitals, therefore, would be disadvantaged while others may seek to avoid treating these patients. Faced with increasing financial stress, hospitals and their physicians could also deviate from the longstanding practice of providing care based on patient needs rather than payer source. If so, the uninsured, and perhaps the beneficiaries of lower paying government programs, could see the quality of their care deteriorate.

Managed competition without budget limits or universal coverage would hasten the development of networks with integrated financing and delivery systems. The new systems would compete for enrollment of a price-conscious insured population. As a result, employers and third party payers, or health plans, would exert even more control over employee and subscriber choice of providers. Since managed competition relies on capitated payment, hospitals would have less opportunity to obtain excess revenues from some payers to compensate for shortages from others and would be dependent on the network or plan of which they were a part for needed revenues. Their financial success, therefore, could depend on their negotiating skills or power within the network or plan. The development of integrated delivery systems could accelerate the trend to hospital diversification, further eroding the unique position of the hospital. It may also lead to a reduction in bed capacity as the merged institutions seek greater control of their costs. The networks also might be able to exert more effective control over the growth in spending for non-inpatient hospital care and foster more efficient use of total capacity.

A comprehensive reform strategy would have the greatest effect on hospitals, combining universal coverage with effective limits on spending growth. Comprehensive reform, however, requires the government to take a more active role in the financing of health care than the public has previously endorsed. The government role could include funding, as well as mandating through the private sector, health insurance coverage for all Americans. The effects would also be determined by decisions regarding the inclusion or exclusion of government programs such as Medicare, Medicaid, CHAMPUS, and the Department of Veterans Affairs health system. The government is also the only entity with the power to set and enforce limits on total spending. The policies concerning government program participation, universal coverage, and spending limits would set the total pool of health care dollars available and the rate spending would increase over time. The aggregate result of these policies could be the same with a single-payer (or all-payer) rate setting system and a managed competition approach. Rate setting and managed competition, however, could have very different effects on the distribution of total spending across geographic areas and across and within types of providers.

Managed competition with a global budget, as proposed by President Clinton, would allocate funds to state and sub-state regions. Current total spending patterns could be locked in place unless significant reallocations were made. Such reallocations, however, may prove to be politically difficult to accomplish. Therefore, while this approach would reflect historic spending preferences at the state and local levels, it would also perpetuate very large and unexplained geographic differences. The financing of hospital care would be determined by the allocation decisions of the individual plans, reflecting the relative power and influence of hospitals and other providers competing for available revenue. It is likely, therefore, that hospitals would compete with physicians to form and control provider networks and plans. Hospitals would also share in the financial risk of covering the plans' subscribers. To compete effectively, many hospitals would continue to evolve into full service providers, as traditional inpatient care progressively declines as a share of total spending.

This market-based approach has the flexibility to meet local needs and circumstances and to control the supply of services through plan allocation decisions. It also has the potential to disadvantage providers that furnish costly, specialty care to needy patients. Plans could attempt to avoid financial risk by restraining the availability of costly services, such as neonatology or advanced cancer therapy, to discourage enrollment of high risk individuals. They could also limit the supply of these services to their subscribers. Hospitals or plans that care for a disproportionate share of sicker and more costly patients would also be disadvantaged if payments did not reflect an appropriate adjustment for their increased risk. A payment system intended to maximize gain and market position through price competition could control the growth in spending and excess service capacity. It could also adversely affect the availability of care for the most vulnerable populations if it did not take account of the unique needs of hospitals located in underserved areas. The acceptability of such a system to the American public would depend on the willingness of policymakers to make needed adjustments and the capacity to develop proper adjustment mechanisms. It also would depend on the capacity of the public to make informed choices based on the ability of the plan, and its member hospitals, to provide access to quality care.

With a rate setting system, the allocation of funds across geographic areas and providers will be determined by payment rates and the services furnished by each provider. Consequently, the system could result in large changes in the distribution of spending. Hospitals and other providers would be dependent on the ability of rate setters to adjust and update payments to reflect circumstances beyond the provider's control. Policy choices regarding the number of sectors and the application of budget limits would also affect the revenue available to hospitals. Hospitals could be at special risk for increases in the volume of services that they, as well as other providers, furnish. Very likely those hospitals that could profitably furnish services for the payment rate would attempt to become full service providers, while others may choose to specialize in certain inpatient services or a more limited range of inpatient and outpatient care. A rate setting system would also allow policymakers to adjust payment rates to reflect broader societal goals, including medical education and access to care in rural or other underserved areas.

The decisions of policymakers will determine whether all Americans are guaranteed financial protection against catastrophic losses due to illness. Policy choices may also set the relative priority for the resources assigned to health care as opposed to other important societal goods. The choice of specific reform strategies will govern the financing for, and thus, the availability of, hospital and other services in the future health care system. Comprehensive health care reform will result in major changes for hospitals and create a renewed period of instability in the delivery of services. Policymakers must consider, however, whether failure to act now will create even greater instability as the crisis in health care financing accelerates and the traditional mission of the hospital erodes. Clearly, change is necessary, now, or at some approaching time. The future of the cherished institution Americans have known as a hospital, and the people it serves, hangs in the balance.

Notes

1. Sylvia Law, *Blue Cross: What Went Wrong?* (New Haven, CT: Yale University Press, 1974).

2. Herman Somers and Ann Somers, *Medicare and the Hospitals: Issues and Prospects* (Washington, D.C.: Brookings Institution, 1967).

3. Suzanne Letsch, Helen Lazenby, Katharine Levit, and Cathy Cowan, "National Health Expenditures, 1991," *Health Care Financing Review* 14(2) (Winter 1992): 1–30.

4. Prospective Payment Assessment Commission (ProPAC), *Medicaid Hospital Payment Congressional Report C-91–02* (Washington, D.C.: ProPAC, October 1, 1991).

5. The Kaiser Commission on the Future of Medicaid, *The Medicaid Cost Explosion* (Baltimore, MD: The Kaiser Commission on the Future of Medicaid, February 1993).

6. Prospective Payment Assessment Commission (ProPAC), *Medicare and the American Health Care System: Report to the Congress* (Washington, D.C.: ProPAC, June 1992).

7. Congressional Budget Office, *Responses to Uncompensated Care and Public-Program Controls on Spending: Do Hospitals 'Cost Shift'?* (Washington, D.C.: U.S. Government Printing Office, May 1993).

8. John Iglehart, "The American Health Care System: Private Insurance," *The New England Journal of Medicine* 326(25) (June 18, 1992): 1715–1720.

9. Ronald L. Numbers, *Almost Persuaded: American Physicians and Compulsory Health Insurance, 1912–1920* (Baltimore, MD: Johns Hopkins University Press, 1978).

10. Stuart H. Altman and Donald A. Young, "A Decade of Medicare's Prospective Payment System—Success or Failure?" *Journal of American Health Policy* 3(2) (March/April 1993): 11–19.

11. Congressional Budget Office, *Trends in Health Spending: An Update* (Washington, D.C.: U.S. Government Printing Office, June 1993).

12. Antonio Legoretta, Jeffrey Silber, George Costantino, Richard Kobylinski, and Steven Zatz, "Increased Cholecystectomy Rate After the Introduction of Laparascopic Cholecystectomy," *Journal of the American Medical Association* 270(12) (September 22/29,1993): 1429–1432.

13. Steven A. Schroeder and Joel Cantor, "On Squeezing Balloons: Cost Control Fails Again," *The New England Journal of Medicine* 325(15) (October 10, 1991): 1099–1100.

14. Steffie Woolhandler, David U. Himmelstein, and James P. Lewontin, "Administrative Costs in U.S. Hospitals," *The New England Journal of Medicine* 329(6) (August 5, 1993): 400–403.

15. General Accounting Office, *Canadian Health Insurance: Lessons for the United States* (Washington, D.C.: GAO, June 4, 1991).

16. Donald A. Redelmeier and Victor R. Fuchs, "Hospital Expenditures in the United States and Canada," *The New England Journal of Medicine* 328(11) (March 18, 1993): 772–778.

17. Jack Hadley, Earl P. Steinberg, and Judith Feder, "Comparison of Uninsured and Privately Insured Hospital Patients: Condition on Admission, Resource Use, and Outcome," *Journal of the American Medical Association* 265(3) (January 16, 1991): 374–379.

18. Helen R. Burstin, Stuart R. Lipsitz, Steven Udvarhelyi, and Troyen A. Brennan, "The Effect of Hospital Financial Characteristics on Quality of Care," *Journal of the American Medical Association* 270(7) (August 18, 1993): 845–849.

19. Howard E. Freeman, Robert J. Blendon, Linda H. Aiken, Seymour Sudman, Connie F. Mullinix, and Christopher R. Corey, "Americans Report on Their Access to Health Care," *Health Affairs* 6(1) (Spring 1987): 6–18.

20. Alain C. Enthoven, "The History and Principles of Managed Competition," *Health Affairs* (Supplement 1993): 24–48.

21. Cynthia B. Sullivan, Marianne Miller, Roger Feldman, and Bryan Dowd, "Employer-Sponsored Health Insurance in 1991," *Health Affairs* 11(4) (Winter 1992): 172–185.

22. Employee Benefit Research Institute, "Sources of Health Insurance and Characteristics of the Uninsured—Analysis of the March 1992 Current Population Survey," *Issue Brief Number 123* (Washington, D.C.: EBRI, January 1993).

23. Prospective Payment Assessment Commission (ProPAC), "The Trend and Distribution of Hospital Uncompensated Care Costs, 1980–1989," *Technical Report I-01–04* (Washington, D.C.: ProPAC, October 1991).

24. Congressional Budget Office, *Estimates of Health Care Proposals from the 102nd Congress* (Washington, D.C.: U.S. Government Printing Office, July 1993).

25. Prospective Payment Assessment Commission (ProPAC), *Global Budgeting: Design and Implementation Issues*, Congressional Report C-93–01 (Washington, D.C.: ProPAC, July 1993).

26. Katharine R. Levit, Helen C. Lazenby, Cathy A. Cowan, and Suzanne Letsch, "Health Spending by State: New Policy Estimates for Policy Making," *Health Affairs* 12(3) (Fall 1993): 7–26.

27. Robert H. Brooke, Rolla E. Park, Mark R. Chassin, David H. Solomon, Joan

Keesey, and Jacqueline Kosecoff, "Predicting the Appropriate Use of Carotid End-arterectomy, Upper Gastrointestional Endoscopy, and Coronary Angiography," *The New England Journal of Medicine* 323(17) (October 25, 1990): 1173–1177.

28. Charles E. Phelps, "The Methodologic Foundations of Studies of the Appropriateness of Medical Care," *The New England Journal of Medicine* 329(17) (October 21, 1993): 1241–1245.

7

Physician Fee Controls

Paul B. Ginsburg

Physician payment has been one of the most rapidly evolving aspects of the health care system. Among public payers, the Medicare program changed from determining physician payments by calculating prevailing rates charged in each locality to establishing a resource-based fee schedule, with conversion factors updated through an expenditure-target mechanism. Medicare also shifted from leaving physicians and beneficiaries to work out any additional payments beyond the program's allowed charge (balance bills) to a participating-physician option and tight limits on balance billing for unassigned claims.

Among private payers, a growing proportion of payment is governed by contracts between health plans and physicians. In preferred provider organizations (PPOs), the typical arrangement involves a fee schedule, agreements by physicians to accept those fees as payment in full, and incentives to patients to use physicians who participate in the network. Health maintenance organizations (HMOs) have numerous payment methods, including capitation for primary care physicians and fee-for-service, which is used extensively for specialist services. The evolution among public and private payers is linked in that many of the latter have been introducing the relative value scale from the Medicare Fee Schedule into their own payment mechanisms.

In considering physician payment under health care reform, its importance as a policy issue depends on the type of proposal being considered. For those proposals that emphasize managed competition, such as the bills introduced by the Conservative Democratic Forum, and the Senate Republican Health Task Force,[1] physician payment is not mentioned. These proposals envision that competing health plans will contract with physicians. While other arrangements, such as traditional indemnity insurance, are not precluded, the sponsors of these proposals presume that under competition most consumers would prefer health plans that do not expose them to unpredictable balance bills.

Proposals for a single-payer system, such as the American Health Security Act,[2] envision a fee schedule developed by the government that would apply to all physicians' services. Although these proposals contain few details on physician payment, the model appears to be the one used in Canadian provinces. Balance billing is not permitted. In contrast to Canada, however, these proposals would provide for substantial opportunities for individuals to enroll in HMOs. It is not clear whether contracts between physicians and HMOs would be governed by the public fee schedule.

The Clinton Administration's proposal[3] includes elements from both the managed-competition and single-payer approaches. It draws from the former by emphasizing competing health plans and attempting to structure a competitive market for choice of health plans. But it attempts to assure a degree of provider choice by requiring HMOs and other plans that have a physician network to offer a point of service option to obtain care outside of the network and by requiring that at least one "fee-for-service" health plan be offered in each alliance. Such a plan would have the same cost sharing apply to all providers and would not require patients to obtain authorization for specialty care by a primary care physician.

Under the Clinton plan, fee schedules would be developed by either the regional health alliance or the state government. These fee schedules would apply to all services in the fee-for-service plan and to out-of-network use in other plans. Balance billing would be prohibited. The fee schedules would be negotiated with providers, who are given antitrust protection to engage in these negotiations, but are specifically precluded from organizing a boycott.

This chapter begins with a discussion of physician fee schedules. Much attention is given to the recent Medicare experience with developing and implementing a resource-based fee schedule. The next major discussion is devoted to all-payer rate setting for physicians' services. This includes discussions of its potential for cost containment and its pitfalls, how rate setting can be linked with global budgeting, and treatment of physician payment by HMOs and PPOs. The final section discusses the fee schedules proposed in the Clinton health plan.

Resource-Based Fee Schedules

In the context of physician payment, a fee schedule is a series of prices that is used by a third-party payer to determine its payment to physicians. Most commonly, it is used as a screen—the payer will not pay more than the physician charges. Fee schedules have three components—a relative value scale, in which the value of each service is expressed in relation to a numeraire service whose value is arbitrarily set to 1.0, a conversion factor, which translates relative values into dollar amounts, and geographic adjusters, which vary the conversion factor by the locale in which the care is delivered.

The use of fee schedules to determine an insurer's payment for physicians' services is not new. Until the mid-1960s, fee schedules were the norm. Though relative value scales were generally based on charges, the California Relative Value Scale, developed by the California Medical Association, incorporated some significant departures, especially for new services.[4] The health care system moved away from fee schedules in the mid-1960s, when Medicare adopted the "usual, customary, and reasonable" (UCR) methodology that had recently been introduced by some Blue Shield plans. Many Blue Shield plans and commercial insurers followed Medicare's lead and replaced fee schedules with UCR to determine payment.

In the 1990s, fee schedules have again become an important, if not the dominant, method of physician payment. The Medicare program introduced its resource-based fee schedule in 1992. Many Medicaid programs, which had used fee schedules all along, have adopted the Medicare relative value scale. In addition, when HMOs and PPOs contract with physicians, they tend to use a fee schedule to determine payment. Many are now incorporating the Medicare relative value scale into their fee schedules. With most of the development in the use of fee schedules surrounding the Medicare program, the Medicare schedule and experience comprise much of the focus in this section.

Resource-Based Relative Value Scale

When the Congress directed the Medicare program to implement a fee schedule, it set out to alter the structure of physician payment. In legislation drafted in 1985 and passed in 1986, the Congress directed the Health Care Financing Administration (HCFA) to develop a relative value scale and created the Physician Payment Review Commission (PPRC) with a mandate to advise it on the structure of payment for physicians' services and other issues. With early results from the resource-based relative value study by William Hsiao and colleagues and a series of recommendations from the Commission in hand in 1989, the Congress enacted legislation requiring a resource-based fee schedule for Medicare.[5,6]

The Hsiao study obtained estimates of relative resource use for various physicians' services by conducting surveys of physicians. A sample from each major specialty was asked to rate the time and *work* involved in a series of vignettes covering the range of services generally provided. The relative values from each specialty were combined into a single scale through identification of services that crossed specialties and were the same or equivalent. Charge data were then used to develop values for services that could not be included in the surveys. This study had major support from the American Medical Association (AMA), which nominated physicians to serve on various technical panels.

The relative values for physician work underwent some significant refinment by the Health Care Financing Administration (HCFA). Comments from specialty societies were elicited and structured panels, comprised of specialty society nominees and medical directors from Medicare carriers, looked for consensus on changes to relative values. Numerous relative values were revised while maintaining the overall structure of payment developed in the Hsiao study.

Some specialty societies complained of systematic distortions in the scale, for example, compression of relative values among procedures, but HCFA chose not to address these methodological issues directly. HCFA asserted that the service-by-service revisions suggested by its review panels would alleviate some of whatever systematic problems existed. Apparently, it felt more comfortable reviewing relative values for individual services by structuring a consensus process with clinicians than refereeing methodological disputes between the Hsiao team and consultants retained by specialty societies.

Physician time and effort only account for slightly more than half of the resources that go into physicians' services. Practice expenses, such as rent, salaries of nurses, technicians, and clerical personnel, equipment and supplies, and malpractice insurance premiums comprise the remainder. Recognizing that estimates of practice expense associated with specific services were not available, the Congress specified that historical charges be used as a basis for the practice expense component of the relative value scale. With a methodology subsequently developed by PPRC, the Congress in 1993 specified reductions in relative value units for those non-office services in which practice expense relative values are highest in relation to physician work relative values.[7]

Despite the use of historical charges for practice expense relative values, Medicare's resource-based relative value scale will lead to substantial changes in the structure of payments. In relative terms, payment rates for evaluation and management services will increase by 31 percent once the transition is complete, while payment for major surgical services will decrease by 30 percent.[8] Payment rates for diagnostic procedures are projected to decrease by 25 percent.

Geographic Adjustment

The payment reform legislation spelled out how payments for a service would vary geographically. A geographic practice cost index (GPCI) was developed that reflects the prices of rent, staff, and malpractice insurance in each payment locality. Other components of practice expense were assumed to have uniform prices nationally. For physician time and effort, an index of earnings of professionals is used, but the geographic variation is reduced by 75 percent. This reflected a compromise between those in the medical community who believe that payments should vary only to reflect differences in practice costs and those who believe that physicians' net compensation per service should vary in accordance with cost of living or what other professionals earn.

This geographic adjuster exhibits markedly less variation across localities than did historical charges. Although the formula provides some gains to rural areas on average, its most striking impact is the reduction of variation among urban areas and among rural areas. For example, the adjuster reduces payment rates in New York City, Los Angeles, and Miami but increases them in Chicago, St. Louis, and Salt Lake City.

The smoothness of the process through which the geographic policy has been developed and implemented has been impressive. The temptation for powerful members of Congress to enact provisions that benefit their constituents is great. But in contrast to policy on prospective payment for hospitals, tinkering with the geographic adjustment formula has been resisted. Clearly, the development of the compromise concerning the treatment of variation in the opportunity costs for physician time and effort reflected conflict between members whose constituents would benefit from one treatment or another. But once this compromise was struck, complaints from physician constituents that the formula treats them unfairly have not resulted in any changes. The principal legislative response to pressures from constituents has been provisions to study how to improve the system and directives to HCFA to incorporate better data as soon as it becomes available. Some of the complaints are valid. For example, the absence of reliable national data on office rents has led to use of data on residential rents for subsidized housing as a proxy. But rather than specify a rough increase for a particular state or locality, the Congress has directed HCFA to give high priority to the development of better data. This response may reflect a discipline by experienced leaders who know that once legislative exceptions are made, many others will follow and in the end, any sense that the payment system is fair will be lost.

It should be noted that the Congress has not tinkered with the relative value scale either. Even during the years before the Medicare Fee Schedule was implemented, when the Congress listed "overvalued procedures" for payment reductions, it never deviated from the detailed recommendations of the PPRC.

Another aspect of geographic adjustment is the drawing of boundaries around payment localities. In Medicare, each carrier drew boundaries for localities, often in consultation with local medical associations. A national policy outlining principles for drawing boundaries had never been adopted. The result was the use of almost every conceivable principle in drawing boundaries.

In Medicare physician payment reform, the Congress decided to defer the development of a national policy for locality boundaries. Instead it set up a process to convert some states to statewide localities. Physician organizations were given the opportunity to petition HCFA to convert to a statewide locality. The organizations had to demonstrate physician support for the change from many parts of the state (not just the areas that would benefit). Under this provision, Minnesota, Oklahoma, North Carolina, and Ohio have changed to statewide localities. My perception is that physicians in general have supported a reduction of geographic differences in payment. The initiatives to switch to statewide localities are consistent with this. HCFA has also supported this development, as data requirements are reduced.

Expenditure Targets

In the Medicare Fee Schedule, the initial conversion factor was calibrated so that spending would be the same as projected under the prior system (called *budget neutrality*), but an expenditure target mechanism was developed to update the conversion factor. Under Volume Performance Standards (VPS), a goal is set for spending on physicians' services in the following year. After the period is over, actual spending is compared to the goal (the performance standard). The percentage difference between the performance standard and actual spending is then added to or subtracted from an index of physician input prices (Medicare Economic Index) to determine the update.

This expenditure target has the potential to accomplish two things. First, it can augment the ability to budget the program. The performance standard is really a budget. To the degree that it is overshot or undershot, adjustments in the update will lead to achievement of planned spending, albeit with a two-year lag. Second, the mechanism places the medical community at risk for the cost implications of its practice patterns. While any one physician's impact on future updates is negligible, physicians' organizations have an incentive to work with government to contain costs.

Balance Billing

The restructuring of payment rates brought about by the Medicare Fee Schedule forced a resolution of the decades-long debate about balance billing. Since its inception, the Medicare program had permitted physicians to decide on a claim-by-claim basis whether to accept assignment, which means getting paid directly by the Medicare program and agreeing not to charge the patient for any amount that exceeds what the program approved, or to bill the patient without limit and have the patient in turn be reimbursed by the program for the allowed amount. Beneficiary groups have continually pushed for mandatory assignment, while physician organizations have resisted fiercely.

Various payment reductions in the mid-1980s led to the development of limits on charges for unassigned claims. When Medicare payment rates were frozen from 1984 through 1986, physicians were prohibited from increasing their charges. Exempted from this restriction were participating physicians—those who agreed in advance to accept assignment for all claims. When the freeze ended, nonparticipating physicians faced limits on the rate at which they could increase charges. Those physicians whose charges were less than 115 percent of the allowed charge were permitted to increase charges toward this level over four years while those above the level were allowed only nominal increases. Other legislative provisions reduced the allowed charge for specific services (the first reduction was for cataract surgery) and simultaneously limited charges for those services to a percentage above the reduced allowed charge.

This last policy change was a particularly salient indicator of future policies. Members of Congress believed that they could not restructure the pattern of payment without restricting physicians from offsetting reductions in Medicare payments by increasing the amount patients had to pay. Thus, the fee schedule could not be enacted without limits on balance billing tied to the new payment rates.

Other aspects of policy changes from the mid-1980s eased resolution of the longstanding conflict over assignment. The participating-physician option proved popular with physicians and beneficiaries, with increasing numbers of physicians signing agreements each year and a larger proportion of services being provided by participating physicians. The upshot was that by the time payment reform was considered, the assignment rate had increased to approximately 80 percent, implying that broader limits on balance billing would affect only a small proportion of claims. Under the Medicare Fee Schedule, physicians' charges are limited to 115 percent of the fee-schedule amount for nonparticipating physicians, who in turn are paid 5 percent less than participating physicians.

Experience with Payment Reform

For the most part, the implementation of Medicare physician payment reform has gone smoothly. From an administrative perspective, no major interruptions in processing of claims for physicians' services were experienced. This seemed to surprise the carrier community as much as anyone. The realignment in the structure of payment has unfolded very much as predicted. It is striking how close the results of the PPRC's 1992 analysis of the impact of payment reform on category of services are to its 1989 analysis.

One important bump along the road to implementing the reform has been the reaction of primary care physicians and rural physicians to the new system. In general, these categories of physicians who had expected to gain from the reform have been disappointed at the results. Perhaps the most important reason for this reaction has been the large budget cuts applied to Medicare physician payment at roughly the same time. Thus, while the relative changes have proceeded as expected, relative gains have been partially offset by absolute declines in the average payment rate. The fact that the initial conversion factor was calibrated too low (see below) did not help in this regard.

Another reason for the disappointment is lack of understanding of the reform. Some physicians were more aware of Professor Hsiao's early publications of likely impact than the simulations of the legislation as enacted. Few understood the transition, which was quite favorable to family physicians but not to general internists. During the first year of the transition, what the average general internist gained from the relative value scale was almost completely offset by losses from the elimination of specialty differentials.

In addition, perceptions of impact may be distorted. In a 1992 survey, the PPRC asked physicians about the impact of payment reform on their Medicare payment rates.[9] As part of the data analysis, the Commission compared the response to what claims data indicated had happened in the respondent's locality. The respondents' perceptions of payment changes were much more negative than what was indicated by the claims data.

The setting of the initial conversion factor proved highly contentious. HCFA made assumptions which outraged the medical profession concerning how physicians would respond to changes in payment rates. Its actuaries projected that physicians facing declines in payment rates would offset one half of the reduction while those seeing increases in payment rates would not change behavior in response. These asymmetric assumptions led to a 6 percent reduction in the conversion factor (given the transition, this meant a reduction of 3 percent in 1992 payment rates). An additional dispute—about interpretation of language relating to the transition—threatened a much larger reduction, but was amicably resolved.

Fortunately, the VPS provided a mechanism to correct errors in calibrating the conversion factor. If the conversion factor was set too low, spending would be lower than projected and fee updates would be higher. For 1992, spending for physician services was over 7 percent below the performance standard (an 11.3 percent increase from 1991 for surgical services and 5.6 percent for nonsurgical services). PPRC analysis suggested that 4 percentage points of the difference were due to various errors in calibration of the conversion factor—about half was due to a more benign behavioral response on the part of physicians than had been assumed. Although the Congress did trim the fee updates somewhat as part of the budget reconciliation process, the final updates exceeded inflation by 8 percentage points for surgical services, 5 percentage points for primary care services, and 3 percentage points for other nonsurgical services.

The experience with the VPS has led many to begin to assess the merits of such a process. As a budgeting mechanism, the VPS appears to have had success. The process of setting a standard, comparing it with actual spending, and having the difference affect the subsequent update has proceeded generally as planned. Although the Congress trimmed back the update in 1993, it is difficult to conceive of physician payment rates having been increased so much in that year's budget environment in the absence of the VPS.

Needless to say, it is difficult to assess what role the VPS has played in inducing physician organizations to work to contain costs. Activities related to practice guidelines appear to have increased, but other factors may have played important roles.

The VPS has had some significant problems as well. One concerns the different updates by category of services. The 1989 legislation that created the mechanism called for separate treatment for surgical and nonsurgical services, principally to win the support of the American College of Surgeons for the payment reform legislation. In updates for 1993 and 1994, those for surgical services were substantially higher than those for nonsurgical services. Much of the difference had a dubious basis. For example, the same baseline has been used to develop the two performance standards despite a somewhat slower historical rate of growth for surgical services. Errors in projecting behavioral responses to fee changes have also contributed to the differentials.

The Congress has been concerned about this experience having a negative impact on the payment gains for primary care services. Besides shielding those services from many of the budget reduction provisions, it created a third VPS category for primary care services (defined legislatively as office visits and a few other visit categories). But the Congress did not address the problem of different baselines to develop performance standards for each category of service. Since primary care has long had the slowest growth in volume of services, it is likely to get the highest updates on average.

A second problem concerns lags in data. Since the VPS is based on services incurred during the year, the assessment of spending cannot be made until enough of the year's claims have been processed so that an accurate estimate can be made for incurred spending. Thus, the performance standard year conforms with the federal fiscal year (ending in September), but the deliberative process does not begin until mid-April when the Secretary of Health and Human Services publishes data on spending in the previous year and makes a recommendation for updates. The PPRC bases its recommendations on these data and the Congress bases its decision on them. But when HCFA implements the decision, it uses data on spending that are more complete, which often differ noticeably. For example, the 1994 updates announced in early December turned out to be one and one-half percentage points higher than the Congress had anticipated when it made its decisions in July.

Single/All-Payer Rate Setting

Using the Medicare Fee Schedule as a base, a rate-setting system could be developed that governed payment rates to physicians from all sources. This section raises a number of design issues relevant to such a rate-setting system. They include the issue of transition from current policies and practices that include dramatically different payment structures and levels across payers, linking rate setting to a global budget, and the treatment of managed care plans. The section begins with a discussion of rate setting as a cost containment tool.

Cost Containment

Rate setting specifies a series of maximum rates for physicians' services. By setting these rates lower than current rates or allowing them to increase more slowly, the increase in spending can be slowed. How much can be saved depends on both the political commitment to reduce spending and the potential for providers to reduce costs in response to the constraints.

Limiting payment rates can lead to reduced costs in two ways. When prices are reduced for individual services, such as an x-ray or an office visit, physicians may be able to sustain such limitations by becoming more efficient in producing services and by finding ways to pay lower prices to their suppliers. Thus, a medical practice can respond to lower fee levels by using less space and paying lower rental rates, finding ways to provide services with fewer or lower-paid employees, purchasing lower-priced models of equipment, and, ultimately, providing less income to the physician who owns the practice. Systemwide pressure on rates of payment for health care services could expand the opportunities to economize on the prices paid for inputs that are specialized to the health care system.

The second way in which rate setting can induce cost containment is by specifying a unit of payment that is broader than that used under the current system—often an individual service. Bundled payment creates incentives to economize on the quantity of services delivered. These opportunities are most important for hospitals, which can be paid on a per case or per diem basis. A problem with physician payment is that when rates are constrained under fee for service, the experience in the Medicare program and in Canada and Germany has been that the quantity of services billed increases to offset a portion of the reduction in payment rates.[10]

Other bundled payments, such as one covering all physicians' services provided during an inpatient stay, one covering all services associated with a visit, or one covering an episode of care, have been discussed by analysts. With further development, one or more of these could be incorporated into a rate-setting system. But these methods, like use of capitation payments for primary care services, might be carried out more effectively by integrated health plans than by a rate-setting system run by government.

Over time, the degree of constraint on service prices that is practically achievable may not be adequate by itself to meet society's goals for cost containment. Upward trends in medical services per capita, reflecting technologically-driven changes in medical practice, are increasing so rapidly that a slowing of this growth is critical to stabilizing health spending in relation to national income. Thus, at least for the long term, a rate-setting strategy must be broadened to include steps to develop an infrastructure to support improvements in medical practice and steps to limit system capacity.

Under rate setting, the medical profession might expand its role in activities to support more appropriate practice by physicians. To the degree that doctors as a group are put at risk for the quantity of services, their organizations could play a larger role in cost containment. This could range from some of the activities that specialty societies are now undertaking at their own initiative in response to the Medicare Volume Performance Standards to activities in which professional organizations carry out governmental activities to encourage more appropriate practice. Limitation of capacity in the medical care system could be an integral part of a rate-setting strategy. With an extensive research literature suggesting that more physicians per capita leads to more services per capita, policies to restrict physician supply could make a significant contribution to slowing growth in the quantity of services. The Clinton health reform proposal includes a provision to limit the number of residency positions that are funded by Medicare and private payers by specialty.

The potential for rate setting to achieve less than its advocates envision arises in two areas: the ability of the political system to constrain rates substantially over the long term and the effectiveness of programs to slow the rate of growth of the quantity of services. Public decisions to set low rates are understandably difficult. Providers, their suppliers, and their employees are often well organized to resist them. They have the potential to recruit consumers to their side by projecting dire consequences if rates are constrained further. The American political system, in which interest groups are thought to play a larger role than in many other Western democracies, may be less well suited to effective rate setting than those in Canada and in Germany.

If rate setting is to be pursued, the design of health system reform and the structure of decision making must be supportive. For example, making health care spending more visible to the public may be a key factor. Contrast Germany, in which all revenue for health insurance comes from a payroll tax with equal employer and employee contributions, with the current situation in the United States. Here, few employees are aware of how much their employer contributes to their health benefits, the degree to which their wage rates have been held down to finance these contributions, and how much lower their taxes are as a result of the exclusion of these contributions from income taxes. Visibility of costs should be an important concern in the development of financing methods for health care reform.

Even if rates are controlled tightly, the success of efforts to slow the increase in the quantity of services is uncertain. While practice guidelines are being developed with enthusiasm, it is not clear how large a departure from current practices they will prescribe and the degree to which some of the guidelines will call for an increase in services. Also unknown is the extent to which physicians will change their practices. Physicians are justifiably concerned about the hassles involved in some utilization review and cost management efforts, raising questions about the potential for increased use of such tools. Some of the infrastructure to support changes in physician practice is dependent on public funding, which might not be forthcoming on a regular, predictable basis.

The degree of constraint on physician supply that can be achieved in the United States is uncertain. Although the federal government can have substantial impact on graduate medical education, the undergraduate medical education pipeline is more difficult to narrow. In any case, it would take many years for significant changes in training policies to have a meaningful impact on physician supply.

Drawing on experiences with price controls in sectors of the economy other than health, some have raised the prospect that the inevitable errors in setting relative rates will introduce significant distortions into the health care system, such as unintended emphasis on some services at the expense of others, or shortages of services for which relative payment rates have been inadvertently set too low. I have long regarded risks of such distortions as much lower for medical care because of the characteristics of the sector. The fact that most physicians provide a wide range of services in their specialty, and that hospitals cannot specialize in those DRGs that are more highly remunerated in relation to costs, limits the opportunity for distortion.

Transition

Two distinct issues of transition must be resolved. First, the major categories of payers have dramatically different payment rates. Projecting data from 1991 to the present, PPRC estimates that Medicare payment rates average between 60 and 65 percent of rates paid by private insurers.[11] The latter is net of discounts. A few years ago, PPRC estimated that Medicaid payment rates were 64 percent of Medicare rates.[12]

Under a single-payer system, a fee schedule could be developed that reflected the weighted average of these categories, perhaps with a downward adjustment to reflect physician gains from no longer serving patients who cannot pay. But under an all-payer system (or a single-payer system that is separate from Medicare), setting the fee schedule at the average would have significant impacts on public budgets.

Devising a system with different payment rates would probably be easier than finding the public funding to have uniform rates. The problems with some classes of patients being more attractive to physicians than other classes would not be worse than they are today. Indeed, an all-payer system would likely end or even reverse the trend towards widening discrepancies. Such a system would formalize the differences, but policymakers and physicians are already quite aware of the situation.

A related transitional problem concerns estimating what average payment rates are in the private sector. Very few data on private payment rates are currently available. Much of the data that exist require substantial "cleaning" in order to use them in a reliable fashion. The problem is more severe if the estimates must be accurate at the local level as well as the national level, since much of the existing private insurer data do not provide adequate coverage of all localities. Short of implementing a national data system, private carriers would have to be asked to report uniform information on payment rates.

The second transitional issue concerns the structure of payment. When Medicare implemented resource-based payment rates, five years were allowed for transition. Medicare accounts for somewhat more than 30 percent of physician workloads in specialties that treat the elderly. To shift the remainder of payment to a resource-based structure would clearly require a period of transition. A Medicare-style transition could be employed—blending average historical payment rates for a service with the resource-based payment rate. But careful consideration needs to be given to the data requirements of such a transition.

Linkage to Global Budgeting

If rate setting is to be part of health care reform, its purpose will be to enforce a global budget or expenditure limit. As I have pointed out elsewhere, global budgeting is not a cost containment policy per se, but rather a tool to calibrate underlying cost-containment policies.[13] Those policies that lend themselves to calibration on a regular basis include rate setting and limits on premiums.

The basic linkage between global budgeting and rate setting is the expenditure target. The expenditure target will reflect decisions on what spending should be. If actual spending deviates from this target, then payment rates must change so that the budget is realized.

Implementation would be more complex, however. Global budgets are specified not in terms of spending for physicians' services but by a broad range of health services—for example, those covered under a standard or minimum benefit package. Thus, important decisions must be made to allocate the global budget among categories of services before an expenditure target for physicians' services can be implemented.

These decisions must do more than merely maintain current allocations. In a dynamic health care system, patterns of care change. Since the early 1980s, for example, inpatient service use has declined sharply in relation to hospital outpatient and physicians' services. If a global budget had been in place and constant shares maintained, too much pressure would have been placed on physicians' and hospital outpatient services and too little on hospital inpatient services. Thus, a process must be established for making careful allocation decisions.

These allocation decisions are made more easily during the early years of a budgeting process when past service volume trends can be most useful as guides to the future. Extrapolations of trend differentials can be a valuable starting point for allocation decisions, but this will not suffice for long because past trends in expenditures by service category will, over time, reflect nothing more than previous allocation decisions, while past trends in service volume will reveal practice changes made in response to an expenditure target. Good decisions will require substantial study of current and future trends in patterns of medical practice and calculation of their implications for resource allocation among sectors.

This scenario has been observed in Medicare physician payment policy. When the VPS was divided into two (and then three) service categories, a decision had to be made concerning differentials in the performance standard by service category. The default formula did not establish differences among performance standards except to reflect the impact of past legislation—for example, reduction in surgical payment rates from implementation of the Medicare fee schedule leads to a lower performance standard for surgical services.

The PPRC noted that performance standards should differ to reflect changes in medical practice. Based on an analysis of recent data trends, it recommended differential performance standards to account for these patterns. But the Commission pointed out that it could base such recommendations on historical data for only a year or two more. After that, the historical data would begin to reflect performance under the system. Its use would dramatically reduce incentives to contain costs.

Treatment of Organized Systems of Care

One might take steps to ensure that organized systems of care, such as HMOs, are not substantially hindered by rate setting. Group- and staff-model HMOs generally pay physicians salaries and bonuses based on the overall performance of the organization. Independent practice association (IPA) models often contract with physicians on grounds other than fee for service. They often capitate primary care physicians and pool a portion of the fee-for-service payment for specialists. Others pay primary care physicians a per-patient fee for case management. Many HMO managers regard these payment methods as a key means of cost containment.

Allowing HMOs to contract with physicians in ways that differ from how rates are set could be accomplished by making the rate setting optional for all payers or only for a defined category of organized systems of care. Since rate setting is a restriction on what physicians can charge, the real issue lies in determining when they are excused from the restriction. The simplest option would be that any time a physician contracts with a health plan, any rates agreed to would be acceptable. But this might enable many physicians to demand higher rates from health plans by threatening to restrict their practice to patients enrolled in health plans that have agreed to such contracts. This might be a particular problem in smaller communities where a single practice is the only source of care in a given specialty. In a sense, too much flexibility could reduce government's ability to wield the market power needed to counteract the pull of some physicians.

One alternative that is more restrictive is to make rate setting optional only for specified health plans like federally qualified HMOs or those that have Medicare risk contracts. A current example gives Medicare risk contractors the choice of purchasing hospital care through the Medicare fiscal intermediary—at Medicare DRG rates—or directly from the hospital at a contracted rate. To the degree that the definition of types of health plans that were granted this option closely paralleled the universe of health plans that consider alternative payment mechanisms important in their management of care, this would be a satisfactory solution.

Alternatively, the option could be provided for specified types of payment, regardless of the characteristics of the health plan. For example, capitation contracts might be permitted without reviewing whether the payments were more generous than the fee schedule. Some plans might negotiate capitation rates with primary care physicians and pay specialists according to the established fee-for-service rates. Bonuses based on the experience of a pool of physicians might also be explicitly permitted even if the ultimate payment exceeded the fee schedule. Using health plan flexibility as a guiding principle (provided that the power to limit payment rates in the traditional fee-for-service component of the market is not given away), rate-setting entities could decide what types of contracts to permit in order to reflect conditions in each market.

To the degree that exemptions from rate setting succeed in permitting organized systems of care to contract with physicians in ways that are integral to their cost-containment strategies, the potential for rate setting to interfere with managed care will have been avoided. Some have noted that any policy that reduces costs for traditional plans will slow the development of managed care. The statement's logic is inarguable, but its relevance is suspect. Managed care has been marketed as a more appropriate and efficient means of providing medical care, rather than as a mechanism for obtaining discounts from physicians. If some of the latter is lost, the potential to achieve the former is not impaired. Indeed, with cost shifting, a managed care plan's ability to obtain a discount and shift costs to the fee-for-service sector could be seen as an artificial basis for growth.

Rate Setting in the Clinton Proposal

Although best characterized as a managed-competition plan, the Clinton health care reform proposal includes fee schedules for the services of physicians and other providers. The fee schedules would apply to care given to those enrolled in fee-for-service health plans and to out-of-network care provided to those enrolled in managed-care plans.

The Clinton Administration has not adequately explained why fee schedules are included, but I can suggest a number of considerations. First, one of the key themes in selling a proposal oriented towards managed care is maintaining choice of provider. Fee schedules may enhance the impression of choice by barring or limiting balance billing for those obtaining services outside of a health plan's network of physicians, or for those enrolling in a fee-for-service plan. They may also enhance the competitiveness of fee-for-service plans by enabling them to contain costs by paying lower unit prices.

Second, fee schedules may bolster managed care efforts to meet budgetary goals. In markets where managed care does not play a large role, fee schedules can meet some overall cost-containment goals. This includes both metropolitan markets in which managed care currently plays a limited role and rural areas where it may never be viable.

Despite the Clinton proposal's sketchy outline of fee schedules, it does specify what services they apply to (see above) and the process for establishing them. There is no direct link to the global budget.

The schedules are to be negotiated between providers and either regional health alliances or state governments. The state government decides whether the fee schedule will be statewide or whether each regional alliance will negotiate its own schedule. The legislation prohibits boycotts but provides anti-trust protection for providers who participate in such negotiations. The process is to be relatively informal, with alliances or state governments making the final decisions after discussions with providers. This does not render providers powerless because they would have the opportunity to make their case publicly. A more formal process, like that used in Germany, would have to furnish a mechanism for binding arbitration and determine who represents providers.

The legislation provides little explicit guidance concerning payment units, relative value scales, and conversion factors. Clearly, Medicare practices will play a large role. With regional alliances facing many immediate tasks, it would be attractive to adopt not only the Medicare relative value scale, but also the myriad payment policies, such as definition of a global service. These Medicare policies have already been well-received by state Medicaid programs and private insurers. They would also give an alliance the opportunity to standardize the technical details of fee-for-service payment without favoring the system of one private insurer over that of another.

Most attention would likely be devoted to establishing and annually revising conversion factors. The starting point would probably be the existing average payment rates. Obtaining an accurate estimate of current rates would be a formidable technical task, however. Experience at the PPRC suggests that determining average payment rates in a geographic area from private-insurer claims data would be difficult, if not impossible, without prior standardization of data editing among carriers.

In negotiating both initial adjustments from current payment rates and annual updates, there are two important considerations. First, if the proposal's premium caps were binding in an alliance, control of fee levels would be an important tool for keeping premiums within the their limits. If premiums of fee-for-service plans appear to exceed the limits, negotiators would have to decide how much of the difference to close through lower payment rates versus having plans undertake additional efficiencies through claims review and other methods. (The Clinton proposal has a specific mechanism in which a health plan may order a uniform reduction in its provider payment rates to bring its premium down to a required level, but any premium reduction achieved through this mechanism would not lower consumer premium rates.)

The second consideration would be fee-for-service plan competitiveness. Lower payment rates would tend to make fee-for-service plans more competitive. With physician organizations currently lobbying to ensure that these plans continue to play an important role, it is likely that their competitiveness with HMOs would be a factor in physician negotiating strategies.

A challenging technical problem in updating conversion factors is calibrating rate changes by service category. Neither uniform changes in payment rates by service category nor basing differential change on uniform increases in spending by category would be good policy. Today, for example, we expect payment rates per inpatient admission to increase more rapidly than per physician service, but we also expect *spending* on physicians' services to grow more rapidly than spending for inpatient hospital services. Failure to make judgments concerning either differential could lead to serious distortions, while addressing these issues in each alliance or state would only increase the challenge.

The Clinton proposal appears to have resolved the issue of the flexibility of managed care plans to contract with physicians by exempting networks from the fee schedule rather than a category of health plan. Health plans might still be vulnerable to local monopolies. Although this would not present any more problems than under current policies, it could be addressed by giving plans the option to purchase network as well as out-of-network services on the basis of the fee schedule. This would follow the current Medicare policy concerning HMOs and hospital services.

The impact of rate setting in the Clinton proposal would probably vary by market. In alliances where integrated health plans dominate, rate setting would play a relatively minor role. The effect could be significant in rural areas, however, if integrated plans do not serve those markets. In alliances in which integrated plans have a tenuous foothold, rate setting would be looked to as a means of providing most of the cost containment.

Notes

1. H.R. 3222, The Managed Competition Act of 1993 (Cooper); S. 1770, Health Equity and Access Reform Today Act of 1993 (Chaffee).

2. H.R. 1200, S. 491, American Health Security Act (McDermott, Wellstone).

3. H.R. 3600, S. 1757, The Health Security Act.

4. This observation is based on discussions with participants in the CRVS process. I have not seen any published literature on this point. The CRVS activity was disbanded in the mid-1970s as a result of objections by federal antitrust authorities.

5. Hsiao, W.C., P. Braun, E.R. Becker, et al., "The Resource-Based Relative Value Scale," *Journal of the American Medical Association* 258(6) (1987): 799–802.

6. Omnibus Budget Reconciliation Act of 1989 (Public Law 101-239).

7. Omnibus Budget Reconciliation Act of 1993 (Public Law 103-66).

8. Physician Payment Review Commission, *Annual Report to Congress 1992* (Washington, D.C.: March 1992), Chapter 2.

9. Physician Payment Review Commission, *Annual Report to Congress 1993* (Washington, D.C.: March 1993), Chapter 6.

10. Barer, M.L., R.G. Evans and R.J. Labelle, "Fee Control as Cost Control: Tales from the Frozen North," *Milbank Quarterly* 66 (1988): 1–64.

11. Statement of John M. Eisenberg, M.D. before the Committee on Ways and Means, December 16, 1993.

12. Physician Payment Review Commission, *Physician Payment Under Medicaid*, No. 91-4 (Washington, D.C.: 1991).

13. Ginsburg, P.B., "Expenditure Limits and Cost Containment," *Inquiry* 30(4), in press.

8

Cost and Quality Issues

David K. Lawrence and James A. Lane

Group practice health maintenance organizations are a uniquely American institution. For years they have led the way in health care organization and delivery innovation. The concepts on which group practice HMOs are founded—an organized, integrated system built around a multi-specialty physician group with incentives that encourage appropriate care—have effectively and efficiently served many communities for decades. They became the model for the modern health maintenance organization (HMO), thus setting the stage for health care reform.

America is beginning a national debate about health care reform and whether we should have a national health insurance policy. The major focus of the discussion is to assure all Americans of uninterrupted affordable health benefits coverage. To a lesser, but not unimportant extent, the debate also involves attempting to assure that all Americans have access to needed health care services.

The political momentum to develop a national health insurance policy comes from the large number of middle income Americans who are worried about losing health benefits coverage. Of Americans polled in late 1993, 39 percent worry a great deal that they will not be able to afford health insurance, and 31 percent are concerned that their benefits will be reduced.[1] There is also growing anxiety about the estimated 40 million Americans who are without coverage. Two reasons for the lack of coverage are the changing nature of available jobs and the high costs of health care. As the American economy has moved from a manufacturing base to a service base, high paying manufacturing jobs with good benefits have been replaced by lower paying jobs, often with few or no health benefits. Two-thirds of the uninsured are workers or their dependents. The rapid increase in health care costs is exacerbating this trend as both employers and employees are being priced out of the health benefits market.

Those who seek to expand coverage, therefore, are forced to address the cost issue. This is especially true because of the potential inflationary impact of increasing the insured population by about 15 percent. Thus, cost containment is an important part of the debate, and a major question is this: Should costs be controlled primarily through competition among health plans, by regulatory means or by some combination of the two?

The perspective presented here is that an approach that relies upon competition among health plans and market forces is more likely to lead to meaningful reform than one based on government regulatory action. A regulatory approach that featured "global budgets," rate and price controls and capacity limitations—certificate-of-need programs or global capital budgets, for instance—would almost certainly be biased in favor of the status quo. Not only would it be difficult to raise the capital needed for new organizations in such a world, the political nature of the decision-making process would certainly favor existing providers and payment mechanisms over new entrants with innovative approaches to organizing, delivering, and financing health care services.

This would be particularly troublesome at a time when significant reform is already occurring as a result of current market conditions and increasing pressure exercised by sophisticated purchasers. The introduction of heavy-handed regulatory approaches at this time could at best maintain the status quo, or at worst return the system to fee-for-service domination. What is needed instead is an environment in which there are clear incentives for innovation to create new organizations and sustain current ones that are capable of improving quality and containing costs.

For too long, Americans have been led to believe that high cost equals high quality. We believed it in the manufacturing sector until Japan showed us that high quality, in the sense of high performance compared to expectations, means low costs. We still believe it when it comes to health care. As will be discussed below, it is well documented that group practice HMOs provide their members with less hospital care than the traditional fee-for-service, indemnity insurance system, and have done so for years. Although in the past this performance was criticized as low quality, today other HMOs, preferred provider organizations (PPOs) and third-party payers are trying to emulate it.[2] On the other hand, there is evidence of significant variation in medical care use in different geographic areas[3] and studies suggest that many unnecessary procedures may be conducted on patients in America.[4]

Although this evidence is usually presented to show the waste and resulting high costs of American health care, it is seldom taken as proof of questionable quality. Politicians and health care leaders are fond of saying that America has the best health care in the world. Although it may be true that America has the very best practitioners in each category of health care services, it does not mean that it has a high quality health care delivery system.

More importantly, the low quality represented by large amounts of unnecessary care is not just a hotly debated but ultimately benign political issue. It can be dangerous. Hospitals are not good places to be in if one is not sick. If Americans begin to realize the risks that they are being exposed to, they may become as concerned about quality as about costs. Improving the quality of America's health care system needs to be an important part of the reform agenda, for its own sake and because improved quality is the best way to achieve long-term cost containment.

Thus, for those who propose competition among health plans as the optimal approach to assuring quality and containing costs, HMOs are the key element of the strategy. This strategy was made possible by the federal policy developed in the early seventies to provide federal funds for HMO development which led directly and indirectly to the significant growth in the number of HMOs and HMO members (Figures 8.1 and 8.2).

When the Health Maintenance Organization Act passed in 1973, almost all HMOs were based on group or staff models and nearly all HMO members belonged to such arrangements. However, by 1984 group/staff domination began to ebb considerably, and today almost 80 percent of HMOs are individual practice association (IPA)/network models which treat approximately 60 percent of all HMO members. This is not due to the superiority of the IPA/network model. In fact, when measured by either cost or quality performance, IPA/networks are no better than any other model. Instead, their growth results more from certain characteristics of group practice HMOs, namely, that they are more difficult to launch and require more capital than do IPA/network HMOs.

Kaiser Permanente, and other group practice HMOs, illustrates the potential of an organized, integrated system. The elements of health care delivery—physicians, hospitals, home care, support functions, and insurance—are integrated into a coherent whole, making it possible for the system to have a significant impact on costs and quality.

Equally important, group practice HMOs have spawned a variety of imitators and competitors, including IPA/network HMOs. During the past 20 years these HMOs, and their more recent variants (e.g., PPOs and point-of-service products), have changed the framework of health care. In doing so, HMOs created an "American way" to deal with quality and cost issues by setting the stage for major reform based on competition among health plans.

Proposals before Congress range from providing federal tax support for the purchase of health benefits coverage, to casting the federal government as the country's only health insurer. Generally, the former scheme fails to adequately address cost containment, while the latter relies on reg-

FIGURE 8.1 Number of Health Maintenance Organizations by Year

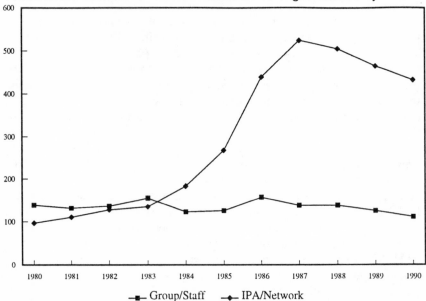

Source: Interstudy Edge, 1991

Figure 8.2 Health Maintenance Organization Membership (000)

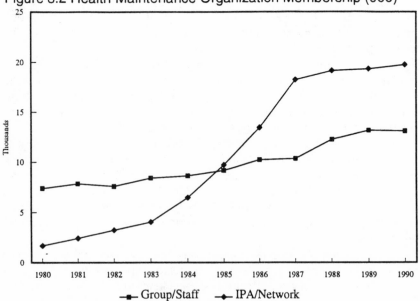

Source: Interstudy Edge, 1991

ulatory cost-control mechanisms. However, the great middle of the political spectrum sees competition among health plans as the preferred mechanism for controlling costs and assuring quality. President Clinton's plan links these proposals by combining competition and premium caps, just in case competition alone fails.

Fair, structured competition among health plans is the best way to assure quality and contain costs. More importantly, competition must focus on health care outcomes. To accomplish real reform existing successful HMOs must be expanded and new organizations must be developed that are capable of competing on the basis of quality and costs. Group practice HMOs have had that capability and it is safe to assume that they will retain it, although in an increasingly competitive environment harder and smarter work will have to be done to remain successful.

However, existing group practice HMOs do not have a large enough capacity to expand, although a number of them have developed innovative approaches to increasing capacity that depend upon strategic alliances with those fee-for-service providers seeking to excel beyond the status quo.

IPA/network HMOs have a substantial capacity for growth, but there is also significant room for expansion in other organizations. Newly emerging organizations that are transforming themselves into capitated group practices—physician/hospital arrangements and fee-for-service groups, for example—can provide added capacity. Existing organizations like community and neighborhood health centers and city and county hospitals, can also become the foundations for new approaches to delivering care on a pre-paid basis. Such transformations can be greatly facilitated if these new organizations are able to vie for members directly through health alliances without having to develop their own capacity to sell to and through employer groups.

The Influence of Group Practice HMOs

The developments of the past 15 years have set the stage for a uniquely American approach to health benefits reform and, ultimately, to health care services. Such reform can be based on the performance of group practice HMOs over the last five decades.

These organizations started in relatively isolated areas just before and after World War II. They were promoted by physicians, consumers, industrialists and a few government officials, with the goal of providing health care in a way that was more satisfying, to both patients and physicians, than traditional fee-for-service, solo practice. They were not designed to contain costs, and it was learned only later that their costs were lower, primarily because of reduced hospital use.

There is little doubt that group practice HMOs have lower hospitalization rates than fee-for-service, indemnity plans. An exhaustive study by
the RAND Health Insurance Experiment looked at the Group Health Cooperative of Puget Sound (a group practice HMO in Seattle, Washington),
and matched its performance against four types of fee-for-service cost-
sharing plans, including one with no deductibles or copayments. Each
participant was randomly assigned to a plan to reduce the impact of individual selection and health status differences. Total cost per member was
28 percent less in the group practice than in the fee-for-service plan with
no cost sharing.[5]

A recent review of group practice HMO studies from over two decades
found convincing evidence that prepaid group practice and staff-model
HMOs reduce hospital use and overall cost relative to indemnity plans,
while maintaining a level of service similar to that found in the fee-for-service system.[6]

More recently Kaiser Permanente's director of special studies, Mark
Blumberg, M.D., completed an analysis of the 1989 National Health Interview Survey (NHIS), a nationwide query of 120,000 persons conducted for
the National Center for Health Statistics. Dr. Blumberg found that after
adjusting for age, sex and self-reported health status, group practice HMO
members had more doctor office visits but fewer non-maternity dis-
charges and hospital days than people covered by either Blue Cross/Blue
Shield or other non-HMO private plans[7] (Table 8.1). The higher rate of
births-per-thousand-members reported for members of group practice
HMOs than for those covered by the Blues and other private plans is
likely to be due to the special appeal of comprehensive group plans to
younger individuals concerned with ongoing care for their growing families (Table 8.2).

There have also been a large number of studies of group practice HMO
quality. Based on an analysis of 27 comparative studies of health care
quality in HMOs versus non-HMOs, and taking into consideration the
populations studied, there is little question that facility-based HMO care
is at least comparable, if not superior, to care in other health facilities.[8]

Official recognition of the relative cost efficiency of group practice
HMOs has come from the Congressional Budget Office. In an analysis of
the cost impact of a "managed competition" approach to health care reform, the Office stated that

> Based on past performance, the Congressional Budget Office would expect
> the prices of staff- and group-model health maintenance organizations to be
> 10 percent to 15 percent below the prices of similar fee-for-service plans.
> CBO estimates that if everyone with health insurance were to enroll in these
> kinds of HMOs and all of them achieved that level of cost reductions, na-
> tional health expenditures could decline by up to 10 percent.[9]

Table 8.1   Ratio of Observed to Expected Annual Utilization by Type of Coverage,
1989 NHIS Population Under 65 with Private Coverage

	Coverage Status				
	Group Practice	IPA	Other HMO	Blues	Other Private
Non-Delivery Hospital Discharges	0.767	1.064	1.132	1.143	1.091
Non-Delivery Hospital Days	0.669	0.982	1.085	1.185	1.074
Doctor Office Visits (truncated at 50 per year)	1.124	1.190	1.091	1.074	1.045

Source: Mark S. Blumberg, "Risk-Adjusted Hospital and Doctor Office Utilization for those Under Age 65 with no Public Coverage," Oakland, CA Kaiser Foundation Health Plan, Inc. (Submitted for publication.)

Table 8.2   Percent of Population Under 2 Years Old by Private Coverage,
1989 NHIS Population Under 65 with Private Coverage

Coverage Status

Group Practice	IPA	Other HMO	Blues	Other Private
3.60	4.25	3.24	2.66	3.00

Note: The variable "children under 2 years old" is used as a proxy for recent births.

Source: Mark S. Blumberg, "Risk-Adjusted Hospital and Doctor Office Utilization for those Under Age 65 with no Public Coverage," Oakland, CA Kaiser Foundation Health Plan, Inc. (Submitted for publication.)

Thus, group practice HMOs are acknowledged to have achieved a significant cost advantage and at least comparable quality when compared to fee-for-service, indemnity plans. They would appear to be the correct foundation for any health care reforms intent on containing costs while maintaining quality. Unfortunately, it is extremely difficult, if not impossible, for existing group practice HMOs to expand rapidly enough to meet the demand likely to be created by a reformed system based on competition among health plans.

Generally, group practice HMOs develop and own health care resources while IPA/networks rely upon the existing delivery system and only organize it in a financial sense to create a network of providers that can be offered to third-party purchasers. Today the HMO world is converging and the models are becoming mixed beyond recognition. Nevertheless, some differentiation is still possible. Launching a group practice HMO requires developing a medical group, organizing support staff and other related services and constructing or renovating medical offices. During the eighties, Kaiser Permanente expanded to six new geographic areas, but only two of those were new starts while the others involved mergers with existing HMOs. (Although all of Kaiser Permanente's original "Regions" have their own hospitals, none of the new ones do.)

In addition, group practice HMOs have generally emerged in areas with large populations and well-developed health care systems as well as physician and hospital surpluses. Kaiser Permanente's expansion criteria have included metropolitan areas of over 500,000 population with a high ratio of physicians and hospital beds to population.

Not all areas are equally hospitable to group practice HMO development. A receptive business environment, health care community and local government are very important. For example, Kaiser Permanente was invited by the business community and the governor to develop a Region in the Raleigh-Durham area in North Carolina. But in Atlanta, Georgia, the business community was generally indifferent and the state's insurance commissioner, concerned that Kaiser Permanente would pose a threat to a number of financially struggling HMOs, delayed our opening. Past resistance by organized medicine to group practice HMOs is also well documented, and it continues today in many parts of the country. During recent expansions into new areas like Kansas City, and outward from existing Regions such as Salem, Oregon, and Akron, Ohio, we have often had difficulty obtaining staff privileges at hospitals and satisfactory arrangements with specialists in the community.

However, Kaiser Permanente's development in the San Francisco Bay Area led to an important proactive response by organized medicine. In 1954, the San Joaquin County Medical Society developed a medical care foundation when its members believed that Kaiser Permanente was going to open in Stockton, California. The foundation model, a forerunner of today's IPA HMO, spread to other counties in California and other parts of the country. It is noteworthy that with few exceptions, strong IPA HMOs and competitive health plan markets were created in areas where there was a strong group practice HMO first.

IPAs and their counterpart network HMOs have provided fee-for-service physicians and other health providers a way to compete more effectively with group practice HMOs. This has become increasingly true during the 1980s as these HMOs have significantly improved their cost-containment practices. PPOs have also become part of the equation as a more competitive health benefits market has emerged.

Through judicious expansion, and by setting high performance standards for other plans to emulate, group practice HMOs can play a key role in covering and increasing the number of health care consumers in their existing service areas. However, as currently configured, they do not have the capacity to absorb a significant increase in membership. That means significant HMO growth will have to occur primarily within the IPA and network HMOs, and perhaps through converted PPOs or newer organizational forms.

While group practice HMOs have been studied at length, much less is known from a "scientific" perspective about newer health care delivery models. Conventional wisdom holds that IPAs and networks maintain their price advantage not through effective hospital utilization controls, but by discounting prices and, because of their "new kid on the block" status, attracting younger and generally healthier members. The CBO appears to have accepted this view and is unwilling to estimate any savings under health care reform proposals for members enrolled in IPA/network HMOs.

A review of the admittedly limited amount of published work on IPA/network HMO performance finds some evidence suggesting that IPAs, networks, or mixed-model HMOs reduce health care use and overall costs where the managed care organization is more than fee-for-service with window dressing.[10] A more recent Mathematica study of performance in the Medicare program concluded that IPAs are as effective as other model types in controlling the use of any service covered by Medicare, with the possible exception of skilled nursing facilities.[11]

Finally, Blumberg's analysis indicates that the hospital utilization performance of IPA HMOs is better than fee-for-service indemnity but not as good as group practice HMOs. IPA HMO members use fewer hospital days than Blue Cross/Blue Shield participants or those with other private coverage, and, like group practice HMOs, they have higher doctor office visit rates and birth rates (Tables 8.1 and 8.2).

Beyond the skepticism surrounding IPA/network HMO cost-containment abilities, a number of other concerns about HMOs in general should be addressed before concluding that they are an appropriate building block for meaningful reform. The questions raised relate to the following issues:

- Favorable selection;
- Inadequate participation in Medicare and Medicaid;

- Reliance on provider volume discounts; and
- Inability to keep cost increases below general health care increases.

Favorable selection. In any reform that relies upon competition among health plans and allows individuals the freedom to choose their own doctor, some players will get more favorable risk ratings than others. A plan's prices depend to a great extent on the health of its members and how well it manages the costs of the services they need. In today's competitive market this economic reality provides a powerful incentive for some HMOs to focus on attracting good risks. However, because of both philosophical and legal constraints, HMOs have "skimmed less cream" than most of their competitors. Still, that does not mean that many of them do not have better than average risks.

There are three factors beyond underwriting techniques that may influence risk. First is the plan's age. Newer HMOs attract younger and generally healthier members who make few demands on provider resources, except for maternity care. Similarly, fledgling HMOs usually have a smaller percentage of older members than their better established counterparts, particularly if they are growing fast. For example, in the last twenty years, Kaiser Permanente's California Regions have aged significantly. In 1972, approximately 40 percent of their members were under 20 years of age and about 25 percent were 45 or older. In 1992, only 30 percent were under 20 while 31 percent were 45 or older. Representing two of the three oldest HMOs in California, these plans have the highest average age of all HMOs in the California Public Employees Retirement System (CalPERS). The median age of Kaiser Permanente's newest Region is five years lower than our California Regions.

Second, plan design can influence choice. HMOs generally have far more comprehensive coverage than the Blues and indemnity plans. This can attract individuals in need of care, especially where there are annual open-enrollment periods. This is clearly seen in maternity use where HMOs have far better coverage and, consequently, higher birth rates than fee-for-service, indemnity insurance (Table 8.2).

A third factor, generally more applicable to group practice HMOs than to IPA/network HMOs, is the use of restricted provider panels. When selecting a plan during open enrollment, individuals currently under medical care are unlikely to switch plans if it means changing their physician or other significant provider. This is almost always the case if a person is considering joining a group practice HMO. It may be the case for an IPA/network HMO, but in many areas, doctors and hospitals belong to a large number of such HMOs.

Of course, such a situation can be a two-edged sword. Once a person belongs to a group practice HMO, he or she is unlikely to leave to join another plan while undergoing care. As noted, any multiple choice plan approach will have adverse selection against some health plans as an inherent feature. That is why those who have studied HMOs have tried to adjust for risk, and why managed competition proposals generally call for risk adjustments among health plans. Initially at least, both prospective and retrospective adjustments will be necessary. In a relatively short period of time, however, adequate prospective risk adjusters will be developed, making selection of little or no consequence in health plan performance as reflected in prices to consumers.

Medicare and Medicaid. HMOs have been criticized for not accepting their "fair share" of Medicare and Medicaid patients. It is true that the percentage of Medicare and Medicaid members in HMOs is lower than that in the general population. However, this is not true of all HMOs, especially where Medicare is concerned. Although only a few HMOs have a sizable Medicaid membership, the percentage of certain group practice HMO members who are Medicare recipients, including that of some Kaiser Permanente Regions, is higher than the Medicare-recipient share of the general population in those areas.

The point must be made that there was no outcry for HMOs to take their "fair share" when organized medicine and other health care providers believed the Medicare and Medicaid programs were a profitable source of income. When the Medicare legislation first passed there was no provision for prepaid group practice reimbursement, in part because of organized medicine's opposition. However, group practice HMOs were able to build an acceptable program, based on provisions in a single line of the statute, allowing those members over 65 years old to retain membership and still receive Medicare. It was not until 1983 that an acceptable Medicare risk contract provision was enacted, and Medicare risk HMOs now have over one million members.

Medicaid experienced a similar scenario with a number of states, including California, leading the way in developing HMO provisions. HMO options for Medicaid beneficiaries fall short in some states, but most legislatures have enacted adequate laws and are developing programs to greatly increase HMO Medicaid enrollment. There is little doubt that HMOs have a proven track record of serving Medicare and Medicaid beneficiaries. The real policy issue is whether these entitlement programs are structured in such a way that HMOs can participate fully and fairly. And in an increasingly competitive environment, with neither Medicare nor Medicaid making adequate payments, all payers must bear their "fair share" of Medicare and Medicaid shortfalls.

Volume discounts. Some believe that some HMOs and most PPOs achieve a significant amount of their price advantage through provider discounts from hospitals, physicians and other providers. Discounts may result from excess bed capacity, which prompts providers to base prices on marginal costs in an effort to increase volume and profits. HMOs undoubtedly receive discounts; however, it is never clear how good or evenly distributed the discounts are. In some of Kaiser Permanente's operating areas with a large number of HMOs and PPOs, it is believed that the only group that does not get a discount is the uninsured who pay cash.

Economists generally dismiss discounts as a reliable health care economic indicator because they do not reflect organizational effectiveness (except perhaps at securing discounts), and result in cost shifting. However, discounts are a fact of life in a competitive environment in which there is substantial excess capacity. More importantly, discounts play a relatively minor role in the pricing policies of some well-established HMOs. Kaiser Permanente's California Regions receive practically no hospital discounts because they own their own hospitals, and consequently cannot bestow discounts on themselves. Yet they retain very competitive cost structures.

Cost increases. Even if HMOs, or at least group practice HMOs, have lower costs than fee-for-service, indemnity plans, they are still criticized for not keeping cost increases on a par with the annual inflation rate defined by the Consumer Price Index. This is especially important because the major cost issue driving reform involves not only the current amount of the Gross Domestic Product devoted to health care, but the rate of increase as well. The argument goes that even if everyone in the country were enrolled in a group practice HMO, there would be only a one-time savings and then the rate of increase would continue unabated. Furthermore, it has been observed that HMO premiums generally have increased over time at a rate similar to health care cost increases.

It is unreasonable to think that HMOs would have had a long-term cost trend significantly lower than health care inflation. HMOs were spawned and continue to swim in a fee-for-service ocean. The highly inflationary nature of the fee-for-service, indemnity insurance system has affected HMOs' cost structures and provided them with a high price ceiling under which they could compete.

HMOs are also affected by cost increases associated with new health care technology. "Big ticket" items like magnetic resonance imaging and organ transplantation are well known, but there are also thousands of other "small ticket" items, for example:

- New immunizations against hepatitis B, measles and chickenpox, which result in significant expenses for vaccine acquisition and administration;
- Drugs for battling human immunodeficiency virus, including AZT and ganciclovir;

- Diagnostic tests such as prostate specific antigen (PSA), which have resulted not only in earlier diagnosis of prostate cancer, but in a marked increase in expensive radical prostatectomies;
- Laparoscopic cholecystectomy, which has increased the frequency of gallbladder surgery;
- Arthroscopes and the subsequent rise in knee and other joint surgery; and
- New catheters that can be inserted into the heart to surgically treat certain arrhythmias.

The list goes on and on. Some of the new technologies actually reduce costs, but most have resulted in gradual and incremental increases. HMOs must and do provide these new technologies and, consequently, bear their expense.

The past performance of HMOs when their major competition was the fee-for-service, indemnity insurance system does not necessarily predict the future. As HMOs become the predominant means of delivering health care benefits, they will no longer have the luxury of the fee-for-service, indemnity insurance price ceiling. If the competitive environment is correctly structured, they will be required to engage in true price competition, and this will provide a powerful incentive to hold costs down.

The Future of Group Practice HMOs

For the reasons discussed above, if there is to be a rapid increase in HMO membership in a short period of time, most of it will not be in traditional integrated group practice HMOs such as Kaiser Permanente's west coast Regions. What then does their future hold? Our answer is that HMOs will continue to set the standard by which health care organization, delivery and financing are measured within the changing context of health care reform and the continuing change in health care delivery and medical science.

They can do this by continuing to grow and expand in their existing service areas, and where possible expand into new areas. This will demonstrate that they are satisfying their members and groups, and will set the competitive standard for other providers to meet.

Organized systems such as group practice HMOs that are responsible for providing health care to a defined population have the capacity to make significant contributions toward improving clinical medicine. Such contributions can result in high-quality, cost-effective care becoming the norm in American health care delivery.

Group practice HMOs can use information about the populations they serve, their health status and the extent to which an HMO's efforts have maintained or improved members' health. They can determine which prevention and health promotion activities are most effective for which members and when.

They can also lead the way in developing measurements like "report cards" that can be used in assessing the performance of health plans. This is important in any health care reform effort that promotes both consumer choice of provider and competition among health plans. Kaiser Permanente is a leader in the effort by the National Committee for Quality Assurance (NCQA) to develop such an assessment system. In fact, Kaiser Permanente's Northern California Region published its own "1993 Quality Report Card" as a first step in this process. This involves a commitment to measure and report what HMOs do, not only to provide a basis for informed choice, but to enable HMO administrators and employees to understand their performance in ways that they never have before. This will provide a platform on which HMOs can launch continuous improvement efforts.

The NCQA "report card" will include information on practices such as mammography and childhood immunization rates, and the percentage of women who first receive prenatal care during their first trimester. It will also include outcomes statistics covering such important variables as neonatal mortality rates, infant birth weights, admission rates for asthma, hysterectomy and caesarean section rates, patient health status following surgery and patient satisfaction data.

This and other data, combined with newly developed computing and analytic techniques, will mean a major leap forward in our knowledge of what works and what doesn't in health care delivery. Knowing the outcomes of particular interventions will allow physicians to assess and help patients understand the consequences of clinical decisions. To get at the essential causes of variation in outcomes, scientific research on a substantial scale is required. It demands huge data bases, large populations, and computing and analytic capacity. Large group practice HMOs, such as Kaiser Permanente have, or can develop, all of these.

Kaiser Permanente is already constructing outcomes-based guidelines for clinical decision making. The Southern California Permanente Medical Group is currently working on guidelines for a number of techniques, including the use of radiographic contrast agents, cholesterol management, breast cancer screening, colon cancer screening, magnetic resonance imaging for knee injuries, and prostate cancer screening. Practicing physicians are playing a key role in developing the guidelines, and the ideas, data, and decisions coming out of the project will be shared throughout the Kaiser Permanente system and potentially will be used by others in the health care sector.

Outcomes research can also pinpoint providers who perform exceptionally well. This is a significant change from conventional approaches to quality which focus on the outliers, or "bad apples." Once these top employees and their practice methods are identified, organized systems such as group practice HMOs can quickly adopt, develop and disseminate the exemplary techniques.

Finally, group practice HMOs are well situated to incorporate the lessons of total quality management (TQM) into the health care system. They have the organization and structure that enables them to support quality management activities. Within Kaiser Permanente, hundreds of TQM projects have been launched in the past four years. We are using TQM tools and techniques to improve clinical and administrative processes in a wide range of areas including members' access to physicians, breast cancer diagnosis and treatment cycles, follow-up and rescheduling of cancelled appointments, hospital admitting procedures, and prescription refill turnaround time.

Efforts to improve care and lower costs are reflected in recent work at Kaiser Permanente's Walnut Creek medical center, where a multi-disciplinary team focused on decreasing the length of stay for major joint replacement surgery and improving patient satisfaction with the discharge process. Similar activities are underway in other group practice HMOs throughout the country as well as in other organized delivery systems like major teaching medical centers. Through these TQM efforts and the development of clinical guidelines and outcomes research, a true science of health care delivery is being built. Such a discipline is vital if we as a nation are to achieve the health care reform goal of providing demonstrably effective, high quality health care that is affordable and accessible to all Americans. It is hoped that as policymakers craft solutions, they do so with an eye toward moving the health care system forward, rather than maintaining the status quo.

Group practice HMOs are uniquely American. For years they have led the way in health care organization and delivery innovation. Other types of HMOs are now emulating them and even improving upon their performance. These organizations, and the ones that will be developed to compete with them, hold the key to reform.

True health care reform will depend upon the cumulative performance of all American health care delivery organizations. Public policy should establish a framework within which all such groups are challenged to innovate so that quality of care is continuously improved and the cost of health care becomes affordable to all.

That is best accomplished by creating an environment in which health plans compete for members based on their ability to provide high quality health care at affordable cost. Such an environment is being created today

166 David K. Lawrence and James A. Lane

by the actions of purchasers, HMOs and others that seek to emulate group practice HMO performance. The challenge for national health care reform is to build on these efforts and create a climate in which positive changes will be accelerated and sustained.

Notes

1. Commonwealth Fund/Henry J. Kaiser Family Foundation, "Health Interview Survey," Lou Harris and Associates, Inc., 1993.

2. "Kaiser Permanente has been criticized for delivering inferior, or at best, ordinary medical care; scolded for being impersonal and even rude; and chastised for lowering costs at the expense of the patient's welfare," *American Medical News*, September 13, 1971.

3. John E. Wennberg and Alan W. Gittelsohn, "Small Area Variations in Health Care Delivery," *Science* 182 (December, 1973): 1102–08; W. Pete Welch, et al., "Geographic Variation in Expenditures for Physicians' Services in the United States," *New England Journal of Medicine* 328 (March 4, 1993): 621–7.

4. Robert H. Brook, et al., "Predicting the Appropriate Use of Carotid Endarterectomy, Upper Gastrointestinal Endoscopy, and Coronary Angiography," *New England Journal of Medicine* 323 (March 7, 1991): 1173–7; Centers for Disease Control and Prevention, "Rates of Cesarean Delivery—United States, 1991," *Morbidity and Mortality Weekly Report* 42(15) (April 23, 1993): 285–9; Mark R. Chassin, et al., "Does Inappropriate Use Eaxplain Geographic Variations in the Use of Health Care Services?" *Journal of the American Medical Association* 258(18) (November 13, 1987): 2533–7; Madelon Lubin Finkel and David J. Finkel, "The Effect of a Second Opinion Program on Hysterectomy Performance," *Medical Care* 28(9) (September 1990): 776–83; Lucian L. Leape, "Unnecessary Surgery," *Health Services Research* 24(3) (August 1989).

5. Willard G. Manning, et al., "A Controlled Trial of the Effect of a Prepaid Group Practice on Use of Services," *New England Journal of Medicine* 310 (June 7, 1984): 1505–10.

6. Robert H. Miller and Harold S. Luft, "Managed Care: Past Evidence and Potential Trends," *Frontiers of Health Service Management* 9(3) (Spring 1993): 13.

7. Non-maternity hospital use is used because hospitalization for birth is rarely discretionary. Group practice HMOs had only 56 percent as many non-delivery days as the Blues. The results presented are indirectly standardized. The standard includes those with no private coverage who hospital use was significantly lower than expected in all three utilization categories presented, but slightly higher than expected in births.

8. Frances C. Cunningham and John W. Williamson, "How Does the Quality of Health Care Compare to That in Other Settings?" *The Group Health Journal* 1(1) (Winter 1980): 13.

9. Congressional Budget Office, *Managed Competition and Its Potential to Reduce Health Spending* (Washington, D.C.: U.S. Government Printing Office, May, 1993), p. 35.

10. Robert H. Miller and Harold S. Luft, "Managed Care: Past Evidence and Potential Trends," *Frontiers of Health Service Management* 9(3) (Spring 1993): 13.

11. Randall S. Brown and Jerrold Hill, *Does Model Type Plan a Role in the Extent of HMO Effectiveness in Controlling the Utilization of Services?* (Plainsboro, NJ: Mathematica Policy Research, Inc., May 10, 1993), p. 1.

PART THREE

Public Programs

9

The Role of Medicare in Reform

Marilyn Moon

Medicare is a critical piece of our current health care system. In fact, many reform proposals treat Medicare's basic structure as "untouchable," suggesting only modest changes in the program while significantly altering many other aspects of the health care system. Nevertheless, it would be a mistake to view Medicare as irrelevant to the reform process. First, Medicare's experience offers important perspectives—both positive and negative—for reform. Moreover, changes elsewhere in the system will have an effect on the Medicare program; it is not possible to enact reforms that dramatically change the delivery of care without also affecting Medicare, even if no formal provisions of the program are altered. And the one area in which most proposals would affect Medicare—cuts in payments to providers to help fund other expansions—may place the program at risk.

Medicare also has a number of problems, acknowledged by even its most fervent supporters, that might be improved as part of overall health care reform. At a minimum, changes in Medicare ought to be considered to ensure its coordination with the rest of the new system. Furthermore, many observers predict that if there is major legislation in the next year or so, we are unlikely to revisit this issue again for some time. If that is the case, major reforms that could improve Medicare deserve attention.

The Importance of Medicare

Medicare serves those most in need of medical care—the elderly and disabled. It remains one of the most popular federal programs, having changed little in its first 27 years. But this important program also carries a substantial price tag; spending in 1993 totaled about $144 billion for 34 million enrollees. Expenditures of over $4,000 per enrollee accounted for over 18 percent of total spending on health services.[1] As a large and visible part of our health care system, Medicare's importance should not be underestimated.

Medicare as a Provider of Mainstream Services

At its passage in 1965, the overriding goal of the Medicare program was to assure access to mainstream care for persons over the age of 65. The elderly were underserved by the health care system, largely because many older persons could not afford care. Insurance coverage as a part of retirement benefits was often the exception, not the rule.[2] Moreover, private insurance companies had shown a reluctance to offer coverage to older persons, even when they could afford it. Even in the 1960s, risk selection was a barrier to achieving broad coverage. In the early part of the decade, the country began to separate into two camps, the health care haves and have-nots, as defined by access to insurance protection. The elderly comprised a disproportionate share of the have-nots.

Strong opposition to a public program by groups like the American Medical Association meant that most of the attention was devoted to allaying fears about government control. Consequently, the rules established to govern Medicare did little to disrupt or change the way that health care was practiced or financed in the United States. Claims processing resembled the method used in the private sector, and Medicare statutes specifically assured free choice of provider and no interference in the routine practice of medicine. Payment rates also were similar to those followed by the private sector, both in the mechanics and the level of remuneration. Physician and other provider groups would at least not be put at a financial disadvantage if they participated in the new program.

By most accounts, Medicare achieved the goal of improved access to health care for the nation's elderly and disabled. Boycotts, which had been threatened by groups of health care providers, did not take place. By 1970, Medicare had enrolled nearly all of the elderly, and after 1972 it added a substantial number of disabled people.[3] However, the relative success of the program contributed to a rapid growth in federal costs, thus ushering in the second phase of Medicare—a concern for cost containment. Attention turned to restraining the growth in program spending.

While critics are quick to point out Medicare's rapid growth, which has outpaced all cost projections, they ignore the fact that this was not the most important element of Medicare in the early years. When attention did turn to costs in the late 1970s, Medicare continued to grow faster than the rest of the system, perhaps in part because of the program's unique aspects, which will be discussed below. But in the late 1980s, Medicare's rate of spending growth declined faster than the rate of health care spending for the entire population, as indicated in Figure 9.1.[4] Thus, even in the area of cost containment, Medicare deserves more credit than its critics often allow.

Positive Lessons from Medicare

Over the last 27 years, Medicare has had a considerable record of success that offers some positive lessons for those who would reform the health care system. While the Clinton Administration's proposal consciously takes an approach quite different from Medicare, many others have incorporated pieces of the program into their proposals, particularly the benefit package and some of the cost-containment mechanisms.

One of the most important lessons of Medicare is that government programs can be viewed favorably by the population they serve and by the public-at-large. In general, Medicare is well liked by its beneficiaries and has significantly enhanced their economic well-being and access to mainstream health care. Medicare is consistently rated as one of the most valued government programs, its benefits are clear and highly visible, and it is supported by a dedicated revenue source that constitutes a popular means of financing. Despite the Clinton Administration's skepticism about a publicly funded "single-payer" system, Medicare demonstrates that such a program can operate successfully in the United States.

Medicare's innovations include new payment mechanisms for providers, and while hospital administrators and physicians have grumbled about the changes, they have generally adjusted quickly to these new incentives. As a result, Medicare has been relatively successful in holding down costs, particularly those of hospital services in the late 1980s. The prospective payment system for hospitals has been widely accepted as an improvement over the old cost-based method. It changed the basic incentives which guided hospitals and made them more conscious of ways to improve efficiency. In addition, the new Medicare fee schedule for physicians, while controversial, is likely to become a standard for physician payment.[5]

These two reform efforts, particularly hospital reform, reflected major changes in the way payments were made and required new accounting systems and behavioral responses to the new incentive structures. While not all the responses were positive, the delivery of health care did change rapidly. For example, the average number of days in a hospital stay dropped dramatically when hospitals were paid on a per case rather than per diem basis.[6] While a study of the response to these hospital reforms uncovered some problems, particularly regarding patient stability upon discharge, it concluded that quality was not seriously compromised.[7]

Figure 9.1: Ratio of Per Capita Medicare Benefits to Per Capita Spending on Health

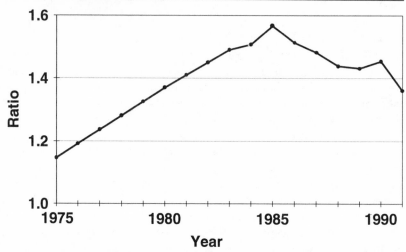

Year

Source: U.S. Congress, Committee on Ways and Means, <u>1993 Green Book: Overview of Entitlement Programs</u> (Washington D.C., USGPO, July 7, 1993).

Overall, these transitions suggest that the health care system can respond to change without experiencing significant disruption of services or quality of care.

Finally, one of the major Medicare successes is its low administrative overhead, which accounts for less than 3 percent of spending compared to about 10 percent for private health insurance for large groups and as much as 40 percent in the small-group market.[8] Proponents of a completely public system of health care use these administrative cost differences to calculate what could be saved by moving away from private insurance. While these comparisons can be overblown (and admittedly, Medicare is sometimes faulted for too little beneficiary service), Medicare administration is often cited as a positive model for the rest of our health care system.

Unique Issues Confronting Medicare

Medicare differs from other parts of our health care system in a number of aspects which pose unique challenges for reform and may argue for some special considerations, especially regarding cost containment. First, as a publicly funded program, Medicare is vulnerable to the pressures of budget reduction efforts. And although public financing may increase support for tighter restraints on Medicare than on the rest of the health care system, there are major factors that boost the costs of the program—the demands on services near the end of life, the aging population, advancing technology, and the consequences of omitting long-term care services from Medicare. These constraints need to be considered when assessing how Medicare should be treated relative to the rest of the health care system, particularly with regard to expected rates of growth.

The Special Pressures on a Public Program

Relative to total health care costs, Medicare performed rather well in the 1980s, but it is still viewed as a runaway line item in the federal budget. Since Medicare is funded with tax dollars in an era of anti-tax sentiment, it gets more scrutiny than health expenditures paid for by individuals or businesses. Moreover, its absolute size and rate of growth distinguish it from most other domestic programs. In the 1970s Medicare accounted for only 3.5 percent of the federal budget; by 1990, it consumed 8.6 percent. Even with the cuts instituted in 1993, Medicare's budget share in 1995 will likely total more than 11 percent.[9] In the view of many policymakers, Medicare may be crowding out expenditures on other domestic programs and/or standing in the way of curbing the overall growth in federal outlays. Critics often argue that Americans will only accept a certain level of public spending, so if Medicare grows rapidly, it hurts other programs even if it has its own revenue source. This alone makes it a potential mark for budget reduction.

The most recent example of Medicare as a target is the Penny-Kasich budget amendment. Offered in the fall of 1993, it aimed to further slash Medicare spending by $37 billion for the purpose of reducing the deficit.[10] This cut would have come over and above the $56 billion, five-year savings included in the Omnibus Budget Reconciliation Act (OBRA) of 1993. The Penny-Kasich amendment failed by just a few votes in the House of Representatives; similar measures will likely surface in the 1995 budget cycle regardless of the status of health care reform.

A second fiscal pressure faced by Medicare is linked with the status of the Hospital Insurance (HI) trust fund. Current law provides a fixed source of funding for HI, and these revenues are not growing as fast as the level of spending, thus creating a likely future crisis when the trust funds are exhausted. That day of reckoning has been postponed several times, thanks to cost-cutting efforts and an increase in the wage base subject to taxation. The last formal projection placed the trust fund's expiration at 1999,[11] but that will probably be delayed for a few years by the OBRA 1993 provisions. Thus even strong supporters of the Medicare program face the prospect of further alterations involving either an increase in the payroll tax rate devoted to Medicare or a reexamination of the program itself.

In addition to these budget pressures, Medicare is treated to the same skepticism about government spending that affects Americans' view of all public programs. There is a perception that, because it is a government program, Medicare is by definition bureaucratic and wasteful. In fact, the evidence suggests that while Medicare is not perfect, in some cases its shortcomings may stem more from too little spending on administration rather than too much. For example, complaints about poor services and program complexity may result in part from tight claims-processing budgets. (As mentioned above, Medicare administrative costs are comparatively low.)

Under the reform proposals of the Clinton Administration and others that rely on a private/public system of financing, Medicare would retain its unique position as a highly visible public program, while the rest of the system would essentially be kept "off budget." Medicare is thus more likely to be a target in each fiscal year's budget, over and above proposals designed to restrain health care spending. Ironically, for some of the reasons detailed below, Medicare spending may be more difficult to control than other types of health spending.

The End of Life

Since Medicare covers the population over the age of 65, and since most Americans now live into their 70s and 80s, many who die each year were Medicare beneficiaries. Medical expenses in the last year of life are quite high on average, resulting in high average spending levels for Medicare. Average acute care spending for persons over age 65 is about 3.8 times as great as that for those under age 65, and Medicare expenditures on behalf of the disabled are even higher than those for elderly beneficiaries.[12] Many casual observers suggest that controlling the use of services in the last year of life may be the "magic bullet" needed to control health care spending. But like most "magic bullets" aimed at the health care system, there is more to the story than just excessive spending on hopeless cases. For instance, are we devoting an increasing share of health resources in vain attempts to forestall death, often through use of new technology? Certainly, few numbers sound as compelling as the widely quoted statistic that 28 percent of Medicare spending went to the 5 percent of enrollees living their last year of life.[13] Such statistics are cited by those who believe that a key to controlling health care costs will be to limit spending on the very old.

But a careful look at the data suggests that the answer is not nearly so simple. First, if technology is being used extensively in futile cases involving the very old, the share of resources devoted to health care in the last year of life should be rising. The evidence, however, does not support this claim. Anne Scitovsky discovered that high expenditures were not a new phenomenon; in fact, they preceded Medicare's introduction in 1965. More recently, Lubitz, updating an earlier study, found that between 1976 and 1985, a period of enormous cost growth in health care, there was no increase in the share of Medicare resources going to those in the last year of life.[14] The proportion of decedents increased slightly but the proportion of Medicare dollars fell slightly.

Further disaggregation of Medicare data also reinforces this analysis. Looking at Medicare expenditures by age, the familiar pattern of more spending on the very old emerges again (Figure 9.2), thus seeming to support claims about disproportionate spending on the very old. However, the data show exactly the opposite pattern for persons in their last year of life, with considerably more spent on 65 to 69 year olds who died than on decedents over age 85. That is, more is spent on younger Medicare beneficiaries who are more likely to recover—a result consistent with reasonable health care policy. Since life expectancy at age 65 is now about 17 years, spending on the younger old is not necessarily just "cheating death" for a few months, but rather treating patients with many useful years left.[15]

These findings suggest several important points. First, physicians do not always know that death is imminent when making health care spending decisions. And since people often die after being ill or requiring medical treatment, it is only natural to see extraordinary health care spending for those in the last year of life, as well as for those who survive a major illness. More appropriately stated, the issue is whether or not we spend inordinately on those with no chance of survival, and whether such outlays contribute substantially to the boom in health care spending. Here the evidence is much weaker. Compared to the young, there does seem to be a dip in spending on the very old in their last year of life, suggesting that decisions are being made to resist heavy acute care expenditures.

The dilemma of excessive use of medical care by the elderly thus is overstated. Probably the most that can be said is that we should expect expenditures to be high for those who are gravely ill and at risk of death. Certainly, some things could be done to try to reduce these expenditures, but quick and dirty solutions are probably not the answer for Medicare or the rest of the health care system. However, Medicare does face some unique challenges in assessing inappropriate care and in finding ways to manage a disproportionate number of high cost cases.

Figure 9.2: Per Capita Medicare Spending by Age as Compared to Overall per Capita Medicare Spending

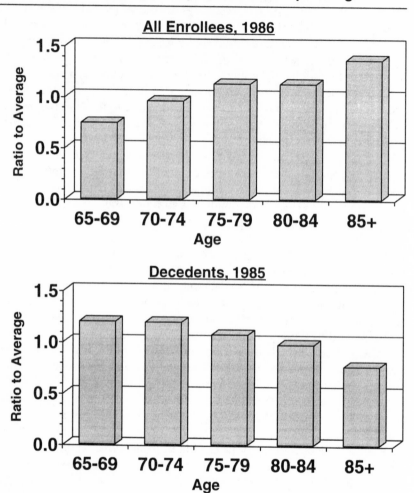

Sources: U.S. Department of Health and Human Services, Health Care Financing Administration, Medicare and Medicaid Data Book, 1990, HCFA Pub. 03314 (Washington D.C., USGPO, 1991); and James Lubitz Use and Costs of Medicare Services in the Last Year of Life, 1976 and 1985 (mimio, Baltimore, May 11, 1990).

The Aging Population

It is not just end-of-life spending that leads to higher costs for Medicare than for the rest of the population. The number of Medicare enrollees is growing at a faster rate than the population in general, and most of that growth is occurring among the very old who have higher than average levels of expenditure. As a result, we should expect more rapid growth per capita, as well as on a population basis.

The aging of the population probably adds about 1 percentage point to the growth of Medicare spending each year relative to the rest of the population.[16] This is not a large amount, but it will become more significant as pressures rise to hold down the cost of care. And it means that just to keep Medicare on an even footing with the rest of the health care system, spending growth per capita should be higher for Medicare.

The Role of Technology

One of the significant pressures on health care spending arises from the use of new technology, but these pressures may be disproportionately large for the Medicare population. Technology has given us new tools such as computerized tomography (CT) scans and magnetic resonance imagers (MRIs), and new procedures such as endoscopies and arthroscopies. These new sources of health care spending tend to operate as extra goods and services consumed rather than as replacements for old technologies or procedures. For example, people may now receive x-rays, CT scans *and* MRIs to diagnose a problem where before only x-rays (and perhaps exploratory surgery) were available. And it is now as easy to subject a blood sample to 30 or 40 different tests as it is to one. These new technologies are often less invasive, and consequently less risky, than earlier means of detecting illness. For example, an MRI is often safer than exploratory surgery for many older or disabled patients. Thus it is no surprise that these new tests constitute the fastest rising categories of services under Medicare.[17]

Although increasingly more complex and expensive over time, the use of surgery and other technical procedures also continues to grow. For example, cardiac bypass surgery rates for men over the age of 65 rose from 2.6 per 1,000 in 1980 to 10.4 per 1,000 in 1989.[18] The increasing success rates for procedures such as hip replacement and cataract surgery translates to lower surgical risks and improved outcomes. In such cases, higher rates of use would certainly be appropriate since the value of these procedures to individuals has increased over time. And again, lower risks mean that older or disabled patients are particularly more likely to benefit. It should not be surprising then that cost of care for these groups is rising rapidly.

With such changes pervading the U.S. health care system, technology may have an even greater impact on Medicare spending and rates of service use within the older population. The combination of an aging population and the special benefits of new technology for frail populations underscores the belief that Medicare will have difficulty holding down its rate of growth, both absolutely and relative to the rest of the population.

The Challenges Posed by the Need for Long-Term Care

Although Medicare covers only acute care services, recipients are also likely to need long-term care. Because such services are expensive and public coverage is limited to the welfare-based Medicaid program, available acute care services may be substituted for inadequate long-term care. As the major insurer affected, Medicare likely has higher costs as a result of this misuse. For example, Medicare's home health benefit is intended to provide rehabilitation and other medical services, but it may also serve as a long-term home care benefit. Rapid growth in home health care since eligibility regulations were eased in 1989 may be attributable to its increasing use as a chronic care, as well as an acute care, benefit.[19] Pressures to use skilled nursing facility beds to meet long-term care needs also have helped raise Medicare spending, particularly since 1988. And before hospital reforms shortened lengths of stay, Medicare often paid for extra inpatient days while patients waited for nursing home placement.

Expansion of long-term care coverage merits more careful analysis, and any revision should be well-coordinated with other reforms. While improved long-term care coverage makes sense for meeting the needs of the elderly and disabled and to reduce inappropriate reliance on acute care services, its prohibitive costs probably preclude significant relief in this area. However, if little expansion of long-term care is included in reform, the pressures to misuse Medicare will persist.

The Lack of an Integrated Approach in Reform Options

One of the most troubling aspects of the Clinton Administration's health care reform proposal is its attempt to establish an elaborate new structure for young, nondisabled families and individuals while keeping Medicare a separate program.[20] But the Clinton proposal should not be singled out for criticism; except for the single-payer approach of Senator Wellstone and Congressman McDermott, the other major reform proposals now being debated would also keep Medicare separate while cutting its expenditures. There are two compelling reasons for this: (1) the strong, early signals from interest groups that Medicare beneficiaries did not want their program to be part of this new "experiment," and (2) the costs of fully integrating Medicare with the rest of the plan.

Nevertheless, the separation is likely to create at least the *perception* of inequity and to generate undesirable complications. Once the reality of the discrepancy in benefits and cost sharing is realized by Medicare beneficiaries, there will likely be an enormous outcry. The Clinton approach to reform also maintains, and perhaps enlarges, a "wedge" between what Medicare and the proposed insurance purchasing alliances for younger families would pay for physician, hospital and other services. This arises from the use of Medicare savings to help fund expansions in the rest of the program. Any modification of these two parts of the Clinton proposal would be enormously expensive, however. Consequently, the costs of full integration into a single health care system might require some changes that Medicare beneficiaries would find undesirable, such as greater contributions toward the cost of expanded care.

Perceived Inequities

Although the Clinton proposal would improve benefits under the Medicare program by adding new prescription drug coverage, beneficiaries are likely to compare their benefit package to that guaranteed to younger families and individuals. What they will soon discover is that while the list of benefits is comparable, required deductibles and protections for catastrophic expenses are more generous in the Clinton proposal. The benefit package for those in the alliances is intentionally established to be equal to or better than 80 percent of existing private, employer-sponsored plans. This was done to replicate or improve the coverage of working families and thus gain middle-class support. But because reform would enrich insurance coverage for many Americans, basic coverage for the under-65 population would exceed protections for the disabled and for those over 65 in the two areas of deductibles required before benefits and limits on out-of-pocket expenses would begin (referred to as "stop loss" protections). Medicare currently has no stop loss protection, while the Clinton plan provides a $1,500 limit per individual. Moreover, one of Medicare's weaknesses is its complicated deductible and cost-sharing structure. Beneficiaries now pay a $676 hospital deductible (with the chance of more than one such charge per year) and a $100 deductible for physician and ambulatory services. This compares to a $200 deductible for all services under the Clinton proposal.[21]

Thus, one of the great ironies of this plan is that despite $65 billion in proposed new spending on the Medicare prescription-drug benefit in the first five years of implementation, and about $64 billion in new monies for long-term care that would largely go to the Medicare population, there will likely be complaints from beneficiaries over both the diminished generosity of Medicare relative to the under-65 plan, and new cost-sharing requirements for drugs, home health care, and laboratory services. Supporters of the Administration's proposal can rightly claim that there would be substantial improvements in benefits under Medicare; but this may afford little solace to those who will strenuously object to a less-generous benefit package for persons who need coverage the most.

The problem would be most visible for those turning 65 after health reform begins under the Clinton proposal. Becoming Medicare eligible would mean choosing between lower benefits under Medicare or substantially higher premiums in an alliance. This discontinuity between the alliance system and Medicare would dramatically highlight the two-tiered system created by the proposal. This awkward transition mechanism is a major weakness of the Administration's plan.

The Medicare "Wedge"

Medicare's current payment levels are lower than the amount allowed by most private insurers. Indeed, much criticism has been leveled at the current system over "cost shifting"—the process which results in some private payers being charged more to help compensate providers for the low payment levels of Medicare and Medicaid. Under the Clinton proposal, Medicaid beneficiaries would receive a health security card exactly like that given to workers; doctors and hospitals would receive the same payments for these patients regardless of who helps to pay for their insurance. Only Medicare would have a completely separate payment system. Because Medicare payments are now substantially below those for the private sector,[22] and since both Medicare and the rest of the system would experience stringent limits on spending growth, a payment differential would initially be "locked in place" at the outset of reform. This effectively institutionalizes "cost shifting."

The Administration contends that, because there is no current problem with providers refusing to take Medicare patients, this payment differential can be maintained until payments for the rest of the system are brought into line with Medicare.[23] It is anticipated that payments and fees in the alliance plans would be rapidly reduced, but it is difficult to determine with certainty what would happen. First, while the differential as a proportion of payment might remain the same, if both Medicare and other payment levels come down over time, providers may not view such changes as business as usual. Providers who feel squeezed from all sides may favor non-Medicare patients for whom fees are not as low. The current cost-shifting "cushion" provided by generous payments to private-sector providers would be reduced. In such circumstances, providers might not be as willing to overlook the differential.

Second, while limits on Medicare growth are intended to be slightly higher than limits on premium growth in alliance plans, the rates of growth are not very different. The Administration's stated goal is to reduce the differential to 0.5 percentage points. Consequently, it would take many years for this mechanism to yield similar payment levels. For example, if payments in Medicare were 80 percent of the level of the alliance sector, and Medicare payment rates rose at 6 percent per year compared to 5 percent per year for alliance plans, it would take about 25 years to equalize the payment levels.

It is even possible that the "wedge" between payment levels might acutally force them further apart. If this happens, specific reductions in payment levels for Medicare could be enacted into law, or cost containment in the rest of the system might be enforced by caps on the rate of premium growth so fees might not be as directly affected. Whether payment rates will converge depends on how alliance plans reduce costs. Some of the claims about obtaining savings in alliance plans emphasize greater efficiencies in the delivery of care and lower administrative costs. If that occurs, payment levels could remain higher for alliances than for Medicare indefinitely, and the percentage gap might actually widen. On the other hand, by obtaining provider discounts managed care plans have had great success in holding down costs.

The provider-payment differential creates a problem only if it affects patients' access to care. While an undetermined amount of discrimination may occur, the differential could reduce access to care if, for example, doctors refuse to accept new Medicare patients. And the entire health care system could be affected if hospitals that serve a disproportionate share of Medicare patients become trapped in such a tight financial bind that they are forced to close. If this occurs in underserved areas, all patients, not just Medicare beneficiaries, would suffer.

Meeting the Challenges

Even if Medicare remains largely intact after reforms in other parts of the system, the program needs to be coordinated with the imminent cost-cutting alterations in coverage for those under 65 years old. Including Medicare in reform could also offer an opportunity to treat all groups fairly and to reduce or eliminate distinctions based on age. These changes would substantially raise the cost of any reform option, however. If Medicare were included in overall reform, it would be reasonable to also raise contributions from beneficiaries and, ultimately, to subject Medicare to the same cost containment methods used in the rest of the system.

The Benefits Structure

Ideally, the generosity of basic benefits under reform would be balanced between Medicare and the rest of the system. Prescription drug coverage, preventive services, and stop-loss protections are considered essential elements of reform under most plans, but not all of these would be added to Medicare. For example, the Clinton proposal would only expand coverage for prescription drugs.[24]

In the interest of fairness, Medicare enrollees should be treated the same as younger insured groups, perhaps not in terms of identical benefits, but at least through consistent criteria. And in instances where cost is an issue, it would be more equitable to cover fewer expanded benefits for everyone than to offer enhanced coverage only to the young, while arguing that a lack of funding makes the same package unavailable for Medicare beneficiaries.

One of the most troubling omissions for Medicare beneficiaries is the lack of stop-loss protection for limiting catastrophic burdens. Although stop-loss protection was undervalued by the elderly when it was provided in the Medicare Catastrophic Coverage Act (later repealed), it is part of any good insurance program and should be provided under Medicare. However, this is one area where a case might be made for a different limit for older persons than for the young on grounds of expense. A larger proportion of Medicare beneficiaries will exceed the upper limit on cost sharing than will nondisabled individuals under the age of 65, consequently, the same stop-loss limits would benefit more elderly than young persons. On the other hand, if stop-loss limits were expressed as a share of income, the elderly and disabled need as much or more protection than others in the U.S. Making treatment "consistent" may imply different rules depending upon one's starting assumptions. But the decision would be very important because of the high potential costs. For example, if the stop loss were set at $1,500 (the level in the Clinton proposal), Medicare costs would rise by at least $10 to $12 billion per year.[25]

Premiums and Cost Sharing

Expanding Medicare coverage to be consistent with coverage for the young would require additional resources. Therefore, it is not only reasonable, but equitable, to include the elderly and disabled in revenue raising for such expansions. At present, Medicare's required premium is 25 percent of the cost of Part B (physicians') services. If viewed in the context of all Medicare spending, premiums now total only about 10 percent of costs.[26] Contributions by working families would be set at about 20 percent in the Clinton proposal. Thus, it may be reasonable to substantially raise the premium on the basic program, as well as to assess a premium contribution for any expanded benefits.

Asking that Medicare beneficiaries contribute to the program on the basis of ability to pay would represent another change consistent with health care reform for working-age families. Premium requirements under many proposals vary by income, and it makes sense to change Medicare in that direction as well. In fact, tying Medicare reform to health care reform for the under-65 population may lower one of the major obstacles to more progressive financing of Medicare. That is, one of the objections to the Medicare Catastrophic Coverage Act was that a small group of the elderly and disabled were being asked to subsidize the poor in their own group. When the entire population is involved and new financing mechanisms are being considered, it will likely be easier to make the case for fairness and spread the responsibility across all age groups so that no one group feels overburdened.

Medicare cost sharing is also imbalanced—for example, deductibles are unusually high for hospitals and nursing facilities and low for physician services. Hospital care deductibles do little to discipline use of services and, at $676 in 1993, the deductible is well above that found in private plans. A higher deductible on physicians' services (or a combined deductible) could help control the use of physician services and would not be unduly harsh. Cost-sharing for home health services, which are growing very rapidly, may be in order. In this area, even a cost-neutral change—raising some cost-sharing requirements while lowering others—would lead to better coordination with benefits for younger families and a more rational cost-sharing policy.

Improved protection for those with low and moderate incomes should occur simultaneously with changes in cost sharing. Those with modest incomes now have difficulty paying Medicare's cost sharing, thus reducing their access to the program. The Qualified Medicare Beneficiary (QMB) program now pays the premiums, deductibles and coinsurance of Medicare beneficiaries whose incomes are below poverty. By 1995, it will also cover premiums for those with incomes of up to 120 percent of poverty. QMB protection should extend beyond the poverty line, particularly if protections for younger families are established at 150 percent of the poverty level.

The Clinton proposal does provide some changes in what Medicare beneficiaries would pay, including adding coinsurance for home health care and laboratory services and a new income-related premium for persons with incomes over $90,000.[27] But these changes are part of the $124 billion in savings aimed at funding not only the new prescription drug benefit but also expansions elsewhere in the system. More generous treatment of Medicare benefits might thus require even more dramatic increases in premiums and cost sharing.

Cost Containment Reforms

Cost containment mechanisms, to be effective and to reduce complexity in administration, ought to be applied equally throughout our health care system. The most obvious example is payment of providers. If there are limits on payment or volume of services allowed, the rules should apply equally across all payers of health care. This would mean that providers cannot shift costs from one source of payment to another. For example, as a result, providers would have to seek greater efficiencies in the provision of care, rather than charging private insurers more to make up for Medicare's restrictive payments. Or, in the case of the various proposals for reform which continue a differential between Medicare and other payers, the differential may lead to discrimination against Medicare beneficiaries. Cost shifting is undesirable currently and locking it in place for Medicare for the purpose of saving federal dollars does not make good policy sense.

On the other hand, moving Medicare immediately into a managed competition framework would create disruption and uncertainty that many advocates of reform wish to avoid. Consequently, most proposals leave out Medicare and assume it will continue to operate much as it does now. But, if we move to a system of managed competition for the working-age population where private insurers make arrangements with health care providers individually and with no overall controls, Medicare could be caught in the bind of being out of sync with the rest of the system. Its current low payment levels (from 25 to 40 percent below the current private sector) could mean that beneficiaries will find it increasingly difficult to obtain care from providers of their choice. Moreover, it is possible, for example, that many providers would join formal network delivery systems and thus limit their availability to Medicare patients. Medicare, as a fee-for-service model and with strict price limits on its providers, would subject elderly and disabled beneficiaries to a system very different from one that emphasizes organized delivery systems. Thus, even if Medicare is kept on a separate track, changes in the delivery system for the rest of the population will certainly affect how beneficiaries receive care as well.

The application of practice guidelines or limits on ineffective treatments will also be substantially more effective if done in a concerted way. Since such activities will be most effective if they change the attitudes of both providers and patients, efforts to influence practice must be viewed as a systemwide activity and not just a gimmick by one public program to hold down its own costs. Patients are more likely to accept constraints if they feel they are equitably applied rather than being part of a group which has been singled out for special treatment. It is easier to make the case that a change will lead to better health care if it is applied to everyone. And certainly to hold down Medicare's costs over time will require close scrutiny of the *use* of services in addition to limiting the payment levels for providers.

Thus, one necessary step for successfully implementing the "next generation" of cost restraint will likely be the presence of more universal controls and coordination. Otherwise, Medicare may suffer. Including Medicare in the broad strategy for reform is likely a desirable approach, as long as it allows a gradual transition to managed care.

Administrative Streamlining

Another change that might initially add to Medicare's costs, but should improve the efficiency of the system over time, would be administrative streamlining. Simplified billing and administration of Medicare could substantially improve the program in the eyes of beneficiaries and providers. And, almost by definition, it makes sense to do this in conjunction with changes in the rest of the system. Medicare beneficiaries (along with all other Americans) could be given a card to be presented to providers. *All* billing could be done via the card so that beneficiaries would not have to file separately or handle multiple forms. The government could require that all doctors use the same forms for billing patients, thus ensuring uniformity. Imagine an environment in which the patient presents a card to the physician in the same way they now use credit cards. A simple computer link would provide information on how much would be paid by insurance and how much would be owed by the patient in the same way that merchants now run the card through a scanner to obtain approval. Separate insurance claim would be unnecessary—the physician would only have to complete a simple form signed by the patient concerning what services were delivered, and the system could track use of health services in a uniform way. It could track the plans and requirements of multiple insurers as well, much like the system that accepts credit cards regardless of type or issuer.

Beneficiaries could receive one or two bills per month and would pay just once per month for any cost sharing owed. Clear language would indicate what Medicare contributes—helping to underscore the substantial amount that Medicare provides—and what is paid by private insurers. Streamlining the billing process could lead to administrative savings, both in terms of lower health care spending, and by saving time and frustration for patients and health care providers.

Conclusion

At first glance, leaving Medicare largely out of the process of health care reform seems to make sense. The program already guarantees nearly universal coverage for all persons over age 65 and most long-term disabled persons. It is a popular and stable program. And since health care reform poses many daunting problems and promises to disrupt the system for many, why add Medicare at this time? The answer is that there undoubtedly will be enormous pressure from interest groups to add the same benefits guaranteed to everyone else and there are strong practical reasons to make cost containment efforts apply to everyone. The uneasy relationships that would result from keeping Medicare separate suggest a very unstable environment for achieving the broad goals of health care reform. But better integration of Medicare would make it more difficult to keep the costs of reform "off the books." Beneficiaries and/or taxpayers would have to be asked to directly contribute more. Unfortunately, the current environment for reform may preclude a careful debate over the dilemma that Medicare poses for reform.

Notes

1. U.S. Congress, House Committee on Ways and Means, *1992 Green Book: Background Material and Data on Programs Within the Jurisdiction of the Committee on Ways and Means* (Washington, D.C.: U.S. Government Printing Office, June 1992).

2. Karen Davis and Cathy Schoen, *Health and the War on Poverty: A Ten-Year Appraisal* (Washington: The Brookings Institution Press, 1978).

3. Robert Myers, *Medicare* (Homewood, IL: Richard D. Irwin, Inc., McCahan Foundation Book Series, 1970).

4. Marilyn Moon, *Medicare Now and in the Future* (Washington, D.C.: Urban Institute Press, 1993).

5. Physician Payment Review Commission, *Annual Report to the the Congress* (Washington, D.C.: U.S. Government Printing Office, 1993).

6. U.S. Department of Health and Human Services, National Center for Health Statistics (NCHS), *Health, United States, 1990* (Hyattsville, MD: Public Health Service, 1991).

7. Katherine Kahn, Lisa V. Rubenstein, David Draper, Jacqueline Kosecoff, William H. Rogers, Emmett B. Keeler, and Robert H. Brook, "The Effects of the DRG-Based Prospective Payment System on Quality of Care for Hospitalized Medicare Patients," *Journal of the American Medical Association* 264 (1990): 1953–1955.

8. Congressional Research Service, *Health Insurance and the Uninsured: Background Data and Analysis*, Senate Committee on Education and Labor, Print 100-2, 122–23, 1989.

9. Ways and Means, *Green Book.*

10. Penny/Kasich Bipartisan Task Force, *A Common Cents Plan*, Washington, D.C., mimeo, October 27, 1993.

11. Board of Trustees, Federal Hospital Insurance Trust Fund, *1993 Annual Report of the Board of Trustees of the Hospital Insurance Trust Fund* (Washington, D.C.: U.S. Government Printing Office, 1993).

12. Diane Lefkowitz and Alan Monheit, *Health Insurance, Use of Health Services and Health Care Expenditures*, AHCPR Pub. No. 92-0017, National Medical Expenditure Survey Research Findings 12, Agency for Health Care Policy and Research (Rockville, MD: Public Health Service, 1991).

13. James Lubitz and Ronald Prihoda, "Use and Costs of Medicare Services in the Last Two Years of Life," *Health Care Financing Review* 5 (Spring 1984): 117–131.

14. Anne Scitovsky, "The High Cost of Dying: What Do the Data Show?" *Milbank Memorial Fund Quarterly* 62 (1984): 610–615; and James Lubitz, "Use and Costs of Medicare Services in the Last Year of Life, 1976 and 1985," Health Care Financing Administration, mimeo, May 11, 1990.

15. Ways and Means, *Green Book*.

16. Ways and Means, *Green Book*.

17. Robert Berenson and John Holahan, "Sources of Growth in Medicare Physician Expenditures," *Journal of the American Medical Association* 267 (February 1992): 687–691.

18. NCHS, *Health USA*.

19. Moon, *Medicare*.

20. U.S. Congress, Senate, *S. 1757*, Health Security Act, November 1993.

21. U.S. Congress, *Health Security Act*; and Moon, *Medicare*.

22. Mark Miller, Stephen Zuckerman, and Michael Gates, "How do Medicare Physician Fees Compare with Private Payers?" *Health Care Financing Review* 14 (Spring 1993): 25–39.

23. Bruce Vladeck, Department of Health and Human Services, testimony before the Committee on Ways and Means, November 18, 1993.

24. U.S. Congress, *Health Security Act*.

25. Author's calculations using the National Medical Expenditure Survey.

26. Moon, *Medicare*.

27. U.S. Congress, *Health Security Act*.

10

Lessons from the Medicaid Experience

Diane Rowland

Medicaid is the nation's major public financing program for providing health care coverage to low-income families and long-term care to low-income elderly and disabled people. Since its enactment in 1965, this means-tested entitlement program has been on the frontline in meeting the health care needs of our country's most vulnerable citizens. As a safety net for the needy, Medicaid serves one in ten Americans and pays eleven cents of every dollar spent on health care. Though its enactment was a tremendous step forward in financing and providing health care to the poor, Medicaid has been attacked for shortcomings in who it covers, how it serves its beneficiaries, and escalating costs that strain federal and state budgets.

The Medicaid experience teaches us about meeting the health needs of the poor through a separate means-tested program, with eligibility tied to welfare, and a program design that combines federal guidelines and state flexibility. As the nation debates the shape of its health insurance system, an examination of Medicaid's impact on the health care of the poor can provide policymakers with valuable lessons and insights.

The Role and Structure of Medicaid

Although it has traditionally been tied to the welfare categories for coverage of the poor, Medicaid is the country's major program for providing health insurance coverage to the low-income population. Enacted as part of the War on Poverty and as a legislative companion to Medicare, Medicaid has grown to be a major source of health care financing for 30 million low-income Americans.

Prior to Medicaid's passage, the poor were essentially outside mainstream medical care. Individuals who could not afford treatment from private practitioners relied on a meager combination of charity care, public hospitals and clinics, and limited public welfare-based assistance for the financing and provision of health care. The difficulties associated with receipt of care resulted in fewer services being provided to the poor than to the non-poor, despite the former's lower health status.[1]

To remedy these disparities, Medicaid was established to provide health coverage to recipients of welfare assistance who were without traditional employment-based health insurance coverage. Authorized under Title XIX of the Social Security Act, the program was designed as a federal and state partnership to eliminate financial barriers in access to medical care by providing a broad scope of benefits to eligible individuals with limited financial resources.

Medicaid's responsibilities have gradually expanded and become more complex since its beginnings as a health care financing program primarily for welfare recipients. Throughout its history, decisions about the program's scope and the comprehensiveness of its benefits have been continuously pitted against pressures to curb spending. Despite these pressures, Medicaid's thrust and framework have been expanded by incremental reforms that have broadened coverage and extended its impact beyond the traditional welfare population.

Medicaid is today the key provider of health insurance for four very distinct population groups: low-income families lacking insurance; low-income elderly people who need help with filling gaps in Medicare benefits; disabled elderly who need long-term care services; and the non-elderly disabled population who need acute and long-term care services. In 1992, Medicaid served nearly 30 million people. The program is the chief source of health insurance coverage for some 20 million people in low-income families, with one in five children receiving health care coverage through Medicaid. Medicaid also supplements Medicare coverage for roughly four million elderly and disabled persons and is the only substantial source of financial assistance for long-term care provided primarily in nursing homes.[2]

The federal statute requires Medicaid to cover cash assistance recipients under the Aid to Families with Dependent Children (AFDC) program and most aged and disabled recipients of the Supplementary Security Income (SSI) program. As a result, standards and eligibility categories from these cash-assistance programs shape Medicaid's core eligibility rules. The federal government sets broad eligibility criteria specifying what categories of individuals are eligible for federal matching payments. These categories are then further defined by state policy.

To become eligible for Medicaid, an individual must meet categorical, income and asset requirements. In 1992, the income eligibility level for a poor family of three averaged $5,106, or 44 percent of the federal poverty level.[3] These levels vary across states due to state discretion in determining AFDC levels and state flexibility in setting Medicaid eligibility. For the aged, blind, and disabled, federal SSI standards set minimum assistance levels and asset limitations. The federal eligibility level for SSI benefits for eligible individuals is about 75 percent of the federal poverty level.[4]

Federal expansions of program coverage have broadened eligibility beyond the welfare population to include other low-income pregnant women and young children. The Medicaid eligibility level for for pregnancy-related services and for children under the age of six is a family income below 133 percent of the federal poverty level. By 2001, states will have to cover all children under age 19 in families with incomes below the poverty level. The federal government provides states with matching funds for certain other eligibility groups if the state chooses to cover them. One of the major eligibility options is to cover medically needy persons who meet the categorical requirements but have incomes that exceed welfare income levels. States also have the authority to broaden coverage of pregnant women and infants with incomes exceeding the federally-mandated standard of 133 percent of poverty, up to 185 percent of poverty. As of January 1993, 33 states have made use of this option; 24 had set their income limits at the maximum level of 185 percent of poverty.[5]

The Medicaid program covers a wide range of services, furnishing medical services commonly offered through traditional private health insurance to low-income families. Some benefits, such as physician, hospital, and nursing home coverage, are federally mandated for all Medicaid beneficiaries. Others, including prescription drugs, intermediate care facilities for the mentally retarded, and vision care, may be offered at the state's discretion. States are permitted to impose nominal copayments or deductibles for services and to set the amount, duration, and scope of services they will cover.

For the elderly and disabled with Medicare, Medicaid serves the somewhat different function of providing assistance with cost sharing and premium payments under Medicare as well as meeting the long-term care needs of beneficiaries. Medicaid also expands the Medicare benefit package for SSI recipients by covering items such as prescription drugs and dentures.

Medicaid is a major purchaser of health care services. In 1992, the program spent $120 billion—12 percent of the nation's health care spending. The Federal government contributed $66 billion toward the programs's costs while the rest came from the states. The federal share of expenditures for Medicaid services is derived from a formula based on state per capita income. While nearly three-quarters of Medicaid beneficiaries were in low-income families in 1992, they accounted for only a third of program expenditures. The bulk of Medicaid spending (68 percent) is for aged and disabled beneficiaries who have high per capita expenses due to their use of nursing home and institutional care.[6]

Federal guidelines place requirements on states to provide benefits and coverage for specific groups of people, while giving them the option to cover others. Within federal guidelines, each state and the District of Columbia design and administer their own Medicaid program. States are responsible for determining who will be covered, what services will be paid for, how much providers will be paid, and how the program will be administered. As a result, there are essentially 51 similarly structured but differently configured Medicaid programs.

Medicaid's Accomplishments

In its nearly 30 years of operation, Medicaid has much to its credit. It has reshaped the availability and provision of medical care to the poor and, in the absence of alternative insurance, has had a positive effect on health status, access to care, and satisfaction with the health care system. Medicaid is also a source of financial assistance for long-term institutional care, pioneering the development of community-based long-term care systems and new approaches to caring for individuals with severe mental and physical impairments.

These achievements demonstrate the crucial role Medicaid plays in our health care system. Financing care for a poor and diverse population within the constraints of a means-tested eligibility program with a high enrollment turnover rate is a formidable undertaking. Medicaid performs its tasks, which are beyond the scope of private insurers, remarkably well.

Protection for Vulnerable Populations

Medicaid demonstrates the importance of designing flexible program structures and benefits to meet the needs of diverse and complex populations whose health needs extend beyond basic benefits. Medicaid is a safety net for the nation's most vulnerable populations, caring for individuals who would otherwise have few options available to meet their health needs. With Medicaid, poor children and their parents have access to a broad scope of health care benefits, especially important preventive services. Nearly two out of three youngsters in poor families receive Medicaid assistance.[7] In addition, Medicaid makes Medicare work for low-income elderly and disabled beneficiaries who cannot afford Medicare's financial requirements and need benefits that are outside the Medicare package.

In the absence of public or private alternatives, Medicaid has also emerged as our national safety net for long-term care services. Medicaid remains the single source of public assistance for nursing home care. For the disabled who live in the community, Medicaid can be an essential source of a broad array of in-home health and social services that enables them to remain in this setting. States have been forerunners in the design and organization of community-based care systems for the aged and disabled with long-term care needs.

Improved Access

As the primary source of health financing for the poor, Medicaid clearly has shown the importance of insurance in obtaining access to care. Having a source of insurance boosts utilization of health services significantly. Before Medicaid, access to physician and hospital care for the poor lagged considerably behind that of the non-poor. Since the enactment of Medicaid, steady progress in narrowing these gaps in access has occurred.

In 1964, the poor averaged 3.8 physician visits per year compared to 4.7 visits for the non-poor.[8] For people who do see a physician at least once in a year, there is very little difference in the number of visits between those at the low and high ends of the income scale; 6.0 visits and 6.3 visits, respectively. In fact, Medicaid recipients under age 65 with at least one visit in the year actually have a higher mean annual physician visit rate than the non-poor—7.7 physician visits for the non-elderly Medicaid population compared to 6.3 for the non-elderly non-poor population.[9] Children with Medicaid are more likely to have regular physical exams than the non-poor, reflecting the emphasis that Medicaid has placed on preventive care for children.[10]

The higher overall utilization rates for Medicaid beneficiaries reflect the lower health status of that population and the greater proportion of disabled people who are high users of health care services in the Medicaid population compared to the general population. The higher use rates also reflect a comprehensive benefit package and minimal cost-sharing requirements that help promote access to care.

The value of Medicaid is underscored by the contrast in outcomes between the poor with Medicaid and the uninsured poor. For most indicators of access to care, the uninsured lag well behind those with Medicaid or private insurance. The poor with Medicaid coverage are more likely to have seen a physician in the past year and generally see physicians more frequently than the uninsured poor.[11] Women with Medicaid coverage have better access to pregnancy-related services than those without insurance.[12] Among low-income children, the uninsured were less likely to see a physician and averaged one less visit per year than children with Medicaid or private insurance.[13]

Having insurance also helps to promote a regular source of care and the receipt of primary and preventive care. Among low-income families, only 16 percent of insured families, compared to more than a third of the uninsured, report being without a regular source of care.[14] Although they still lag behind the privately insured in terms of the adequacy of prenatal care, women with Medicaid coverage have better access to pregnancy-related services than those without insurance. Poor children with Medicaid are more likely to have regularly scheduled physical examinations and dental care than poor children without Medicaid.[15]

Medicaid has helped break down many of the barriers to care experienced by those without insurance. In a 1993 survey, a third of the uninsured reported that they went without needed care during the past year, compared to only eight percent of those with private insurance and 10 percent of those with Medicaid. Moreover, 71 percent of the uninsured, in contrast to 21 percent of those with private insurance and 28 percent of the Medicaid population, reported that they postponed needed care.[16]

Medicaid also improves access to medical care for the low-income elderly by providing assistance with Medicare's cost-sharing obligations. Those with Medicaid coverage use physician services at rates comparable to elderly people with private insurance to supplement Medicare. The elderly with Medicare only use lower levels of care and are less likely to seek physician care than those with similar health needs and a source of supplementary insurance.[17]

Reduced Financial Burdens

The families who rely on Medicaid are already in a precarious financial situation. A recent Kaiser Family Foundation study showed that nearly half of all adult Medicaid beneficiaries had problems finding a job, nearly one-third had difficulty paying the rent, and more than one-fourth reported problems buying food.[18] Having insurance coverage is one of the highest priorities of the poor because medical expenses, even for routine care, generally exceed their limited disposable income. One in three low-income Americans expressed concern about being able to pay doctor and hospital bills. Paying medical bills was a problem for 22 percent of Medicaid beneficiaries. However, those without insurance faced the most severe financial stress; 40 percent of the uninsured said they had problems finding enough money to pay doctor or hospital bills.

For those with Medicaid coverage, the program offers relatively generous coverage with minimal or no cost sharing, and helps to reduce financial burdens for medical care. By contrast, private insurance coverage is often limited in scope and can require significant enrollee cost sharing in the form of annual deductibles and copayments. For many poor families with private coverage, out-of-pocket expenditures are more likely to limit the amount of preventive services received, as well as result in a greater degree of catastrophic medical burdens than for those with Medicaid protection. Out-of-pocket expenditures for children as a percent of family income were 15 times greater in families below the poverty level without Medicaid coverage as in comparable families with Medicaid.[19]

Medicaid Drawbacks

Medicaid has had many successes in meeting the health needs of the population it serves, but it has also fallen short when measured as a source of comprehensive coverage for the nation's poor. Its reach has been limited by program design—coverage of essentially the welfare population rather than the poverty population—and discretion over eligibility levels by state. Its impact on access to care has similarly shown that Medicaid clearly improves utilization of care by the poor and, most notably, that the poor with Medicaid coverage fare substantially better than the uninsured poor. Yet differentials in access to care continue to exist when comparing the privately-insured non-poor population to the poor with Medicaid.

In assessing the Medicaid experience, it is important to evaluate both the issues related to coverage of a low-income population, including their greater health needs and financial and non-financial barriers to care, as well as the structural framework of Medicaid itself. Both factors are critically important in drawing lessons from the Medicaid experience with regard to coverage of the poor, scope of benefits, access to care, and cost of care that can be applied to reform.

Coverage of the Poor

One of the most persistent criticisms of Medicaid is that it fails to cover everyone in poverty. Nearly 15 percent of all Americans—32 million people—had incomes below the poverty level in 1991 ($10,860 for a family of three). As the safety net to the nation's poor, Medicaid covers only 48 percent of the poverty population under age 65 and 31 percent of the poor over age 65.[20] Nearly 19 million poor Americans are without Medicaid assistance.

By design, Medicaid is a program for targeted groups of the poor, not for the entire impoverished population. The program's structure leaves many needy people outside of its reach. The rules governing Medicaid's operations and the federal-state relationships that determine eligibility, benefits and financing provide coverage only for specific groups of individuals, excluding equally poor individuals who fall outside the groups eligible for federal matching payments.

While the Medicaid program provides a logical financing vehicle for covering the poverty population, the maze of categorical, income, and asset criteria dictating who is eligible keeps many poor people, especially poor single individuals, childless couples, and adults and children in two-parent families, from obtaining coverage. Some are excluded because federal requirements generally limit state matching funds for those eligible for welfare assistance. Therefore, no matter how poor, many adults are excluded since they do not have children. Only by becoming disabled could they qualify for Medicaid assistance.

Others are barred because state income eligibility levels for Medicaid are below the poverty level and asset criteria are highly restrictive. Since Medicaid eligibility levels for low-income families are derived from state-determined AFDC eligibility standards, a state's decision on where to set cash assistance levels makes a major difference in Medicaid eligibility. While the national average in 1992 for Medicaid coverage was 44 percent of poverty, actual Medicaid levels vary by state and are based on AFDC eligibility standards. AFDC eligibility ranged from $1,788 for a three-person family in Alabama to $11,076 in Alaska.[21] No state sets its eligibility income criteria high enough to cover the entire poverty population.

Medicaid is not a universal national program. The state-based nature of the program has resulted in variations in scope of coverage and program benefits. In any given state, the percentage of the population with Medicaid coverage reflects the extent of poverty there, as well as the income and asset requirements for program eligibility. Those living in poorer southern states often face the most stringent income thresholds. As a result, the percent of the poor covered is lowest in the states with the highest poverty.

Access to health care services and the level of services largely depends on the poor person's state of residence and the scope of its Medicaid program. Low-income people receive less care if they reside in states with limited Medicaid programs.[22] Among Medicaid beneficiaries, the average number of visits to physicians is lower for those residing in states with coverage restrictions and benefit limits than for those in states with more generous assistance.[23]

Limitations in Covered Services

The health status of the low-income population is worse than that of people with higher incomes. The association between poverty and poor health is reflected in high rates of acute and chronic conditions among the poor. Heart disease and diabetes are nearly twice as prevalent among the poor as among the non-poor.[24] Poverty is associated with low birthweight, which is a major correlate of infant and childhood mortality.[25] Poor children are also more likely to suffer from conditions associated with impaired mental and physical development, such as high lead concentrations in the blood.[26]

The greater prevalence of these conditions among the poor emphasizes the need for early intervention and education, and for more intensive treatment and follow-up. Medicaid, however, falls short of providing these services in several critical areas. Although the Medicaid benefit package includes a range of services, many beneficiaries are either unaware of available coverage or have difficulty gaining access to services. Providing continuous and coordinated preventive and primary care is further complicated because Medicaid is means-tested, which results in high turn-over rates as economic and family circumstances fluctuate.

Since Medicaid's inception, preventive services have been recognized as a critical benefit for low-income children. With Medicaid's Early and Periodic Screening and Diagnostic Treatment (EPSDT) program, children are guaranteed appropriate preventive services to meet their medical needs, but not all eligible youngsters are enrolled. For too many children on Medicaid, EPSDT is a key that is not being used to open the door to comprehensive benefits.

For adults, preventive and primary care services are increasingly recognized as an important component of the benefit package. Although the poor suffer from many conditions that are responsive to early detection and treatment, such as breast and cervical cancer, they have less access to early care. Though most state Medicaid programs cover pap smears and mammographies, access to services is often limited by providers' unwillingness to furnish care at Medicaid's low payment levels. Among adults, women with household incomes below $10,000 were consistently less likely than wealthier women to have had both a Pap smear to detect cervical cancer and a breast exam or mammogram to detect breast cancer.[27]

Limitations in Access to Care

Medicaid is a major purchaser of physician, hospital, and nursing home services for its beneficiaries, but its impact on the health care market differs substantially by provider type. Despite sizable expenditures on care for the poor, Medicaid accounts for only 11 percent of personal health care spending on hospitals and 4 percent of spending on physicians. In contrast, Medicaid paid 45 percent of the $53 billion spent on nursing home care for the elderly and disabled in 1990.[28] This, plus the absence of other third-party purchasers, makes the program a dominant force in the nursing home market. Medicaid has less leverage with physicians and hospitals because of its limited market share. As a result, payment policies have often created barriers to access to mainstream medical care for some Medicaid beneficiaries. This is particularly a problem with access to private physicians, an area where states have had the broadest discretion over payment levels. Within federal guidelines, states determine the method of payment and the amount they will pay for physician services to Medicaid beneficiaries. Participating providers must accept the state reimbursement for care as payment in full and cannot charge beneficiaries additional fees.

Compared with Medicare and private insurers, states have paid physicians lower rates for similar services under Medicaid. For example, Medicaid's payment level for a routine office visit averages 60 percent of Medicare. Similarly, Medicaid pays only 60 percent of the private rate for obstetrical care.[29] Due to these low reimbursement levels, Medicaid beneficiaries often face serious difficulties in locating a provider willing to accept Medicaid as a payment source. Physicians often cite billing complexity, inadequate continuity of coverage, and difficult and litigious patients as reasons for not participating in the Medicaid program.

Increasingly, physicians are choosing either to not accept Medicaid patients or to limit the extent of their Medicaid practice. Only about one-third of the nation's physicians participate fully in the program. Roughly another third limit their complement of Medicaid patients, and a quarter report they will not accept Medicaid patients at all. Another 5 percent who see Medicaid patients will not accept any new ones.[30]

This problem is particularly serious for pediatricians and obstetricians/gynecologists, the two specialties whose services are most needed by the women and children in low-income families. Among pediatricians, a specialty group that has had one of the highest Medicaid participation rates, the percentage of doctors limiting their Medicaid caseloads has increased in the past decade. In 1989, 23 percent of pediatricians did not participate in Medicaid at all and another 30 percent limited their practices.[31] With one in five American children receiving health care coverage through Medicaid, non-participation among pediatricians has serious access implications.

To overcome some of the obstacles that beneficiaries face in obtaining care, Congress in 1989 required states to prove that obstetrical and pediatric services are as available to Medicaid beneficiaries as they are to the general population. Many states are boosting reimbursement rates to pediatricians and obstetricians to improve access. Nevertheless, whether payment hikes will increase physician participation remains an open question.

With limited access to private physicians, many Medicaid beneficiaries turn to community health centers and clinics for care. These federally funded centers afford comprehensive care to low-income families and are often the only available source of care in underserved communities. Hospitals, especially public ones, and their out-patient clinics are also vitally important as a source of care to indigents.

Unlike physicians, hospitals do not have the option of refusing to serve Medicaid patients, although lower payment rates may translate to different levels of service for Medicaid patients. Inadequate payment levels may also lead to fiscal strain on particular providers serving a high proportion of low-income and Medicaid patients. Allowance is now made to permit higher payments under Medicaid to hospitals serving a disproportionate share of low-income patients.

Rising Costs

A review of Medicaid's history reveals a program constantly struggling with rising costs. Efforts to curb escalating program costs began as early as 1972 with the repeal of an original provision requiring that Medicaid be comprehensive in scope of services and eligibility for welfare-covered groups by 1975. Throughout its history, there have been repeated cycles of cutbacks in response to fiscal pressure in the states and concern over increasing program costs. Today, Medicaid spending is consuming an expanding share of both state and federal budgets and is cutting into states' ability to finance other important social welfare programs.

Federal and state Medicaid spending has more than doubled in the past four years, increasing from $54 billion in 1988 to $120 billion in 1992. Over this period, total Medicaid spending accelerated sharply with an average annual growth rate of 21.8 percent. From 1990 to 1992, Medicaid spending increased by $43.9 billion, accounting for more than two-thirds of the total Medicaid spending growth over the four year period from 1988 to 1992. Current projections indicate that total Medicaid spending will exceed $140 billion in 1993.[32]

Medicaid's role as a safety net is the chief factor driving Medicaid spending. The single largest contributor to higher spending was increased enrollment, which grew by six million people between 1990 and 1992, and accounted for 41 percent of the rise in payments. Although pregnant women and children made eligible by federal expansions in Medicaid eligibility represented one-third of the growth in enrollees between 1991 and 1992, they accounted for less than six percent of spending growth.[33] Dominating the growth in expenditures is the increase in enrollment-related spending for groups traditionally eligible for Medicaid—low-income families, and aged and disabled beneficiaries. Aged and disabled beneficiaries are particularly costly to cover because they tend to be sicker and use more health services, especially expensive institutional care, than do low-income families.

The pressures to expand the safety net that Medicaid provides to vulnerable populations place the program squarely at the center of the cost control debate. Yet, Medicaid has limited ability on its own to control overall health care cost increases, and when it restricts payment levels in an effort to contain costs, access to care is often reduced. The Medicaid experience demonstrates the importance of applying cost controls to the whole population rather than separately to low-income and publicly supported populations. It also underscores the importance of recognizing that chronically ill and disabled patients are expensive to care for in our health system, and the cost of any program covering their health needs will reflect these higher expenses.

Lessons for Reform

Although Medicaid has made remarkable progress in improving care of the poor, it faces criticism for several key flaws—falling short in covering all of the needy, failing to deliver appropriate services, and lacking control of program costs and financing. Despite the program's accomplishments, beneficiaries appear to experience barriers in obtaining some types of services and in receiving care in the most appropriate setting. Improving access to care for the Medicaid population is constrained by limited physician participation in the program, the reliance of many program beneficiaries on clinics and emergency rooms for care, and the lack of coordination and accountability of services provided under a fee-for-service system. Gaps in continuity of care due to interrupted eligibility for coverage weaken the program's effectiveness in providing primary and preventive care, while reliance on expensive institutional services constrains development of long-term care alternatives in the community.

Medicaid's experience in providing medical care to the poor offers many lessons in serving needy groups. Medicaid has achieved significant advances in financing and providing health care to the poor, and expanded access has resulted in lower mortality and improvements in health. Yet, the program has fallen short of realizing equal access for both the poor and non-poor. Most notably, Medicaid's impact is limited because a significant segment of the poverty population has been legislatively barred from entering the welfare-based program and because coverage varies across states. Progress in eliminating access differentials between the poor with Medicaid and the non-poor has been remarkable, but such improvement has been uneven across the states and has left the uninsured poor behind.

Medicaid's experience is particularly instructive in matters of program design and structure, as well as on access to care. It provides both a working model of a means-tested program jointly administered and financed by the federal and state governments, and a notable contrast to the universal and federally run Medicare program for the elderly and disabled. From this disparity between Medicare and Medicaid, differences in program impact can be evaluated from the perspective of access to care and public support of the program. These lessons can help inform the policy debate over treatment of the low-income population in national health reform.

Implications of a Means-Tested Program

Medicaid is a means-tested program for individuals who fit the welfare-based categories of assistance and meet state-determined income and assets criteria for eligibility. It was not designed to provide health coverage to the entire poverty population. Single individuals, childless couples, and most two-parent families are excluded from coverage, no matter how poor. Once enrolled, coverage is dependent on income eligibility standards, resulting in high turnover of the covered population. Many who are eligible for the program do not enroll because they are either unwilling to apply to a welfare program or are discouraged by procedural and informational barriers. In essence, Medicaid is not a "user-friendly" program.

The Medicare program, which covers the elderly regardless of income, provides a useful comparison to the means-tested Medicaid program. Medicare enrollment is based on eligibility for social security benefits. It is not income tested. Furthermore, it is national in scope and does not vary by state. The Medicare benefit package, as well as provider payment standards, are also constant throughout the country.

When examining the differences between the universal social insurance approach of Medicare and the targeted means-tested approach of Medicaid, it is apparent that the Medicare model offers more positive results in improving access and integrating the poor into the mainstream of medical care than does the Medicaid model. Medicare coverage of all elderly people assures full program participation and provides a broad and powerful constituency to ensure that program benefits are maintained and improved. Conversely, the means-tested and state-financed Medicaid program has been vulnerable to cutbacks and is subjected to habitual political assault.

Under health care reform, eligibility for low-income assistance should be separated from welfare and extended to all individuals based solely on income qualifications. Use of an assets test in addition to income-based eligibility is not necessary because of the close association between low-incomes and limited assets for the non-elderly low-income population.[34]

In addition, the Medicaid experience demonstrates that equitable coverage of the low-income population across states requires federal standards for eligibility to achieve uniformity. Coverage of the poor with sliding-scale assistance for the near-poor can best be achieved with federal standards and financing to eliminate differential policies in the states.

Mainstream Care for Low-Income People

Medicaid was intended to bring the poor into the mainstream of medical care by opening the private marketplace and expanding the range of providers willing to treat the poor.[35] Medicaid financing has clearly helped move many of the poor into more mainstream-care settings by replacing dependence on charity and free care with financial access to both public and private providers. The Medicaid experience shows us that a separate program for the poor inevitably encounters problems in bringing the population it serves into the medical care mainstream. Most notably, when payment policies for the poor lag behind those of other programs and private rates, the poor will not have comparable access to conventional medical care. Under Medicare, with its universal coverage and standard payment rates, low-income and high-income elderly have comparable access to care.

For the non-elderly, access is clearly better for those with Medicaid coverage than for the uninsured, but not to the same sources of care available to the privately insured. Even with Medicaid coverage, the poor still rely much more on emergency rooms, clinics, and the outpatient departments of hospitals for their care than do those with private insurance. Areas where the poor live are often medically underserved and require assistance to develop clinics and other medical resources. Financing alone appears to be insufficient for placing medical resources in most underserved communities.

Under health reform, access to care for the low-income population can best be assured by eliminating separate treatment of the poor. Comparable benefits and payment policies for all individuals, regardless of income, will help assure equitable access by eliminating payment differentials and reducing provider incentives that favor treatment of the non-poor. However, additional outreach efforts, coupled with the development of health resources in the underserved areas where many of the poor live, may still be required to assure equitable access.

Federal and State Governments: Sharing Responsibility

Embodied in the debate over the future of Medicaid and health care for the poor is the relationship between the federal government and the states with regard to program design and financing. The current Medicaid structure provides flexibility for the states to determine income levels and coverage options within federal guidelines for matching funds. Recent federal legislation has begun to limit state flexibility by specifying national income standards for eligibility for specific groups and standardizing coverage for these groups in all states.

The balance between eligibility standardization versus retention of state discretion—which ultimately results in variations in coverage—is a critical aspect of health reform. The Medicaid experience shows that, when given discretion, states will make fundamentally different decisions regarding scope of coverage, benefit package, and provider payment policies. Although such autonomy allows programs to be structured according to state priorities and funding levels, it has also created pressure to shape the program to more common national standards, as reflected in congressional mandates imposed on states in the early 1990s.

From the Medicaid experience, health reform efforts should note that uniformity is more likely to occur if supported by federal dollars. States are increasingly reluctant to accept federally mandated spending requirements. The matching-funds financing of Medicaid creates a constant tension between the states and the federal government over program configuration and direction. Establishing a core of federally financed services with supplemental services provided by the states would clarify lines of responsibility and provide more equity in terms of treatment of the poverty population.

Political Support for Health Care for the Poor

Medicaid enjoys neither popular support nor a strong political constituency. It has come under attack both as an inadequate insurer, from the perspective of the poverty population, and as a costly and growing share of the budget, from the perspective of the state and federal bill payers. The program's welfare base has left it with a weak political constituency and a vulnerability to cutbacks and retrenchment.[36] With few allies and proponents, Medicaid survives mainly because of its critical role in financing indigent care.

In contrast, Medicare, with its universal coverage of the elderly, has enjoyed widespread public support that has often protected the program from cutbacks in service and scope. Programs that serve the poor are more likely to be maintained and adequately funded if they are part of broader initiatives that have a wider base of political support, like Medicare. Separate programs for the poor seem to result in substandard programs for the poor. Broadening the constituency for the needy to include the middle class under health care reform is important for providing full coverage and an adequate benefit structure that is both politically viable and maintainable.

The Clinton Plan: Medicaid and the Low-Income Population

The Clinton health reform plan proposes universal coverage for all U.S. citizens and legal residents through a standard, comprehensive set of medical and health benefits. To assure such coverage, the plan combines two mandates, one requiring all employers to offer and contribute to the cost of health insurance coverage for their employees and dependents, the other requiring all individuals to purchase insurance. Enrollment in a plan would occur primarily through regional health alliances that would negotiate with health plans on behalf of consumers and employers.

Under the Clinton plan, those in the low-income population, like all other Americans, would receive coverage through health plans offered through regional health alliances. The Clinton plan would cause a major restructuring of responsibilities and benefits for the low-income population. Medicaid acute coverage would be replaced by the new system, employer responsibility for their low-income workers and their dependents would increase, and coverage of current Medicaid beneficiaries would be shared by state governments and the new alliances. Long-term care services, as well as coverage of the dual Medicare and Medicaid eligibles, would remain the purview of Medicaid.

The Clinton proposal significantly improves coverage of the low-income population by mandating universal coverage and a standard benefit package. It provides health insurance protection to 36 million uninsured Americans—60 percent of whom have incomes below 200 percent of the poverty level—and eliminates the risk of being uninsured for millions more. Today, one-third of poor Americans and 29 percent of near poor Americans are uninsured—covered neither by Medicaid nor private employer-based insurance. Under the Clinton plan, they will now be covered by their employer or through their regional health alliance.

By providing the poor with the same coverage offered to all Americans, the Clinton approach takes a major step toward accomplishing mainstream medical care access for the low-income population. The poor would be covered just like everyone else; through their employer, if working, or through regional alliance. Most significantly, by providing universal coverage the plan offers protection to the millions of low-income people not eligible for Medicaid. Full protection for all regardless of income, and elimination of a separate program with state variations and payment limits for the poor, would surmount many of the structural problems that have limited Medicaid's effectiveness.

The Clinton plan takes a bold step forward in its commitment to universal coverage and comprehensive benefits, with an emphasis on primary care and preventive services. Full coverage regardless of income level, employment status, or state of residence will end Medicaid's current variations in eligibility and coverage. Bringing all Americans under the same health care umbrella is the first step toward eliminating the inequities of today's health care system.

Notes

1. Karen Davis and Cathryn Schoen, "Health, Use of Medical Care, and Income," in *Health and the War on Poverty: A Ten-Year Appraisal* (Washington, D.C.: Brookings Institution, 1976), pp. 18–48.

2. Kaiser Commission on the Future of Medicaid, *Medicaid at the Crossroads* (Baltimore, MD: Henry J. Kaiser Family Foundation, 1992).

3. National Governors' Association, "State Coverage of Pregnant Women and Children," (Washington, D.C.: National Governors' Association, 1992).

4. Committee on Ways and Means, *Overview of Entitlement Programs: 1993 Green Book* (Washington, D.C.: U.S. Government Printing Office, 1993).

5. Committee on Ways and Means, *1993* Green Book, p. 1635.

6. Kaiser Commission on the Future of Medicaid, "Medicaid Spending Growth Snapshot: 1991 to 1992," Policy Brief No. 1 (Baltimore, MD: Henry J. Kaiser Family Foundation, 1993).

7. U.S. Bureau of the Census, *Poverty in the United States: 1990. Current Population Reports,* Series P-60, No. 175 (Washington, D.C.: U.S. Government Printing Office, 1991).

8. David Rogers, Robert Blendon, and Thomas Moloney, "Who Needs Medicaid?" *New England Journal of Medicine* 307 (July 1, 1982): 13–18.

9. Kaiser Commission on the Future of Medicaid, *Analysis of the 1987 National Medical Expenditures Survey* (Baltimore, MD: Henry J. Kaiser Family Foundation, 1993).

10. Paul Newacheck and Neil Halfon, "The Financial Burden of Medical Care Expenses for Children," *Medical Care* 241 (December 1986): 1110–1117.

11. Kaiser Commission on the Future of Medicaid, *Analysis of the 1987 National Medical Expenditures Survey.*

12. U.S. Government Accounting Office, *Prenatal Care: Medicaid Recipients and Uninsured Women Obtain Insufficient Care* (Washington, D.C.: U.S. Government Printing Office, 1987).

13. Margo Rosenbach, "The Impact of Medicaid on Physician Use by Low-Income Children," *American Journal of Public Health* 79 (September 1989): 1220–1226.

14. Kaiser Commission on the Future of Medicaid, *Analysis of the 1987 National Medical Expenditures Survey.*

15. Paul Newacheck and Neil Halfon, "The Financial Burden."

16. Kaiser Foundation Health Reform Project, The Commonwealth Fund, and Louis Harris and Associates, *The Americans and Their Health Insurance II Survey*, administered September 10, 1993 (Baltimore, MD: Henry J. Kaiser Family Foundation).

17. Congressional Budget Office, *Updated Estimates of Medicare's Catastrophic Drug Assistance Programs* (Washington, D.C.: U.S. Government Printing Office, 1989).

18. Robert Blendon, Karen Donelan, Craig Hill, Ann Scheck, Woody Carter, Dennis Beatrice, and Drew Altman, "Medicaid Beneficiaries and Health Reform," *Health Affairs* 12 (1993): 132–143.

19. Paul Newacheck and Neil Halfon, "The Financial Burden."

20. Kaiser Commission on the Future of Medicaid, *Analysis of March Current Population Survey 1992* (Baltimore, MD: Henry J. Kaiser Family Foundation, 1993).

21. National Governors' Association, "State Coverage of Pregnant Women."

22. Robert Blendon, Linda Aiken, Howard Freeman, Bradford Kirkman-Liff, and John Murphy, "Uncompensated Care by Hospitals or Public Insurance for the Poor: Does It Make a Difference?" *New England Journal of Medicine* 314 (May 1, 1986): 1160–1163.

23. Embry Howell, "Low-Income Persons' Access to Health Care: NMCUES Medicaid Data," *Public Health Reports* 103 (1988): 507–516.

24. Kaiser Commission on the Future of Medicaid, *Analysis of the 1987* National Medical Expenditures Survey.

25. Barbara Starfield, Sam Shapiro, Judith Weiss, Kung-Yee Liang, Knut Ra, David Paige, and Xiaobin Wang, "Race, Family Income, and Low Birth Weight," *American Journal of Epidemiology* 134 (1991): 1167–1174.

26. U.S. Department of Health and Human Services, *The Nature and Extent of Lead Poisoning in Children in the United States: A Report to Congress* (Atlanta, GA: Agency for Toxic Substances and Disease Registry, July 1988).

27. Andrea Piani and Charlotte Schoenborn, "Health Promotion and Disease Prevention: United States, 1990," *Vital and Health Statistics* 10 (1993): 88.

28. Kathryn Levit, Helen Lazenby, Cathy Cowan, and Suzanne Letsch, "National Health Expenditures 1990," *Health Care Financing Review* 13(1) (Fall 1991): 29–54.

29. Physician Payment Review Commission, Annual Report to Congress: 1991 (Washington, D.C.: Physician Payment Review Commission, 1991).

30. American Medical Association, "Physician Participation in Medicaid," *Physician Marketplace Update* 2 (July 1991).

31. Barbara Yudowsky, Jennifer Cartland, and Samuel Flint, "Pediatrician Participation in Medicaid: 1978 to 1989," *Pediatrics* 85 (April 1990): 567–577.

32. John Holahan, Diane Rowland, Judith Feder, David Heslam, "Explaining the Recent Growth in Medicaid Spending," *Health Affairs* 12 (Fall 1993): 177–193.

33. Holahan, "Explaining the Recent Growth," p. 190.

34. Marilyn Moon, *Assets and Limits in Medicaid* (Washington, D.C.: The Urban Institute, April 1993).

35. E. Richard Brown, "Medicare and Medicaid: The Process, Value and Limits of Health Care Reforms," *Journal of Public Health Policy* (September 1983): 335–356.

36. Robert Blendon, "What Should Be Done About the Insured Poor?" *Journal of the American Medical Association* 260 (December 2, 1987): 3176–3177.

11

Federal and State Public Employees Health Benefits Programs

Cathy Schoen and Lawrence Zacharias,
with Gloria Santa Anna and Susan Kelly

State and federal public employee health insurance programs covered an estimated 19.3 million people in 1993, with annual expenditures in excess of $33 billion. This chapter examines these programs with two goals in mind: (1) to draw on the experiences of these plans to inform the national health care reform policy debate; and, (2) to understand options for the future of the public employee plans under comprehensive national health reform.

Introduction: Access and Cost Control and
the Role of Purchasing "Alliances"

National health care reform debates center on two critical issues: how to provide universal access, and how to improve control over total costs while preserving or enhancing quality. In stark contrast to national health insurance debates during the 1970s, when proponents were primarily concerned with equitable access to health care services, escalating expenditures throughout the 1980s have made cost control the critical test for health reform proposals in the 1990s.[1] An emerging, central strategy for addressing both access and cost issues is to reorganize insurance by replacing individual and small, employer-based group policies with broad social or community "alliances"[2] that pool risk across a large membership and consolidate purchasing power. At their most basic level, alliances are designed to reverse the demise of community-based health insurance in the United States by bringing together groups large enough to share risk when contracting with insurance carriers or health maintenance organizations (HMOs).

Conceptually, the creation of new alliances for the purpose of health coverage is a goal shared by most national health reform proposals that promote universal access. The proposals diverge, however, on how to use the resulting group-purchasing and budget power. Such plans emphasize one of two approaches to controlling costs: using market power to run insurance programs directly—a method similar to that employed by Medicare or Canadian and European health insurance systems; or relying on market incentives to make consumers choose between competing insurance plans. The Clinton reform proposal draws from each.

The direct approach is advocated by so-called "single-payer" proponents. Their proposals would organize an entire state or region into one community group, and then pay for medical service directly through the use of negotiated or legislated fee schedules, capitation, institutional budgets or prospective rates (e.g. fixed payments based on diagnosis or global fees), and total expenditure hospital budgets. Such proposals mirror the Medicare program and add the discipline of total expenditure budgets.[3]

At the other end of the spectrum, "managed competition" proposals would create alliances, acting as either active or passive purchasing agents, that would contract with multiple health plans to offer coverage to a plan's members. These proposals would rely on premium incentives and consumer choice to force plans to compete on the basis of cost and service. Under this approach, purchasing alliances would compel plan members to shop for the best coverage. The resulting free market would act as a cost control mechanism. Managed competition proposals generally prevent alliances from using their power to implement direct budget controls or to directly negotiate fees with physicians, hospitals or other care providers.[4] Unlike single-payer approaches, which require all members to belong to the "social" or "community" insurance pool, managed competition allows some part of the insured population to participate voluntarily in alliances. Such elective membership would, in effect, promote a degree of competition among the alliances themselves.

Federal and state employee health benefit plans provide the closest model available for evaluating the concept of health insurance purchasing alliances. With group membership roles ranging from 20,000 to nine million people, all are large enough to pool risk and exert significant influence over insurance markets (see Table 11.1). Public employee plans have also been under considerable pressure to control costs while trying to provide access to a diverse membership that cuts across a wide range of occupations, income classes, ages and ethnic groups.

This chapter explores public employee plan experiences. In Section One, we examine the nine-million member Federal Employees Health

Table 11.1   Federal and State Employee Health Benefits Programs, Fiscal Year 1993

	Total Members	Total Budget
Alabama	84,000	$ 143,989,238
Alaska[a]	54,350	113,640,914
Arizona	136,650	177,795,628
Arkansas	57,646	73,633,729
California	920,000	1,500,000,000
Colorado	92,811	124,327,553
Connecticut	145,000	333,676,087
Delaware[aa]	90,800	138,000,000
Florida	344,061	500,700,000
Georgia	482,268	713,600,000
Hawaii	164,800	222,956,011
Idaho	43,059	44,318,551
Illinois[a]	318,075	610,625,800
Indiana	92,300	159,389,000
Iowa	76,250	106,406,435
Kansas	75,744	145,157,046
Kentucky[a]	201,284	234,000,000
Louisiana	163,007	346,395,128
Maine	46,000	75,800,000
Maryland[aa]	198,800	223,916,500
Massachusetts	240,493	530,941,457
Michigan[d]	187,575	360,000,000
Minnesota	143,980	214,297,000
Mississippi	83,956	99,300,000
Missouri	67,014	106,300,000
Montana	29,202	28,874,770
Nebraska	34,077	59,461,712
Nevada	38,696	64,903,685
New Hampshire	34,625	65,000,000
New Jersey	884,447	1,319,503,893
New Mexico[aa]	61,100	60,515,900
New York	1,073,000	1,850,000,000
North Carolina	473,907	630,102,852
North Dakota	47,783	56,878,884
Ohio[d]	320,647	202,701,738
Oklahoma	117,037	171,024,883
Oregon[c]	106,276	140,351,530
Pennsylvania	250,000	417,110,560

Table 11.1 *Continued*

	Total Members	Total Budget
Rhode Island[aa]	59,275	75,000,000
South Carolina	317,723	415,211,045
South Dakota	32,225	28,700,000
Tennessee[aaa]	254,550	$ 229,908,480
Texas	448,758	774,576,000
Utah	96,000	115,300,000
Vermont	19,576	26,750,000
Virginia	275,943	365,100,000
Washington	295,154	422,000,000
West Virginia[b]	178,400	258,922,800
Wisconsin[a]	197,270	236,400,000
Wyoming[b]	31,596	34,609,560
State Total	10,187,187	15,348,074,369
Federal Total[e]	9,137,767	17,600,000,000
Total	19,324,954	$ 32,948,074,369

Notes: Unless otherwise noted source is authors' survey and computations. People counts above include employees, retirees and dependents. Authors calculated dependents where data was not available from plan, using 2.5 per employee and 1.5 per retiree. Budget counts include retiree costs unless unavailable.

[a] Budget from Segal Company, 1993 Survey of State Employees Health Benefits Plans, Advance Copy of Data Tables, active only. People include retirees, from authors' survey.
[aa] People and budget from Segal.
[aaa] Tennessee data from Segal with authors' estimate of total budget to include state plus other public.
[b] Budget from State and Local Government Benefits Association, 1992-93 SALGBA Survey, SALGBA, 1993.
[c] Authors' computation based on survey data.
[d] Michigan and Ohio budget is for active only. People includes retiree counts. Ohio retirees are in a separate system.
[e] Celinda Franco, Health Care Fact Sheet: Federal Employees Health Benefits Program, Congressional Research Service, April 22, 1993.

Benefit Program (FEHBP), a relatively passive purchasing alliance which has been unable to control costs despite relying on a consumer-choice strategy throughout its 34-year history. The FEHBP case study is a clear reminder of what can go wrong if an alliance pursues a market approach without a coherent strategy for overcoming unforseen obstacles, and it highlights the fact that market approaches to cost containment and quality maintenance tend to undermine large-group insurance principles by dividing communities along lines of health risk and income class.

Although most state employee plans have not moved beyond the FEHBP's role as a passive health plan broker, a few have become more active in serving their membership, with the intention of controlling costs without unduly limiting members' access to care. Section Two delves into some of these plans' experiences to uncover implications relevant to the health reform debate. It would be an exaggeration to claim that the available evidence on state plans supports one or the other approach. Since no state employee plan has evolved to the point of being a single-payer style plan, a comparison of health reform proposals based on the federal and state experience is not yet possible. Nevertheless, activist plan evidence suggests that market approaches will not achieve even limited success unless alliances develop group-purchasing strategies (contracts with health plans), while at the same time directly operating their own competing health plan.

Section Two also discusses the state employee program experience with risk selection, including adverse selection in voluntary alliances that seek to bring additional public and non-profit sector employee groups into the core pool of state employees. These discussions draw on internal plan documents, case studies and examples cited by states in a survey conducted by the authors in the fall of 1993.[5]

While both sections address broad issues of national health reform in light of federal and state employee health plan activity, Section Three attempts to answer the following narrow question: Should health reforms accommodate the continued autonomy of these large, long-running plans, or should such plans be incorporated into the larger reorganization of the national health system?

Section One: The Federal Employees Health Benefit Program

With nine million beneficiaries, FEBPH is the largest purchaser of employee and retiree health insurance in the nation. Advocates for reform based on simple, consumer-purchasing alliances cite the program as a model of cost-effective consumer choice.[6] However, the program possesses neither effective cost controls nor satisfied members. It is, in fact, an example of the pitfalls inherrent in a market approach that forces individuals and families, rather than more knowledgeable and resourceful plan administrators, to assess all the comparisons and trade-offs involved in choosing a health plan.

Although internal and external critiques of FEHBP have emphasized different concerns, there is consensus about five serious programmatic flaws:[7]

1. The program has failed to control costs.
2. It encourages segmentation of beneficiaries into biased risk pools. Consequently, costs are unnecessarily high, insurance principles are undermined, volatile switching between plans occurs, and plan administrators and members are unable to make meaningful evaluations and comparisons of competing plans.
3. Meaningful choice is illusory. Members would prefer fewer plans and less complexity. Costs are a barrier to choice for lower-income families.
4. The FEHBP's passive approach to purchasing has increased administrative costs, despite the fact that such an alliance has the potential to reduce such costs.
5. The program's governance lacks the independence and accountability needed to focus on total costs and service.

It is hoped that national reform can learn from the FEHBP experience and avoid repeating its shortcomings should reforms create new purchasing collectives.

An Experiment with Consumer Driven Competition

Generally speaking, purchasing alliances can foster competition at two levels: they can bring a variety of health care alternatives to their members' attention (i.e., passive brokering), thus encouraging plans to compete directly for enrollees on the basis of price and performance characteristics; or they can set performance standards for service and negotiate with competing plans before allowing them to offer their plan to the program's population (i.e., an active purchaser). In the latter case, consumers choose between plans, but only after program administrators are convinced of their value to large, randomly selected risk pools.

The FEHBP is the closest model available of a relatively passive broker. The program, administered by the Office of Personnel Management (OPM), has historically emphasized competition at the consumer level. In fact, FEHBP is barred by law from using a competitive bidding process or renewal negotiations to control a plan's entry into the program.[8] Plans qualify for participation by meeting certain statutory requirements and insurance reserve standards, but not threshold cost, quality or service standards. By 1993 the program offered members approximately 420 options, including seven nationwide point-of-service indemnity plans and 300 HMO plans.[9] In any given geographic area, members could choose from among as many as 35 different plans.

OPM has allowed plans to compete for members by varying benefits and cost-sharing requirements as well as structure.[10] To a greater extent than its' private sector counterparts, FEHBP enforces consumer price sensitivity by exposing its members to a high share of premiums and out-of-pocket costs.[11] By law, the federal government sets its maximum dollar contribution at 60 percent of the average of the "big six" plans and caps the percentage it will pay of any plan at 75 percent.[12] A member's share of premiums varies significantly depending on plan choice. For example, for 1993–94 rates, a family's share of annual premiums ranged from a low of $411.00 to a high of $4,336.80, or 54 percent of the premium. At fiscal year 1994 (October, 1993 through September, 1994) rates, members would have had to spend at least $810 annually if they chose a nationwide point-of-service indemnity plan.[13] Overall, members pay 30 percent of total program costs out-of-pocket.

Failure to Control Costs

As a cost-control model, FEHBP receives low marks. The plan expects to spend $17.6 billion in fiscal year 1994, following average cost increases of 13 percent per year since 1986 (see Table 11.2). Program costs escalated 12 percent per year between 1980 and 1989, despite major cuts in benefits in 1982.[14] During the 1990s, annual rates of increase have remained around 10 percent despite increased cost sharing, conversion of open-choice fee-for-service plans into network plans, and the fact that HMO enrollment tripled in a decade as a proportion of total members.[15]

Throughout the years of cost increases, FEHBP administrators have remained relatively passive. As late as 1990, OPM's major cost-control recommendation was to change the way premiums were paid in order to reduce the federal government's share of total costs. The agency has neither pursued more aggressive scrutiny and control of the plans themselves, nor has it sought to use its potential market power to negotiate on behalf of plan members.[16] Studies of the FEHBP have concluded that a passive, broker-type approach to managing competition is not a viable cost reduction strategy. Many of the same studies recommended restructuring of the program to facilitate administrative scrutiny of plans (and so foster competition for entry into the program), and aggressive negotiation on behalf of plan members. Even some ardent managed competition proponents apparently agree with this assessment.[17]

Table 11.2   Federal Employee Health Benefit Program
Nine-Year Cost History

Year	Cost Per Enrollee	Percent Change
1986	$1,592	--
1987	$1,869	17%
1988	$2,260	21%
1989	$2,731	21%
1990	$3,107	14%
1991	$3,314	7%
1992	$3,518	6%
1993	$3,811	8%
1994	$4,179	10%
Cumulative Change	$2,587	163%
Average Annual Change	$323	13%

Source: Authors' calculation based on, "Employees Health Benefits Fund, Budget of the United States, Fiscal Years 1990-1994."

A Case Study of Biased or Adverse Risk Selection

Any national or state health care reform proposal offering a choice of competing health plans must decide how to manage the problem of adverse risk selection. Advocates for and against managed competition agree that "biased selection is the Achilles heel of market-oriented proposals to reform the health care system."[18]

In general, the purpose of pooling or alliances is to spread insurable risks. Biased risk selection undermines this purpose with negative consequences for both cost control and access. The following discussion describes the problem.

Biased selection occurs when relatively healthy members of a population group, acting on the low probability that they will need expensive, specialized care, choose health plans that may only cover catastrophic expenses or provide easy access to routine care but more restricted access to specialized services. Conversely, higher risk, sicker members will seek more comprehensive coverage and wider access to specialized care, reflecting their expectations of high and frequent medical bills. If program rules allow health plan premium costs to reflect the risk mix of their members, such selection patterns will force plans with higher-risk members to raise prices, while plans with better risks can charge less. Over time, price will divide the pool in such a way that risk will no longer be shared by the entire population. Since the price differential between plans will now reflect risk selection, biased risk will also undermine purchasers' ability to assess the value of competing plans and could result in higher-cost plans being driven out of business, even if such plans control costs more efficiently.

The problem is especially acute for health insurance markets since a relatively small proportion of the population in any given year accounts for a major share of total costs. Recent national data on the concentration of health expenditures reveal that the sickest 1 percent of the population accounts for 30 percent of all expenses, while the sickest 10 percent accounts for a 72 percent share. Meanwhile the healthiest half of the population accounts for only 3 percent of total expenses.[19]

Using this data, Table 11.3 illustrates the nature of the problem with a hypothetical two-plan example. The table shows that, all other variables being equal, two 5,000-member plans would have the same premiums if both shared population risks proportionately. If, however, Plan B succeeded in drawing away 10 percent of Plan A's healthier members, the selection bias would produce a 21 percent differential in premiums. In such an event, Plan B could provide a less efficient delivery system and still appear to be less expensive. Biased selection thus not only undermines group and individual ability to compare or evaluate costs, but ultimately harms efforts to control total costs.

Biased selection also undermines access. If groups are divided into risk segments, premium differential can be extreme as elderly and chronically ill members are forced to share high risks among themselves, regardless of ability to pay. As differentials grow, lower-income group members may be forced into plans that fail to address their health needs.

The erosion of group insurance. The FEHBP is an example of a program that has no systematic mechanism for offsetting adverse selection. A 1988 study commissioned by OPM, in fact, began its critique with the statement: "The history of FEHBP is a study in the erosion of the group insurance principle by risk selection."[20] Risk segmentation is so severe that premiums vary by 246 percent although the expected value of benefits differ by only 46 percent.[21] For example, using retirement as a proxy for higher-risk health needs, retirees accounted for as much as 76.6 percent of some

Table 11.3 How Biased Selection Can Affect Premiums

Case One: No Risk Bias, Two Plans With 5,000 People

Case Two: Biased Selection Occurs
Plan A Loses 500 of Its Healthiest Members to Plan B

Claims/Risk Group	People Plan A	People Plan B	Costs Plan A	Costs Plan B	People Plan A	People Plan B	Costs Plan A	Costs Plan B
Sickest 1%	50	50	$3,750,000	$3,750,000	50	50	$3,750,000	$3,750,000
Next 1%	50	50	$1,375,000	$1,375,000	50	50	$1,375,000	$1,375,000
Next 3%	150	150	$2,125,000	$2,125,000	150	150	$2,125,000	$2,125,000
Next 5%	250	250	$1,750,000	$1,750,000	250	250	$1,750,000	$1,750,000
Next 20%	1000	1000	$2,375,000	$2,375,000	1000	1000	$2,375,000	$2,375,000
Next 20%	1000	1000	$750,000	$750,000	1000	1000	$750,000	$750,000
Healthiest 50%	2500	2500	$375,000	$375,000	2000	3000	$300,000	$450,000
Total	5000	5000	$12,500,000	$12,500,000	4500	5500	$12,425,000	$12,575,000
Plan Premium Per Person			$2,500	$2,500	Premium Average		$2,761	$2,286
					Plan A Premium Compared to Plan B		20.8%	

Source: Marc L. Berk and Alan C. Monheit, "The Concentration of Health Expenditures:
An Update," Health Affairs, (Winter 1992) (11) 4: P.145. Distribution of cost based on national data.

plans' total FEHBP enrollment while in others, retiree enrollment accounted for only 21.5 percent of its FEHBP members.[22]

Simply put, the relatively healthy, well-informed segment of the FEHBP population has learned to switch in and out of plans based on their expected medical care needs, while higher risk, sicker members are concentrated in a few plans. The problem is exacerbated, according to OPM internal reports, by competing plans' use of tactical and subtle benefit differences to improve their risk mix.[23] Frequent switching is also a problem. Plans have experienced a "roller-coaster ride of sudden expansion and equally sudden contraction."[24] Selection against plans has forced several nationwide insurers to withdraw from the program.[25]

Without some offsetting policy, competing forces defeat the main purpose of group insurance and render the alliance ineffective.

Alleviating biased risk. Internal and external analyses by OPM, as well as Congressional investigations, have concluded that risk selection has undermined the program's ability to either compare or control costs. Reforms are clearly needed, and the following recommendations for FEHBP also apply to national health reform policies: (1) standardize core medical benefits; (2) prohibit variations that would raise barriers for high-risk families; (3) limit the number of choices to high performance, high quality plans only; and, (4) risk-adjust rates to avoid penalizing or rewarding plans based on members' health risk.[26]

The Illusion of Choice

Member choice of plans is a core element of FEHBP. The primary argument for providing a broad array of plan choices is that it will improve membership satisfaction. In practice, however, members have not been satisfied. From their perspective, FEHBP has two major flaws: Meaningful choice is illusory since members lack information about quality and subtle restrictions may block access to a needed benefit; and, for all but the highest-income members, cost differences (mostly due to adverse risk selection problems) may preclude rational or effective choices, whether or not plans are available that match members' needs.

Informed choice among plans would require that FEHBP members compare a variety of complicated plans based on expected health needs and the projected value of each plan's servicing of those needs. At one point, OPM provided side-by-side comparisons of benefits and copies of booklets for all participating plans during open enrollment. However, the number of plans and variations today makes this practice too costly and complex.[27] Instead, OPM recommends that members themselves obtain booklets and contact health plans before making their decisions.

A 1989 survey of FEHBP membership found that what individuals and families most want are simple choices and guaranteed protection if they need medical care. A vast majority of employees answered "yes" to the question of whether comparing plan benefits was a problem, and 62 percent of those with an opinion said they wanted the program to be simpler with fewer choices. Reflecting the difficulty of making meaningful comparisons, respondents said that familiarity, rather than price, benefits or recommendations, was the reason they chose their plan.[28]

Income inequities and premium regressivity. Members' income and health status further limited choice. The analysis of FEHBP enrollment reveals that workers with higher incomes tended to enroll in more costly plans than did lower-income workers, although premiums as a percent of their incomes were much lower. Specifically, a Congressional study found that premiums paid by low-income workers (those with an annual income of $10,000 to $15,000) amounted to 6 percent or more of their salary, compared with the 1.5 percent of salary paid by higher income ($60,000 to $66,000) families. At the same time, high income families chose plans that cost an average of $350 more than plans selected by low income workers. Across income groups, older workers tended to choose more expensive plans and devoted a higher percentage of their salary to health benefit costs.[29]

This finding underscores a fundamental problem that FEHBP shares with any competitive approach that would require individuals and families to choose a health plan based in part on cost: Those on the lower rungs of the economic ladder have little choice because their low incomes force them to select the most affordable plan. At the same time, those at the upper end of the income scale will be relatively insensitive to price, since even the higher premiums amount to a relatively insignificant share of their incomes. Unless premiums are related to income or substantial subsidies are provided for low-income purchasers, market-driven competition at the family level is likely to divide health plans by income class as well as by health risks.

High Administrative Costs and Lack of Control

FEHBP's guiding principle of multiple-plan availability at prevailing market prices has not only failed to control costs, segmentation by risk, and choice restrictions on low-income members, but it has also increased administrative costs.

The General Accounting Office found that plan administrative costs were 89 percent higher per $100 dollars of benefits than those of comparable large, private sector group plans. Administration expenditures in the

FEHBP program averaged 8.5 percent of total costs, compared with 4.5 percent in the private sector.[30] Analysis revealed a three-hundred percent variation in 1990 administrative costs per contract, from a low of $135.54 to a high of $371.67.

FEHBP's admission of multiple indemnity plan carriers also undercuts the program's capacity to leverage group size in contract negotiations with carriers. In recommending that FEHBP assume more insurance administrative functions (including self-insurance), the studies cite private-sector large-group experience and the federal CHAMPUS' success in reducing administrative costs by consolidating plans. CHAMPUS reduced administrative overhead 25 percent by restructuring its insurance administration contracts from 100 carriers to three regional contractors.[31]

The studies of FEHBP conclude that one of the clear potential advantages of such a large purchasing alliance should be its ability to eliminate "middlemen" costs by using competitive bidding for some administrative functions and by assuming others directly. In addition, an alliance the size of FEHBP should be able to develop innovative methods to evaluate and monitor competing plans' performance and to use the knowledge to bargain more effectively with carriers. It is in this area that several state plans have adopted apparently successful reforms.

Toward a More Independent, Accountable Program

Whatever the core strategy, all national health reform proposals must select an organizational governance structure that purchases or administers health insurance on behalf of the population. If alliances become central to a reorganized national health care system, questions still have to be addressed about the administrators' flexibility, range of powers and accountability to individual members as well as to the general public's need for accessible, affordable health care.[32]

As a model for national reform, FEHBP's greatest strength has been its ability to provide nine million federal employees and retirees with an integrated and relatively stable (except for costs) health insurance system. At the same time, the FEHBP program offers little to inform national policy on the general governance issues of adaptability and accountability, except for potential weaknesses to avoid. Studies and testimony in Congressional hearings have sharply criticized those weaknesses, recommending that a new agency or independent board, governed by informed enrollee and employer representatives, be given program control. Indeed, some state employee plans have advanced far beyond FEHBP's passive and unresponsive bureaucratic governance model, in part because of stronger collective bargaining pressures at the state level.

Section Two: State Employee Health Plans

Next to the FEHBP, state employee health benefit programs are among the nation's largest group purchasers of health insurance. In the aggregate, the 50 state employee health programs spent more than $15.3 billion in fiscal year 1993 to insure more than ten million employees, retirees and their dependents. The state plan is usually the single largest purchasing group by size of membership, excluding Medicaid, in the state: Twenty-two enroll more than 150,000 people, 15 cover more than 250,000, and six have more than 400,000 (see Table 11.1).

These health benefit plans were initiated in an era when healthcare cost inflation was not a significant problem, and the percentage of payroll expenditures devoted to healthcare was relatively low. Public sector employers began including healthcare benefits to improve their ability to compete with private sector employers and to address emerging problems with health care access among their own and other public sector employees and retirees.

Elusive cost control. Over the past decade, the biggest concern has been the escalating cost of healthcare services. As Table 11.4 illustrates, state health plans as a group have not been successful despite their considerable efforts to incorporate market incentives and managed care principles. In most states, the inflation rate for base plans accelerated over the fiscal years 1988 to 1993.[33] The average annual rate of increase for these five years was 23.4 percent, compared to an 11.1 percent average annual increase over the past decade. If state plan premiums continue to escalate at even the ten-year rate, plan costs will double every seven years.

This experience has run counter to predictions at the beginning of the decade that making employees more sensitive to costs would enforce stronger market discipline and help control costs. Many states which contributed a more generous share of premiums (80 to 100 percent) and cover benefits more comprehensively have achieved lower rates of increase than those which exposed families to relatively high premium shares.[34] Nevertheless, with a handful of exceptions, cost control has been elusive.

Relying on consumer choice and managed care is not enough. The state experience supports a central lesson for national reform: No state that has fashioned its program along passive broker lines, such as FEHBPs, has successfully controlled costs, regardless of the size of its alliance. Furthermore, as in the federal program, reliance on consumer choice and competition has produced biased risk selection problems that have undermined access and increased total costs. In contrast, some states that have transformed their programs from passive brokers into aggressive agents appear to be making headway against escalating costs.

Table 11.4   State Employee Indemnity Plan Premium History, Employer Paid Premium Share and HMO Participation

	Family Plan 1993 Monthly Cost	Average Annual Percentage Change Basic Family Plan		Percent Employer Share of Family Premium	Percent of Members in Basic Plan
		1983-93	1988-93		
Alabama	$ 363.00	10.0	20.6	58	92.0
Alaska[a]	384.59	6.5	2.0	100	100.0
Arizona[b]	462.90	11.5	21.4	84	12.0
Arkansas	338.64	12.6	33.5	56	100.0
California	590.00	10.4	20.4	69	17.0
Colorado	396.22	9.5	48.4	56	42.0
Connecticut	573.42	15.6	21.3	81	63.0
Delaware	558.46	12.5	19.7	81	40.0
Florida	361.72	11.3	24.1	74	62.0
Georgia	347.50	10.9	20.6	75	89.0
Hawaii	334.76	13.0	28.4	60	74.0
Idaho	243.08	5.7	28.4	78	93.0
Illinois	416.00	7.2	34.6	69	64.0
Indiana	414.27	9.6	18.4	83	61.0
Iowa	452.14	8.7	27.3	69	89.0
Kansas	579.24	12.4	39.0	62	76.0
Kentucky	383.01	12.7	36.9	44	69.0
Louisiana	329.08	10.1	24.3	50	59.0
Maine	494.54	15.2	28.0	77	100.0
Maryland	355.29	7.1	12.6	85	61.0
Massachusetts	607.20	13.8	15.9	85	30.0
Michigan	704.73	11.5	18.9	95	65.0
Minnesota[b]	392.46	11.0	18.6	78	42.0
Mississippi	286.00	14.5	31.8	45	100.0
Missouri[b]	458.31	13.3	38.8	58	82.0
Montana	249.00	7.0	16.7	70	100.0
Nebraska	518.01	13.5	25.6	79	64.0
Nevada	420.21	9.6	25.3	51	79.0
New Hampshire	566.22	13.6	20.6	100	85.0
New Jersey	563.78	18.6	25.9	100	70.0
New Mexico[c]	337.85	10.3	18.3	70	100.0
New York[d]	334.48	8.8	2.4	81	80.0
North Carolina	360.78	11.2	30.9	40	85.0
North Dakota	304.00	8.5	9.7	100	99.0
Ohio	467.66	9.3	19.3	90	69.0
Oklahoma	383.16	9.2	33.0	42	64.0
Oregon[a]	322.91	8.2	13.9	100	39.0
Pennsylvania[a]	307.56	7.5	8.1	100	85.0
Rhode Island	418.65	13.5	8.5	100	77.0
South Carolina	376.87	12.8	37.0	62	89.0
South Dakota	370.10	10.2	44.3	38	100.0

Table 11.4 *Continued*

	Family Plan 1993 Monthly Cost	Average Annual Percentage Change Basic Family Plan		Percent Employer Share of Family Premium	Percent of Members in Basic Plan
		1983-93	1988-93		
Tennessee	$ 348.59	13.6	18.1	80	96.0
Texas	514.60	9.8	38.2	67	58.0
Utah	443.79	19.6	16.1	90	94.0
Vermont	406.14	12.9	24.4	80	72.0
Virginia	479.00	10.7	26.7	68	93.0
Washington[a,b]	286.76	9.9	8.7	100	45.0
West Virginia	417.00	10.8	17.2	90	96.0
Wisconsin	624.06	13.2	22.5	68	12.0
Wyoming	321.90	7.0	26.3	45	100.0
Average	$ 419.39	11.1	23.4	73.7	72.7

Notes:
[a] Composite premium, same for individual and family. Oregon for BUBB plan only.
[b] Arizona, Minnesota, Missouri, Wisconsin costs vary by county.
[c] New Mexico employer premium share higher for low income employee.
[d] Costs do not include prescription.

Source: The Segal Company, Annual Survey of State Employee Plans, 1983-1993.

State employee plans have overwhelmingly incorporated managed care and competition into their programs. All but eight states offer a choice of HMO and use premium incentives to encourage members to pick the least expensive plan. By 1993, 37 state programs had converted their fee-for-service plans into point-of-service network plans in which participants pay considerably higher deductibles and co-insurance if they use providers outside the network of "preferred" hospitals, physicians, pharmacies and clinics. All but four or five states use utilization review and case management of expensive illnesses, as well as pre-authorization of elective hospital admission.[35]

Pressure to cut plans is countered by pressure to protect access. Intensified cost pressures have occurred during a time when most state budgets were in crisis; the recession decreased revenues while it increased the demand on state human services programs. Most states, like their private sector counterparts, have tried to ease this squeeze by shifting the cost increases onto their employees.[36]

Unlike private sector employers, however, state employee health insurance programs seeking to cut costs at the employees' expense face strong opposition. One reason is that any state action is a matter of public policy, so health coverage reform has implications beyond the narrow issue of state employees' benefits. Strategies adopted for state employee plans may be seen as government endorsement of similar policies for the general population. Moreover, state employees are better organized than private sector workers: Nearly 40 percent of state employees are unionized, compared with 12 percent of private employees.[37] States with unionized workforces are subject to substantial employee pressures, through either collective bargaining or the legislative process.[38]

Finally, state employee health benefit plans are far more likely than private plans to be accountable to commissions, boards or advisory committees that include employee representatives. By the end of 1993, 25 states operated with some form of participant oversight: six were part of retirement systems with independent boards, 13 operated as independent commissions, authorities or trust funds, and at least six included joint labor-management committees with authority to monitor or approve plan changes, even though those plans continued to be administered by personnel or administrative divisions of the state executive government. Opposition to reduced access and financial protection has meant that state employee plans have maintained relatively comprehensive benefits with substantial employer participation in premium sharing. Table 11.5 shows that in 43 state plans the employer paid 80 percent or more of the employee individual premium, while in 21 states employers also paid 80 percent or more of dependent coverage. Deductibles are $150 in the majority of plans, although most require use of network providers for lower deductibles to apply.

The resulting pressure on state public employee plans in itself is instructive for national health reform policy decisions. For many state plans the countervailing power of organized constituents, coupled with the bright sunshine of public scrutiny, has effectively foreclosed the "easy solution" of cost shifting. The constant pressure of accountability has kept program managers from focusing only on the employer's share of costs and instead has forced more collaborative attention to total program costs.[39]

In several states, plan managements have been compelled to move from passive acceptance of cost increases to more activist approaches on behalf of their constituents. While it is too early to draw conclusions about the likelihood of long-term gains, California, Minnesota, Massachusetts, Pennsylvania, New York, Washington and Utah have had marked success. Each has held average annual cost inflation rates below 10 percent over the past four to six years. Washington and Minnesota are currently

Table 11.5   Summary Description of State Employee Health Benefit Programs

Number of State Plans with Each Characteristic

Premium Share Paid by Employers	Employee Plan	Dependent Plan	Retiree Plan	Retiree Dependent
80 to 100%	43	21	28	15
70 to 80%	4	8	1	5
50 to 70%	3	15	4	5
Under 50%	0	6	4	11
None	0	0	13	13

State Plan Deductibles, Indemnity or Network Plan

Deductible	Total Plans	Number of Total Plans Where Deductible Applies to Network
$100 or Less	24	9
$101 to $200	17	2
$201 to $300	9	0
More Than $300	1	0

Coinsurance Features of Plan

Paid by Plan	Total Plans		Number of Total Plans Where Deductible Applies to Network	
	Hospital	Medical	Hospital	Medical
90% or More	33	22	17	16
80% to 90%	15	25	5	6
Less Than 90%	3	4	0	0

Notes: Minnesota, Wisconsin, Arizona, Missouri and Washington vary premium coverage by county. Employer share based on lowest cost plan.

Source: The Segal Company, 1993 Survey of State Employee Benefit Plans Advance Copy, (Atlanta, GA: Segal, 1993) Tables 3,4,5 and 6 and authors' survey.

fashioning their public employee programs into foundations for statewide reform.

Before turning to the activist public program experiences, two caveats are in order. First, it is impossible to judge to what extent these large groups' success has been achieved at the expense of a broader population as a result of health plans' increasing rates to others to offset concessions to large purchasers. Second, none of the programs reviewed has had to take into account more general health and public welfare concerns. Although large, they remain a relatively small share of the total market.

Mixing Competition and Direct Control

In contrast to the national debate which tends to polarize alternative cost-control approaches (i.e., market incentives versus direct negotiation, rate setting and control), closer examination of the relatively successful state plans moves us toward a more complex strategic discussion. Whatever the label assigned to the strategy, activist state plans have pursued a mixture of direct control and competition in their efforts to manage program costs.

Toward more direct control. Activist state plans that have met with some cost control success share common characteristics—they are running health insurance programs directly (or with tight rein over an administrative agent), and they are intensively supervising and negotiating with competing health plans that wish to enroll public employee members. These efforts have evolved from earlier, less aggressive program strategies.

More activist public employee programs tend to be large enough to support their own health plan. In all the states reviewed below, the public employee program operates a health plan, either by contracting directly with medical care providers or through an administrative intermediary that acts under the policy guidance of the state program. The public employee program itself retains control over reimbursement policies and medical service provider participation standards to establish a provider network to serve as a statewide "indemnity" plan offered to public employees. Even where a third party administrator is a partner in the plan's development, the parent public employee program has given the statewide indemnity/network plan a separate identity and name to indicate that the plan, including its participating network providers, is controlled directly by the public employee program.

Activist public employee programs have also used their directly controlled statewide plan as a standard by which to evaluate other managed care plans competing for public employee enrollment. Programs with effective cost controls have been able to aggressively negotiate HMO rates, in part because of the expertise and comparative cost information provided by their own, self-insured plan.

Our case histories lead to an interpretation of an implicit strategy driven by the development of what Washington State calls a public "benchmark" plan.[40] In this respect the strategy is remarkably similar to Medicare's. The following brief descriptions sketch the achievements of these plans and strategies.

California and Minnesota: Not Just Purchasers

Although California and Minnesota are touted as models of managed competition, neither successfully controlled costs until they abandoned predominantly purchasing strategies.[41] Incursions of competing managed care plans failed to curb rates of increase until the state programs set up their own managed care plans and moved aggressively to negotiate plan rates using the threat of exclusion. Until 1990–91, both California and Minnesota saw costs escalate at or above national rates, despite the fact that 75 percent of California's plan members and 57 percent of Minnesota's belonged to competing HMOs. It required budget pressures *plus* the development of statewide network plans *plus* aggressive rate negotiations with HMO plans to bring 1992–93, 1993–94 and projected 1994–95 rates down to annual levels not exceeding 5 percent. The examples below illustrate a range of approaches and some emerging innovative reimbursement strategies.

Utah and global rates. Utah's public employee program covers 90,000 state and local public employees, retirees and their dependents. The Group Insurance Division, the program manager, self-insures and self-administers its basic health plan known as PEHP (Public Employees Health Plan). In addition it offers two HMOs through competitively bid contracts. PEHP has included a preferred network of providers with discounted fee-for-service rates since 1985. Beginning July, 1993 the Utah state employees plan introduced a "designated service plan" where providers, chosen for their high quality care, agree to give high cost, high volume services for a negotiated global rate, including hospital, physician and associated services. The plan uses its own claims data bank, which includes information from HMOs, to analyze quality and to aggregate fee-for-service costs, and then negotiates all-inclusive global rates. The Utah plan now offers its members this special category of "designated-service" providers, in addition to its network hospitals, physicians and pharmacies. The strategy, according to Linn Baker, director, is "to put the state-run plan in direct competition with the two HMOs we offer." During the past six years the plan has held annual cost increases to 7 percent.[42]

South Carolina—prospective payment for outpatient services. South Carolina's public employee plan covers some 300,000 state, school and county public employees, retirees and their dependents. Like Utah, the program contracts directly with providers for network arrangements, rather than delegating the task to an intermediary. It operates a fee schedule for participating physicians, and in 1992 it began paying for inpatient hospital services on a DRG basis. In 1993, South Carolina began implementing prospective payment rates for outpatient services to extend its control over hospital-related costs. The plan uses a third-party claims administrator to pay claims and act as a "partner" in running networks.[43]

Washington. With help from the University of Washington, Washington State has developed DRG payments for hospitals and a relative value fee schedule for its statewide plan that will be shared with Medicaid, the

Workers' Compensation Program, and new local-government and private-employer risk pools. Through the new Washington State Health Care Authority, the plan will be available for all school employee groups, local governments, non-profit agencies, low-income families, and small private employers. State employees, Medicaid recipients and Workers' compensation claimants also are members of the plan. As of 1993, Washington legislation also calls for implementation of expenditure caps.[44]

New York. The New York State Health Insurance Program covers over one million people, including all state and local government enrollees and their dependents. Since the mid-1980s, the program's statewide plan, known as the Empire plan, has established a fee schedule for non-hospital medical services. Providers that agree to accept the fee schedule receive preferred status, with bills paid in-full except for small patient-visit copayments ($5 to $8). For hospitals, the Empire plan relies on New York State regulatory controls to set rates, but imposes managed care controls on use. For rates in effect for 1994, the program held the premium increase to under 2.2 percent overall; between 1989 and 1994, the average annual increases per person have been under 6.5 percent.[45]

Pennsylvania. The Pennsylvania Employees Benefit Trust Fund (PEBFT) plans to develop networks using the state's information on hospital quality and cost. Initially, the Trust will contract with vendors to develop the network, but the Trust plans to retain a direct contractual relationship with providers in order to maintain control. PEBTF has held average annual increases to 8 percent since 1988 as a result of aggressive administrative controls and expects networks to improve this performance.[46]

As program managers have become more sophisticated in analyzing HMO internal plan costs and performance, they have begun to question the need for intermediary contracting organizations. More active state programs can revise strategies as they learn, and growing expertise can open the door to more direct control of previously contracted activities. Managers of large public employee programs reported that even those states cited as models of managed competition may choose a parallel strategy of more direct control. For example, comparative analysis of administrative costs has led California Public Employees Retirement System (CalPERS) administrators to question whether eliminating some of their HMO network intermediaries in favor of the state's own network plan (administered by Blue Shield) would reduce total and administrative costs and improve performance evaluation capabilities.

Direct administrative control to decrease costs. State public employee programs have reached the same conclusion as those studying the Federal employee program: Administrative costs could be reduced by assuming at least some of the functions traditionally performed by insurance carriers—34 programs self-insure their plans, and four have also taken over all or part of the administration of claims.[47]

More direct control over traditional insurance functions has dramatically decreased administrative costs for indemnity plans. Ten states report indemnity plan administrative costs of 5 percent or less of plan expenses, while four operate insurance plans with administrative costs of under 3 percent. These rates are much lower than both the 14 percent national average for private health insurance administrative costs as a percent of total expenses, and the 13 percent administrative/profit cost average reported by HMOs.[48] Pennsylvania has been able to use gains in administrative efficiency alone to keep average annual cost increases at 8 percent since 1988 while paying for 100 percent of employee premiums and maintaining a comprehensive traditional indemnity plan.

Public Employee Plans Provide a Base for Expanding Access and Consolidating Purchasing Power

Whether or not public employee plans move toward more direct provider contracting and development of fee schedules, activist public employee plans are considering enhanced group purchasing power as part of a general access and control strategy. Some have looked internally, sounding out their state governments for opportunities to consolidate and simplify the purchasing policies of state health programs. Others are opening their doors to a broad array of public employee groups and, in three instances, private individuals and groups.

Integration of state health policy. At least four states—Washington, West Virginia, Missouri and Nebraska—are under legislative mandates to integrate their state employee, Medicaid and Workers' Compensation programs.[49] Except in Washington, integration refers to reimbursement policies, including a requirement that medical providers participate in all programs if they want to participate in any. However, this does not extend to the risk pool, which remains separate for each of the programs. Integration is meant to enhance group purchasing power, simplify administration (paperwork and differing reimbursement methods as well as rates), and expand access by requiring that participating providers serve all members. Both the public programs (as payers) and hospitals, physicians, clinics and HMO plans (as providers) are expected to see a reduction in administrative overhead.

Expansion to cover non-state employee groups. As part of the strategy to expand alliances, state employee plans have been opening up to non-state employee groups. These additional groups generally consist of local government and educational personnel, though in three cases they also include employees not strictly in the public sector. In addition to the 19 plans that have historically been open to non-state public employees, the Missouri, Kansas, South Carolina, North Dakota and Washington programs are now developing unified public employee programs.[50] Missouri and Washington will admit quasi-public and non-profit agencies receiving state funds, as well as other public employee groups.[51] The Washington State Health Care Authority will also operate a small-employer and individual private-employee pool as a separate group, with access to plans developed and operated on behalf of the large public employee group. Minnesota has similarly expanded its scope and now manages separate group plans for other public employees and private, small employers.

As a result of this expansion, public plans in 13 states will be open to any public employee group in the state; three of these will offer a plan to private employee groups as well. Another 11 will be open to public education employees and/or retiree groups and/or some subset of other public groups. Six other states are studying such innovations.[52]

For some programs, these efforts have more than doubled their group size, with further growth still possible. California, for example, would add an additional one million members to its current 920,000 if all school groups participate. Advocates for state plan expansion cite the potential cost savings as a mutual gain for state and local government alike.[53] The state employee group enhances its own purchasing power, while smaller governmental units gain access to more affordable care. Notably, Minnesota and Washington have incorporated expansion of their state employee plans into more general, far-reaching health reform strategies. At any rate, expansion of the core alliance of state employees, whether through voluntary measures or mandates, has direct implications for the institutionalization of broader alliances under national health reform proposals. We return to this issue in Section Three.

Biased Risk Selection and Plan Competition

As noted earlier, a principal weakness of the FEHBP market incentive system was its inability to respond to the inevitable problem of biased risk selection that follows when competing plans segment the larger population into smaller risk pools. Without risk adjustment of premiums to offset the impact of biased selection, competition strategies which force enrollees to choose plans based on costs could penalize plans that serve those most in need of care while rewarding plans that succeed in avoiding risk.[54]

State plans have experienced some of these problems, although no state begins to match FEHBP's array of 420 healthcare plans. Still, all but eight state employee plans offered a choice of HMOs as well as indemnity or point-of-service basic plans. In response to our survey, the majority of program managers who had analyzed their plans answered "yes" when asked whether adverse risk selection was a problem.[55] State public employee plans confirm our earlier assertion that any national health reform featuring competing health plans must develop a risk adjustment methodology.

Biased selection can be severe. California's and Massachusetts' program data on plan enrollment by age illustrates the potential severity of the problem. As illustrated in Figures 11.1 and 11.2, HMOs in both states enjoy an enrollment mix with a far greater proportion of younger people, while indemnity plans were left with a high proportion of older lives. In Massachusetts, HMOs served a mix of state members and their dependents in which 42 percent of the group is under 30 years old while only 16 percent is over 49. In contrast, 41 percent of indemnity plan members are older than 49 and only 27 percent are under age 30. Figure 11.1 shows that significant age mix differences may exist between HMOs in contrast to more open-choice indemnity plans. Kaiser, a staff model HMO in operation since the 1940s, has a significantly older mix of members than the newer, network model HMO. However, the indemnity plan, known as PERSCARE, has a wildly disproportionate share of older members: By 1993, the average age in the basic point-of-service indemnity plan was 51, compared to 43 for those enrolled in CalPERS' HMOs.[56]

While age is not sufficient to evaluate risk, such major disparities in age groups will produce significant cost differentials. Based on actuarial values used in a study of federal employees, we can calculate the effects of age alone on premiums: In Massachusetts average HMO premiums ran about 25 percent below the indemnity plan, and in California the staff model and IPA model HMOs could expect to be 19 and 24 percent respectively—less expensive than the PERSCARE indemnity plan.[57]

Massachusetts is acutely aware that plan risk mix accounts for a substantial share of the premium differentials between plans. Two studies of the plan found that the problem goes well beyond age. One study found that people who switched into HMOs had been relatively low cost users the previous year, while people who switched back into the indemnity plan had previous year use rates above average.[58] More recently, a comparative analysis of indemnity plan and HMO claims revealed that 70 percent of high cost patients (over $20,000 for expensive and chronic illnesses) were enrolled in the indemnity plan, even though the plan covered only one-third of the state employee population. The indemnity plan had three times more seriously ill participants than anticipated, while HMOs as a group had only half the expected incidence of serious illness.[59]

Risk distortions can increase total costs. State programs provide evidence that the resulting distortions in premiums can drive up total costs as well as undermine risk pooling and access.[60] Examples from New York's and Maine's state employee plans illustrate the problem.

New York. A study of HMO plans participating in the New York State Health Insurance Program (NYSHIP) showed that for 15 out of 29 participating HMOs, the program paid more than it would have if participants had remained in the statewide Empire plan. Although savings from the other 14 HMOs outweighed the excess costs, the study concluded that

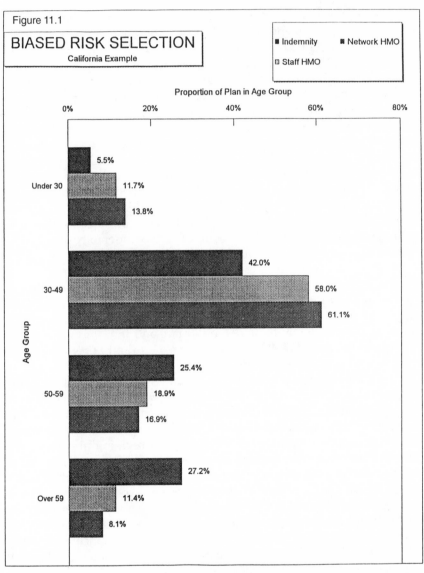

Figure 11.1

BIASED RISK SELECTION
California Example

■ Indemnity   ■ Network HMO
▫ Staff HMO

New York could reduce costs if it reduced the number of participating plans to those with demonstrated efficiency. (New York law prevents the NYSHIP plan from negotiating HMO premiums based on experience).[61]

Maine. In 1992–93, competitive bidding for the entire 44,000 member Maine State Employee Health Insurance Program pitted its point-of-service indemnity plan against an HMO. Prior to the bidding, state program administrators had concluded that an HMO bid, based on prevailing HMO rates, would lower the program's overall costs. To their surprise,

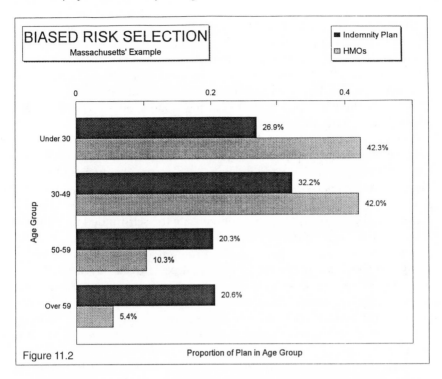

BIASED RISK SELECTION
Massachusetts' Example

■ Indemnity Plan
▨ HMOs

Age Group

Under 30	26.9% (Indemnity) / 42.3% (HMO)
30-49	32.2% (Indemnity) / 42.0% (HMO)
50-59	20.3% (Indemnity) / 10.3% (HMO)
Over 59	20.6% (Indemnity) / 5.4% (HMO)

Figure 11.2   Proportion of Plan in Age Group

the HMO bid, once it was forced to cover the same risk pool as the indemnity plan, came in at 10 percent higher than the indemnity/POS plan. The higher costs reflected the HMO's higher overhead. Had the second bid been competitive, it would have ended Maine's status as one of only eight states that has kept its entire state and retiree group in one plan.[62]

Reflecting a general concern about HMOs—that they initially attract a younger and healthier population, making it difficult to evaluate efficiency and driving up costs—several state employee plan managers shared the view expressed by a South Carolina representative: "We have been losing income to HMOs, but not claims costs."[63]

States begin to confront risk adjustment. If an alliance's population is large enough to allow evaluation of expected costs for health risk given age, sex, health status and geographical medical cost variations, it should be administratively feasible to make adjustments to offset risk disparities among pools. Health plans enjoying a healthier enrollee mix can, for instance, be assessed a surcharge to subsidize the necessary costs of plans with a disproportionate share of poor health risks. This practice would narrow the spread of premiums to more closely reflect relative efficiency and quality rather than risk mix. It would also reduce the temptation for health plans to compete by avoiding risk since such a tactic would now entail a surcharge.

State employee plans, in theory, provide fertile ground for developing such risk adjustment methodology. In fact, a review of more activist plans uncovered some initial attempts to mitigate perceived risk selection problems. However, the limited number of examples proves that even large employee groups have not yet addressed the problem systematically. Only one state, Washington, is attempting to develop a risk adjustment methodology compatible with managed competition.

North Carolina. In our review of 51 alliances which are large enough to develop a practical application of such risk adjustment, we found only one, North Carolina, that had implemented a cross-subsidy methodology. North Carolina enacted legislation in 1987 that required its Teachers and State Employees Comprehensive Major Medical to assess HMOs administrative fees plus a risk charge to "compensate the self-funded plan for the loss of better health risks to HMOs." After first standardizing its HMO benefits to facilitate comparison, the program in 1990 implemented a straightforward surcharge based on age mix: HMO's pay a fixed per-age category for members in several categories from age four to 49. The methodology increases HMO premiums by some 5 percent while decreasing the self-insured indemnity plan costs by 1 percent. Thirteen percent of the program's 473,907 members are currently enrolled in HMOs.[64]

Washington State Health Care Authority Study. Washington has initiated a research study that will develop a methodology for the entire Authority, which integrates payment policies for Medicaid and Workers' Compensation as well as the 295,000 member public employee plan.[65] The plan aims to cross-subsidize competing pools on a more scientific basis than North Carolina's current system.

Experience rate HMOs. Illinois, Georgia, Texas, Minnesota, Washington, Utah and Massachusetts state plans report that they use analysis of age and sex mix in negotiations with HMOs to reduce rates to what would be expected from experience rated plans. Washington risk adjustment negotiations in 1993 reduced rates by 12 percent.[66] Massachusetts has been using age/sex adjusted data for HMOs for several years to help evaluate internal performance. The Massachusetts' state program plans to implement a claims data base, which it would manage, that would merge claims data from all its participating plans to enable age, sex and health-risk adjusted comparisons for its entire population. Currently, the program is dependent on summary reports provided by HMOs rather than on a claims data base linked to plan membership. Rates of increase in Massachusetts' HMO plans have recently exceeded the program's indemnity plan.[67]

Voluntary Alliances: Adverse Selection
Against the Entire Group

National health insurance programs in most industrialized nations allow individuals or families to pay for care themselves or to buy separate, private insurance, but they are still required to contribute to the collective system.

A central issue in the U.S. health reform debate is whether or not participation in collective insurance alliances should be mandatory for the entire population, or for all but those groups that are themselves large enough to form their own social insurance arrangement. So-called "single-payer" proponents advocate the former, while managed competition supporters generally favor multiple alliances as a hedge against the inflexibilities of one centrally administered plan. State employee health plans that operate voluntary alliances (that is, allow smaller groups to choose whether to join a core alliance of state employees) provide insights into the disadvantages of preserving a degree of market pluralism in the administration of health alliances.

Adverse risk selection revisited. The arguments surrounding voluntary alliances emphasize two values: On the one hand, optional entry allows satisfied customers to maintain their current insurance arrangements; on the other hand, entry and exit pressures may improve the accountability and performance of alliance managers and staff. Analysis of potential benefits along these lines are beyond the scope of this chapter, since the data is not available to evaluate the relative efficiency of existing state public programs compared with the arrangements made by eligible groups who chose to stay out. State plan internal experience can, however, speak to the central argument for making alliances mandatory. Namely, that allowing voluntary alliances would undermine the principles of equity, pooled risk, and cross-group sharing of health care risks. In other words, adverse selection would work against the core alliance unless it could impose complex entry and exit regulations.

A number of key factors exist that are crucial for protecting the core alliance against adverse selection resulting from voluntary entry and exit. These include preserving the size and composition of the core population and developing internal operating rules that limit cyclical exit and entry patterns based on risk. The following state plan stories highlight the issues that arise when a core statewide public employee alliance allows groups to join voluntarily rather than mandating participation.

Geographic cost variation and sub-regional markets. State employee "alliances" are statewide by definition. In theory, programs could pinpoint premiums for sub-regions if costs varied substantially across the state, but in practice state plans pool geographic cost disparities among all enrolled members. Sub-regional rates exist only to the extent that an alliance offers HMO plans which serve discrete geographic areas.

The practice of pooling geographic disparities creates potential problems when exit and entry rules allow local government groups to join a statewide plan at statewide average premium rates. In states like New York, where sub-regional geographic health care costs vary significantly, the statewide rate will be a bargain for any "average" group living in or near New York City, but excessive for those groups living in lower cost areas. New York's state public employee program provides a case example of what can happen if an alliance decides to offer a statewide rate and then allows voluntary entry and exit by local governmental employee groups.

The New York state employee alliance was first opened to local governments in 1957, when insurance practices made it difficult for smaller, local governments to obtain affordable group coverage. As a result, voluntary enrollment led to early, rapid expansion of the alliance: nearly half of all eligible local public agencies, accounting for some 500,000 members, joined the plan. Today "participating agency" membership is down to 330,000 of the plan's 1 million members, with nearly all located in or near New York City and Albany. Adverse selection due to geographic cost variations has increased costs for the core group of state employees and retirees. A 1990 study documented that the average costs for voluntary participating agency (PA) employees run 29 percent to 32 percent higher than average costs for state employees.[68] PA groups have also been able to leave the plan at the point they incurred a deficit, leaving the remaining members of the state employee alliance to make up for past claims. The consultant report concluded that, as a result of design decisions and voluntary entry/exit rules, the state plan "has lost those who should have benefited the most and lost those with the best experience."[69]

As illustrated by efforts in Pennsylvania, addressing subregion variations can be difficult. The Pennsylvania Employees Benefit Trust Fund wants to enroll municipal government employees. Based on internal analysis of its statewide groups, four sub-regions exist. Nevertheless, the Fund would like to use one state rate in order to maintain solidarity across the state and simplify administration. However, the rate would be particularly attractive in urban areas. Although there are groups waiting to join, expanded access requires decisions on how to avoid the destabilizing effects of adverse selection on the current state employee group.

Risk selection and stability. Voluntary entry and exit also risks exposing core state employee alliances to relatively sick groups that may join if charged an average rate. At the same time, relatively healthier groups would stay out, regardless of the relative efficiency of the plan's administration. Two examples below show that while these concerns are real, the risk to the plan depends on the size of the group entering compared to those required to participate.

South Carolina. Legislation opened South Carolina's 300,000-member plan to counties in 1989. By 1993 half the counties had joined the plan, accounting for some 5 percent of the plans' membership. According to the plan's manager this group costs 25 percent more than they pay in premiums due to higher health costs. However, the impact is minimal given the group size.[70]

Kansas. Kansas enacted legislation in 1991 to open its state employee plan to schools, other local governments, and entities that received state grant funds such as health centers and mental health clinics. The State plan then discovered that many schools had adopted a practice of paying employees to leave the school's health plan. Analysis revealed that employees who took the cash option tended to be healthier, leaving schools with a pool of relatively sicker employees in need of coverage. With a potential 60,000 new school-employee members coming into their 75,000 member plan, the legislature feared a drain on state resources that could destabilize the state employee plan. As a result, it amended the legislation to postpone the opening date until enrollment rules could be established. Since the intent of expanding coverage was to improve access and a public sector alliance, Kansas is looking for ways to avoid outright experience rating. Rules under consideration include prohibiting entering groups from exiting for at least the next five years and prohibiting entry for groups with a cash-out policy.[71]

Stability is also a concern if groups enter and leave without restriction. To reduce volatility, some state voluntary public alliances have imposed rules limiting entry and exit, including waiting periods, separate risk pools, deficit allocation agreements, required minimum entry contracts, and other restrictions that have in practice restricted and slowed the growth of public alliances.[72]

Implications for national reform. National reform proposals that would create voluntary alliances are likely to face problems even more severe than those experienced by these state employee groups. Without regulations mandating participation of a large core group, and rules to share health risk and smooth geographic cost variations, voluntary alliances are unlikely to provide a stable base for reform.

Section Three: Comprehensive Health Care Reform and the Future of Public Employee Benefit Programs

Any national reform proposal will have to adopt policies regarding the future of these fifty-one public employee health benefit programs. Conceptually, three alternatives exist: (1) reorganize public employee programs to provide coverage for an expanded population; (2) dissolve separate public employee health benefit programs in favor of new, region-wide coverage of citizen or general population alliances; or (3) give these programs the option either to continue operating as separate insurance programs for public employees, with new legislated minimum standards, or to join the larger regional alliance.

A Potential Foundation for Reform

Due to their size alone, the FEHBP and most state public employee health benefit programs offer a foundation for building new statewide or region-wide health insurance programs that would serve a broader population. Moreover, unlike Medicaid these programs are likely to have a positive image in the eye of the larger populations and thus a more viable base for expansion. Given the fact that state governments also run Medicaid and workers' compensation programs, and purchase health services for other health programs (including those for prisons), reorganization of state public employee plans to serve a broad population also offers the opportunity to consolidate reimbursement policies across a sizeable portion of total state health expenditures. Washington is one state that has acted on this opportunity as part of its comprehensive reform initiative.

An indirect advantage of building on existing public employee programs is that such reform would avoid the issue of what else to do with these giant membership groups. As our discussion of the alternatives indicates, other choices raise major policy concerns.

Evaluating potential. Determining whether or not such a strategy would be viable in other states or the FEHBP is beyond the scope of this chapter. However, our comments below describe what we see as critical issues in such an evaluation.

Public employee programs differ widely in the extent to which they have moved beyond benefit manager functions as extensions of personnel departments to develop the expertise, staff and administrative capacity to run large, complex health insurance programs (whether as purchasing agents or direct administrators). Thus, a key concern in evaluating whether these plans, or the FEHBP program, provide a viable base for reform depends on an assessment of the extent to which the existing program has developed a capacity worth building on. The critical issue is what expertise, staff, data, research and administrative capacity exists in the program itself, rather than through contracts with other entities. To the extent that an existing program primarily relies on outside consultants and insurance carriers for policies and administrative functions, any new program could transfer such contractual arrangements over to the new entity.

Another critical issue is the capacity of the current program to provide a viable structural base for expansion. As noted in our discussions of

FEHBP and state programs, freedom to act, and a governance structure which includes beneficiaries to ensure accountability, are critical concerns. To the extent that the program is part of an internal state personnel or employee relations department, it would have to be reorganized into a more independent public entity to provide a stable underpinning for broad expansion.[73]

State public employee programs have recognized the need to restructure as they expand. Recent expansions in Washington, Missouri and Kansas have resulted in new health authorities, commissions or trust funds to run the program under the guidance of a board of trustees. Based on interviews and our survey, at least 10 to 15 public employee programs are sufficiently independent and well-developed enough that they could, if reorganized, provide a base for reform. The question is, will national health reform proposals provide the opportunity?

Fold Public Employee Programs into New Regional or National Programs

The Clinton proposal, and all "single-payer" proposals, would place public employees in new insurance programs covering all residents in a given geographic area. Such proposals would sever the link between place of employment and insurance coverage in favor of new insurance pools covering the entire population.

Regional Versus Statewide or National Insurance Programs

Public employee programs currently operate a uniform program on either a statewide, or in the case of FEHBP, national basis due to the scope of their employment base. The programs operate a centralized, unified, umbrella program for all employees and retirees. Members have one set of informational phone numbers, a single set of enrollment rules, and statewide or national plans whose rates do not vary by region and regional plans whose rates are uniform across broad geographic areas. In addition, each program has at least one insurance plan capable of serving all participants wherever they might live or work. Reform proposals that would create insurance pools on regional or sub-state levels and require state and federal employee participation would divide currently integrated groups. Depending on how these regional program lines are drawn, integration decisions must address the following issues.

Portability. How will regional plans cover members who live and work across regional lines or switch places of residence? The problem is particularly acute for retirees and families with college-age students.

Equity for members employed by the same employer. Currently, federal and most state public employee plans provide a uniform premium policy and choice of plans across all regions covered by their programs.[74] If under re-form, regional lines do not match current program coverage, state or fed-eral employees working for the same employer could end up paying dif-ferent rates when choosing the same health plan or receiving dissimilar health plan options.

For the state or federal government as the employer, the resulting vari-ations in premium rates and lack of a plan that fits the scope of their em-ployee and retiree group will also require solutions.

Re-enrolling 20 million people. Proposals must also address transition is-sues. Typically, large public employee plans manage relatively stable health plans with only a small proportion of members transferring from one plan to another during annual open enrollment periods. Decisions to drop a major health plan or switch administrative carriers do not come easily to these programs, due to their size and the administrative com-plexity of re-enrolling thousands of members into a new plan.

National health reform proposals that would require the entire group of 20 million federal and state public employee plan members to re-enroll into new entities must address the transition issue on a much larger scale. One solution would be to phase in the largest existing employment-based groups last, in order to put the necessary administrative capacity in place. Whatever the decision, disruptions in coverage must be minimized.

Remaining separate. Allowing large public employee programs to re-main separate would raise several concerns. First, such a policy would miss opportunities to build on the past, such as using restructured exist-ing programs as building blocks for reform, drawing on existing public expertise and relatively stable administrative mechanisms, and building onto a group already large enough to manage complex programs.

Unless the decision to allow a public employee group to remain sepa-rate was part of a strategy to build mandatory statewide public and pri-vate sector alliances, allowing public employee programs to opt out of new entities could risk a second-class image for the fledgling groups. In essence, the federal or state governments would be creating rules and en-tities that apply to others, but not themselves. Moreover, any decision to leave public employee plans separate would undermine opportunities to integrate Medicaid with other state-run health programs and transform it into a reformed delivery and financing system.

Conclusion

Although a few activist public employee plans have succeeded somewhat in improving costs and access, our relatively short review testifies to the need for national reform to bring the potential of collective action to the general population. The fact that we could find only a small number of tentative success stories among 51 large purchasing alliances with strong incentives to control costs should quiet those still calling for market competition to solve access and cost problems without major reform. On the other hand, public employee alliances can provide some lessons for the national health policy debate.

First, to the extent that public employee programs pursue a "competitive" cost control approach, they have had to move beyond passive purchasing agents. And they have done so from a base where they also exert direct control over their own "public" plan. In all those public employee plans with more successful cost control records, a program-run benchmark plan similar to the national Medicare program appears to be critical to success.

Second, premium and consumer driven strategies are not essential for achieving cost control success. Public employee plans have decreasing inflation rates, even where no choice exists and where premiums are fully covered. Conversely, costs have continued to escalate even where programs impose substantial premiums on members and rely on competition at the consumer level.

Third, competitive approaches go hand-in-hand with biased risk. If reform provides for competing plans, it must establish a mechanism to risk-adjust premium rates and protect against new access barriers. The issue is not just a technical concern but is central to preserving access and improving efficiency and cost control.

Fourth, more attention must be given to governance and accountability. Accountability to members has exerted considerable control over public employee plans and has kept managers focussed on controlling total costs while protecting access. Moreover, the wide variety of public employee plans' governance structures offers the opportunity for research into the implications of reform.

Finally, national reform options should recognize the possibility that reorganized public employee plans could provide a base for expanding access and integrating policies. Where viable administrative structures or innovative methods exist, national reform and state policies should try to consolidate. Careful study of Washington State's ongoing reform efforts should prove particularly instructive.

Notes

The author has developed a set of case studies drawn from the states of California, Minnesota, Pennsylvania and Washington to detail the evolution and experience of a variety of forward-looking state public employee health benefits programs (Appendix A). She has also prepared a table describing the extant public employee health insurance plans in each of 50 states (Appendix B). Both documents are available to the interested reader; please address requests to The Eisenhower Center,

Columbia University, 475 Riverside Drive, Suite 248, New York, NY 10115 (attn: Christopher Zurawsky).

1. To contrast the current debate with the 1970s national health insurance proposals see Karen Davis, *National Health Insurance* (Washington, D.C.: Brookings, 1975).

2. "Alliances" is the term used by the Clinton health reform proposal for large groups that have joined together as a single community group to purchase health insurance. Alternative managed competition proposals call these "purchasing cooperatives." Single-payer plans avoid the term, instead using phrases like "social insurance." Throughout the text we opt for "alliance" when discussing health plans that pool a diverse, large population group into a single group for insurance purposes. These groups are central to the Clinton proposal and competing Democratic and Republican national health reform proposals. For a comparison of proposals see Beth C. Fuchs and Mark Merlis, *Health Care Reform: President Clinton's Health Security Act*, (Washington, D.C.: Congressional Research Service, November 22, 1993); and Beth C. Fuchs, Coordinator, *Health Insurance Legislation in the 102nd Congress: Part II* (Washington, D.C.: Congressional Research Service Report, October 4, 1993).

3. Advocates for single-payer approaches emphasize the international success of such approaches and the social justice or equity of including all residents in single, integrated health insurance systems. For a discussion of cost control potential and values see Morris L. Barer and Robert G. Evans, "Interpreting Canada: Models, Mind-Sets and Myths," *Health Affairs* 11 (Spring 1992): 44–61. For a discussion of budgeting see Joseph White, "Markets, Budgets and Health Care Cost Control," *Health Affairs* 12 (Fall 1993): 44–57.

4. The Clinton proposal combines elements of both approaches. For the theory of managed competition strategies see Alain C. Enthoven, "The History and Principles of Managed Competition," *Health Affairs* 12 (Supplement 1993): 7–23. The entire issue is devoted to managed competition issues.

5. The authors contacted all fifty states during October, November and December 1993, by telephone or in writing, with questions relating to plan size, governance, total and administrative costs, whether the plan admitted groups other than state employees, program practices to manage costs and risks, recent innovations and plans under consideration with relevance to the Clinton proposals and national reform. All but five states responded. Where the survey is the source of information, we refer to it as "Authors' Survey."

6. See for example Stuart M. Butler, "Rube Goldberg, Call Your Office, Health Care Second Opinions," *New York Times*, September 28, 1993, A25.

7. The FEHBP has been the subject of repeated studies and analysis in its thirty-three year history. For an early study see House Committee on Post Office and Civil Service, *Review of the Federal Employees Health Benefit Program*, Committee Print 97th Congress, 2d Session (Washington, D.C.: U.S. Government Printing Office, 1982). The text draws primarily on analysis of program data and three recent comprehensive studies: U.S. Office of Personnel Management, Towers, Perrin, Forster & Crosby, Inc. (TPF&C), *Study of Federal Employees Health Benefits Program* (Washington, D.C.: OPM, April 22, 1988); Congressional Research Service (CRS), *The Federal*

Employees Health Benefits Program, Possible Strategies for Reform, House Committee on Post Office and Civil Service, 101st Congress, 1st Session, Committee Print 101– 5, 1989; *The FEHBP*, the Metropolitan Life Insurance Company study, reported by John Creedon, "Statement of the Consultants of the Committee on Post Office and Civil Service before the Subcommittee on Compensation and Employee Benefits," in *Recommendations for Reform of the Federal Employees Health Benefits Program*, Hearings Before the House Committee on Post Office and Civil Service, Serial No. 102– 56 1992:8–31.

8. TPF&C, *Study of FEHBP*, p. 6.

9. The number of options exceed plans because plans offer a choice of high and low coverage. Celinda Franco, *Health Care Fact Sheet: Federal Employees Health Benefits Program* (Washington, D.C.: Congressional Research Service, 1993).

10. For example, dental, mental health/substance abuse, prescription drugs, transplants, and extended care services. FEHBP rules do not require standard benefits. For the 1993–94 plan year deductibles more open point-of-service plans ranged from none to $300, coinsurance from none to 30 percent, and out of pocket limits from $1,500 to $5,000 per person in addition to varying limits on mental health services. The plan guide instructs members to obtain plan booklets for details. U.S. Office of Personnel Management, *1994 FEHBP Guide, 1993 Open Season For Federal Civilian Employees* (Washington, D.C.: OPM, 1993). Here after OPM, *1994 FEHBP Guide.*

11. Federal employees pay a higher share of premiums and have less generous benefits than large group in the private sector. Hay/Huggins Company, Inc., *Comparison of Federal and Private Sector Employee Benefits, 1991*, Prepared for Congressional Research Service, June 1992:3.

12. The six originally included two major nationwide indemnity plans, the two largest associations and two largest HMO plans. Since Aetna pulled out in 1990, FEHBP has used a "shadow" premium value to calculate the maximum dollar contribution. U.S. General Accounting Office, *Letter to Senator Graham, Information on Federal Health Benefits Costs* GAO/GDD-92–18R (Washington, D.C.: GAO, June 23, 1992), p. 6, here after GAO, *Graham.*

13. Point of service plans provide beneficiaries with a list of network physicians, hospitals and other medical care providers. These plans impose significant cost sharing for use of non-work providers. However, members may choose whether or not to use the list. Premium rates for 1993–1994 are the authors' calculation based on OPM, *1994 FEHBP Guide.*

14. Cost data for 1980 to 1989 from CRS, *The FEHBP*, p. 18. Data for 1988 to fiscal year 1994 from the U.S. Office of Management and Budget, *Budget of the United States Government, Fiscal Year 1990, 1991, 1992, 1993 and 1994*, Appendix, Tables for Employees Health Benefits Fund, (Washington, D.C.: GPO, 1989, 1990, 1991, 1992, 1993), pp. IX7–IX8; A1073–1074; Part Four 1049–1050; Appendix One 907–908; Appendix 1016–1017.

15. Total membership was stable during this period at nine million members. The proportion of retirees, however, grew. GAO, *Graham*, p. 8.

16. Constance Berry Newman, Director, Office of Personnel Management, "Testimony," *A Checkup on the Federal Employees Health Benefits Program*, Hearing before

the House Subcommittee on Federal Services Post Office and Civil Service, S. Hrg. 101-849, APRIL 20, 1990:75–81.

17. Alain C. Enthoven, "Effective Management of Competition in the FEHBP," *Health Affairs* 9 (Fall 1989): 33–50.

18. James C. Robinson, Harold S. Luft, Laura B. Gardner, and Ellen M. Morrison, "A Method for Risk Adjusting Employer Contributions to Competing Health Insurance Plans," *Inquiry* 28 (Summer 1991): 107.

19. Marc L. Berk and Alan C. Monheit, "The Concentration of Health Expenditures: An Update," *Health Affairs* 11 (Winter 1992): 146.

20. TPF&C, *Study of FEHBP*, p. 2.

21. CRS, *The FEHBP*, p. 90.

22. TPF&C, *Study of FEHBP*, pp. 58–66 and 69–75; and Congressional Research Service, "Testimony of the Federal Employees Health Benefits Team," in *A Checkup on the Federal Employees Health Benefits Program*, Hearing before the House Subcommittee on Federal Services, Post Office and Civil Service, S.Hrg. 101-849, APRIL 20, 1990:82–94.

23. TPF&C, *Study of FEHBP*, p. 69–70.

24. TPF&C, *Study of FEHBP*, p. 59.

25. Aetna left in 1990; four other nationwide plans left after 1990.

26. For a longer discussion see Chapter 6, CRS, *The FEHBP*, pp. 171–202.

27. Lynda Gurnett, Missouri Consolidated Health Plan, telephone interview 8 December 1993 and written communication 16 November 1993 to authors told us that their recent mailing of booklets and provider lists to members cost $6 per mailing because of the sheer volume of material. Yet, members found the complexity confusing and choices unclear.

28. OPM 1989 attitude survey reported in GAO, *Graham* Enclosure V:13–16.

29. CRS, *The FEHBP*, pp. 344–346.

30. U.S. General Accounting Office, *Federal Health Benefits Program, Stronger Controls Needed to Reduce Administrative Costs*, GAO/GGD-92-37 (Washington, D.C.: GAO, 1992), p. 27; and U.S. General Accounting Office, *Letter to Honorable Gary L. Ackerman, Information of Federal Health Benefits Costs*, GAO/GGD-92-11R (Washington, D.C.: GAO, 1992).

31. GAO, *FEHBP*, p. 37–38.

32. For a discussion of concerns about the structure and accountability of alliances see Robin Toner, "Alliance to Buy Health Care: Bureaucrat or Public Servant," *New York Times*, December 5, 1993, 1, 38. For a discussion of governance forms see Walter A. Zelman, "Who Should Govern the Purchasing Cooperatives," *Health Affairs* 12 (Supplement 1993): 48–57.

33. State fiscal years usually run from mid-year to mid-year. Thus, premiums for fiscal year 1993 would be those that went into effect mid-year 1992. All premium and plan detail information is from: The Segal Company, *Annual Survey of State Employee Health Benefit Plans, 1983, 1988, 1989, 1990, 1991, 1992, 1993* (Atlanta, GA: Segal Company, 1983–1993). Segal surveys plan in effect in January of the survey year, hereinafter Segal *Survey*.

34. Section Two discusses further.

35. Authors' Survey and Segal *Survey*, Tables 8, 9, and 11.

36. Authors' Survey and Segal *Survey* show reductions in coverage and shifting premium shares.

37. Barry T. Hirsch and David A. MacPherson, "Union Membership and Coverage Files from the Current Population Surveys: Note," *Industrial and Labor Relations Review* 46 (April 1993): 577.

38. State legislators also provide resistance since they are often in the same plan as employees and are loath to cut their own benefits.

39. For an analogy to the Canadian and European experience that countervailing power can lead to more effective collective action, see Cathy Schoen, "Paying Too Much, Buying Too Little: U.S. Medical Care on the Critical List," in *Labor in a Global Economy, Perspectives from the U.S. and Canada*, ed. Steven Hecker and Margaret Hallock (Eugene, OR: University of Oregon Books, 1991), pp. 278–285.

40. Margaret Stanley, *Statement Before Congress, Controlling Health Costs and Expanding Access to Care: The Value of Purchasing Cooperatives*, Washington State Health Care Authority, Testimony, November 2, 1993, p. 8.

41. Enthoven, "History," p. 37.

42. Linn Baker, Director Utah Group Insurance Division, telephone interview with author, 30 November 1993; see also Paul J. Kenkel, "Utah Employees' Health Plan Aims for Wiser, Thriftier Patients," *Modern Healthcare*, August 30, 1993, 68–70.

43. Robert Tesler, South Carolina State Division of Insurance, telephone interview with author, 3 December 1993.

44. Washington State Health Care Authority, *Results of State Purchasing Strategy* and *Overview Health Services Act of 1993, July 1993*, slide presentations of internal documents (Seattle, WA: Washington Health Care Authority, 1993).

45. New York spending per person increased an average of 5.5 percent in the two-year period from 1989 to 1991, Alexander and Alexander Consulting Group, *A Comprehensive Study of New York State's Health Benefits Structure, Final Report*, January 1991, p. 13. Author's calculation for more recent years based on total costs per person.

46. Paul Krissel, Trustee, telephone interview with author, 22 November 1993.

47. Louisiana, Missouri and Utah administer their own indemnity plan claims. Pennsylvania administers Major Medical and Medicare supplemental claims. Fall, 1993 telephone survey by authors. Authors' Survey. Self-insurance means that the plan establishes a reserve for paying unexpected claims and claims incurred at earlier dates. Self-administered means a plan has staff to pay claims and perform other administrative services rather than contracting with an intermediary.

48. Authors' calculation based on private health insurance costs reported in Suzanne W. Letsch, "National Health Care Spending in 1991," *Health Affairs* 12 (Spring 1993): 104. For HMOs, Marsha R. Gold, "HMOs and Managed Care," *Health Affairs* 10 (Winter 1991): 197.

49. Authors' Survey.

50. California, New York, New Jersey, North Carolina, South Carolina and a handful of other state employee health benefit programs have long been open to public schools or local government groups as well as state employees. New York, for example, opened its plan in 1957 in response to private insurance reluctance to offer benefit plans to small municipal and governmental employers. California

opened its state health benefit program in 1962 as part of an umbrella retirement system which had been established in 1936 to provide pensions for state and local employees. Alexander and Alexander, *Objective Two Report*, Consultants Report to N.Y. State Health Insurance Program, September 1990:37 and Service Employees International Union, *The CalPERS Experience and Managed Competition* Issue Brief (Washington, D.C.: SEIU, March 1993), p. 3.

51. Lynda Gurnett, Missouri, interview.

52. Authors' Survey.

53. For example the William E. Curry, Jr., Comptroller, Connecticut Office of the Comptroller *Health Care Cost Relief for Distressed Municipalities: A Legislative Proposal* (Hartford, CT: Comptroller Office, Summer 1991). The proposal estimated municipalities could reduce their benefits' costs by 14 percent.

54. Retirees and families with older, college-aged children have a particular need for the portability provided by more open-choice point-of-service or indemnity plans. Others with rare health conditions may find their specialized physicians participating only in certain plans. If this occurs, and sicker patients gravitate to plans with particular specialists or reputations, premiums will diverge irrespective of delivery system efficiency or quality.

55. Fourteen out of the 17 states who had analyzed risk distribution answered yes. Another 16 states indicated that they had not evaluated their plans or that they did not know the age and sex distribution across plans. Authors' Survey.

56. See case study in Appendix A.

57. Authors' calculation based on age distribution and relative age cost values used by TPF&C in *Study of FEHBP*, p. 3.

58. Massachusetts Taxpayers Foundation, *Special Topics: Managing State Employee Health Care Costs, State Budget 1993* (Boston, MA: Mass. Taxpayers, February 1992), p. 7. For studies with similar findings for private sector plans see: Jack Scanlon and Neil Austin, "Bringing HMOs in Line With Cost Management Goals," *Business and Health* (December 1987): 12–17; and Ira Strumwasser, et al., "The Triple Option Choice: Self Selection Bias in Traditional Coverage, HMOs, and PPOs," *Inquiry* 26 (Winter 1989): 432–441.

59. Michelle S. Alkon, William Mercer, letter to Cathy Schoen, 2 April 1993 regarding the results of the analysis of high cost claimants in the Massachusetts state employee plan.

60. Roger Feldman, Bryan Down, and Gregory Gifford, "The Effect of HMOs on Premiums in Employment-Based Health Plans," *Health Services Research* 27 (February 1993): 779–811.

61. The Alexander Consulting Group, *The Financial Impact of Health Maintenance Organizations on Total Medical Benefit Costs for New York State Employees*, Appendix III, Report to NYSHIP, July, 1990, p. 9.

62. Harvey Sobel, *Maine Health Commission Meeting Documents* (Boston, MA: William M. Mercer Company, May 12, 1993), p. 3.

63. Tesler interview.

64. Paul Sabo, telephone interview with author, 2 December 1993 and untitled plan documents for 30 June 1993. For legislative language see North Carolina G.S. 135-39.5B, 1987.

65. Chuck Hitchings, Washington State Health Care Authority, telephone interview 16 December 1993 and written summary of risk adjustment proposal.

66. Authors' Survey.

67. Charles Slavin, Research Director, and Dolores Mitchell, Executive Director, Massachusetts Group Insurance Commission, personal interview with author, 12 November 1993.

68. Alexander and Alexander, *Objective Two Report*, p. 40.

69. Alexander and Alexander, *Final Report*, p. 45 and Alexander and Alexander, *Objective Two Report*, pp. 37–40. For PA groups of 500 employees or less the consultant report found that the state plan is much more efficient than the group could buy on their own.

70. Tesler interview.

71. Dave Charay, Administrator, Kansas State Employees Health Care Commission, telephone interview with author on 6 December 1993.

72. Examples include the following: North Dakota amended its legislation in 1989 to require that local governments stay in the plan for at least two years and to impose a two-year waiting period for those who had withdrawn but wished to re-enter in reaction to unstable membership and risk concerns; the New Jersey plan's discovery that brokers were promising lower rates to groups who left the plan, only to have the groups re-enter several years later, led the state plan to impose rules limiting entry and exit; Illinois and Minnesota have tried to avoid selection problems for state employee groups by establishing separate, parallel risk pools for local governments and imposing entry standards (these pools are growing slowly); in Illinois in 1993, after four years of operation, only 350 local governments, representing 17,000 people, participated; South Dakota ended its voluntary alliance altogether after a five-year experience of volatile entry and exit—the plan is considering reopening with rules governing participation; and finally, adverse selection against the Nevada state employees' plan in early 1993 led to a separation of state and local public employee risk pools. Non-state public enrollee claims averaged 15 to 24 percent more than the state group during 1992 and 1993. Authors' Survey.

73. New Jersey, for example, reports that because its nearly one-million member program lacks the independence to act, it is severely understaffed and has failed to automate tasks critical to effective administration. Nelson Figueras and Peter Burkhardt, telephone interview with author, 15, 18 November 1993.

74. Minnesota, Arizona, Washington, and Missouri have recently departed from this policy. Employer premium contributions in these public programs instead are pegged to the lowest cost plan available in each county. As a result two workers working side by side could receive higher or lower contributions rates when choosing the same plan depending on what other plans are available where they live. The Missouri display of the cost of plans to employees runs some 40 pages due to the county by county variation. Authors' Survey.

12

Public Data Systems

Lynn Etheredge

For those interested in the long-term future of the U.S. health care system, the current reform debate can seem like an episode of the television series *This Old House*. In the show, homeowners are energized by plans for the future—adding a sunny family room, enlarging the kitchen, or perhaps installing a downstairs bath—although they know that basic repairs will be needed before new construction can begin. Then the experts take over, loosening boards to see what is underneath, investigating the basement, and checking the roof for leaks. In due course, the homeowners learn that their humble abode needs preliminary rehabilitation, from stronger ceiling joists to new heating, plumbing, and/or electrical systems. Often, the structure's deterioration can be traced to previous owners who found it easier to slap on another coat of paint than to incur major repair expenses.

Similarly, health care reform will require a great deal of time, effort and expense to deal with deteriorating conditions before visions for the future, like a fully-insured population, can be realized. Growing public demands have led political leaders to call in the experts, and major rehabilitation projects are now being proposed for health insurance coverage, benefits and markets, as well as health professions training, primary and preventive care, delivery system organization, quality assurance and government regulation. The next several years, at least, are likely to be spent creating solid financial foundations and well-functioning component systems for the health sector's future. This is vitally important work, and for those faced with the daunting prospect of investing so much sweat, brain power and money in problem-fixing, an infusion of inspiration is needed if the task is to be carried to completion. Therefore, let us not lose sight of the bright possibilities that these efforts present for improving individual and community health—the important long-term payoffs of national health reform.

How can the nation move beyond repair of what is failing to a health system that makes unmet health needs a fading memory and continuous improvement in health outcomes, quality and efficiency a concrete reality? Clearly, assured health insurance coverage and better health insurance markets, health professions' policies, and organized delivery systems are important foundations. Appropriate use of incentives and regulation will have a large, although as yet undetermined, role. But new public data systems—the focus of this chapter—should also play a major role if society is to reach beyond today's insurance-based paradigms toward ever-better performance and results.

Advocates for new public data systems include among their ranks some of the most visionary reform enthusiasts, as well as some of the toughest-minded pragmatists. Although seldom the focus of media attention, elements of a major national health data strategy are now emerging in health reform proposals; they deserve serious discussion among those concerned with the health system's future. These appraisals need to consider how to use information to identify unmet health needs, achieve effective accountability, and create powerful dynamics for improved performance. These discussions may also help forge consensus on broader reform issues by moving from a short-term "winners and losers" focus to an awareness of how successful reform can lead to improved individual and community health.

Two public data system options are discussed in this chapter: performance "report cards" for the health system's providers, communities, and financing and delivery organizations; and, economic data on prices, quantities and expenditures. Both of these initiatives will involve national legislation to assure that data are available, comparable and useful. Neither is linked exclusively to any one proposal for health care reform, and both are widely compatible with the leading bills of different sponsors. Indeed, a case can be made that these two kinds of public data initiatives are essential, under any reform approach, to assuring a better-performing health system and well-functioning cost control strategies. A case can also be made that, without these data initiatives, health care reform could lead to an increasingly troubled health system, with poorly designed cost control policies choking the possibilities for serving unmet needs and underserved populations. Thus national data strategies, refined in the forthcoming legislative process, may well emerge as key elements of a broadly supported, non-partisan reform agenda.

The following discussion considers the rationale for these public data system initiatives. Specific mention is made of exemplary work that has already occurred in developing the technical and consensual base for these data initiatives, although a thorough analysis of the competing proposals and technical issues is not intended. A final section suggests caveats about implementation.

"Report Cards" for Accountable Performance

A growing number of reformers and legislative proposals suggest that the nation adopt a "report card" strategy for organized health care systems, health insurers and health care providers. Each of these entities would be required to report on key performance indicators with respect to quality (including health outcomes), costs and service. Government authority, such as a new National Health Board, would mandate the basic data elements and how they would be measured, assure that information was collected and audited for accuracy, and see to it that the information was delivered in a useful, comparative form for consumers, employers, public officials, and others.

This "report card" idea, as a central reform concept, is new to today's health care debates. It is intended to benefit the majority of Americans who already have health insurance coverage and access to care, as well as those who are uninsured or underserved.

As a way to understand the important role advocates see for this report card, a useful analogy can be drawn between health system performance reports and standardized achievement tests of educational performance. If there were no standardized education testing, politicians and spokespersons for American education would undoubtedly still be proclaiming that the U.S. education system is the best in the world, if only because it is American. If queried about performance of a particular school, the local school board might cite its spending rates per pupil, curriculum changes, computers in the classroom, or the school's accreditation and teachers' credentials. Pressed too hard, they might include a glowing report on the football team's recent successes.

Of course, there is no question that many elements of American education are excellent. But the fact that the U.S. has world-leading science research institutions, first-rate liberal arts colleges, and other notable strengths clearly does not mean that inner-city schools are achieving basic literacy levels or offering appropriate technical training for those students not headed for college. Nor does it mean that one's local school system is providing mathematics and science education on a par with Japan or Germany. We know the extent to which our educational system is falling short because there are valid and reliable measures of educational achievement. Only with objective measures has the nation been able to overcome self-interested obfuscation and identify where expenditures do not match performance, formulate reform agendas, and motivate national, state and local initiatives.

Similarly, our concern for the health of the general population—as well as our own health—should lead to a demand for objective, publicly available performance measures for the health care system. In the absence of such performance measures, one still hears politicians and special-interest advocates assuring the public that the U.S. health system is, of course, "the best in the world." As evidence, they note that foreign heads of state regularly seek care at America's leading medical institutions. Query a hospital administrator about the health of her institution, and you are likely to receive a briefing on its accreditation, the board-eligible and board-certified status of its physicians, budgets and rates of increase, recent investment in expensive technologies, and the addition of new services. Numerous studies have shown, however, that such indicators do not accurately define performance levels.

Despite the valid positive points to be made about the U.S. health system, there remain too many disturbingly bad or neglected problems. For instance, this country's abundance of world-class tertiary care centers does not necessarily mean that a particular inner-city's infant mortality and childhood immunization rates are better than (or even equal to) that of some Third World countries. Even affluent suburban communities cannot rest assured that their community hospital's high-tech equipment or relatively low patient volume necessarily places their quality of service substantially above that of less well-appointed, higher-volume institutions.

Politicians and providers will almost certainly not be able to tell you how health care services are improving a community's health status, or how one community's measures compare to another's, because they have little concrete information to work with. That the health system—at a household and local level, where key individual and public decisions are made—now lacks even rudimentary performance measures is one of the unfortunate, lingering consequences of an "insurance" paradigm based on unquestioning payment policies. Basic performance indicators like those found in the educational system are strikingly underdeveloped for health care.

As Arnold Relman has noted, the health care system must move into an era of assessment and accountability.[1] With valid report cards it should be possible to identify both excellence and serious problems—individuals, employers and other purchasers will be able to make better choices, public health can be accountably linked to organized delivery systems and individual providers, and professionalism and self-interest can be engaged for continuous performance improvements. To realize these potential gains, however, it will be necessary to have both useful, valid and reliable measures, as well as a willingness among major players to alter their usual patterns of activity if better information dictates such a shift. Are these conditions for a successful initiative already in place, or are they forthcoming? A brief review of some current proposals for national data systems can help answer this question.

What Data Should Be Included in "Report Cards"?

Like opponents of standardized education testing, opponents of public accountability measures for the health care system argue that quality of care is ineffable, or at least multi-dimensional, and only validly judged case-by-case: that medical care is at least as much art as science, and that overall statistical indicators are likely to be misunderstood and misused by non-professional purchasers or users. Nevertheless, as large businesses have become more sophisticated health care buyers, they have reached beyond these "white-coat" routines to insist on reliable quality measures, and have found a number of the nation's leading health care institutions willing to work with them to develop comparative performance measures for health care providers. Trail-blazing work is now being done by employer- and managed care-sponsored organizations, research think tanks, specialty societies (e.g., American College of Physicians) and accrediting organizations (e.g. Joint Commission on Accreditation of Healthcare Organizations), government agencies, individual researchers and research teams, foundations, and data specialty firms.

Three of these efforts—designed for public accountability—are described below to illustrate measures that can be adapted for report card initiatives, their specific rationale, and how different measurement concepts could work together. They are the Health Employer Data and Information System (HEDIS), the Outcomes Management System, and the *Healthy People 2000* indicators.

In mid-1993, the National Committee for Quality Assurance (NCQA) published its proposed HEDIS 2.0 data set for performance measurement of health insurance plans.[2] The proposal reflects a multi-constituency effort, primarily led by large employers and the managed care industry in consultation with many groups and experts from across the country, to develop immediately useful measures for comparing health plans' performance. The HEDIS 2.0 document has been finalized, and a national pilot project is underway with some twenty health plans. Top companies, such as Kaiser Permanente, have begun to publish their ratings on key measures; additional data elements are being planned for a HEDIS 3.0 release. NCQA intends to audit individual health plan data for accuracy, consistency and objectivity.

The HEDIS measures fall into four major categories: quality, access and satisfaction, membership and utilization, and finance. The following are selected items from the more than forty proposed measures in the draft report:

Quality of care. Childhood immunizations, mammography screening, first trimester prenatal care, Pap smears, cholesterol screening, asthma admissions/re-admissions to emergency room/hospital; diabetic retinal exams, treatment following myocardial infarction;

Access and patient satisfaction. Visit rates in previous two years for specified age categories, member satisfaction survey results;

Membership and utilization. Enrollment/disenrollment, frequency and average cost of five selected procedures—laminectomy, hysterectomy, coronary artery bypass grafts (1–4 arteries), angioplasty, and cardiac catheterization; Cesarean-section rates;

Finance. Various measures of solvency, efficiency, and compliance with statutory requirements.

The HEDIS 2.0 effort does not fully realize a report card for health quality and health outcomes measures. But it reflects the practical intent of its designers in incorporating data elements that can be readily implemented and does not drive "beyond the headlights." Certainly, the emphasis on specific preventive services for defined populations, such as immunization rates and pre-natal care, highlight key measures where there is professional consensus that the health care system's performance needs to be improved. The early performance reporting shows that plans that are generally regarded as high quality also have significantly better-than-average indicators. That is encouraging, even if the indicators fall short, in some cases, of management targets. Such differentials can enhance the push toward excellence, while providing a warning to the public about poorly-rated plans.

A second data system initiative, reflecting a leading-edge effort to measure patient functional status and medical care outcomes, is the Outcomes Management System. Developed by Interstudy in the late 1980s, with further development and implementation now led by a spin-off enterprise, the Health Outcomes Institute (HOI), this approach systematically tracks and assesses patient health outcomes. Data include objective clinical measures, as well as patient-reported functional status and well-being. Developed by leading researchers and clinicians, the following 17 Technology of Patient Experience (TyPE) instruments (general and condition-specific questionnaires and data collection protocols) are now available:[3]

Angina, asthma, carpal tunnel syndrome, cataract, chronic obstructive pulmonary disease (COPD), chronic sinusitis, depression, diabetes, hip fracture, hip replacement, hypertension/lipid disorders, low back pain, osteoarthritis of the knee, prostatism, rheumatoid arthritis, stroke, and substance abuse disorder.

Three consortium efforts, involving more than forty specialty and multi-specialty clinics and thirty companies and managed care organizations, are now field testing one or more of these TyPE instruments. Many other organizations are closely studying the outcomes-based data. HOI, the American Society for Testing and Materials (ASTM), the Joint Commission on Accreditation of Healthcare Organizations, the Health Care Financing Administration and others are working toward data element standardization to assure comparability among outcomes data bases.

Outcomes have a strong theoretical claim as the ultimate measures of health system performance; as specific data elements are proved valid, reliable, and useful, they may strongly influence the report card movement. As in education, where student development is the primary concern, so too in health care, where our real concern needs to center around individual health status. Again like education, however, many confounding factors affect health outcomes—individual motivation, social culture and environment, for instance—thus signalling a continued need for multiple performance indicators.

Advocates for patient outcomes data believe they can have a major impact on quality assurance philosophy, clinical practices, and patient results in the health sector. They note that quality assurance practices in the health care sector, insulated by insurance payments, have lagged several generations behind other sectors. Quality leaders in other national sectors have reconceptualized their efforts several times during the past century, starting from a procedure-based focus on standards for well-trained personnel and equipment and expanding to production process assessment and end-of-the-line measures. Starting with counting "defects," this shift evolved first toward statistical quality control of normal, or non-outlier, processes, then again to an emphasis on key management responsibility (rather than worker-only accountability) and institution-wide interdependencies in the total quality management/continuous quality improvement philosophy. Most recently, quality assurance has reached beyond institutional boundaries to assess quality by a products value to the customer.

Viewed against this progression of paradigms, the health care systems' practices still stand at the earliest stage of quality-assurance (i.e., individual procedures); most insurers' and judicial oversight efforts are only somewhat farther along, stalled at efforts to identify and punish individual outliers, or defects. The Medicare DRG classification system for non-outlier payments—inspired by the industrial quality control tradition—embodied a paradigm shift to conceptualization of hospital care as a production line process by applying modern statistical quality management techniques. Its intended use as a quality management tool, however, is only partly realized. Statistical profiling techniques for selection and management of networks, as well as practice guidelines, are now being developed by many in the health system.

Each stage in the evolution of quality control thinking has occured through the mastery of previous stages; the progression to newer philosophies and methods has been necessary for continuously-improving performance. For the U.S. health system, such shifts toward outcome-based performance measures may also move provider and institutional mentalities from a narrow focus on individual procedure competency, insurance payment and judicial review, to a broader outlook that counts improved patient health status as a top priority.

A third major data initiative proposed for the U.S. health system's future—developed over several Presidential administrations—is a tracking system directed toward the major goals of *Healthy People 2000*, a health program developed by the U.S. Department of Health and Human Services.[4] The initiative quantifies current national baselines and achievable goals in twenty-one health promotion, health protection, and preventive services categories, that would markedly improve the well-being of the U.S. population. Many of the indicators can be affected by personal responsibility and public health activities, as well as by health care provider activities. Some examples of community health goals that are linked to the two earlier report card elements are listed here:

- Increase childhood immunization levels to at least 90 percent for 2 year-olds (a 20 percent increase over current levels);
- Increase first trimester prenatal care to at least 90 percent of live births (an 18 percent increase);
- Increase clinical breast exams and mammography every two years to at least 60 percent of women aged fifty and older (a 140 percent increase);
- Decrease the Cesarean delivery rate to no more than 15 per 100 normal deliveries (a 39 percent decrease);
- Decrease activity limitations due to chronic back conditions to no more than 19 per 1,000 people (a 13 percent decrease); and,
- Decrease disability from chronic conditions to no more than 8 percent of the population (a 15 percent reduction).

The *Healthy People 2000* goals underscore the rationale for taking seriously both "report card" proposals and the push for improved health system performance. There is enough intellectually credible work in this initiative and its supporting documentation to warrant anticipating that the nation's health can be markedly improved if a successful strategy, focusing the health system on quantifiable objectives with performance accountability, is implemented.

Who Are the Potential Users of Report Card Data?

There are at least four groups of potential users for report card data: individuals; group purchasers and "systems integrators" (e.g. employers, purchasing coalitions, insurers, health maintenance organizations, preferred provider organizations and other organized delivery systems); managers and professionals in health care systems; and community health planners and public officials. The ultimate impact of performance data would combine the effects of their responses.

For consumers, comparative information about quality, costs and service completes a "consumer choice" paradigm that assures that consumers have the purchasing power to obtain health care and allows them to make rational choices in their own interest, using the best available information. Personal experience, word-of-mouth, inertia and other factors will influence consumer choices. But not all consumers need to be supremely rational "early switchers" for a report card initiative to influence provider behavior. The prospects that a poorly-rated plan will experience a steady, if gradual, loss of market share can prompt remedial action by the plan's administrators. Consumers may also be aided by the media and new publications like *Health Pages*, which provides a comparative consumer guide to local health plans and providers. It is hoped that such health care purchasing information will reach the level of depth and sophistication available to purchasers of such non-essential goods as automobiles and stereo equipment.

Large employers and other group purchasers who buy health care services, in effect, at "wholesale" prices may ultimately have more impact on report card initiatives than individual consumers who pay "retail." Indeed, in most markets it is at the wholesale purchasing level, featuring professional buyers purchasing in large scale, where the techincal aspects of quality, as well as tough price competition, are most effectively assured. (For example, a large retail concern like Sears is able to negotiate performance specifications and prices for Kenmore appliances and Craftsman tools.) Therefore, it is no surprise that large employers, business coalitions, and various managed care organizations and other system integrators have been in the forefront of the report card and statistical profiling movements. This suggests that they are also likely to take the lead in optimally utilizing these performance data. Providers who do not measure up to the standards of "wholesale" purchasers may find themselves left out of networks and delivery systems being developed for the "retail" market.

A third group of report card data users is likely to be the managers and professionals within health care organizations. To manage organizations properly, explicit goals and supportive cultures are required. Report card measures can help system managers identify activities that their organizations need to improve; they may also enhance motivation and culture development. For example, Peter Drucker, an authority on corporate culture, has noted that non-profit organizations must be managed by values rather than by the profit motive. Report card elements can provide a rich and engaging menu for defining an institution's missions in serving its local community and the patients who rely on it. Professionals who feel that they are "fighting the system" when they try to fulfill unmet health needs should find universal health insurance, coupled with properly done report cards, particularly salutary. If report cards can successfully illustrate the distinctions between "doing good" and "doing well" they will create a powerful dynamic—much loved by economic theorists—that augurs well for the future of any enterprise.

A similar aspect of report card influence may be professionally generated pressures to excel, i.e., given valid measures of health system performance, health professionals may push their organizations toward continuous improvement in meeting or exceeding community standards. This perspective was recently offered by a psychiatrist who spoke with me after a presentation on managed competition theories. He expressed the view that the report card concept—much more than economic incentives—would be the critical element needed to make national health care reform work. He believed that, given physicians' professional self-concepts and their very high degree of competitiveness, none would want to be judged by objective measures as providing second or third-rate care. He felt that, if the report cards were done correctly, a professional-competition dynamic would become the key factor leading to improvement of the health care system.

Finally, there are important potential users for report card data among community public health leaders and other officials. With universal coverage in insurance plans or programs, each with a defined enrolled population, reported performance can be an element of a consolidated community report card. The *Healthy People 2000* community-level goals can thus be linked with health plan performance. This opens up new potential working relations between health providers and traditional public health agencies, particularly in a universal health insurance environment where unmet health needs are no longer tolerated. Such a relationship was highlighted in a recent presentation by Dick Davidson, President of the American Hospital Association, to hospital executives, medical directors and trustees. During the talk, he posed a 10-question pop quiz regarding the audience's readiness for reform. Among his questions were, "Does your institution's leadership meet a least once a year with its local health officer to discuss your community's health needs and your institution's role in meeting them?" and, "How many of you know who your local health officer is?" His point was that, with universal health insurance coverage, many hospitals can reorient themselves away from cost-shifting and avoiding unfinanced patients and toward targeting a community's health needs. In a competitive environment that includes performance report cards, success in meeting such health needs will become an even more important factor in a hospital's success.

Health Sector Economic Data

The second major public data initiative is enhancing the capacity to track and assess—on a national, state and local level—health care expenditures, prices and quantities. These data will be needed both to design and to (re)calibrate health cost control strategies. Given the scale, complexity, diversity and rate of change of the U.S. health system—with expenditures of over $1 trillion annually—this task, like the performance report cards, will pose a considerable challenge.

Beyond national health expenditure estimates, there is a striking scarcity of useful data about levels and trends in health care spending. If one queries what changes in clinical practice have accounted for the recent $100 billion annual increase in health care spending, there is no systematic data to answer the question. The national summary government analysis simply subtracts inflation indexes and population growth from national spending estimates and ascribes the balance to "intensity." (The Medicare actuarial reports used to describe this figure as the "net residual"; the shift in terms does not indicate better data.) Of course, there is no shortage of experts now opining that the increases are clearly not worth the money, but one would feel more assured if there were solid data to describe the changes that the critics have concluded were wasteful.

One might assume that there would be greater amounts of useful information at the state and local levels, but the opposite is the case. Few states (and even fewer localities) now provide timely estimates of health care spending in their geographic area, while about once per decade HHS has attempted to estimate state level spending. In mid-1993, expedited estimates were released for 1991. These figures include only approximated expenditures on hospitals, physicians services and prescription drugs, with unknown state-level error rates. They also calculate spending within the geographical boundaries of a state, not by its resident population; the differences are substantial in many states where border-crossing to receive medical care is common.[5]

If the nation is as serious as it should be about dealing with health care costs, then a rational policy needs a good data system on health care expenditures as its foundation. Ideally, this system should provide national estimates to track levels and rates of change in health care spending, prices and service volumes at the national, state and local levels. Indeed, one would almost have to consult a political psychologist to explain why health policy discussions so often seem to rehash centuries-old debates on liberal versus conservative political philosophies rather than proceeding rationally from the collection and analysis of objective data. Absent such data, misguided political decision makers may fail to intervene appropriately when dealing with unnecessary spending, or they may mistakenly forestall use of the health system's new financial capacity to satisfy community health needs.

The ability to produce state-level estimates is vital because of the great diversity among states in spending and rates of change. For example, recent HHS data indicate that per capita spending on health care in 1991 varied state-to-state by a ratio of nearly 2:1, ranging from $2,402 in Massachusetts to $1,234 in Idaho. The national average was $1,877. As a percentage of per capita income, spending proportions fluctuated from a high of 12.9 percent (Louisiana, North Dakota, and West Virginia) to a low of 7.4 percent (New Jersey). As observers have noted, these differences reflect an even greater disparity in health cost problems *within* the country than between the United States and nations like Canada and Germany. Underlying these differences are many related variations in supply of health care resources, state economies, market shares of prepaid group practices, teaching facilities, demographics and health status, and many other factors.

Disaggregated data are also needed because national HHS analyses can seriously mislead decision makers into thinking that the U.S. health care system is changing uniformly, rising everywhere at about the same rate of price inflation and population, plus the well-known "intensity" factor. But, in fact, the available data show there are wide year-to-year fluctuations in sub-national data. The Medicare data system, which tracks actual spending rather than estimates, illustrates these surprising variations, which occur even in a price-controlled program. In 1989, Medicare spending increases exceeded 24 percent in two states (Alabama and Rhode Island), while falling in three states (Illinois, North Dakota, and New Jersey). Even over the three year 1985–1988 period, two states recorded double-digit annual increases (Virginia and New York), while four states showed declining expenditures (Nebraska, Rhode Island, Missouri, and Oregon).[6] On a more disaggregated basis, Table 12.1 shows a greater than 3:1 variation in six-year rates of increase for Part B expenditures.[7]

Lynn Etheredge

Table 12.1   Medicare Part B Annual Expenditure Growth by State, 1986–1992

Highest States		Lowest States	
South Carolina	+ 15.9%	Illinois	+ 7.1%
Delaware	14.2%	New York	7.0%
Kansas	13.4%	Oregon	6.9%
Nevada	13.3%	Hawaii	4.7%
North Carolina	13.0%	California	4.3%

Source: U.S. Health Care Financing Administration.

It is not necessary to belabor the current data problems to realize that for any comprehensive national, state and local strategy for dealing with health care spending, very serious implementation hurdles lie ahead unless far better data are made available for decision-making and trend analysis. Indeed, on the basis of the above numbers, the toughest issues facing a successful cost-containment policy may involve variations and rates of change in clinical practices rather than service pricing. If so, health cost containment may prove far more difficult than many price-control advocates, working without an adequate national data base on clinical practice variations and changes, have presumed.

Even were the nation to pursue a market-oriented reform strategy for the next several years, however, rapid development of economic data-gathering capabilities will still be necessary to assess how well it is working and to devise targeted interventions where it is not working. In truth, no responsible analyst can guarantee that any of the major cost-control strategies now being debated in Congress will work well, produce efficiency, make appropriate trade-offs among competing objectives, perform similarly in all areas, and be found to do more good than harm. Initial health cost control policies will need accurate and timely economic data for assessment, (re)calibration and potential redesign.

What kind of data are needed, and how can they be collected? Fortunately, there has been a great deal of work done within the private sector, and with both the Bush and Clinton administrations, on these issues; a solid technical base exists for moving ahead with a new national data system for health expenditures. The core of these initiatives will be a common claims form for insured services, with standardized information and coding. That form can produce detailed, comparable and timely transaction data to be cumulated for area, state, and national reporting. The data can be efficiently collected using individual "health security" cards, similar to credit cards, and electronic claims transmission. Given the clamoring for good economic data, and the health sector's 15 percent claim on net national output, users for these data should be plentiful.

This initiative needs to go beyond information collection, however, to assure that data are analyzed and made available for public and private sector users. At the state level, a health agency could produce annual health-sector analyses of levels and rates of change in spending, prices, and service volumes/clinical practice patterns, including intra- and cross-state comparisons and assessments. It could also develop options for appropriate policy actions. Indeed, this capacity to develop and employ differentiated policies is one of the important reasons to invest in better health data systems and their analysis. With good health price and volume data analysis, it should be possible to identify antitrust problems and deal with them through antitrust remedies, to pinpoint needs for better medical guidelines and effectiveness research and respond appropriately; to deal with unmet health needs through public health initiatives and plan performance goals; to target price controls in situations where markets cannot function; to highlight insurer premium limits when it is insurer performance that needs to be shaped up. To return to the *This Old House* analogy, trying to deal with health care costs without better information is like trying to rehabilitate a house without being able to look behind the walls or in the basement and attic. If one wants to guarantee solid foundations, non-leaky roofs, and safe wiring, it makes sense to enable experts to look carefully at what needs to be done, and to make use of an array of tools and materials—perhaps even beyond those now "on the shelf"—for the particular jobs at hand.

Implementation

There is growing recognition that a national health reform agenda needs to include public data initiatives such as those outlined above. The leading Clinton, Chaffee, and Cooper-Breaux bills, for example, all subscribe to major initiatives in these areas: the Clinton plan is a truly ambitious national design. But there is a great deal of work still to be done. The country is fortunate that there has been so much cooperative work done already on both report card and economic data issues that can facilitate bipartisan agreement and implementation.

There are many lessons from previous public data system initiatives that can inform these efforts. The most important caveat, in my view, is to make sure that the data required are actually useful. It would be better to start with a few key indicators, like immunization rates or prenatal care delivery, than to respond to potential interest group demands for dozens, if not hundreds, of indicators. Similarly, it is quite easy for data hounds ("let's collect everything and decide what to do with it later") and management information system enthusiasts ("data allows us to control the system") to swamp decision makers with numbers, only to discover that quality control has suffered so much that no one trusts the information. For evidence of such information overload one need look no further than the thousands of computer tapes of unused data collected by the Medicare and Medicaid programs.

A sensible approach would be for a new National Health Board to build on pre-existing multi-constituency efforts—like those of the NCQA and the Workgroup for Electronic Data Interchange—in much the same way that the Securities and Exchange Commission relies on the private sector Financial Accounting and Standards Board, co-sponsored by users and producers of data, for proposed national financial reporting standards. Given the importance of community-level action, national data strategy might do well to keep universally-mandated elements at a basic level, while allowing states and communities to supplement report card and economic data requirements according to their needs and priorities.

Conclusion

The nation has much reason to hope that health systems reform—building on efforts to deal with the problems of declining health insurance coverage and runaway costs—will lead to a much brighter future, better health status, improved individual and community health and intelligently-designed initiatives tailored to local circumstances. Such a future is possible, provided that the nation makes a major investment in public data systems.

Notes

1. Arnold Relman, "Assessment and Accountability: The Third Revolution In Health Care," *New England Journal of Medicine* 319 (1988): 1221–1222.

2. National Committee for Quality Assurance, *Health Plan Employer Data and Information Set and User Manual, Version 2.0* (Washington, D.C.: National Committee for Quality Assurance, 1993).

3. Health Outcomes Institute, *An Introduction to the Health Outcomes Institute's Outcomes Management System* (Bloomington, MN: Health Outcomes Institute, 1993).

4. U.S. Department of Health and Human Services, Public Health Service, *Healthy People 2000: National Health Promotion and Disease Prevention Objectives* (Washington, D.C.: Government Printing Office, (PHS) 91-50212, 1991).

5. Katharine Levit, et al., "Health Spending By State: New Estimates For Policy Making," *Health Affairs* 12:3 (Fall 1993): 7–26.

6. U.S. House of Representatives, Committee on Ways and Means, *1993* Green Book (Washington, D.C.: Government Printing Office, WMCP 103-18), pp. 220–221.

7. Physician Payment Review Commission, *Expenditure Limits* (Washington, D.C.: Physician Payment Review Commission, staff paper, July 1993), p. 62.

PART FOUR

Private-Public Sector Roles and Responsibilities

13

Private Health Insurance and the Goals of Health Care Reform

Stan Jones

The leading group of health care reform proposals before Congress argues that the way to bring about broader access to care and contain the costs and assure the quality of health care is to "improve the markets" for health insurance and health care in the country. Proposals by the Clinton administration, the Conservative Democratic Forum (Cooper), the Senate Republican Health Task Force (Chaffee), and others[1] maintain much or most of the basic structure of our current private employer-based health insurance system. This distinguishes them from other proposals, such as single-payer approaches, that virtually eliminate the employers' and insurers' roles in the health insurance market in favor of publicly financed and administered health insurance.

The proposals vary in how much "improving" they think the market needs in order to accomplish cost containment, quality assurance and full access to insurance, and in how much federal or state government action is required. But they all pin the nations' hopes on insurers and health plans competing in this new market. It is ironic that health insurers, the target of some of the Clinton administration's most stinging criticism, should be given this critical role under reform.

In this chapter we will discuss briefly the kind of market these reform proposals intend to create, then look at some of the practices in the current private-employer based insurance market that undermine access, cost containment, and quality assurance, and finally examine the several levels of federal or state government intervention proposed to restrain these practices.

How an "Improved Market" Would Work

In these proposals, "improving the market" requires encouraging employers and individuals to shop for health care and health insurance based on its price and quality, and regulating what insurance is sold and how it is priced and marketed so as to encourage health insurers, plans, and providers to compete for customers by containing costs and assuring quality of services.

Those who have shaped these proposals argue for what I have called a "domino theory" of cost containment and quality assurance:[2]

Domino Number One. If purchasers of health care were to shop among health plans for the best price and quality they could get for their money, it would force insurers to compete based on those variables;

Domino Number Two. Health reformers could mobilize an army of such buyers by encouraging or directing more people to buy health insurance, and offering them a choice of competing insurers and health plans. By regulating insurers so they cannot reduce their premiums by cutting coverage or by favoring healthy and avoiding sick people, these health reformers would take away the more destructive forms of price competition in the current private health insurance market;

Domino Number Three. To keep their premiums at competitive levels, insurers would have to find ways to constrain the rising costs of health care by working with doctors, hospitals and other providers of services to better manage the services.

Market reform advocates argue that the popularity of managed care among insurers and providers is indicative of the potential for physicians, hospitals and insurers to develop new interrelationships and novel cost-containment methods. Many advocates also contend that staff- and group-model HMOs dominate the managed care system because they are vertically integrated. That is, their physicians and other providers are part of, or are closely tied contractually to an insurance or health plan and both parties share the financial risk. Ideally, the insurer and providers collaborate to jointly manage both the clinical and financial aspects of providing health care, as well as the insurance programs.

The market reform approach to health care would accelerate the pace at which insurers and providers move toward these vertically integrated managed care arrangements in order to constrain year-to-year increases in health care costs. The Clinton proposal sets "targets" (read: caps) for this consolidation, with the intention that insurance premiums will fluctuate within the following limits: no more than 1.5 percent faster than the Consumer Price Index (CPI) in 1996, with an allowance for changes in population; 1.0 percent or less in 1997; 0.5 percent in 1998; and equal to or less than the CPI in 1999 and 2000. These low rates of annual premium increase would be virtually unprecedented in the recent history of U.S. health care and health insurance.

Current Private Employer-Based Health Insurance Market Characteristics That Undermine Market Performance

Policymakers state that their health care reform proposals will improve access to health insurance, contain rising health care costs and assure the quality of health care through competition among health plans. Reform is needed because of the following structural characteristics of our current health insurance market that undermine its capacity to achieve these goals without reform.

Health Insurance Is "Employer Based." Most health insurance in the United States is arranged by employers for purchase by their employees.[3] When health insurance was first marketed by Blue Cross and Blue Shield, employers offered relatively standard insurance packages whose premiums varied little from employer to employer.

These business plans gave way to those with widely varying benefits as each employer fashioned its own agreement with the labor unions, or as they followed diverging coverage trends in their particular industry in order to compete for employees. Industries that required more highly skilled workers (or had stronger unions) offered better and better benefits; others offered weaker coverage—or none at all.

The original standard, or "community-rated," premium has also all but disappeared. As actuarial sophistication grew in the health insurance field, insurance companies could offer more attractive premiums to large employers with lower-than-average past health care claims "experience." This enabled insurance companies to lure these employers away from insurers—usually Blue Cross and Blue Shield plans—that persisted in community rating. With the further expansion of such coverage, fostered in large measure by the growth in private insurance claims data bases, insurers could offer fully or partially "experience-rated" premiums to companies employing as few as fifty people.

While such rating is the standard for most of the insurance industry today, it also has led to widely diverging premiums for employers and their workers based on their past claims experience. This development results from health insurance being arranged or purchased by individual employers who are motivated to pay only the health costs of their own employees. The insurance industry has responded by developing employer or employer-class experience rating techniques and benefit packages that help them recruit or retain the type of employees they need for their particular business. Relentlessly rising health care and insurance costs have made employers more determined than ever to limit their health expenditures to their own employees needs, thus creating the fragmentation of insurance benefits and premiums that we face today.

Such practices have undermined the insurance market's capacity to provide access to health coverage. The high premiums for large employers with "bad experience," and for some small employers who are part of a group with chronic "bad experience" (in the insurer's judgement), has prompted them to purchase less coverage or none at all.

The Uneven Distribution of Individual Health Care Costs Invites Medical Underwriting and Risk Selection. In most insurance plans, up to 50 percent of health care costs are incurred by as little as 4 percent of the subscribers. Moreover, 25 percent to 30 percent of the subscribers will incur few costs other than the occasional doctor's office visit. This wide disparity invites several insurance practices that undermine the performance of the entire market.

First, insurers have grown more adept at "medical underwriting." They will now refuse coverage because an employee or dependent has a particular medical condition, has a record of "high claims experience," or is likely to file numerous or expensive claims in the future. Insurers believe they can identify such "bad risks" fairly accurately based on a questionnaire or even a medical examination. By excluding these risks, insurers have been able to offer lower premiums to small employers and to healthier individuals. Competition by medical underwriting, of course, has undermined the insurance market's capacity to provide access to affordable health insurance to those who stand a better-than-average chance of needing costly health care. Some people, in fact, cannot buy health insurance at any price in today's market.

Second, the uneven distribution of health care costs among individuals invites insurers to compete by "risk selection" in large employer groups. In many such groups, employees choose their health insurance coverage during "open seasons" from among competing plans. "Risk selection" occurs when an insurer enrolls subscribers who use more (adverse selection) or less (favorable selection) health care than the average for the whole group. The insurer with the sicker people will have to work harder than the plan with the healthier people to keep its premium at a competitive level. Favorable risk selection can afford a very large premium advantage, as was seen in a recent study of competing Federal Employees Benefits Plans.[4] Although all the plans used identical managed care techniques, premiums varied by 100 percent while benefits differed by only 5 percent.

Although risk selection tools and medical underwriting techniques have not been perfected, they are gaining credibility in the industry. Health plans can implement any or all of the following ten patient-recruitment devices:

1. Invest in opinion research on what makes healthy and sick people join or leave plans, interviewing people whose health care utilization levels are known from their claims data;
2. Offer or emphasize benefits known to attract healthier or lower-utilizing subscribers;
3. Increase staffing for family practice, internal medicine, or pediatric and obstetric services, in order to decrease waiting times. Similarly, staff can be cut back for specialty services, especially for the chronically ill, thus increasing waiting times;
4. Try to avoid including physicians in their panels who have established practices dealing with the sickest and toughest cases in town; they may bring their patients along with them;
5. Contract with prestigious teaching hospitals in order to advertise quality, but establish tough protocols for referrals to those institutions;
6. Market themselves as the plan for healthy people, or those not worried about security, while deemphasizing services for the chronically ill;
7. Market and make services most accessible to geographic areas, work sites, and institutions where healthier people, on average, are found;
8. Avoid placing brochures in doctors offices or clinics;
9. Operate an informational "800 number" during open-enrollment season where trained counsellors ask questions of potential subscribers that subtly nudge high users (who are security conscious) away, while encouraging low users into the plan; and,
10. Angle advertising in a way that feeds the known anxieties of low users considering leaving your plan.

Risk selection in large groups undermines the insurance market's cost containment abilities in several ways. First, risk selection's power as a competitive tool weakens the incentive for insurers and health plans to compete by containing the costs of health care in order to offer low premiums; it allows insurers who do not have the capacity or will to truly manage costs to prosper by risk selection.

Second, competition by risk selection has actually increased employers' costs. This is because health plans have converted savings from favorable risk selection into more benefits or lower out-of-pocket costs for their subscribers, not into savings for the employer. This has allowed them to increase their attractiveness to employees choosing among plans in open seasons. Today, however, employers are finding ways to make risk selection save money for them and to shift more of the cost to the employee. They do this by limiting their employer's share of the premium of the plan an employee selects to the premium of the lowest cost health plan available, which is often the plan with the most favorable risk selection. This shifts more of the costs for sicker employees onto the sick employees themselves by increasing their share of the premium for their health plan.

Insurance Is Built on a "Claims Payment Chassis" That Discourages Joint Ventures with Providers. For both Blue Cross and Blue Shield Plans and commercial insurance companies, much of the business of health insurance is built on the skeleton or "chassis" of claims payment. Insurers review billions of paper or electronic claims against differing insurance contracts in order to pay agreed amounts if they judge, based on their rules, that the service was covered and appropriate. In this role, the insurer acts as a financial and accounts administrator on behalf of the subscriber.

The claims processing machinery represents a huge investment by the insurance industry. It includes computers, complex software, coding systems, forms, rules for reviewing and judging what services are "medically necessary and appropriate," and a growing armamentarium of computerized "algorithms" for reviewing whether a claim should be singled out for special review or paid.

Insurers have built much of so-called "managed care" on this chassis, rather than on the vertical integration sought by reformers, and have consequenly increased the industry's commitment to claims payment. This claims payment chassis is supported by an insurance culture that argues that business with providers should be conducted "at arms length," with both parties being restricted to the roles of buyer and seller. In fact, insurers often have succumbed to a "cops and robbers" mentality when dealing with care providers. They police claims and provider practices to "apprehend" fraud and abuse and prevent the bad guys from cheating their subscribers. The dynamic of such a system leads to more codes and distinctions among procedures and more detailed rules in order to ensure that the claim is fair and appropriate, and to catch and deny inappropriate claims.

In recent years insurers have seen the need for closer relationships with physicians. Larger insurers are moving to endorse staff and group model HMOs, replacing "arms length" with "joint venture" and "shared risk." But the vast majority of health insurance plans remain welded to a "claims payment" chassis that only undermines insurance market efforts to contain costs. It discourages movement toward the vertically integrated health plans in three ways. First, it creates resistance to global or budgeted payments to providers in vertically integrated systems that would idle the computers and all the investment and powerful insurance executives that go with them. Second, "arms-length" managed care encourages such deep hostility between physicians and insurers that getting them into the same board room or at the same negotiating table becomes increasingly difficult. Third, reviewing care on a transaction-by-transaction or claim-by-claim basis discourages the type of interactive responsibility and shared effort required to assure quality.

Insurers Are Conservative Risk Managers. Because insurers assume financial risk they are, by necessity, risk managers. In recent years it has been popular to claim that insurers are no longer at risk because of the rise in "self-insurance," where the employer assumes the risk that health claims in an upcoming year may exceed the premium set in advance (or budgeted) to cover them.

However, insurers still carry a great deal of risk in the small-employer and individual-insurance markets. In addition, HMOs competing for employees' enrollment in even large employer groups have always been at risk. As more insurers "get religion" and move toward HMOs, an increasing proportion of the market will be carried by insurers on an "at-risk" basis. By accelerating this movement, market reform proposals greatly increase the risk insurers must assume.

Health insurance risk derives from many factors. The most basic is that insurance premiums are set six to eighteen months in advance, based on claims data which is three to six months old. The more changes and fluctuations in this most recent data, the more difficult it is for the actuary to estimate future claims costs with precision. If the actual claims incurred in the forthcoming year exceed the revenues collected by the premium, the insurer must pay the difference when he is "at risk." A difference of a few percentage points in predicting claims costs can amount to a great deal of money given the volume of health care claims. If the insurer or HMO sets its next year's premium on the high side to cover uncertainty about future costs, it may not be able to compete with other plans. If it sets its rates too low, it increases the chance that it will incur losses.

An insurer's capacity to take risks of this kind is measured by the amount of its tangible financial reserves. If reserves are available to cover potential losses, it can afford to offer a competitive premium. If its reserves are low, it may need to make a high offer—or none at all.

Such "risk" considerations in a financial institution foster a reluctance to accept change and rapid innovation. Insurance risk is reduced only by slow and steady evolution that does not disrupt established trends. It also encourages strenuous efforts to "manage risk," i.e., to reduce the range of projected costs. For example, risk is reduced by avoiding quick changes in benefits, methods of managing care, or other practices, until the insurer accumulates good experience and claims data. It is also reduced by limits on the number of new subscribers an HMO or other health plan will enroll in an open season, through underwriting or risk selection techniques that avoid the higher users of care, and by agreements with providers that put them at-risk for some of the cost.

Because it goes to the heart of the insurers financial role, risk management takes precedence over "managed care," and there are many health insurers who only practice risk management. Furthermore, most of the above "risk management" techniques slow the transition to a market where insurers compete to contain costs and assure quality.

Employers (Purchasers) Poorly Manage Plan Competition. In recent decades, large employers have offered employees multiple choices of health plans, including staff and group model HMOs, in order to provide better coverage and encourage cost containment through competition among plans. However, their efforts have been undermined by the risk-selection process described above.

More recently, many employers are avoiding risk selection and its costs by reducing the number of health plans from which their employees can choose, often giving their business to one insurer who offers several different plans or a "point-of-service" choice option that allows enrollees to select a fee-for-service provider outside the plan. Many employers have moved away from their HMO options and back to fee-for-service alternatives. Some have found ways to capitalize on favorable risk selection to reduce their premiums by shifting costs to their employees, as described above.[5]

Often, the larger employer's savings in this area are attributable to cost shifting to the employees rather than to cost containment. The most popular such devices include increasing the employee's premium share or cost sharing, and reducing benefits. As with insurers, it is easier for the employer to effect savings in these ways than to encourage competition among plans. In any case, increases in employer premium rates have not demonstrated their effectiveness in managing competition.[6]

It is difficult to understand why large employers have brought so little sophistication to managing competition between plans given the high cost of the benefit. Perhaps it is a matter of overall compensation. If costs of health insurance were reduced it would be converted ultimately into higher wages, so it matters too little to the employer to force real effort. Perhaps it is the difficulty of convincing employees to accept changes in physicians and health care practices associated with the more vertically integrated versions of "managed care."

It is clear, however, that the insurance market's capacity to contain costs has been undermined by the failure of large employers to manage competition, and particularly risk selection.

What Level of Federal or State Action
Would Improve the Insurance Market?

Reform proposals based on improving the health insurance market can be seen as falling into five levels of increasing government intervention. The purpose of categorizing them in this manner is to be responsive to the political dictum that holds that government should do no more than needed to accomplish public goals. Policymakers, particularly elected politicians, often require that proposals for dealing with thorny issues be laid out in successive steps, from the least painful solution to what could be termed the most "invasive." Therefore, the following six proposals for improving the insurance market are offered incrementally, based on the level of required government intervention:

1. Regulate insurers and encourage employers;
2. Regulate insurers and mandate employer and individual purchasing;
3. Charter insurers and replace employers;
4. Make insurers the equivalent of public utilities (i.e., all-payer rate setting or the "German Model");
5. Replace insurers and employers with the government (i.e., the single-payer or Medicare model); and,
6. Replace insurers and employers and hire providers—an approach similar to socialized medicine and the Veterans Administration model.

This chapter focuses only on the first three levels, or "market-improvement" proposals. The Clinton proposal, which includes possible government regulation of providers as a back-up plan, falls somewhere between Levels Three and Four (denoted later as "Level Three and One-Half"), the Senate Republican Task Force proposal is in Level Three, the Heritage Foundation proposal is in Level Two, and the Conservative Democratic Forum proposal and most other market-improvement proposals are in Level One. Each successive level includes most of the policies of earlier levels.

Level One: Regulate Insurers and Encourage Employees

Level One reform involves regulating insurers to limit experience rating, medical underwriting, and benefit design practices that have undermined the insurance market's capacity to provide access to insurance for small groups and individuals. Almost all proposals for market reform would require insurers to: accept all applicants for insurance; exclude no specific medical or pre-existing conditions; offer all applicants a basic or standard benefit package; limit to a certain range how much premiums can vary from employer to employer (e.g., 25 percent to 50 percent); restrict variations in year-to-year premium increases; and, cut administrative costs through the use of standardized forms and procedures.

Reform at Level One also takes steps to encourage small employers and individuals to purchase more insurance on a voluntary basis by establishing subsidies of various amounts for small employers and low income individuals through tax breaks or direct government payments. Some would set up "medical IRAs" that allow individuals to pay a portion of their cost sharing or other medical costs with tax-exempt dollars.

Such reform proposals would also encourage small employers and individuals to set up voluntary joint purchasing arrangements to buy insurance on behalf of larger numbers of employees or individuals. Furthermore, some would require employers to arrange group coverage for their employees, but would not mandate an employer contribution to such a plan.

Level One reform proposals clearly address some of the practices in the employer-based health insurance market that undermine accessibility to good health insurance. By regulating insurers, it encourages employers to offer better coverage to more employees and urges individuals to purchase insurance for themselves. Supporters argue that the influx of new buyers, and the constraints on insurers' competitive tactics, will cause more competition in the market to constrain health care costs. The argument against Level One reform is that it does not go far enough to assure access to good health insurance for all, nor to contain rising health care costs.

Experience with experimental efforts in state governments to encourage employers and individuals to purchase insurance voluntarily through Level One proposals indicates a low likelihood of success.[7] The difficulty seems to be that in many low wage and unskilled labor markets, employers are not obliged to offer any insurance to obtain the employees they need. Moreover, the employees and individuals in these markets, who account for the lion's share of the nation's uninsured, have so little disposable income that they can purchase little or no coverage unless it is highly subsidized.

Critics also argue that Level One proposals offer too little hope for rapid progress toward cost containment by insurers. The proposals do not address the issue of risk selection in the large employer health insurance market. Indeed, Level One proposals seem to regard large employers as models of how to manage risk selection and competing health plans. In fact, large employers seem to be abandoning these tactics, or use risk selection and other techniques to shift costs to their employees rather than contain them. Nor do Level One proposals seem to create strong enough incentives for insurers to move from their "claims payment chassis" toward vertically integrated managed care.

Some legislators argue for starting with Level One reform, and seeing what it can do. Many others insist on moving toward greater government intervention.

Level Two: Regulate Insurers and
Mandate Employer and Individual Purchasing

Level Two reform moves from encouraging employers and individuals to purchase health insurance to mandating that they do so. At Level Two, some proposals, such as President Clinton's, require that the employer pay a substantial portion (possibly 80 percent) of the premium for their employees coverage; and they require the employee to accept the coverage and pay the remaining share of the premium. Individuals likewise are mandated to buy. Other proposals, such as that of the Republican Senate Health Task Force, mandate that the employee or individual purchase insurance if it is not offered voluntarily by the employer.

Proposals that mandate coverage also recommend the following measures: standardize coverage specifically so the employer and the individual know what they are required to purchase; constrict more tightly the range of private insurance premiums that can be offered (the Clinton proposal requires insurers to offer everyone the same "community rate"); establish higher subsidies to employers and/or individuals so the mandate does not inflict undue financial harm such as lay-offs, wage cuts, and other dislocations; regulate health insurance more broadly to encourage competition designed to contain future cost increases; and, encourage voluntary participation by small employers in purchasing alliances or cooperatives in arranging health plans and managing competition between them.

The effect of the employer and individual mandate is to override the employer's narrow interest in providing only those benefits and paying those costs that apply specifically to his employees. Under the purchasing requirement, all employers would buy at least the same standard coverage for their employees. Thus, the mandate corrects one of the fundamental practices undermining access to health insurance in the current employer-based health insurance market.

Advocates of Level Two reform argue it also will help contain costs. They contend it will encourage health plans to vertically integrate in order to offer lower premiums to attract the new, cost-conscious employers and employees who now have to buy insurance. Standardizing benefits eliminates one of the primary means of risk selection in large groups, as well as one of the factors that often confuses consumers who attempt to comparison shop for insurance.

Level Two reform is a political watershed. To require employers and or individuals to purchase insurance from a private vendor is a great step foward into government regulation. In the face of constituent or colleague opposition, many politicians simply revert to Level One reform and argue for giving it a try before going to the drastic step of sanctioned Federal control. But other legislators see Level Two as too weak to achieve cost containment. They argue that it still fails to adequately address the problem of risk selection, gives too little incentive to insurers to move toward vertically integrated managed care as a means of containing costs, and leaves it to employers to voluntarily join coalitions which might have a better chance of managing competition. These provisions portend relatively slow progress by insurers toward cost containment.

Slower progress becomes doubly worrisome to policymakers once they have moved to Level Two and mandating. If premiums were to continue to rise as in the past, very high subsidies would have to be paid in the future to keep insurance affordable under the mandate and to avoid inflicting more financial harm on employers and individuals. Higher subsidies mean higher on-budget costs and higher taxes, both politically unpopular measures.

Once at Level Two, therefore, the policymaker must propose a credible program for containing costs so they do not rise to levels requiring new taxes. Indeed, the cost containment program should be designed to achieve long-term savings sufficient to offset the short-term costs of subsidies needed to assure universal coverage. The Clinton proposal, for example, predicts a surge in health care spending as a percent of GNP for the several years immediately following enactment of health care reform legislation, but a slowdown in increases in subsequent years more than offsets the initial costs.

These pressures to accelerate market reform in order to contain cost more rapidly, rather than levy taxes, push many policymakers inexorably to Level Three reform.

Level Three: Charter Insurers and Replace Employers

Level Three reform charters insurers—that is, it limits the number of competing health plans to those that have the capacity to better manage care. In addition, it effectively replaces many or most employers with new health plan purchasers who, it is hoped, would more effectively manage health plan competition, contain costs and assure quality. These new purchasers are known under various bills as "alliances," Health Plan Purchasing Coalitions (HPPCs), or simply purchasing cooperatives. Clinton would have them purchase health insurance on behalf of all employers of less than 5,000 people—in other words, broker coverage for 78 percent of all Americans. The Cooper bill would focus on employers of fewer than 100 employees, or roughly 50 percent of the population.

Level Three proposals include all of the insurance regulation of Level One, and the employer and/or individual mandates, standardized coverage and subsidies of Level Two. They also recommend the following:

- State government certification of health plans based on criteria, established by a national board, that would be conducive to cost containment and quality assurance;
- Mandating that alliances or HPPCs be the exclusive source of health insurance and that they offer a choice of health plans to all eligible parties during annual open seasons, as well as guaranteeing that employees and individuals have clear and standardized descriptions of competing health plan premiums;
- Giving vertically integrated health plans the opportunity to offer richer coverage (lower cost sharing) at a competitive premium to employees in order to allow them to lure more of the market into more tightly managed care; and,
- Providing alliances or HPPCs with the tools for controlling and adjusting risk selection among health plans. In addition to standardized benefits, these devices include a prohibition on discriminating among subscribers and providers based on likely use of services, standardized marketing, monitoring of insurer activities, and formulae that takes favorable and adverse selection into account when adjusting premium revenues among insurers.

The goal of these reforms is to address several more of the insurance practices that undermine cost containment in the present market. They aim at reducing risk selection as a competitive practice by insurers in large groups, and create stronger market pressures on insurers to move away from their claims-based chassis to vertically integrated managed care.

There is reason to worry that these proposals do not adequately address these insurance practices and therefore may require time and or refinement in order to contain costs. One of the key problems is adjusting for risk selection. The proposal establishes mechanisms for developing risk adjustment algorithms that explain more than the 20 percent of risk selection currently achievable. There is no guarantee this is possible. Lack of a powerful risk adjustor argues for limiting the number of competing plans in each alliance and allowing the alliance to act more as a business negotiator. This raises political problems by further limiting the number of insurance plans that would survive after health reform; and it raises market concerns by making it hard for new and innovative vertically integrated systems to enter the competition.

Another obstacle is the role of "risk" in health insurance. The insurance industry needs financial reserves in order to take risks. Insurers have spent down their reserves in recent decades as more and more employers have self-insured. Many reform proposals require the insurers to apply "at-risk" variables to much of the population, and many eliminate the alternative of self-insurance for most employers. At the same time, they change the proportion of their business for which they must assume risk, with most reform proposals altering the incentives and market climate to such a great degree that actuaries will face a difficult time setting premiums for future years based on past trends. The insurers will need more financial reserves than are presently available in the industry if they are to set premiums low enough to meet the cost containment targets set by health care reform proposals.

With inadequate reserves and, as noted earlier, a marked aversion to rapid change, insurers and health plans may well respond to the reform proposals by setting high premiums or limiting the number of people they will enroll in an open season, based on their capacity or financial stability. The Clinton proposal allows them to establish such limits. Others will necessarily permit it. Such risk issues could result in too few openings in health plans to accommodate meaningful competition and choice by people in an alliance or HPPC.

Yet another problem with Level Three reform is the difficulty inherrent in setting up and staffing scores of new alliances or HPPCs. The nations' largest employers have found this approach to cost containment difficult and many are abandoning it. To achieve it in the time frame envisioned by some of the proposals seems a stiff challenge at best.

There are, at present, no completely credible Level Three proposals for restraining the insurance practices of risk selection, poor management of competition, and inadequate risk reserves, all of which undermine or greatly delay cost containment. Changes and improvements to the proposals will be needed if they are to succeed in these areas.

Like Level Two reform, Level Three would mark a new chapter in the annals of government intervention in health care. It may well produce a market where many and perhaps most present insurers cannot compete. It may also create what seems to many politicians to be large, new bureaucratic structures, namely, purchasing alliances and health boards.

These concerns with the workability of cost containment in Level Three, and with the damage to important political interests, could lead to a reshuffling of policy positions. For example, The Cooper bill maintains much of this Level Three cost-control structure, but retreats from the mandate of employers and employees out of concern that costs will not be contained and that government and private costs will be unaffordable. If an individual or an employer of fewer than 100 people chooses to buy insurance, it must do so through the HPPC, but the purchasing is still voluntary.

The Republican Senate Health Task Force allows the system twice as much time (until the year 2005) to set up and achieve credible cost containment through market reform. It phases in mandates and subsidies to employers and individuals over time as it becomes clear that costs are in fact being contained.

The Clinton bill also takes into account the possibility that market reform may not produce the level of cost containment needed in the near term to make universal access affordable; but it does so by moving toward more aggressive government intervention, rather than less, to ensure that enough money is saved to pay for access for all Americans.

Level Three and One-Half: Market Reform Backed by Government Regulation of Providers

The Clinton proposal incorporates a transition from market-based reform strategies for cost containment to government regulation of physicians, hospitals, and other providers. More specifically, the Clinton plan provides for an all-payer rate setting system for fee-for-service health insurance plans as a back up cost containment system. Other provisions include requiring alliances and or state government to establish standard fees for hospitals, doctors and other providers, which must be used as a basis of payment by health plans that are not vertically integrated—this could easily constitute over 50 percent of the insurance market. The Clinton plan would also set very tight limits on year-to-year premium increases by health plans, and automatically impose reductions in the above rates or other plan payments if the plans' annual premium increases threaten to exceed the limits specified through the year 2000.

These provisions are justified in two ways. First, they give the market an opportunity to operate on its own, while still creating a structure of government regulation that comes into play automatically if the market fails to constrain costs at the rate targeted by the proposal. The underlying assumption seems to be that this price-setting approach can serve as a last resort for achieving the level of cost containment needed to assure universal access to health insurance.

Second, advocates of this rate-setting system argue it creates an environment so distasteful to physicians, hospitals and other providers they will be all the more motivated to form vertically integrated systems and contain the cost of care in a more rational and professionally satisfying manner.

Can Private Health Insurance Achieve the Goals of Health Care Reform Given These Proposals?

While Level Three market reform would seem to achieve the goal of access to insurance for all, it is not as reliable as a cost containment mechanism. Its proposal to eliminate risk selection, for example, seems to move in the right direction, but how quickly it can be made effective is not clear. The political logic of paying for improved access to insurance by containing costs, rather than raising taxes, requires that insurance reform move not only effectively, but rapidly.

Through its strict year-to-year premium increase targets, the Clinton bill requires the most rapid rate of change within the insurance industry. These targets seem to have been based more on what savings are needed to make the political case, than on a careful assessment of what the insurance industry can achieve under market reform incentives. Some critics argue that the limits and rate-setting system of the Clinton plan distort the market incentives, and that health plans will compete not with each other, but with the government-set limits.

The industry may not be able to meet the Clinton limits or the Cooper targets. If it does not, the reasons are implicit in the practices and characteristics of our employer-based health insurance market, as described above, which has long undermined this market's capacity to achieve access, cost containment, and quality assurance. It is ironic that the most criticized institution in our health care system, health insurance, should be given the task of effecting so much of the system's reform.

Notes

1. H.R.3600, The Health Security Act (Clinton Administration); H.R.3222, The Managed Competition Act of 1993 (Cooper); S.1770, Health Equity and Access Reform Today Act of 1993 (Chaffee); H.R.3080, The Affordable Health Care Now Act (Michel); S.1743, Consumer Choice Health Security Act—to be introduced (Nickles); The Comprehensive Family Health Access and Savings Act (Gramm).

2. Stan Jones, "Regulation Under A Consumer Choice Approach To National Health Insurance: The Domino Theory of NHI," *National Center for Health Services Research: Research Proceedings—Effects of the Payment Mechanism on the Health Care Delivery System*, Proceedings of a Conference Held at Skyland Lodge Shenandoah National Park, Virginia, Nov. 7–8, 1977.

3. Congressional Budget Office, *Projections of National Health Expenditures: 1993 Update* (Washington, D.C.: Government Printing Office, 1993), p. 22.

4. Congressional Research Service, U.S. Library of Congress, *Federal Employees Health Benefits Plan: Possible Strategies for Reform*, prepared for the U.S. House of Representatives Committee on the Post Office and Civil Service, 101st Congress, First Session, Committee Print 101-5, May 24, 1989.

5. Stan Jones, "Perspective: Can Multiple Choice Be Managed?," *Health Affairs*, Fall, 1989.

6. Stan Jones, "Multiple Choice Health Insurance: The Lessons and Challenge to Private Insurers," *Inquiry*, Summer, 1990; Alain Enthoven, "Multiple Choice Health Insurance: The Lessons and Challenge to Employers," *Inquiry*, Winter, 1990; Stan Jones, "Some Pre-Surgery Notes on Alain Enthoven's Helpful Second Opinion," *Inquiry*, Winter, 1990.

7. W. David Helms et al., "Mending the Flaws in the Small Group Market," *Health Affairs*, Summer, 1992.

14

The Administrative Perils of Political Progress: Implementation Challenges in the Clinton Health Plan

Lawrence D. Brown

It's fun to have fun.
But you have to know how.
— The Cat in the Hat

Some polities view public administration as a high and noble calling, and those who practice it enjoy an elevated social status. The United States is not one of them. American political culture, which distrusts both government in general and the elected politicians who run it, reserves an especially hard place in its heart for appointed officials—"bureaucrats"—who apply the dead, heavy hand of public regulation to citizens who cannot hold them directly accountable.

In a rational cosmos, a nation that is determined to constrain its officialdom and minimize the authorities entrusted to it would command powerful efficient policymaking institutions that elicit cogent legislative measures from its elective cadres. Those who prefer not to give administrators wide scope to interpret and improvise should say plainly what they mean in statutes. The U.S. political system falls well short of this ideal. Political arrangements that divide formal power among three distinct branches of government and fail to integrate them informally by party or other mechanisms find it necessary to build ad hoc coalitions that are often strengthened by obscuring key issues that then pass into the administrative process—the bureaucracy—for elucidation. The necessity and legitimacy of administrative discretion seem to vary inversely, however, as the Right condemns bureaucracy for public intrusions in private prerogatives and the Left attacks it for selling out to private power centers.[1] American administrative norms thus add the injury of large and complex delegated tasks to the insult of strong popular distaste for the public servants who are expected to discharge them.

For these reasons the U.S. administrative process rarely affords a pretty site for policy implementation. Rather, it generally entails a jumbling and skewing of the key variables of organizational analysis—constituencies, goals, missions, technologies, structure, and more—in decidedly un-Weberian configurations. Across a range of cases at least three regularities that may be especially telling for national health reform seem to emerge.

First, policymakers repeatedly encase legislation in administrative vessels that provide political insulation from the conflicts that significant programmatic innovation triggers, but do so by clouding the lines of accountability that link citizens, program administrators, and political leaders. Second, because securing a majority coalition often demands fudging decisions on the most complicated and controversial issues, policymakers often pass laws that for their successful implementation require administrators to tackle tasks they do not know how to perform. Third, the designers of policy continually devolve onto administrators implementation challenges that cannot be met without a tenable equilibrium between the goals and intents of law—often multiple, ambiguous, or inconsistent—and the preferences of those real-world players who live with and under those laws. Therefore, administrators often find themselves in tension both with lawmakers (who wonder why their goals were subverted and displaced) and stakeholders (who complain that they have been left uncertain about what is expected of them, or that what seems to be expected is unreasonable). These three patterns may be captured in shorthand as issues of structure, technology, and environment, respectively. These administrative perplexities more or less go with the territory of policymaking in the United States; if pressing social problems compel a policy response one has little choice but to proceed in spite of them. Nonetheless, those who would tread boldly onto new strategic turf might want to ponder the possible fate of their proposals in these bureaucratic thickets, the political and substantive costs of triggering a particularly severe bout of administrative conflict and confusion, and feasible means (if any) of easing implementation frictions that are unavoidable in the best-laid plans.

Administrative Challenges of Health Policy Reform:
An Overview

Reformers discount administrative obstacles to the implementation of their health policy goals at their peril. Health care adds to the generic

American aversion to bureaucracy the "scientific" objections of well-heeled, strongly-organized provider constituencies to governmental instrusion in their professional affairs; deeply-entrenched bad habits integral to the nation's laissez-faire tradition in health policy (which has thusfar rejected efforts to build a coherent federal policy framework around actors who have played by rules largely set by and for themselves); and easily inflamed suspicions in the popular mind that "government" and "reform" are mutually exclusive constructs. The public also apparently wants federal leadership in fixing health care arrangements that need substantial repair—but without markedly enlarging federal regulating and taxing powers. All this cognitive and political dissonance could be a prelude to a flamboyant reprise of the administrative dysfunctions noted above, namely, reform schemes that furnish political insulation by obscuring administrative accountability, that dump into administrators' ill-prepared laps questions that proved too thorny to resolve legislatively, and that subject administrators to the debilitating cycle of public sector disappointment and private sector discontent. These are neither the only nor the main issues in evaluating the Clinton administration's health reform proposals, but they ought to be somewhere on the checklist.

Unfortunately, administrative concerns have had little visibility in the intensifying health reform debate.[2] This may be natural enough: To proponents of "fundamental" and "comprehensive" change, it is self-evident that the health care problems the nation confronts are "systemic" and demand bold new policy concepts and constructs now that a window of opportunity has finally opened. Getting the grand plan right is surely the top priority; institutional "details" can wait.

Systems analysts fashioning macro-level reforms might concede, however, that policy ideas mean little if they are not implemented effectively by the system's diverse operatives, and they might agree too that a reputation—deserved or not—for managerial incapacity can erode popular confidence in government, as it did in the 1970s, when dozens of assessments chronicled federal faltering in the implementation of Great Society programs. Both short-term program efficacy and the longer-range viability of public sector innovation argue for timely, sustained monitoring of administrative challenges.

It might be argued that the notion of policy and administration as discrete entities is misconceived. Every fin de siecle observer understands that they are inseparable, that administration is replete with policy content and political causes and correlates. That these are inseparable processes does not, however, make them indistinguishable. Administration is the means by which appointed officials try to make sense of the policy directives entrusted to them by their political superiors. Precisely because these directives are so often vague, contradictory, excessively specific, or otherwise problematic, administration is the art of making policy work as well as possible in the real world—a challenge that generally demands mediation between, and modification in, both policy and its objects.[3] When these adaptations and improvisations break down, so does policy. And, arguably, the more audacious, speculative, creative, and demanding is the policy adopted, the greater the burdens—and the higher the stakes—of successful administrative mediation between government and society.

The Clinton health reform initiative may be as audacious, speculative, creative, and demanding a policy initiative as has ever hit the top of the action agenda of U.S. domestic policy. The plan tries to do what some think is impossible: Deliver to the electorate the big change it seems to seek in the health care system without increasing unacceptably the role of big government, taxing, and spending. In a dramatic attempt to square this circle, the Clinton administration has offered up an ingenious and eclectic combination of markets and regulation, of familiar features of the present system and fresh institutional machinery, and of public and private functions, new, old, and revised. Although the plan aims to simplify the current melange of financing and delivery mechanisms, an effort to touch so many bases while soothing so many interests inevitably creates complexities of its own. These intricacies of vision and design in turn pose administrative challenges that could turn out to be minor bumps along the road to reform or obdurate barriers that cannot be easily overcome, and therefore call into question key policy tenets of the proposal itself.

This chapter explores some administrative challenges of the Clinton plan by contemplating structure, technology, and environment. On all three counts the proposal presents dilemmas. By seeking to introduce major change into the system without raising the spectre of big government, it incorporates institutions that promise political insulation (that is, decisionmaking at a comfortable remove from political leaders and overt political processes). These decision structures, however, raise questions of democratic accountability (that is, who really runs them and how voters/consumers can trace salient health care events and outcomes to policy and its makers). By inventing new organizations and processes that mediate between government and a private system that is "broken" but resists significant measures of direct governmental repair, the plan seeks societal comfort (and political cover) in revitalized markets and restructured incentives. It thereby presumes that a range of organizations will tackle new tasks for which they may lack adequate administrative technologies. And by inventing a new synthesis of market and regulatory forces to negotiate a better balance among cost, quality, and access, the proposal risks a scenario of administrators perpetually at odds with public superiors and private stake-holders with images of "correct" balancing that conflict with those of administrative intermediaries.

Political Insulation and Democratic Accountability: Structural Dilemmas

The basic purpose of the Clinton plan—and the sine qua non of any health reform worthy of the name—is to introduce a set of federal policy rules that stand a chance of making the system's otherwise fragmented and undisciplined elements cohere. The key policy tools are employer mandates, broad insurance reform, health alliances as purchasing agents, and budget targets.[4] These (and other) tools would be deployed administratively at four main levels. First, a new National Health Board (NHB) would set budget targets and baselines, promulgate risk adjustment methods, establish mechanisms for monitoring and assuring the quality of care, and more. Second, the states, working within the new federal policy framework, would determine the number of regional health alliances within their borders, set rules for their composition and governance, and certify health plans. Third, new regional health alliances within each state would negotiate terms of trade with health plans, ensure that plans eschew preferred risk selection in their marketing and enrollment practices, and work to keep regional health costs within budget targets. Fourth, health plans must themselves play within these and other federal rules or risk exclusion from the menu of plans that health alliances offer to their members (that is, consumers under their jurisdiction). All four levels—the federal government, states, alliances, and plans—become partners in the quest for affordable universal coverage, which integrates new financing provisions, new mechanisms for shopping for and buying care, and new budgetary and insurance regulations.

In the aggregate, this schema marks a significant departure from the status quo. At the same time, proponents insist, it preserves important elements of existing arrangements and introduces incremental changes consistent with the American policy style. The plan therefore tempers (or hedges) its policy breakthroughs with various forms of political insulation that deflect both charges that the Clintons are contriving a major governmental "take-over" and the heat of conflicts that change will generate. All employers would for the first time be required to pay at least 80 percent of the cost of insuring their workers, but the system would remain "employer-based" (firms with fewer than 5,000 workers would pay into the regional alliances, those that are larger would continue to make their own arrangements for worker coverage). Less well-off firms and workers would get subsidies, and all employers are promised a cap on the percent of payroll that health coverage could consume. New rules would presumably end the most odious discriminatory practices of the health insurance industry, but the industry would survive (as it would not in a single-payer system) and its leading lights will probably own or manage many health plans. (And—icing on the compensatory cake—small insurers thrown out of work by consolidations in the insurance market may even find new jobs working for the health alliances.)

Market forces would be the best, but not last, hope for cost containment; should they fail, the Clinton plan calls a budgetary "backstop" into play. This regulatory strategy, however, does not involve direct manipulation of or negotiated agreement on fees and charges of doctors and hospitals but rather imposes a cap on the rate of growth of health insurance premiums. Forcing health plans to discipline providers apparently affords political insulation that public sector rate setting lacks. The Clinton proposal has high hopes for improving quality by gathering and publicizing data on the performance of individual plans and their providers, and by using these data to "empower" consumers shopping among plans. Such doings, touchy when placed in governmental hands, would be the province of regional councils that handle quality-related tasks. These and related expedients may make change more saleable by cushioning—insulating—both the general public and special constituencies from the inevitable shocks of a systemwide overhaul.

This blend of innovation and incrementalism may make sound centrist political sense, but these structural concoctions carry a potential administrative challenge—the diffusion of responsibility and accountability, that is, a clear sense among the citizenry as to who does what, why, and in what chain of command. The fuzziness starts with the NHB, an entity more reminiscent of French central planning than of U.S. practice (there seem to be no clear analogues in housing, education, environmental protection, or other key policy arenas) whose ontological status and mission are vague. The United States already has, of course, a "Ministry of Health," namely, the Department of Health and Human Services (HHS), which would probably be entrusted with broad national rule setting. HHS, however, is a notorious "bureaucracy," with formal channels of accountability straight to the President (and Congress), and these connections, doubtless a virtue in administrative theory, are a defect in political practice.

As first proposed, the NHB was to be a paragon of insulation, composed not of bureaucrats but of experts, independent of direct executive and legislative control. But its functions would be multiple and complex, leaving one to wonder how these jobs could be done wisely and well without significant bureaucratic support; how competent generalist masters on the board would be to control their staffs; whether the board would parallel, duplicate, or interfere with activities and staff at HHS; and whether an operation of this magnitude and importance should be detached from political leadership. Evidently the Clinton team had second thoughts of its own about independence. The latest iteration makes the board an executive agency run by seven presidentially-appointed members with staggered terms. It is nebulously described as a "steering committee,"[5] but one that would still stand above the political fray, enjoying immunity from administrative and judicial review of its cost containment decisions. Predictably, these modifications have failed to allay the anxieties of conservatives, who reject what they depict as a powerful new bureaucratic presence that will try to run the health care system from Washington, D.C. A new health care game surely requires new rules, and, therefore, a well-constituted administrative structure responsible for setting them in Washington. A convincing case that the NHB fills that bill has not yet been made.

Supporters of the Clinton plan invoke that most hallowed form of insulation, the U.S. federal system, by insisting that Washington's role as rule maker will be confined to functions that require national standard-setting, as much action as is consistent with affordable universal coverage will be devolved to the states. The states, for instance, can choose between an alliance-based system or a single payer model, can make the alliances agencies of state government or non-profit corporations, determine the number of alliances and (within federal constraints) their structure, and certify health plans. Many of these decisions will be political hot potatoes. For example, the number of health alliances and their boundaries will shape the distribution of risks within them, and therefore the costs that must be covered by employer premiums. Moreover, once the alliances are up and running, the states' role(s) in overseeing them are unclear. For instance, seeking political insulation of their own, the states, speaking through the National Governor's Association, refused responsibility for enforcing budget limits on health alliances, so the NHB will apparently shoulder that painful duty. But what happens when the states' initial decisions about the alliances' numbers, jurisdictions, governance, and organizational locus come under fire? Who sets criteria for "adequate" performance, and can state decisions be modified at will? Whose will? (That is, who is "the state" for these intents and purposes?) Are states expected to monitor the operations of health alliances and extend technical assistance when they think it is needed? Do state departments of health and of insurance have the staff capacity and expertise to do so? If competitive rigors force health plans to the financial wall (or out of business), should the state help them find their way or prop them up? If collection, communication, and clarification of data on health plan performance is essential to informed consumer choice, should states have a hand in discharging these functions? In most states health alliances will be unfamiliar creatures, and it is not easy to visualize the state administrative structures best suited to put them in place and speed them on their way.

The health alliances, which will act as health insurance purchasing agents for small firms (now defined as those with fewer than 5,000 workers) and individuals, raise accountability questions of their own. These entities are at once the ultimate in political insulation and the truly crucial element of the scheme, for they mediate among new government entitlements, cost-conscious pooled purchasers, health insurance administrators, and (of course) providers, effectively disciplined at last by these new arrangements. It falls to the alliances to strike policy tradeoffs heretofore unthought of or unthinkable but now made acceptable by their market clout and strategic acumen. States could make the alliances agencies of state government, but their mainly private sector constituents may not want to be represented in this fashion. The alternative—not-for-profit corporations run by boards composed equally of employers and consumers (with providers confined to an advisory role)—may be more comfortable in orientation, but poses problems of its own. These nonprofit bodies would work under the general oversight of the states but would be answerable mainly to their own boards. Employers and consumers are not homogeneous categories, however: with so much money on the line one anticipates a lively intraorganizational politics. How will conflicts over the fairness of representation and the wisdom of substantive decisions be negotiated? What would be the division of authority between the states and the self-governing boards? How much expertise will business and consumer members bring to their jobs, and how much time will they commit to them? Why should the economists' worst, and usual, case scenario—capture of feeble regulatory bodies by the canny, well-financed special interests they supervise—not emerge here? Is it feasible to limit providers and their kin to purely advisory roles in a political economy that spends one dollar in seven on health care? The United States has been down a similar road before—nonprofit Health Systems Agencies endowed with (supposedly) consumer-dominated boards and a broad mission—with disappointing results,[6] and it is hard to say whether the alliances' power to channel billions of dollars and make "real" decisions will cure or compound the organizational liabilities evident in the HSAs.

The bedrock protection for accountability in this refashioned market system adds another layer of political insulation with the sanction of another hallowed American ideology: The consumer's right to choose among health plans certified by the states and offered by health alliances permits disaffected customers to vote with their feet. But, as President Clinton himself observed, choice and movement among plans will not be cost-free. Those who want more generous plans will have to pay more—a bit of a problem for the less well off, who may not be able to afford the out-of-pocket costs they would incur in plans other than HMOs. Nor is accountability for the performance of plans and providers between open enrollment periods a negligible concern. The rules of the new game presume that plans will offer—will have to offer—reasonable access to good quality care at "efficient" rates. To date the nation has shrunk from pushing cost containment hard, so no one knows what modal responses, and what range of variations, to expect when health plans are compelled to cover all enrollees, deliver good results on health "report cards," and do so at bids that stay within the budget limits the alliance elects to set or the premium caps it must honor.

In principle, states and alliances will monitor the adequacy of access and quality within guidelines set by the NHB and other advisory groups; will make risk-adjusted payments that preclude financial disaster in plans with high numbers of poor risks; and will rely on the managerial capacity of plan administrators not to damage their reputations and market positions by striking inappropriate balances among access, quality, and cost. These expectations assume in turn that good data are available and ready to be packaged, analyzed, and communicated to multiple audiences; that state and alliance administrators will be prepared to monitor and steer plan performance in a newly competitive marketplace; that plan managers will recognize "inappropriate" balancing when they see it; and that they will be disinclined to chance it even when the financial risks are strong and the affected constituents are weak. All these assumptions are speculative: useful data are not available on a national and regional scale for a wide range of pertinent variables; the interpretation of the data on hand is often controversial; and the likely administrative behavior of states, alliances, and health plan managers in balancing cost, quality, and access is largely unpredictable.[7]

It should be noted too that these structural questions apply only to a subset of a larger system that would remain considerably fragmented. The regional health alliances under the oversight of the NHB mainly cover smaller firms and individuals. Larger firms could choose to join the regional bodies or to constitute themselves as "corporate" alliances under the supervision of the Department of Labor, which would be expected to enforce the requisites of affordable universal health coverage for this clientele. Meanwhile, HHS would continue to run Medicare, and undocumented aliens, veterans, Indians, and various other populations would remain under yet other administrative auspices.

The Clinton plan promises the security of health care that can never be taken away. But security inheres not only in formal financing entitlements but also in practical perceptions of the interplay between financing provisions and delivery patterns. It is far from clear that public opinion will agree that broad reformulations of the delivery system are an acceptable price for universal coverage achieved (allegedly) without major new taxing and spending. Consumers who are moved to examine the current system may deplore the arbitrary impact of employer policies on the contents and continuity of coverage; the constrictions of provider choice well underway; and the carte blanche extended to insurers to raise rates, drop coverage, and exclude bad risks, and conclude that the President's plan looks highly attractive by contrast. Some, however—especially middle class types satisfied with their coverage and providers and in no hurry to cross-subsidize others—may be troubled by a plan that makes their options contingent upon decisions trickling down from an NHB, states, alliances, and plans whose structural properties remain vague and whose political accountability is hazy.

Decisions in Organizational Uncertainty: Technological Dilemmas

Clever policy inventions mean little if those who must implement them do not know how to proceed. This issue is often glossed over. After all, policy innovators are generally pretty confident that their theories will work well enough in practice if only practitioners put their minds to it. Moreover, they can usually point to "prototypes"—successful, albeit miniaturist, examples of some facsimile of their recommendations, in at least a few sites. And organizational learning is obviously (and tautologically) possible if the right conditions (carrots and sticks) support it. The nature of the learning curve is vitally important, but inherently unknowable, so the proper inference is anyone's guess. Should policy be geared to best practices and creative incentives that bring laggards up to speed, or should it be aimed at the middle of the administrative performance curve, lest innovation overtax implementers and invite disappointment across a highly variable and weakly-controlled federal system?

The Clinton plan takes the expansive view. It would require a wide range of organizations to tackle tasks that will be new for most and difficult for many. The NHB's agenda is broad and complex:

> ... implement the comprehensive benefit package, oversee cost containment, put in place standards for the coverage of individuals and families, establish quality and information standards, set up requirements for participating states, monitor participating states' compliance, establish premium class factors, develop risk-adjustment methodology, encourage the reasonable pricing of breakthrough pharmaceuticals, establish minimum capital requirements, and set up grievance procedures for enrollees.[8]

None of this is unproblematic. Most analysts contend, for example, that the risk adjustment methods now available are rather basic, which complicates fair compensation of health plans for higher risks, a premise that is critical to the Clinton proposal's assault on preferred risk selection.

The Board would also set a national framework for quality assurance, a quantum leap from current national efforts that advance slowly and not always steadily, to generate consensus on medical practice guidelines and information about health outcomes. The NHB would create a National Quality Management Program, to be run by a National Quality Management Council, for which the NHB would provide a staff; set up and monitor regional professional foundations with a sizable agenda of their own; establish and appoint the (eleven) members of a National Quality Consortium; implement health information systems that would "collect, regulate, and disseminate a broad range of information," safe-guarding individual privacy all the while; and set standards for the "form, manner, and frequency" of information collection and transmission. Luckily, a 15-member National Privacy and Health Data Advisory Council would also be created to help the NHB with these duties.[9] Likewise the Board would establish "baseline" budgets for health alliance regions, from which permissible future spending growth would proceed. This task may be difficult not only for obvious equity reasons—lower bases for past "efficient" performers seem to penalize the good guys—but also because data on spending patterns are far from complete and are not always useful for regulatory purposes.

The states too may find many tasks assigned them by the Clinton plan beyond their technical ken. Despite understandable acclaim of state health policy innovations over the last five years or so, it is worth noting that the approaches of the reform leaders—Hawaii, Oregon, Massachusetts, Florida, Washington, Minnesota, Vermont—differ markedly from one another, and that none save the Washington legislation closely resembles the national blueprint in the Clinton plan. (Florida's Community Health Purchasing Alliances, for instance, are voluntary and limited to firms of 50 workers or fewer.) None has yet organized mandatory health alliances, whose purview runs the gamut of delivery and financing issues. Few have much track record in certifying, monitoring, advising, and perhaps resuscitating health plans. With the exception of modest and largely superficial ventures in health insurance regulation and in the launching of (mostly voluntary) managed care programs in Medicaid, the states have trod lighly on this turf. Organizing and interpreting data to "empower" consumers in a competitive marketplace are likewise embryonic activities in most state health bureaucracies. If 50 laboratories of democracy are to play workable variations on the new national themes, they may need a good number of new sophisticated staff—not easy when budgets are tight and hiring procedures cumbersome—and must train existing staff to adapt quickly.

The states have the advantage of administrative staffs and routines now in place, available for improvisation and "reform" (an advantage that can equally be read as a recipe for Thorstein Veblen's "trained incapacity" for major innovation). The health alliances must start from scratch and face a wide range of technically-complex and politically-charged tasks. As shoppers and buyers in the small-group market, they must, among other things, set fee schedules for fee-for-service plans, assure that plans contract adequately with academic medical centers for specialist care, and digest and use the products of the many new quality-promoting institutions the reform would create. Each year the alliances would furnish to each interested plan such pertinent information as:

> ... demographic characteristics of persons eligible for enrollment; the uniform per capita conversion factor for the regional alliance; the premium class factors; the regional alliance inflation factor; the risk-adjustment factors, reinsurance methodology, and payment amounts to be used by the regional alliance in computing blended plan per capita rates; the plan bid, AFDC, and SSI proportions; the AFDC and SSI per capita premium amounts; and the alliance administrative allowance percentage.[10]

Because they are as yet legal fictions one can picture alliances as one pleases, and some administration planners prefer to depict them as leanly-staffed bodies mediating modestly between purchasers and plans. Minimalism could carry costs of its own, however. The Clinton plan wants to see all citizens enrolled in plans that offer everyone reliable access to good quality care under a basic benefit package. Will the health alliance staffs know how to ensure that all such services are in fact appropriately available to all enrollees, and not merely on paper? If they question the management decisions of one or another plan (seeking to make its way in a tough market newly constrained by fiscal pressures of price competition and premium caps) will they be prepared to negotiate or demand improvements? Will their staffs acquire detailed performance information (some of it perhaps viewed as proprietary) from health plans, know what to make of it, translate it into cogent reports to consumers, and help them make sense of it all? How much outreach, counseling, and intervention will alliances be expected to furnish consumers who no longer take their orders or cues from employers? Will alliances have waiting rooms?[11] The alliance's broad agenda will demand board members and staffs with a so-

phisticated understanding of data and their (mis)uses, insurance principles and practices, evaluation methods, government programs, health
plan management, and more. Will the right people be available when and
where the alliances want them?

Ironically, organizational technology may be as challenging to the
health plans as to their institutional superstructure. The managed care
"revolution," sometimes viewed as the basic system transformation that
the Clinton approach would incrementally expand, has given health plans
little experience with price competition, still less with operating within
budget limits designed to shrink spending growth rates rapidly. The
fastest growing segments of the managed care market—not traditional
HMOs, but rather PPOs, IPAs, and indemnity plans with utilization review and related components—have not departed far from the norms of
fee-for-service, third party payment medicine. (That may be why they
have grown quickly.) Most health plans have so far faced the same opportunity, indeed competitive imperative, to practice preferred risk selection
just like the rest of the insurance industry. Covering all consumers for a
defined benefit package within firm cost constraints will be a new task for
most of them. It may be true that huge quantities of "fat" await squeezing,
and that contractions that would be politically impossible if engineered
directly by government will be tolerated when contrived by market
forces. Yet, with the possible exception of some group and staff-model
HMOs, few plans have displayed high "profiles in courage" in separating
medical wheat from chaff. Denying tests and procedures, closing facilities, managing queues, reducing work forces, and refusing specialist con-
sultations may be no less controversial because they are market-driven.
How plans will respond to broad new service mandates coupled to firm
new cost constraints is anyone's guess, but how they can respond
sucessfully without significantly enlarged micromanagement of the behavior of consumers and providers is hard to imagine. Plans may face intensified levels of intraorganizational conflict that will demand adroit
management, both administrative and medical, far transcending the casual expedients that suffice in today's weakly competitive and regulated
system.

In its forthright commitment to affordable universal coverage, the Clinton plan is a dramatic and welcome break with the political past. Its dependence on speculative organizational dynamics to achieve these goals
outside the glare of the political spotlight is, however, disturbingly consistent with policy patterns of the last two decades. The formula—evident in
federal policy for HMOs, PSROs, and HSAs—goes roughly as follows.
Agree to inflate an organizational skeleton into a national policy blueprint; postulate national penetration by this new institutional type; assign
the organization a long list of goals, many of them unclear, controversial,

or mutually inconsistent; turn hundreds of the new entities loose in pursuit of these goals with little preparation and inadequate staffing, training, and funding; revisit the enterprise a few years later to discover that most of the organizations have performed disappointingly; spread blame broadly across the explanatory spectrum from ill-advised legislative provisions imposed by one's partisan and ideological antagonists to lack of savoir faire by local administrators; and set about inventing programmatic repairs nearly as speculative as the original gambit.[12]

The federal government is not congenitally incapable of organizational innovation that reliably advances policy reform. The Prospective Payment Assessment Commission and the Physician Payment Review Commission, for example, have helped guide into place radical alterations in the mechanisms by which Medicare pays hospitals and physicians.[13] These, however, are national bodies with central staffs, not entities expected to take root in hundreds of state and local jurisdictions. They deal with one dimension of one program—payment rules in Medicare—not the balancing of access, quality, and cost for most of the population. And although they mediate among interests, experts, and policymakers, they perform an advisory function in making decisions for which the President and Congress retain clear accountability.

The administrative architecture of the Clinton plan risks a reprise of the familiar pattern of political insulation cum organizational confusion on a much enlarged scale with vastly higher stakes. The generalizability of prototypes should be considered carefully in the context of the capacities of average- and under-achievers before one can begin to judge whether the plan is a prudent leap of faith within the reach of organizational technologies or the latest in a series of federal invitations to administrative frustration.

Mediating Between Government and Groups: Environmental Dilemmas

The key goals of the Clinton plan, universality and affordability, have long eluded U.S. society. The reason may be that no one—until now—has been clever, committed, and resourceful enough to devise a comprehensive Pareto-optimal reform strategy, under which relations among groups, administrators, and political leaders should fall into line without crippling conflict. Or the reason may turn not on wit but on major disagreements over values and interests that are inherently hard to manage—and especially so for the weak institutions of American government. In this case, reform probably portends pitched battles over who bears its costs and enjoys its benefits, battles that will strain relations among groups and government, leaving administrators caught in the cross fire.

As James Morone remarked, controlling costs and improving access "partially contradict one another," encouraging Congress "under political pressure to leave its primary goal ambiguous—tossing the most fundamental matter into the lap of implementing agencies."[14] As administrators figure out what to do with this "most fundamental matter" they will be strongly influenced by their environment—patterns of political support and opposition by private groups and public leaders who follow their work and try to influence it by means both of clear and present signals from formal authorities and informal power holders and of the subtler dynamics of the law of anticipated reactions. They may well find that environment unsettled and unsettling.

If universality is to be squared with affordability, the medical and lay executives of the health plans must manage aggressively both the demand for and supply of care. Likely strategies include: limitations on consumer demand (gatekeeping and higher out-of-pocket costs for those outside managed care plans), supply side contractions (reducing duplication of facilities, encouraging regionalization), and, probably most important, depressing the rate of growth of payments to professionals, health care institutions, and those employed by them. These measures could trigger severe conflict between plan enrollees and providers on one side and plan administrators on the other, especially if all plans end up constrained by premium caps, and few consumers discern a ready "exit" from new constraints.

The health alliances are expected to be willing and able to monitor the plans in their portfolios and to ensure that they meet their budget targets while also maintaining access and preserving (in fact improving) quality. This presumably requires, among other things, investigating the availability of services and the adequacy of staffs and facilities and translating data into materials useful for empowered consumers. Such tasks hold a strong potential for conflict both with the plans monitored and with the insurance companies that are expected to own and run many of them. Nor are alliances likely to avoid internal conflict on various counts: Neighborhood, class, race, and other social cleavages may cut across each other, and consumer members dedicated to broad benefits and easy access may clash with business members working to hold the line on their premium contributions. It is not farfetched to picture new, tentative, thinly-staffed health alliances locked in combat with health plan administrators, providers, insurers, employers, and consumers as they collectively encounter the strains of wringing value for money from the U.S. health care system.

Who will manage these conflicts if they spill over the boundaries of the alliances and into the press and the public arena? The states perhaps, for they are entrusted with many basic decisions for these regional bodies and (presumably) will have authority to amend and revise in the light of experience. The plan is not clear about such flexibility, however, and its exercise would in any case generate political heat and legal challenges once initial structures were put in place. Moreover, the states' apparent unwillingness to enforce budget caps suggests that health plans and alliances may find themselves getting mixed signals—from the states on delivery issues, from the NHB (or other federal authorities) on cost containment matters. Market devotees cherish Charles Schultze's tenet that markets obviate the need, supposedly constant in public sector reallocations, to indemnify the losers from policy change.[15] But if market reforms produce many losers, with a deep sense of loss, their anger is likely to be turned on the closest politically-accountable targets, who will stay their heavy governmental hands at their electoral peril. All these doings channel sizable sums here and there among claimants with deep economic stakes and fervent principled rationales for their positions. They are bound to be political, and the best-plotted schemes to force conflict down to the levels of markets and administrators cannot ensure that it will obediently stay there. If the states are a prime center of action, the result could be dozens of federal-state battles over the terms of waivers that will allow states to modify this aspect of the federal rules and jettison that one. But, then again, the states may decline to iron out the wrinkles in Washington's blueprint.

If the states prefer to insulate themselves from such conflicts, they may direct antagonisms toward the NHB, whose interpretations of the benefit package, risk adjustment methods, baseline budgets, and other weighty questions should generate some controversy of their own. National political leaders might reiterate that the NHB was designed to stand above the fracas and insist that it take the heat, but if the heat grows too intense for sizable electoral blocs policymakers may become disillusioned and start damping it. Like the rest of the administrative apparatus, the NHB has no magic formula for the harmonious equilibria it is expected to devise. If it holds fast to the postulated cost constraints by enforcing premium caps, it risks conflict with an insurance industry made perhaps more powerful through consolidation and control of health plans, and with a wider range of actors suffering the pains of contraction. If it eases the cost controls to allow a kinder, gentler adjustment to universal coverage, political leaders may criticize its indulgence. The health plans, alliances, states, and NHB may pay a significant price for the political insulation envisioned by and for their political superiors in Washington, namely, a life of friction with myriad aggrieved constituents in an agitated administrative environment.

Conclusion: Administrative Perils of Political Progress

One regrettable side effect of the upsurge in health reform sentiment is the assumption that health policy analysts can insightfully forecast the consequences of the numerous innovations proposed in more than 1,300 pages of draft legislation. The great majority of these consequences are unpredictable. The uncertainty may be especially great on administrative questions, which turn on nuances, little understood, in 50 states and thousands of communities. Perhaps the administrative requisites of the Clinton plan can be met with relatively little pain and much social benefit. Perhaps the pain will be severe, but the ensuing confusion no worse than the status quo. Perhaps the plan will trigger administrative chaos, but the price will be well worth paying to achieve universal coverage—a goal whose harmonization with cost containment is, after all, an object of constant debate and adjustment even in systems that dedicated themselves to it long before the United States. Or perhaps the administrative dilemmas of the plan highlight truly problematic features of its political and conceptual underpinnings.

Affordable universal coverage has five main ingredients: a clear entitlement of all citizens to care, a basic benefit package that defines (at least in general terms) what care is covered, financing mechanisms that validate the entitlement, far-reaching insurance reform that eliminates many practices now standard in that industry, and a plausible framework for cost containment. From an administrative viewpoint, the shortest distance from the current system (which fails on all five counts) to one honoring these objectives is probably a single payer model that finances care with public revenues, eliminates private health insurance and (therewith) the many complications that attend its revision and regulation,[16] and meddles very little in a delivery system founded on fee-for-service medicine, third party payment, and broad freedom of choice for patients and providers. The Clinton plan takes a very different route, far more tortuous administratively, that preserves both employer-based financing and the private health insurance industry, and hopes to achieve afforable universal coverage by market reform of the delivery system. The approach rests in good part on the political judgment that a system like the Canadian would not fly in the United States and that something more centrist and homegrown must be offered up instead. The Clinton plan therefore proposes an "American solution to American problems," one with abundant political insulation and a determination to avoid such familiar bugbears as "big government" and "tax and spend" policies, and the conservative brickbats they provoke.

This political reasoning may be impeccable but it asks a great deal of organizational and administrative capacities to assimilate and improvise innovations in response to policy directives from above. The Clinton plan risks diffusing accountability for important administrative decisions throughout a complex organizational universe constructed in part to furnish political insulation from conflict. The organizations within that universe may be asked to implement policies that are not sustained by decisionmaking technologies now at hand. And administrators may find themselves damned if they do and if they don't as they steer toward a better balance among cost, quality, and access within a skeptical-to-hostile environment of interest groups and public sector superiors poised to blame them for failing to make sense of the new policies. As often happens in U.S. politics, the Clinton plan risks deferring to administrators basic conflicts of value and interest whose attempted legislative resolution might stop policymaking in its tracks. Whether this is American politics as necessary and appropriate or (and?) an invitation to an implementation debacle that discredits policy itself is impossible to judge prospectively.

Administrative perplexities, though hardly lethal to the appeals of the Clinton plan, may be salient enough at least to make one wonder whether the implicit premise of the policy debate over the two years or so—that the strategic choice lies between a single payer system and managed competition—has not enforced a premature foreshortening of the options. Is there no policy "center" that might hold politically without demanding the administrative conjectures of the Clinton plan? Cross nationally, single payer systems are few and full-blown models of managed competition are nonexistent. Most western democracies finance care by social insurance mechanisms (payroll taxes on employers and workers) and contain costs by national regulation of payments to providers—a combination of budget caps and structured negotiations—complemented by supply side regulation with teeth.[17] The closest U.S. analogue that might point toward a reform "model" is the Medicare program, which rests on social insurance financing, retains private insurers in the minor roles of fiscal intermediaries and carriers, and regulates payments by means of the Prospective Payment System for hospitals and the Resource Based Relative Value Scale fee schedule for physicians. Much can be said for and against this model, but Medicare has been reasonably successful in covering the eligible population, holding down administrative costs, and (lately) curbing the rate of growth of payments to providers.

Regulated multipayer social insurance systems have their problems, to be sure. Critics say that their policy and administrative foci center too heavily on the fiscal concerns of budget and insurance ministries and too little on prevention, education, promotion, and kindred endeavors that transcend mere sickness insurance and promote positive measures to improve the public's health. Equally important, such systems increasingly fear excessive, inappropriate, and costly utilization patterns and volumes

of service that constraints on freedom of choice and practice and more sophisticated information on the clinical efficacy of services might redress.

Social insurance (as well as single payer) systems have watched with
fascination U.S. experiments with managed care, medical guidelines, and
outcomes research, but so far they have resisted the comprehensive reorganization of the delivery system embraced so warmly by many influen-
tial American analysts and by the Clinton plan. Their reticence probably
reflects both supply and demand considerations. Recognizing how hard it
is to fine tune incentives and reorient entrenched delivery patterns, other
nations may doubt the ability of their administrative systems to pull it off
well. They also show a healthy skepticism as to whether public opinion
wants or would accept such changes. In the United States, the support of
sizable numbers of public opinion poll respondents for "fundamental
change" in the system has convinced reformers that the populace shares
their own "systemic" diagnoses and cures, but a large dose of caution
might be in order. It is quite unclear what people mean by such answers or
what concrete tradeoffs they might be prepared to endorse. Very likely the
average citizen thinks mainly about the system's parts, not the whole, and
is persnickety about what parts he or she wants fixed and which left in
place. (High on the latter list is freedom of choice of provider.)[18] Thence,
perhaps, the rub: both the administrative capacity to supply fundamental
delivery reform and the public's demand for it are problematic, but the
Clinton plan makes it the centerpiece of both the affordability of universal
coverage and the political centrism of its policy initiative.

If this approach could be riding for an administrative fall (quite possibly preceded by a legislative tumble), why not revisit social insurance financing coupled with central regulation of multiple payers as an alternative centrist scheme that could assume an acceptably American shape and
might avoid some of the administrative complications in the Clinton plan
as well? The answer seems to be, first, that social insurance financing
evokes (payroll) taxes in ways that employer mandates do not, and, second, that structured negotiations within budget caps look like Big Government whereas premium caps enforced through regional health alliances and local health plans will pass political muster. These political calls
may or may not be accurate. Employer mandates are highly controversial
and the subsidies proposed to make them more palatable are hard to define equitably and to administer efficiently. The ponderous administrative
machinery required to revitalize competition locally and regionally while
managing it within firm federal rules may be more vulnerable to attack
from right-of-center than some suppose. In politics, as in policy, there is
no free lunch. If the potential administrative costs of the Clinton plan are
not justified by the political benefits its design confers, then one might
conclude either that the U.S. public is still not ready to face the tradeoffs

"true" reform entails or that the canvassing and debating of strategic alternatives—including ones with greater administrative simplicity—ought not to quit quite yet.

Notes

1. On the cultural background and history see James A. Morone, *The Democratic Wish* (New York: Basic Books, 1980).

2. For some useful ruminations by soon-to-be insiders see the special issue of *Health Affairs*, "Managed Competition: Health Reform American Style?" 12 (Supplement 1993), especially Walter Zelman, "Who Should Govern?", Paul Starr, "Design and Development," and Richard Kronick, "Federal/State Roles," pp. 49–64, 87–98.

3. See Frank Thompson, "The Enduring Challenge of Health Policy Implementation," in Theordore J. Litman and Leonard S. Robins, eds., *Health Politics and Policy*, 2nd ed. (Albany, NY: Delmar, 1991), pp. 148–169.

4. Details of the Clinton plan are taken from Commerce Clearinghouse, *President Clinton's Health Care Reform Proposal: Health Security Act as Presented to Congress on October 27, 1993* (Chicago: Commerce Clearing House, 1993).

5. Ibid., p. 52.

6. On the HSAs see Morone, *Democratic Wish*, pp. 253–321; and Lawrence D. Brown, *The Political Structure of the Federal Health Planning Program* (Washington, D.C.: Brookings Institution, 1982).

7. For a searching critique of the Jackson Hole variant of managed competition as a means to these ends see Thomas Rice and others, "Holes in the Jackson Hole Approach to Health Care Reform," *Journal of the American Medical Association* 270 September 15, 1993): 1357–1362.

8. Commerce Clearing House, *Reform Proposal*, p. 66.

9. Ibid., pp. 101–107; quotations at pp. 104–105.

10. Ibid., pp. 56–57.

11. This and several other good questions come from Karen Davis, "Health Care Reform: Implications for Urban Health," in *Health Care in Underserved Urban America: Implications for National Reform*, proceedings of a Conference sponsored by Columbia University, June 7–8, 1993, pp. 128–135.

12. For cases in point see Lawrence D. Brown, *Politics and Health Care Organizations: HMOs as Federal Policy* (Washington, D.C.: Brookings Institution, 1983), and "Political Conditions of Regulatory Effectiveness: The Case of PSROs and HSAs," *Bulletin of the New York Academy of Medicine* 58 (February 1982): 77–90.

13. David G. Smith, "Paying for Medicare: The Politics of Reform" and Thomas R. Oliver, "Analysis, Advice, and Congressional Leadership: the Physician Payment Review Commission and the Politics of Medicare," *Journal of Health Politics, Policy and Law* 18 (Spring 1993): 114–174.

14. James A. Morone, "Administrative Agencies and the Implementation of National Health Care Reform," in Charles Brecher, ed., *Implementation Issues and National Health Care Reform: Proceedings of a Conference* (New York: Josiah Macy, Jr. Foundation, 1992), p. 54. For an account of the efforts of state Medicaid managers

to cope with these and related tensions, see Michael Sparer and Lawrence D. Brown, "Between a Rock and a Hard Place: How Public Managers Manage Medicaid," in Frank J. Thompson, ed., *Revitalizing State and Local Public Service* (San Francisco: Jossey-Bass, 1993), pp. 279–306.

15. For instance, Alain C. Enthoven, "The History and Principles of Managed Competition," *Health Affairs* 12 (Supplement 1993), p. 40.

16. Morone, "Administrative Agencies," pp. 68–69.

17. For a detailed account of these systems see William A. Glaser, *Health Insurance in Practice* (San Francisco: Jossey-Bass, 1992).

18. William A. Glaser, Letter to the Editor, "City Managed Competition Cannot Be Enacted," *Health Affairs* 12 (Fall 1993): 277–78.

15

Global Budgets and the Competitive Market

Harold S. Luft and Kevin Grumbach

"Regulation" and "competition" have been perennial adversaries in the arena of health care reform. Global budgets are in many ways the apogee of the regulatory approach—price controls writ large. Instead of setting prices at the level of small units of service, such as fees for individual physician or hospital services, global budgets regulate payment at the institutional or geographic level. Examples of global budgets are lump sum annual hospital budgets (as in Canada) and regional physician expenditure caps (as in Germany). A different political philosophy is embodied in competitive strategies to control costs. Rather than vesting budgetary authority in centralized "big government," the competitive approach calls for returning greater responsibility for the purchase of health care to individual consumers. This strategy also vests the responsibility for the difficult decisions concerning "how much is enough" and "which providers survive" in the invisible hand of the market rather than the visible hands of regulators and planners.

Periodically in the United States, efforts at conciliation have occurred in the form of policies that seek to blend regulatory and competitive features of health care reform. This hybridization of regulation and competition has most recently found expression in the health care plan developed by President and Mrs. Clinton. Starr and Zelman, key participants in the task force that drafted the Clinton plan, have argued the case for this type of policy compromise as a means to "break the gridlock" in health care reform:

> The debate over health policy has been plagued by a misleading polarization between "competition" and "regulation." Managed competition, we

are told, exemplifies a competitive strategy; global budgeting, a regulatory strategy. This antinomy poses a false choice. With new rules and institutions in the market, we can—and almost certainly will—have both. Managed competition does not just "release" the forces of the market; it reconstructs the market. And even without global budgeting, managed competition involves much new insurance market regulation. Moreover, with its emphasis on capitated health plans, managed competition provides a better platform for global budgeting than exists in the current system.[1]

In this chapter we examine global budgets and competition as cost control strategies. We begin by discussing the use of global budgeting in other nations, evaluating its advantages and potential problems. We then shift the focus to the United States, with its own set of problems and opportunities, and contrast the global budget approach with the most prominent contemporary pro-competitive strategy, managed competition. We conclude by discussing the ways in which the Clinton plan attempts to broker a compromise between global budgeting and market competition, highlighting some of the unsettled questions about this reform model.

Global Budgets

Different forms of global budgeting have existed for many years in Canada and Europe. Global budgeting as an approach to regulating the health care economy continues to gain popularity among governments and other major payers of care in these nations. Although global budgets are most commonly used to pay hospitals, many nations are now experimenting with applications of global budgeting for physician services or for the entirety of health care services within a geographic region.

The notion sometimes held in the United States that nations with organized systems of national health care explicitly allocate an annual global budget for the entire health system is an oversimplification of the global budgeting processes in most of these nations. Even in a nation such as Canada, where a public single payer insurance program controls virtually all third party payments, the budgetary process at the level of allocating overall health system revenues bears a striking resemblance to the Congressional appropriations process for the Medicare and Medicaid programs in the United States. Like U.S. Medicare, the Canadian Medicare system attempts to operate under a planned budget but has traditionally been an "entitlement" program committed to a pay-as-you-go method of raising and appropriating funds. If expenditures in a given year exceed the desired or expected level of growth, the provincial health plans are obligated to raise the required revenues (or increase the federal and provincial debt) to meet their statutory commitment to a solvent health insurance plan. Budgeting at this level of overall revenue appropriations no more acts as a rigid global budget in Canada than it does for the Medicare program in the United States. In addition, similar to the Medicaid program in the United States, budgeting for Canadian Medicare is complicated by joint federal and provincial administration and financing. An American policy maker hoping to emulate the "Canadian" method for establishing a fixed national health care budget might be disappointed to find that there is no annual act of Parliament that declares that the overall Canadian budget will be fixed at a certain percent of GDP.

Rather, the crucial application of global budgets in Canada and other nations occurs in negotiations between providers and provincial health plans or other payers. It is at this level of determining payment to specific provider units and sectors, rather than at the more overarching and less tangible level of developing "national" or "provincial" health budgets, that global budgeting has been exercised by payers attempting to control health care costs.

Global Budgets for Hospitals

The classic model of global budgeting is the lump sum payment of hospital costs that is practiced in Canada. Each hospital negotiates annually its budget for operating expenses with the provincial health plan. The budgets are based more on tradition and politics than on a systematic process of resource allocation. The initial budgets for hospitals at the inception of public insurance in Canada were based on each individual hospital's historical operating costs. Annual increases have usually been applied as a percentage increase in each hospital's budget, with minor variations in annual growth rates for individual hospitals being dependent on hospital volume or addition of new services. Once these prospective budgets are agreed upon, the provincial plan pays each hospital monthly installments of the annual budget. The hospital issues no bills for individual services or for individual patients. The hospital is responsible for controlling its internal expenses within the limits of the global budget. Other than monitoring funds targeted for special services or intervening in cases of repeated budgetary overruns, government intrudes minimally in how hospitals internally allocate their global budgets.[2]

Global budgeting of hospitals has also been used in many European nations, even those without true single payer systems. For example, Germany has a system of multiple privately-administered health insurance plans known as "sick funds." Relationships among the non-profit sick funds are characterized more by cooperation than by competition. Although government plays a minor role in directly financing health insurance in Germany, it oversees national cost containment polices by acting as a referee for all-payer negotiations between sick funds and provider groups. Traditionally, this process focused on establishing a fixed per diem rate for each hospital that would be uniformly charged each fund. The per diem levels were calculated by first determining an overall hospital operating budget and then dividing this budget by the anticipated number of patient days, thus approximating the workings of a global budget. However, by prolonging hospital stays hospitals were able to "game" per diem rates to generate payments in excess of the negotiated global budget. As a result, Germany and other European nations with multi-payer social insurance plans have begun to phase out per diem payments and moved closer to the Canadian method of paying the global budget on a periodic, lump sum basis.[3]

Global Budgets for Physicians

For many years the perceived success of global budgets in Canada and Europe as a mechanism for controlling growth of hospital costs stood in marked contrast to the problem of controlling physician costs in these nations. During the latter years of this century, single payer and multi-payer programs alike relied on fee-for-service methods to pay physicians. In an attempt to contain expenditures for physician services, nations adopted binding fee schedules. However, fee controls had only partial success in containing costs, since the volume of physician services remained uncontrolled. By the late 1980s, many governments recognized that relying solely on price setting under fee-for-service physician payment was a limited instrument of cost control and was creating increasingly fractious negotiations between payers and physicians.

In the 1980s Germany was one of the first nations to apply the lessons of hospital global budgeting to the physician sector. Almost a hundred years ago, Germany had a form of physician global budgeting under which government strictly regulated the total payments to private practitioners. All sickness fund payments for professional physician services were funneled through provincial physician associations, which in turn reimbursed individual physicians on a fee-for-service basis. Because the amount of funds allocated annually to each association was capped, the associations were forced to reduce fees to their members if increases in volume drove the level of physician costs above the expenditure cap. Although this lump sum system of physician payment was abandoned in Germany during the 1960s and 1970s, health care inflation rekindled interest in this approach. In 1986, global provincial physician budgets were reestablished in Germany.[4] Several Canadian provinces also instituted expenditure caps for physician services in the late 1980s in an attempt to impose the economic discipline of a global budget on a fee-for-service payment method.[5]

Global Budgets for Other Services

There are far fewer examples of the application of global budgets to sectors other than hospitals and physicians. Belgium has adopted a system of global expenditure caps for pharmaceutical products, similar in method to the German physician expenditure caps. However, the Belgian case is an exception to the rule: uncapped expenditures for drugs, dental services, and other types of health products and services are not capped elsewhere in Europe or in Canada.[6] The services and supplies tend to be subject to relatively high levels of cost sharing in most national health systems, reducing the incentive for third party payers to take on the political fight of imposing global caps.

Supply Limits as a Complement to Global Budgets

Most nations that rely on global budgeting to control payments to providers have coupled it with explicit public regulation of provider capacity. In both single payer and multi-payer social insurance systems throughout the industrialized world, government has the authority to place limits on hospital bed supply, diffusion of new technologies and other capital improvements, and the number of new physicians entering the workforce. Regulation of supply is born of political necessity in these systems, as enforcement of payment schemes such as hospital global budgets and physician expenditure caps becomes daunting in an environment of expanding capacity.[7] It is difficult to limit the size of the budget pie when the number of providers ordering slices keeps growing.

Advantages of Global Budgets

The main attraction of global budgets is that they erect a firm fence around expenditures. As noted above, attempts to regulate payments at the relatively disaggregated level of fee-for-service or per diem rates leaves payers still vulnerable to unanticipated cost increases if the volume of services exceeds estimated levels. Global budgets, in contrast, pay at the most aggregated unit of service possible. As long as a nation doesn't add more hospitals or more provinces, the volume factor in hospital global budgets or provincial expenditure caps is fixed. Once rates are agreed upon, costs for the year for globally budgeted services are predictable. Because global budgeting requires a single payer or cooperation among multiple payers, it also shifts the balance of bargaining power in favor of payers when negotiating rates of increase. Although in evaluating the success of global budgets as a cost containment tool it is difficult to isolate the effects of global budgeting from other policies and features that may differ among national health systems, many observers have concluded that global budgeting strategies are an important factor in the relative success nations other than the United States have had at slowing health care cost increases in recent years.[8]

A feature of global budgeting that appeals to both payers and providers is its administrative simplicity. Under the purest forms of global budgeting such as lump sum hospital payment, claims processing is reduced to the equivalent of writing one check per month to each hospital. Although hospitals continue to maintain some tracking of individual resources at the patient level for purposes of internal cost accounting, institutions are spared the elaborate expenses of generating and collecting on itemized bills for each patient encounter. Global budgeting explains at least in part why Canadian hospital administrative costs are half those of U.S. hospitals.[9]

Related to the issue of administrative simplicity is the principle that global budgeting permits economic "macromanagement" without third party intrusion into clinical "micromanagement." Global budgeting establishes the boundaries around expenditures. Establishment of these budgetary boundaries in turn gives providers and patients considerable latitude to allocate resources within the perimeter of the global budget. The types of intrusive utilization review activities that have become second nature to third party payers in the United States, and are so deeply resented by United States clinicians, are virtually unheard of in Canada and Europe. In the U.S., lack of third party payer control over aggregate budgets leaves payers little recourse but to attempt to win the cost containment battle by regulating the volume of individual units of service such as surgical procedures and hospital days.[10]

Drawbacks of Global Budgets

Criticism of global budgeting tends to focus on three related concerns: the political nature of the budgeting process, questionable incentives to improve quality and value, and the technical problems of "price error" in the setting of specific budgetary allotments. Global budgeting requires a societal approach to containing costs and is therefore an inherently political process. The global budgeting process substitutes an explicit, collectively undertaken mechanism of aggregate fee setting for the myriad purchasing negotiations which would occur spontaneously in a market system driven by individual consumer choice. Participants must ultimately agree on a budget for a hospital or a group of physicians; all are then obliged to provide and receive care within these socially determined levels of resource allocation.

The budgetary process is only as good as the political processes and institutions that undergird the regulatory mechanisms. The regulatory process may fail to register accurately public willingness to increase re-sources for health care, resulting in excessively austere global budgets. Or the political process may be captured by provider interests or the interests of persons with selected diseases, leading to overly generous payment rates. The viability of global budgeting in other nations reflects the legiti-macy of the political processes for negotiating health care budgets in these nations. In Canada, "good government" is a term emblazoned on the founding declaration of the federal state. Faith in the Canadian govern-ment's ability to manage health care budgets remains high. In European nations such as Germany, the quasi-public rate setting process works only because the individual sick funds, providers, and public all accept this structure for budget negotiations; the threat of direct government as-sumption of rate setting functions serves to motivate the major players to cooperate in this budgetary process. A former Minister of Health of New Zealand once remarked, when queried about the elaborate system of re-gional budget planning boards in his country, that "democracy is a messy business." Most nations have accepted the problematic features of public planning as a tolerable side effect of a global budget pill that is relatively effective at controlling costs with an acceptable level of social equity.

Whether there are political institutions in the U.S. that could maintain legitimacy and public responsiveness in regulating global health care budgets remains a frequently debated question. A particular problem is that the American political process differs substantially from that of a par-liamentary democracy. The absence of "party loyalty" and the powerful role of special interest groups make it more difficult to pass and imple-ment a program "for the good of the public."

Two domestic examples of attempts to establish global budgets, how-ever, may suggest that the politics of global budgeting is not a hopeless cause in this country. The first example is the experience of Rochester, New York in developing a community process for planning global hospi-tal budgets for all local institutions and coordinating the deployment of new technology. The Rochester model shared many of the features of the German hospital budgeting process, with its reliance on cooperation and negotiation among private third party payers and providers in a non-gov-ernmentally run budgeting mechanism. It is important to note that the Rochester area adopted active health planning measures as early as the 1950s and was thus a fairly well integrated regional system prior to its ex-perimentation with global budgeting.[11]

A different model is the recent adoption of volume performance stan-dards for the Medicare program in the United States. Although designed as a somewhat looser target of expenditure control than the more rigid

German physician expenditure caps, the volume-performance policy indicates the willingness of a U.S. government program to introduce regulation of physician expenditures at a more global level than traditional fee-for-service. The implicit budget caps, however, are imposed on physicians collectively and do not discriminate between those physicians who are helping to contain costs versus those specifically responsible for the budget overruns.[12]

Closely related to concerns about the political aspects of global budgeting is the possibility that global budgets lack incentives to improve the quality or efficiency of services. Terms such as "bureaucratic ossification" and "freezing of innovation" make frequent appearances in commentaries about global budgets.[13] Concerns are expressed that as long as institutions know how to play the bureaucratic game of global budgeting, these institutions are assured a relatively stable flow of funds from year to year. In this view, absent the conditioning function of market competition in challenging providers to innovate and remain attuned to consumer interests, the commitment to improve quality and enhance value atrophies. A hospital that improves productivity and ends the year with a budget surplus may reap the "reward" of simply having its global budget reduced the following year in response.

A final concern with global budgeting is that even if the political process arrives at acceptable overall budgetary authorizations, there are technical problems in making allocations to individual provider units.[14] For example, a province may decide on an overall budget for hospital care. This budget must then be allocated in the form of individual hospital global budgets. If hospital A's budget has traditionally been 30 percent greater than hospital B's budget, should the global budgets simply be titrated against these historical cost patterns? Perhaps hospital A has been relatively inefficient, providing the same volume and intensity of services as hospital B but at higher cost. Should hospital A's global budget be reduced as a result? Or should hospital B's budget be raised? How can those responsible for budgeting accurately measure the true costs of care at the two institutions, including adequate adjustments for potential differences in case mix? Should the global budget reward better outcomes? The same considerations apply when allocating global budgets to different regions, for example, regional physician expenditure caps. Tremendous variation in physician expenditures has been found across states in the U.S.[15] How should global budgets respond to such variation? Experience with global budgets in other nations has demonstrated that the simplest part of global budgeting is deciding on annual across-the-board growth factors. Measuring efficiency and adjusting budgets accordingly to individual hospitals or physician groups has proved a politically and technically more difficult task.

Competition

"Managed competition" has emerged as the defining concept in market-oriented health care reforms in the U.S. Although often used to describe an overall reform package that includes financing and other elements, managed competition is fundamentally a strategy for controlling costs. As a method for controlling payments to providers, managed competition can in theory be matched with a variety of financing and coverage mechanisms, from universal tax financing to employer mandates.

In the view of the architects of managed competition such as Enthoven, there are two key flaws in the current economics of health insurance in the U.S.[16] First, open-ended employer and government subsidies for health insurance have insulated Americans from the true costs of insurance. In addition, the enormous variety of benefit packages, coverages, and exclusions makes it impossible to effectively compare health plans. As a result, individuals are relatively price insensitive when purchasing insurance and the dynamic of price competition among plans is severely attenuated. The absence of price competition allows health plans to be passive reimbursers and not make the types of decisions necessary to contain costs. Second, the market for health insurance is too unstructured. Purchasers rarely attain the critical size necessary to effectively bargain with insurance plans, benefits are not standardized precluding meaningful cost comparisons, and insurers have too much latitude to game the market through various underwriting techniques such as experience rating and exclusionary clauses. Simultaneously, health plans frequently represent a very small market share for any provider, so efforts at price negotiation, or more importantly, evaluation of practice patterns are severely hampered.

Managed competition proposes to rectify these flaws through two basic interventions. First, limits must be imposed on the amount of subsidies allowed for health insurance so that individuals are forced to shoulder directly a greater proportion of the cost of enrolling in more expensive plans. The expectation is that greater price sensitivity among consumers will induce a more competitive market for health insurance, restraining overall cost growth and improving value. Second, this competition must be "managed" through the creation of large-scale brokers for the purchase of health insurance, through standardization of benefit packages, and through the curtailment of discriminatory underwriting practices. A basic assumption of managed competition is that large HMOs will be able to exert the requisite level of discipline on providers to compete successfully in this environment.

Advantages of Managed Competition

The advocates of managed competition contend that this route to cost containment can bypass many of the perceived potholes along the global budget route. Enthoven, himself a one-time federal government bureaucrat, has registered a vote of no confidence that American political institutions are up to the task of global budgeting. In Enthoven's view, the regulatory process is too easily influenced by provider interests. As mentioned earlier, the American political process is far more vulnerable to special interest groups and their ability to incorporate loopholes in legislation even when the overall proposal is approved.

It is also important to note that the crucial role of supply constraints in global budgets is responsible for many advocates of a managed competition strategy in the United States. The U.S. health care system is seen as having unique problems of excess capacity requiring "downsizing" to produce a more efficient system. Hospital occupancy in the U.S. is well below that of other industrialized nations, and the spread of technology both within and outside hospitals is virtually uncontrolled. Many more hospitals offer open heart surgery, magnetic resonance imaging, and intensive care units in the U.S. than in other nations. Potentially even more serious than excess hospital capacity is the problem of specialists and outpatient care. In most European nations specialists practice primarily in the hospital and specialized equipment is reserved for hospitals, even if the patient might be treated on an ambulatory basis. Furthermore, hospital departments are usually hierarchically structured, with a limited number of salaried positions. In the United States, specialists practice both in their offices and in hospitals, have their own referral networks, and often their own specialized equipment, such as MRI units, catherization labs, and surgical suites for such procedures as cataract removal and arthroscopy. Establishing global budgets for individual physician office practices or selecting those to be denied specialized technology would be an administrative nightmare. Thus, a global budget is likely to freeze in place existing providers and ratchet down fees.

In the pro-competitive view, market forces will be more successful than regulatory agencies in executing the tough decisions of downsizing. Under global budgeting, detailed determinations of facility-specific service closures would have to be made in the context of global budgets. Even if a regulatory body were to identify services for closure, hospitals would challenge such decisions in the courts and the shrinkage of capacity would probably take decades. If services were not closed, hospitals would attempt to increase volume and increase their budgets proportionately.

Reducing the number of freestanding technologies, such as MRI centers and outpatient catheterization labs, poses even greater regulatory challenges. In terms of changing physician specialty distribution, analyses have shown that regulation of the number of new specialists entering the workforce will not produce significant shifts in the overall physician pool for a generation at least. Advocates of managed competition argue that, through the process of selective physician contracting and hiring, competing managed care plans will effectively drive many specialists out of the market by leaving these physicians with a dwindling number of patients in the fee-for-service sector. Similarly, high cost, low quality hospitals would not survive in this competitive market. In Enthoven's view, government regulators in the U.S. lack the ruthlessness necessary for effective budgetary action. Such action may be more decisively undertaken by private enterprises motivated by the demands of the competitive marketplace: "Hospital rate regulators are notoriously unwilling to force unneeded or inefficient hospitals to close. ... Only impersonal market forces can close down unneeded, inefficient activities."[17]

Pro-managed competition forces contend that in major parts of the country competing health care plans such as HMOs would be able to sign up the physicians and hospitals they thought provided cost effective and high quality medical care. Those providers not recruited into one of the organized health plans would still be able to treat patients in the residual fee-for-service sector, but the number of patients in that sector is likely to fall as more are attracted to the lower cost HMOs.

Competition among plans may also encourage cost-reducing and quality-enhancing innovation, given the appropriate incentives. That is, if measures can be developed that accurately and realistically rate the quality of plans, and consumers choose among plans on the basis of quality and net premium cost, there will be incentives for plans to innovate. This may mean substituting physician assistants and nurse practitioners for physicians, experimenting with increased outpatient and home care, or other approaches. Critics of regulation contend that global budgets combined with regional monopolies provide little incentive for such innovation.

Disadvantages of Managed Competition

One of the most basic concerns about managed competition is that it will not achieve its most ostensible goal—cost containment. Congressman Pete Stark's dismissal of managed competition as a unicorn, wondrous but never seen in this world, may earn higher marks for sound bite rhetoric than incisive policy analysis. Yet his comments reflect serious concerns in many quarters that managed competition is a relatively untested policy lacking the track record of global budgeting.[18]

There are several reasons to question the cost containment potency of various types of managed competition. It is dubious that inducing greater price sensitivity among consumers will have the force to control overall costs. The past decade has already seen employers shifting a greater share of premium costs to employees, especially for dependent coverage, without damping the rate of inflation of employment based insurance. Price competition may simply stratify the market based on ability to pay, with individuals having little disposable income locked into lower cost plans and more affluent individuals paying ever-increasing shares of premium outlays to remain in higher cost plans. The "sponsors" who will be responsible for managing the competition may not be up to the task and may fail to wield sufficient countervailing power vis-à-vis provider groups. Consolidation of the insurance market into a few, monolithic HMOs may create an oligopoly of private plans that collude in keeping costs inflating at a rapid clip. Plans may still be able to compete by skimming off lower cost enrollees rather than by achieving true efficiencies of service. Attempts to develop risk-adjusted payment methods to outflank plans in their marketing strategy may prove unsuccessful because of technical difficulties in devising sufficiently sensitive methods of risk adjustment. More detailed criticisms of managed competition have been articulated elsewhere by a number of analysts, and we simply highlight some of the most important concerns.[19]

In addition to criticism that managed competition may not succeed at controlling costs, the more market-oriented reform strategies inevitably raise concerns about equity. It is a basic expectation of the market that individuals with higher incomes will purchase more and better goods and services than those with lesser incomes. The market may be efficient at distributing goods and services, but its justice is that of an economic meritocracy. Insofar as most contemporary civilizations aspire to at least an approximation of the ideal of health care as a fundamental social right rather than a privilege of social class, market reformers face the challenge of designing policies that can inject sufficient price sensitivity into the health care system without relegating lower income groups to inferior access to care.

Managed competition proposals have attempted to achieve this balance by assuring all Americans a basic subsidy for health insurance. In Enthoven's plan, this subsidy would be at the level of the lowest cost HMO premium in a region. President Clinton's proposal indexes the subsidy to the average cost premium. It is expected, and considered acceptable (and even desirable), that many Americans would be willing to supplement the basic premium subsidy with out-of-pocket premium payments to purchase more expensive plans. Presumably, individuals with more discretionary income, as well as those with chronic medical needs that reinforce allegiance to a long-standing provider relationship, would be most likely to pay extra premium costs. The issue, then, becomes what level of health care will individuals with higher incomes be able to buy? Will the differences between the low-cost (or average cost) plan and the higher-priced plans be primarily a matter of amenities— champagne meals after delivering a baby and medical offices with more convenient parking—or of more meaningful differences in the quality of services? Some variations on the managed competition theme, such as the proposal developed by California Insurance Commissioner John Garamendi, have attempted to control the magnitude of the tiering effect by regulating a maximum level of co-premium that may be charged in addition to the standard, subsidized premium. Regarding the comparative merits and faults of global budgets and competition, the salient point is that the competitive approach, unlike the global budgeting strategy, has a certain degree of income-based inequity built into it that must be countered by various regulatory policies.

Marrying Competition and Global Budgets Under the Clinton Plan

As only the second Democrat to serve in the Presidency in over two decades of nearly uninterrupted Republican administrations, President Clinton has charted a course for the elusive "third way": a mixture of policies that is neither entirely liberal nor conservative but places a premium on pragmatism and political feasibility. Starr and Zelman capture the flavor of this political philosophy in their summary of the development of the Clinton proposal: "... the framework and many details reflect an extended conversation over the past year among analysts trying to break through false ideological dichotomies."[20] The product of these deliberations is what Starr and Zelman refer to as "managed competition under a budget."

Managed competition under a budget could also be called "managed competition ... but." On the one hand, the Clinton plan embraces most of the central tenets of managed competition such as limiting insurance subsidies to induce greater price competition among private health plans and restructuring (i.e., "managing") the market for health insurance through health alliances. Yet drafters of the Clinton plan were not so convinced of the effectiveness of these proposed market reforms that they were willing to rely on the market for voluntary enrollment or do without a back-up cost containment strategy in their plan. For this back-up measure, they turned to global budgeting.

Briefly, the way global budgeting would work in the Clinton proposal is as follows: A new entity, the health "alliance," would be established in each region to serve as an intermediary between the payers of care (individuals, employers, and government) and the competing private health plans. For most insured Americans, funds for insurance coverage would first flow into the alliance and in turn be disbursed to the plan of the subscriber's choice. The required employer contribution would be indexed to 80 percent of the average weighted premium of all approved plans in the region. although employers could offer larger contributions, it is expected that most employees would face some out-of-pocket costs for the premiums of the more expensive health plans. The health alliance would be responsible for adjusting payments to the health plans so that those with higher than average risks would be paid more and those with lower-risk enrollees paid less. Risk adjustment would be designed to address only the costs associated with differences in plan efficiency and quality, rather than in the enrollees' own risk status. The health alliances would also be charged with the responsibility for monitoring quality of care in the various plans and producing "report cards" to inform consumer choices among plans.

In the management of global budgeting, a national health board would establish a spending target for each alliance's total payments to health plans. If competition proves successful, expenditures would remain within the targeted amount. If, however, health plans continued to raise premiums and thereby cause expenditures to exceed the target, the national board would have the authority to regulate premium increases and demand reductions in charges by the higher cost plans. In essence, the Clinton plan's approach to global budgeting is setting a regional expenditure target to be enforced through caps on increases in insurance premium rates.

Starr and Zelman, defending what some have called a "cold-feet" policy of managed competition, explain: "Some may ask why, if we believe that managed competition will work, we also see a need for global budgets. One might as soon ask the designers of a new airplane if their specification of a second engine demonstrates a lack of confidence in the first. Good designs often build in redundancy."[21] The Administration may have also been motivated to include budget caps to provide a guarantee of costs savings for those in Congress (and the Congressional Budget Office) skeptical of the cost saving potential of competition.

Managed Competition Under a Budget

The form of global budgeting proposed in the Clinton plan has several novel features that distinguish it from the types of global budgets typically used by Canada and European nations. The most important distinction is that global budgeting in other nations usually involves budgets directly applied to provider entities, such as individual hospitals or regional physician associations. In general, these nations have not relied on global budgeting at the level of premium payments into private health plans to control overall expenditures. Nations such as Germany with multi-payer social insurance programs utilize "premium caps" only in the sense that financing of plans derives mainly from payroll taxes set at a fixed percent of payroll. This type of financing-defined budgeting is quite different from regulating individual plan premium levels under the complex scheme of variable employer and employee payments included in the Clinton plan.

The fundamental issue with this regulatory model is whether it can make global budgets stick. Enforcing global budgets comes at the political cost of taking on powerful provider interests and, in the case of regulation at the premium level, insurance corporation interests as well. The moral fortitude to join this battle in other nations derives from either of two conditions: One, that the regulators are also the payers, as in single payer government-administered systems; or two, that private insurance plans have willingly ceded to government the authority to regulate (stringently) provider payments, as in multi-payer European systems. The Clinton plan's intention of regulating overall regional third party expenditures in a system of intense private insurance plan competition, with taxpayer dollars only partly at stake, may not have the winning political ingredients for regulatory success. The requirement that all employers pay a share of premiums may help generate the kind of employer support for cost containment that has made for more successful multi-payer alliances in Rochester and Europe.

The premium-regulation style of global budgeting also raises definitional questions. Which payments are included when calculating the global budget? There are several possible alternatives. The budget might only apply to the "base" premium subsidy—the 80 percent of the average weighted premium in the region that defines the alliance's standard level of contribution for health insurance. Another definition would include the consumer share of the premium for the standard benefit package as well as deductibles and co-payments at the point of service. Finally, one could opt for a truly global budget and include the costs of services not included in the standard benefits package. Each definitional level has different implications about where the regulatory process is attempting to hold the

line on costs. In the first definition, the global cap is mainly geared towards placing a limit on mandatory employer and government payments
into the alliance. The implication is that if individuals are willing to pay
extra premiums (and can be persuaded by plans to do so), then government is not obliged to impose caps on these "voluntary" payments. In
particular, the focus on the rate of growth for overall costs in a health alliance precludes a differentiation between one geographic area in which all
plans have a comparable (and excessive) rate of growth and another area
in which cost increases are highly skewed among plans. The second definition of global budget encompasses expenditures from all sources for
covered services. The third captures the total health care costs, irrespective of their coverage under the program. Obviously, the less global the
global budget, the larger the potential escape hatch for plans and providers in the form of cost inflation in areas not under the jurisdiction of the
budgetary cap.

These differences in the scope of expenditures encompassed within the
global budget raise different considerations about the technical requirements for collecting expenditure data. Monitoring and enforcement of
global budgets requires "on line" expenditure information if regulatory
policies are to respond to current year or past year trends. Measuring the
total regional expenditures in terms of the 80 percent premium contribution of the alliance is relatively easy, since these dollars all pass through
the alliance funnel and may be identified in transit from primary payers
through the alliance and on to health plans. Calculating the total costs of
covered services in a region is more difficult, since this will require captur-
ing the services not reimbursed because they are under the deductible.
Measuring total expenditures in a region, including those for non-covered
services, is the most daunting technical undertaking—particularly in a
system that preserves a substantial level of cost sharing. It is the process of
piecing together this type of detailed spending data that explains why the
official government reports on national health care expenditures for 1991
was not issued until 1993.

Who's Doing the Regulating

The "two engine" metaphor of managed competition and global budgets
as a means of holding down inflation of health insurance premiums in
many ways obscures the much more profound role of global budgets in
the evolving competitive character of the U.S. health care system. As we
have emphasized, global budgets have a tradition of being used at the
level of controlling payments to specific provider entities—individual
hospitals, provincial medical associations, etc. It is unlikely that any strategy for controlling payments to health insurance plans, whether competi-

tive or regulatory (or a hybrid), will succeed in the United States without the imposition of some type of global budgets at the level where the rubber meets the road—payments to providers. Specifically, attempts to control health plan premium inflation through greater premium cost sharing or public regulation can succeed only if this cost containment pressure is translated into effective controls at the point of actual service provision by physicians, nurses, and other health care workers and suppliers.

This understanding has not been lost on large HMOs. Major staff and group model HMOs in the United States have the organizational structures that allow them to use the tools of global budgeting within their plans. Group and staff model HMOs in the United States, such as Kaiser Permanente and Group Health Cooperative, apply many of the budgetary tools of a Canadian provincial health plan. They globally budget their own hospitals. They establish an expenditure cap for physicians, either by capitating a well-defined physician group that serves the plan's enrollees exclusively (e.g., the Permanente Medical Group) or by directly employing physician staff (e.g., Group Health). Like Canadian and European systems, these HMOs complement their global budgeting methods with controls over capacity. Both hospital beds and physician staff are kept at a carefully monitored level relative to the number of enrollees, and tertiary care services tend to be regionalized within a large HMO such as Kaiser. It is this ability to apply internally global budgets that will likely confer a competitive advantage on these HMOs in the future medical marketplace.

To the extent that these types of integrated systems merge insurance plan and providers into a single organized entity, regulation of "premium" payments may in essence constitute a global budget for providers at the most aggregate level possible. There are potential advantages to global budgeting for an entire system of providers rather than to specific sectors (e.g., individual global budgets for hospitals and fee-for-service payments to physicians under a province-wide expenditure cap, as in Canada). One of the methods used by HMOs to offer more extensive coverage at a lower overall cost is a relative shift in resources from hospital care to physicians and outpatient services. This type of innovation may be impeded when there are more barriers to diverting resources from one sector to another, such as may occur when hospitals and physicians are trying to preserve their respective global budgets.

Conclusion

The debate between competition and global budgets may obscure areas of growing agreement in the formulation of health policy in the United States. One of these is the recognition that successful cost containment ultimately requires delineation of global spending limits and management of capacity within the health care system. Under traditional global budgeting in Canada and Europe, a governmental or quasi-governmental agency directly allocates global budgets to specific provider groups and public planning processes regulate supply. In American staff- and group-model HMOs, the HMO obtains a global prepayment enrollment fee and then internally allocates budgets to provider units. For private insurance plans that lack the organizational structures to manage internal provider budgets and capacity, the prospects for continued survival in the United States are bleak, whether the future lies with managed competition or single payer. Reliance on such cost containment methods as patient cost sharing at the point of service and utilization management from a distance is unlikely to achieve sustained control of expenditures.

Viewed from this perspective, the following are the two key issues concerning the future of regulation and competition in the U.S. health care system. First, who should be in charge of regulating global budgets at the level of specific provider units? Should public agencies play this role directly, or should allocative decisions about individual hospital and physician group budgets be delegated to a private agency—the HMO—operating under a system of inclusive prepayment? The answer to this question will depend on perceptions of the relative effectiveness and accountability of public vs. private managers in dealing hands-on with health care providers, as well as the advantages and disadvantages of paying at the level of an integrated provider system rather than its component units. Even in a system in which much of the authority is delegated to HMOs to control capacity through selective contracting, public regulatory mechanisms may play a complementary role through such policies as reform of graduate medical education and of the physician workforce and the coordinated regionalization of specialized services.

Second, if authority over global budgets at the provider level is delegated to HMOs, how should the level of payments to HMOs be determined? That is, if payments to an integrated HMO system constitute one of the most global forms of global budgeting, who sets the rates for these budgets? It is in answering this question that the regulatory and competitive strategies most clearly part company. Under price competition, the invisible hand of the market determines rates for individual plans. At the other extreme, a regulatory apparatus could specify uniform budgets for each HMO. Such a system of regulated payments to HMOs under universal insurance has been proposed by both Relman and Caper.[22] The Clinton plan attempts to prevent a total estrangement between price competition and regulation by promoting the former while maintaining some regulatory fail-safe mechanisms. The relative merits of price competition and regulation, and the potential for successfully blending these two approaches are likely to remain contentious issues as health care reform unfolds. Variations among the states in their efforts to implement health care reform may provide natural experiments for comparing the outcomes of different balances of competitive and regulatory strategies.

Notes

1. Paul Starr and Walter A. Zelman, "Bridge to Compromise: Competition Under a Budget," *Health Affairs* 12 (Supplement 1993): 7–23.

2. Robert G. Evans, Jonathan Lomas, Morris Barer, et al., "Controlling Health Expenditures—The Canadian Reality," *New England Journal of Medicine* 320 (March 2, 1989): 571–77.

3. William A. Glaser, *Health Insurance in Practice* (San Francisco, CA: Jossey Bass, 1991).

4. Glaser, *Health Insurance*.

5. Jonathan Lomas, Catherine Fooks, Thomas Rice, and Roberta J. Labelle, "Paying Physicians in Canada: Minding our Ps and Qs," *Health Affairs* (Spring 1989): 80–102.

6. Glaser, *Health Insurance*.

7. Brian Abel-Smith, "Who Is the Odd Man Out?: The Experience of Western Europe in Containing the Costs of Health Care," *Health and Society* (Milbank Memorial Fund Quarterly) 63 (1985): 1–17.

8. Glaser, *Health Insurance*; Abel-Smith, "Who Is the Odd Man Out?" *Health and Society*, pp. 1–17; Evans, Lomas, Barer, et al., "Controlling Health Expenditures," pp. 571–77; Kevin Grumbach and Thomas Bodenheimer, "A Physician's View of Cost Containment," *Health Affairs* 9 (Winter 1990): 120–26; and Henry J. Aaron and William B. Schwartz, "Managed Competition: Little Cost Containment without Budget Limits," *Health Affairs* 12 (Supplement 1993): 204–15.

9. Evans, Lomas, Barer, et al., "Controlling Health Expenditures," pp. 571–77; and Steffie Woolhandler and David U. Himmelstein, "The Deteriorating Administrative Efficiency of The U.S. Health Care System," *New England Journal of Medicine* 324(18): 1253–58.

10. Grumbach and Bodenheimer, "A Physician's View," pp. 120–126; Evans, Lomas, Barer, et al., "Controlling Health Expenditures," pp. 571–77; and Joseph White, "Markets, Budgets, and Health Care Cost Control," *Health Affairs* 12 (Fall 1993): 44–57.

11. William J. Hall and Paul F. Griner, "Cost-Effective Health Care: The Rochester Experience," *Health Affairs* 12 (Spring 1993): 58–69.

12. Grumbach and Bodenheimer, "A Physician's View," pp. 120–126; and Philip R. Lee, Paul B. Ginsburg, Lauren B. LeRoy, and Glenn T. Hammons, "The Physician Payment Review Commission Report to Congress," *Journal of the American Medical Association* 261(16) (1989): 2382–85.

13. White, "Markets, Budgets," pp. 44–57; Alain C. Enthoven, "The History and Principles of Managed Competition," *Health Affairs* 12 (Supplement 1993): 24–48; D. Dranove, "The Case for Competitive Reform in Health Care," in *Competitive Approaches to Health Care Reform*, eds. Richard J. Arnould, Robert F. Rich, and William D. White (Washington, D.C.: The Urban Institute Press, 1993), pp. 67–82.

14. Joseph P. Newhouse, "An Iconoclastic View of Health Cost Containment," *Health Affairs* 12 (Supplement 1993): 152–71.

15. Katharine R. Levit, Helen C. Lazenby, Cathy A. Cowan, and Suzanne W. Letsch, "Health Spending by State: New Estimates for Policy Making," *Health Affairs* 12 (Fall 1993): 7–26.

16. Enthoven, "The History and Principles," pp. 24–48.

17. Enthoven, "The History and Principles," p. 43.

18. Newhouse, "An Iconoclastic View," pp. 152–71; Aaron and Schwartz, "Managed Competition," pp. 204–15; Stuart H. Altman and Alan B. Cohen, "Commentary: The Need for a National Global Budget," *Health Affairs* 12 (Supplement 1993): 194–203; Arnold S. Relman, "Controlling Costs By 'Managed Competition'—Would it Work?" *New England Journal of Medicine* 328 (Jan. 14, 1993): 133–35.

19. Jonathan E. Fielding and Thomas Rice, "Can Managed Competition Solve Problems of Market Failure?" *Health Affairs* 12 (Supplement 1993): 216–28; Thomas Rice, Richard Brown, and Roberta Wyn, "Holes in the Jackson Hole Approach to Health Care Reform," *Journal of the American Medical Association* 270 (Sept. 15, 1993): 1357–62; and Relman, "Controlling Costs?," pp. 133–35.

20. Starr and Zelman, "Bridge to Compromise," pp. 7–23.

21. Starr and Zelman, "Bridge to Compromise," pp. 7–23.

22. Arnold S. Relman, "Reforming Our Health Care System: A Physician's Perspective," *Phi Beta Kappa Key Reporter* 58 (Autumn 1992): 1–5; and Philip Caper, "Managed Competition that Works," *Journal of the American Medical Association* 269 (May 19, 1993): 2524–2526.

16

Goals and Clarifications

Eli Ginzberg

This final chapter, while informed by those that preceded it, is the sole responsibility of the editor, who absolves his fellow authors of any and all responsibility for the analysis and conclusions set out below. No matter what happens in federal health policy reform in 1994, including the remote possibility that Congress will fail to take significant action, the year will represent a major marker in twentieth century U.S. health policy deliberation and probably action, because of the major proposals that President Clinton has put before the nation and Congress to fix a system that he defined as sorely in need of fixing.

The three principal objectives of this retrospective and prospective account are to review the reasons that health reform usurped center stage in 1994; to illuminate some of the more important implications that are embedded in the significant reform program that has been advanced; and to speculate about the many challenges in health care financing and delivery that the nation will continue to face into the twenty-first century no matter how sweeping the reforms that Congress enacts before then. The principal aim of this longitudinal perspective is to make more explicit some of the major potentials and constraints on health reform that derive from the nature of our democratic institutions, the operations of our economy, and our tolerance for inequities between ethnic groups and social classes.

No president, and surely not Bill Clinton who obtained only 43 percent of the popular vote in the election of 1992, would assume the leadership for a major effort such as health reform without a careful calculation that a significant majority of the American people, and therefore its Congressional representatives, would be inclined to follow his lead. Of course, even successful presidents can miscalculate: Franklin Roosevelt did in 1937 when he proposed to enlarge the Supreme Court; so did Woodrow Wilson when he tried to persuade his fellow countrymen that the United States should join the newly established League of Nations.

But there is an important difference between the two failed presidential initiatives cited above and Clinton's health reform proposals. The average citizen had no direct and ongoing experience with the workings of the Supreme Court and even less with the embryonic League of Nations. On the other hand every American has an ongoing and continuing interaction with the health care system from the time that his mother first seeks prenatal care until a physician signs his death certificate, some seventy, eighty or more years later. During this time he or she is likely to have had at least four to five contacts with the health care system *every* year of his/her life.

In light of this direct and continuing interaction between the average citizen and the health care system, it is beyond the pale of American politics for a president to take the initiative to seek to alter the extant system in major regards unless he has concluded that a majority of the voters will welcome and support his reforms. This is surely a critical dimension of President Clinton's thinking and the reason that health reform is *the* domestic political issue of 1994.

The issues we need to explore, if only selectively, are the major reasons for the weaknesses and failings of the extant health care system that disposed the electorate to entertain major reforms. First, the extant system, since the 1930s and particularly since the end of World War II, has been predicated in the first instance on employer-based health care benefits. In the mid-1960s, after a decade of disappointing experimentation to provide broadened access for the elderly, the nation realized that private health insurance had failed as the sole mainstay of health care financing and introduced alongside it a system of social insurance to pay for the health care of the elderly (Medicare) and a joint federal-state tax program to cover selected categories of the poor (Medicaid).

In the subsequent three decades (1965 to 1994) the citizenry became increasingly aware of and concerned about a growing range of shortcomings in this mixed private-public payment system. For a variety of reasons growing numbers of employed persons and their dependents have been unable to obtain private health insurance; half of the nation's poor are not enrolled in Medicaid; increasing numbers of workers with good health insurance are locked into their jobs to retain their insurance; and the three principal payers—employers, the federal government, and state governments—are encountering increasing budgetary pressures in meeting the steep increases in their health care expenditures.

While the President referred to a great many failings of the extant health care system in his address to the Joint Session of the Congress on September 22, 1993, the heart of his argument focused on the following goals and objectives: the urgent necessity to assure all Americans that they would be permanently covered by private health insurance or by Medicare; that everybody would have access to an agreed-to list of essential health care services; and that the future costs of the system would be constrained to a rate that approximates the growth in GDP, not two to three times that rate as has been the case in recent decades.

The President, in constructing the broad outline of his reform agenda, was aware that while most employed Americans and their dependents continued to enjoy good health care coverage as a fringe benefit of employment, the last decade and more had seen many employers pressuring their employees to assume increasing deductibles and copayments to a point of precipitating some of the nation's worst strikes.

An even more acute problem reflected the growing concerns of employed persons with adequate or superior health insurance coverage that if they lost their jobs or voluntarily sought a change they might be able to obtain new health insurance coverage only at a very high cost or not at all. This growing insecurity about the future of their health insurance coverage was the prime motive that led the President to propose a major health reform initiative.

A second important consideration focused on the urgent need of the nation to slow its health care expenditures. In running for the White House and as President-elect, Clinton had called attention to the close linkage between moderating federal health care outlays and bringing the federal budget deficit under control. The latter could not be accomplished unless the former was successfully tackled. But the President was aware that the other key payers also had a growing interest in moderating the rate of their health care expenditures. As a former governor and as the former chair of the National Governors' Association, Clinton had first-hand knowledge of the pressures that rapidly rising expenditures for Medicaid were placing on state budgets, pressures that left many states with little or no new money for high priority needs, from improving public education to strengthening their criminal justice systems.

There was also growing evidence that many of the nation's leading employers, under the co-chairmanship of former presidents Ford and Carter, were lobbying for a more aggressive role by the federal government to provide coverage for the entire public and at the same time to moderate the increases in the nation's annual health care outlays. Such advocacy by many of the nation's leading corporations for greater federal initiative was, to say the least, a striking departure from their conventional policy position.

Finally, households, which paid out-of-pocket for about one-quarter of all health care expenditures, were reporting on numerous opinion surveys that they were deeply disturbed by the remorseless rise in their health care outlays, although most of these outlays were not for physician or hospital services but went primarily for dental care, over-the-counter drugs, and long-term care. Whatever the reasons for their increased outlays, consumers were complaining and worried about what the future held in store for them.

In light of this highly selective and condensed review of the changing political environment it should come as no surprise that a centrist Democratic president decided to make health reform the core of his domestic program. To review once again the widespread public support for such a reform initiative:

- The growing numbers of well-insured Americans who were becoming increasingly uneasy about their ability to remain well-insured in the face of their growing vulnerability in the job market and/or the increasingly aggressive risk-management tactics pursued by the health insurance companies that denied coverage to many with pre-existing conditions or canceled policies once beneficiaries developed a serious chronic illness.
- The awareness of the American people that all other advanced nations provide basic health coverage to all of their citizens and permanent residents at a per capita and total cost considerably below the U.S. level. While acting on the American preference for private health insurance may have been the sensible way for the nation to go at the end of World War II, such ideological support for the private marketplace was severely eroded by the Medicare-Medicaid legislation of 1965. The retrogression in coverage for the poor under Medicaid from about three out of four in the mid-1970s to one in two in 1994 has been a growing challenge to the American public whose historic embrace of the virtues of the private marketplace did not commit them to a philosophy that the poor were not entitled to essential health care.
- The growing concerns of all of the major payers—the federal government, state governments, employers and households—with the unyielding increases in health care expenditures surely helped to convince the President that the time had come, in fact was overdue, for the nation to tackle health reform so that it could achieve two desirable goals—permanent universal coverage and effective cost controls.

This recapitulation of the reasons that the political setting in 1994 is favorable to major health reform can be formulated thus:

- A significant and growing proportion of the electorate no longer has abiding faith in the private health insurance system which provides coverage for most employed persons and their dependents. They have become aware that at any point in time about 40 million are without coverage and that the aggregate figure approximates 66 million over the course of a year. Of course, the number of workers who are uninsured for a year or longer is much fewer but the fact remains that a health emergency can arise at any time so that even a short period without coverage becomes a major threat to the unemployed worker and his or her family.
- The American people are no longer willing to accept the primacy of the marketplace as the price for excluding a significant minority of the population from a legal entitlement to essential health care. They feel that this is a shortcoming in their political fabric that calls for early reform.
- It would be far-fetched to postulate that the majority of the citizenry has a deep understanding of the financing of its health care system and that this knowledge is one of the driving factors pushing for health reform. But it is not far-fetched to state that the estimated expenditure of a trillion dollars for health care in 1994 with a doubling of that amount by 2000 or shortly thereafter has permeated the consciousness of most voters and has helped to predispose them to Presidential and Congressional leadership that promises sometime soon, if not immediately, to moderate the rate of health care spending.

In short, I believe that the American voter is looking to the Congress to act positively on the President's health reform proposal prior to the elections in the fall of 1994. The decision to act is critical but, as economists are fond of reminding the public, even the pursuit and accomplishment of worthwhile goals carries a price, often a high price. Accordingly we will now consider a few of the major complications (real costs) involved in pursuing and achieving the goals of the President's reform proposals.

The first and foremost challenge that the reform must meet and surmount is how to provide universal coverage for all (or almost all since the Clinton proposal does not cover the undocumented). There are some who believe that this objective can best be achieved by the federal government's providing tax subsidies based on personal income so that those who are not insured via their employer can purchase health insurance in the marketplace with the help of the federal tax subsidy. But for a whole series of reasons, the most important of which are the complexity of putting a federal tax subsidy system in place and the uncertainty that most if not all of the uninsured would in fact buy health insurance, the proposal has fallen by the wayside.

There is considerable support inside and outside of Congress for a single-payer system in which all health care expenditures would be covered by federal or federal-state tax receipts. Such a system, the proponents claim, would lead to sizable reductions in administrative costs and would further result in a more equitable way of raising the required health care revenue since it would be linked to the progressive income tax. But the fact that the federal government currently covers about 30 percent of total annual health care outlays and all levels of government about 40 percent would necessitate the federal government's finding a way to add around $600 billion to its annual budget to cover the costs of a single-payer health care system. Of course, most of this large sum is already in the system but rechanneling it into the federal budget would be a herculean task. Small wonder that the President has steered clear of this approach and opted instead for expanding the employer mandate to all employers with ceilings on the amount that employers must pay for health care benefits (3.5 percent of payroll for small employers to a maximum of 7.9 percent) and subsidies for individuals and marginal firms.

There are many small, and some large, labor-intensive firms that do not provide health care coverage at present on the ground that they cannot afford to and, further, that most of their workers prefer a fatter pay envelope to health care coverage and less cash. But as the administration has pointed out, most employers do provide health care benefits and are implicitly taken advantage of by those who do not because the former, through cross-subsidization, must pay more to cover the bills of uninsured workers.

The nub of the issue reduces itself to the prospective job losses that might result from what is obviously a not-so-hidden tax on wages. The estimates of job losses are all over the lot, with some estimates as high as several million, although most economists are skeptical about such pessimistic projections. It would be a mistake to ignore the costs represented by future job losses, but if the nation reaches a judgment that universal coverage is a must and employer coverage is the best, in fact the only, current mechanism to achieve such coverage, then the risk of modest job losses must be accepted.

Universal coverage is only one half of the President's priority goals for reform; the other half relates to the institution of effective cost controls. Here the President has a two-pronged proposal: intensified competition among managed health care delivery plans under the auspices of regional health alliances and a fallback position relying on federal and state caps on the rate at which health insurance premiums can be raised.

As for intensified competition among health care delivery plans, the market has begun to churn as all sorts of actors, old and new, seek to reposition themselves for the reform environment that lies ahead. Many new managed care organizations are being developed and old ones that hold promise of contributing to cost containment are expanding, but it will take considerable time before the evidence is in that intensified competition by itself can constrain costs. If the relationship between the two were so simple and direct, the cost acceleration that has characterized the U.S. health care system since the end of World War II and particularly since the passage of Medicare and Medicaid would not have occurred; in fact, it would have been impossible.

Small wonder therefore that the President's proposal, while stressing the potential of managed competition to contain costs, has a fallback position of global budgets. However, it is far from clear that Congress will approve this part of the President's reform agenda. Many who believe that the time has come for major health reforms may balk at the idea of the federal government's determining the total amount of money that the American people are permitted to spend on health care. The opponents are convinced that such overriding governmental budgetary controls will have severe adverse effects on the raising of new capital and the speed of technological innovation; that they will reinforce the status quo and that they foreshadow the early introduction of broadscale rationing. Each of these fears can be justified and the adverse consequences that the opponents of global budgets fear must be considered.

The issue may well come down to this: how much longer will the United States tolerate a rate of spending for health care that is twice or more the rate of growth of the GDP? Of course, the introduction of global budgeting carries a large number of potential negatives, each of which is serious and collectively are potentially disruptive. But we know from the experience of the past that the nation has reached a point at which the absence of restraints on health care spending can no longer be tolerated. The only question that remains is whether competition in health care markets is to be given a second chance to fail or whether the President must have from the start a fallback position for moderating total health expenditures.

A number of other critical political-economic issues that have shaped the President's reform proposal warrant at least brief consideration in order to understand more fully the dynamics of the major legislative initiatives now before the nation. We will inspect several such determinations.

The first relates to the administration's decision to leave Medicare intact and not risk, at least initially, enveloping it in the new structure. The White House recognized that on balance the elderly hold a favorable view of the current Medicare system. Of course they recognize certain defects in the current system, particularly the lack of long-term care. Nevertheless, most of the elderly are committed to Medicare and believe that they have more to lose than gain from having their special system merged with the structure contemplated for the below-65 population. Given the complexity of the reforms that the administration is proposing, leaving Medicare intact has the added advantage of not further complicating an already very complicated reform proposal.

The over-65 constituency, whose lobbying power on the Hill as well as in the 50 states is substantial, have been able to extract two costly concessions from the administration: a liberal drug benefit and a start on home-care benefits. Despite the administration's emphasis on cost containment it found it politically expedient, even necessary, to add these two benefits, which will carry an additional outlay of over $130 billion during 1995–2000.

This decision to keep Medicare out of the reform package has at least two major drawbacks. It creates many differences in the costs that the younger and older populations will face for the same benefits, with corresponding tensions and frictions. And the potential for optimizing the administrative gains from a more thoroughly integrated financing and delivery system will be thwarted until some time in the future when the two discrete systems are likely to be integrated.

The administration's proposal that only employers with more than 5,000 personnel would be given the opportunity, if they meet the reform plan's criteria, to continue to operate outside the system of the new health alliances is also contentious. There are many among the employer community who believe that the exception is set at much too high a figure and are recommending that the floor be 1,000 or 500 or even less. But if the Congress were to accept a much lower figure, it would probably undermine the ability of the health alliances to become a potent force for providing coverage of good quality health care to all at a competitive price and the ability to cross-subsidize the poor. As is true of almost every aspect of the President's reform proposal, the projected gains carry a cost and the size of the estimated cost depends on who is doing the estimating.

A third challenge to the designers of the reform plan was the realization that universal coverage does not necessarily translate into universal access to essential health care services. At best, coverage is a precondition for access but to turn the promise of good care into a reality, health care providers, particularly physicians and the medical infrastructure, must be readily available where people live. The administration recognizes that a significant gain in access for the uninsured, the underinsured, and low income persons residing in inner-city or outlying rural areas would depend in the first instance on a significant change in the proportions of generalists and specialists that the medical educational system is turning out. The administration has proposed changes in graduate medical education that contemplate increasing the proportion of generalists to 55 percent of all newly trained physicians within the next years.

Under the best of circumstances such a radical shift in the distribution of the new physician supply will take decades to accomplish, but serious questions remain even if this change in output could be achieved. The questions involve such basic matters as whether so large a change is needed or desirable; what other changes in the health care system, such as the relative earnings patterns of generalists and specialists, need to be substantially revised; and finally how are physicians who have long avoided practicing in underserved areas to be attracted to these sites?

It is just short of a quarter of a century since Congress initiated actions aimed at increasing the physician supply in underserved areas, urban and rural. The record of successive initiatives, involving special monetary incentives, special grants for residency training in family practice, linking weaker with stronger service delivery systems and raising the earnings potential of generalists failed to moderate the maldistribution of physicians except at the margin. The question that we must ask now about the proposed Clinton reform is how many more years will be required before the redistribution of the physicians and other health care personnel will transform universal coverage into ready access to essential services for the entire population. The odds are that it will take a long time.

The foregoing represent only a few selected illustrations of the challenges that remain after the broad principles of health reform gain political consensus. In fact, whether and to what extent Congress will agree to the President's many far-reaching proposals will in large measure depend less on how it assesses the social equity of the several proposals and more on how it assesses the costs, disruptions, and opposition of powerful interest groups to the changes in the existing health care system that would be required to implement the key reforms. Agreement in principle about the value of the proposed reforms is a precondition for favorable action. Equally important is the assessment that Congress must make of the costs involved in implementing them, a calculation that will be greatly influenced by the positions adopted by the different groups that have the most to gain or lose from the proposed reforms.

Confronted with the scale and scope of the President's health reform program, there is no possible way for the Congress in a single legislative session to thrash out all of the pros and cons of the infrastructure changes that would be necessary to ensure the success of the new reforms. Many of the details will not be addressed, much less resolved, until some time in the future. As is true for so much of personal as well as public decision-making, once broad choices have been made about the guiding principles, the complex details relating to their implementation must be accepted largely on faith, to be worked out subsequently.

No one in the executive or legislative branch of the federal government was able to foresee at the time that Medicare and Medicaid were enacted that some three decades later the rate of Medicare expenditures would become the major threat to the federal budget. Similarly, no legislator who voted for Medicaid could have anticipated that the new program, after it expanded in the mid-1970s to a point where it covered about three out of every four persons with incomes below the federal standard of poverty, would go into reverse and by the mid-1980s cover no more than two out of five. And no one in 1965 could have foreseen that the principles adopted by Medicare for reimbursing inpatient care would set the stage for a major expansion in the nation's hospital plant to a point where high-tech specialist care would come to dominate the U.S. health care delivery system. These examples of the uncertainties that the future holds in store for major health reforms are that much more relevant in the face of the scale and scope of Clinton's reform proposals.

To summarize this section on the goals of health reform:

- Large-scale reforms such as those proposed by the President must reflect a growing political consensus among the American people that the extant health care system has serious shortcomings. In the absence of such an emerging consensus no political leader would risk proposing a major reform initiative.
- The public's discontent is centered on the uncertainties confronting the large proportion of the population below the age of 65 that is covered by private health insurance, a mechanism that at any time fails one out of every four Americans of working age and that leaves those with good insurance coverage concerned about what the future may bring.
- The vast majority of the population has reached a point where it believes that all Americans must have access to essential health care services based on the principle of entitlement, not charity.
- Most Americans also believe that the rate of national expenditures for health care must be moderated, even while all members of the public must have access to essential services of good quality.

Beyond broad agreement that the nation should pursue and achieve these four goals expeditiously, there are wide differences of opinion among both the better and less informed public about how to achieve these four primary reforms. That is the challenge that the Congress faces and must respond to before November 1994, realizing that having decided on the goals it cannot possibly work out all of the details. Much must be left to later.

This brings us to the final part of the chapter: to look beyond 1994 and to raise, if not answer, some of the pressing questions that will have to be faced "later," questions that are not necessarily included in the reforms that will be passed but are part and parcel of three distinctive cultures—politics, economics, and medicine—that have intersected in the past to shape our health care system and that will continue to reshape it irrespective of the specificity of the reforms that will be enacted in 1994 and how their implementation will proceed in the years ahead. We will focus on selected characteristics of the three cultures that are certain to determine the future, recognizing that most of that future remains hidden from view.

We postulated earlier that the nation's political ideology has reached a point where access of the entire population to essential health care will henceforth be viewed as a national commitment. But this new commitment needs specification. The states in the Northeastern region have been committed to public education for all children since the middle of the 19th century but, as everybody knows, the public schools in the inner cities of Boston, Providence, and Hartford provide a quite different and poorer quality of education than do most schools in the surrounding suburbs. Similar disparities between inner-city and suburban schools are characteristic of most of the metropolitan areas in other regions of the country. There is little or no reason to believe that the American people are willing or even capable of providing in real time an equal level of health care services for poor and affluent alike. What the nation's leaders can set as a national goal and strive to accomplish in the decade ahead is to make available to all income groups a level of essential care.

From the perspective of economics, gross differentials in per capita health care spending are found among neighborhoods, cities, states, and regions. The extent of these differentials is suggested by the 100 percent spread between states with the highest and the lowest annual per capita health care outlays. The question that the nation has barely glimpsed at, much less analyzed, is whether, how, and how quickly it should address these locational differentials in spending. Once again, if public education is a marker, the areal differences in health expenditure levels are likely to persist for years to come.

Alongside the political and economic constraints that will govern the rate of progress that the nation will be able to achieve in reducing if not eliminating the gross differentials in access to essential health care services, account must be taken of the constraints inherent in the culture of medicine and public health. The incidence and prevalence of disease among sub-groups in the population are often substantial, determined in the first instance by the impact of poverty that is reinforced by a low level of education. The health and medical services that different groups require depend at bottom on the principal risks to which they are exposed and the extent that these risks determine their needs for care and cure.

While epidemiologists have stressed the importance of population-based approaches that involve a broadened community perspective in determining the priority health needs of local populations, the dominant health care delivery system long geared to individual clinical pathology and treatment has only recently begun to be modified. It needs to become responsive and of greater value to sub-groups in the population which have special health needs by virtue of the conditions under which they live and work. Responding to such differences in health status and health needs is a further determinant—together with the continuing political tolerance of the American people for inequality in income distribution and the economic constraints of total resource limitations—that the path of major health reform upon which the nation is about to embark will be long and winding.

So far the clarifications that have been at the center of our concern about achieving the goals of health reform relate primarily to the institutional framework which bounds the current U.S. health care system. But if we adopt a lengthened horizon that looks beyond this century to at least the early decades of the next, we must contemplate the probability of a vastly different health care delivery system, responding to new opportunities and new potentials, stemming largely from advances in biomedical research and technique, informed by innovations in the social environment.

Molecular biology and human genetics are at an early stage of development but they hold great promise for the future. Many of the conditions that lead to early morbidity and mortality such as various types of cancer may lend themselves to early corrective treatment by drugs or surgery. Greater understanding of dysfunctional behaviors such as smoking, improper diet, lack of exercise should set the stage for the deferment, if not avoidance, of organ failure. The recent pharmacological advances in the treatment and control, if not cure, of depression and other mental health afflictions is another area of great promise.

Perhaps the most important restructuring of our health care system will be propelled by our society's appreciation that the principal determinants of health status reflect the behavior of individuals, who in turn are primarily influenced by their levels of education and by the conditions governing their work, their living conditions, and their expectations for the future. Unless the individual is educated to a level where he can understand how his future health status will be affected by his behavior; and unless all adults are afforded the opportunity to work and be self-supporting; unless their income is sufficient to protect them against conditions that are injurious to their health; and unless they are able to function as members of a community which can provide guidelines and directions for the future, the odds are against a long and healthy life.

It makes little or no sense for a wealthy democracy such as ours to invest an ever larger proportion of its GDP in the further sophistication of its acute care delivery system when the evidence mounts that—in addition to new research—improved health outcomes depend on improved education and living conditions for those in the lower half of the nation's economic distribution.

By far the greatest contribution to the improved health of the American people in recent decades has resulted from the anti-smoking campaign. The opportunities for future gains in the health status of the nation are many and diverse but they will depend on more than breakthroughs in biomedical R&D, a higher level of education and changes in the behavior of individuals. A critically important determinant will be the commitment of the larger society to provide all groups in the population not only improved access to the health care system but the basic opportunities for education, work, and income which together will determine the health status of the nation.

About the Contributors

Stuart H. Altman, Ph.D., is Sol C. Chaiken Professor of National Health Policy, The Heller School, Brandeis University and Chair, Prospective Payment Assessment Commission, Washington, D.C.

Lawrence D. Brown, Ph.D., is Professor and Head, Division of Health Policy and Management, School of Public Health, Columbia University.

Lynn Etheredge is an independent consultant on health care reform, income security and government policy and Chair, The Health Information Exchange for Health Care Reform, Washington, D.C.

Richard G. Frank, Ph.D., is Professor of Economics, Harvard Medical School.

Paul B. Ginsburg, Ph.D., is Executive Director, Physician Payment Review Commission, Washington, D.C.

Eli Ginzberg, Ph.D., is A. Barton Hepburn Professor Emeritus of Economics and Director, The Eisenhower Center for the Conservation of Human Resources, Columbia University.

Howard H. Goldman, M.D., Ph.D., is Professor of Psychiatry, University of Maryland School of Medicine; Co-Director, Center for Mental Health Services Research; and Associate Director, Johns Hopkins-University of Maryland Center on the Organization and Financing of the Care of the Severely Mentally Ill.

Kevin Grumbach, M.D., is Assistant Professor of Medicine in Residence, Department of Family and Community Medicine, University of California, San Francisco.

Stan Jones is an Independent Consultant on Private Health Insurance and Public Policy and Director, Health Insurance Reform Project, George Washington University.

James A. Lane is Senior Vice President, Kaiser Foundation Health Plan and Kaiser Foundation Hospitals.

David K. Lawrence, M.D., is Chief Executive Officer and Chairman, Kaiser Foundation Health Plan and Kaiser Foundation Hospitals.

Harold S. Luft, Ph.D., is Professor of Health Economics and Acting Director, Institute for Health Policy Studies, University of California, San Francisco.

Thomas G. McGuire, Ph.D., is Professor of Economics, Boston University and Consultant, Johns Hopkins University of Maryland Center on the Organization and Financing of the Care of the Severely Mentally Ill.

David Mechanic, Ph.D., is René Dubos Professor of Behavioral Sciences and Director, Institute for Health, Health Care Policy and Aging Research, Rutgers University.

Marilyn Moon, Ph.D., is Senior Fellow, Health Policy Center, The Urban Institute, Washington, D.C.

Joseph P. Newhouse, Ph.D., is the John D. and Catherine T. MacArthur Professor of Health Policy and Management, Harvard University.

Thomas Rice, Ph.D., is Professor of Health Services, School of Public Health, University of California, Los Angeles.

Diane Rowland, Sc.D., is Senior Vice President, The Henry J. Kaiser Family Foundation and Associate Professor of Health Policy and Management, School of Hygiene and Public Health, Johns Hopkins University.

Cathy Schoen, M.A., is Director, Commonwealth Fund Health Care Reform Program and Special Projects Director, Labor Relations and Research Center, University of Massachusetts.

Donald A. Young, M.D., is Executive Director, Prospective Payment Assessment Commission, Washington, D.C.

Lawrence Zacharias, J.D., is Associate Professor of Law, Policy and Organization, School of Management, University of Massachusetts.